【英汉对照全译本】

AN INQUIRY INTO THE NATURE AND CAUSES OF THE WEALTH OF NATIONS

国民财富的性质与原理

[英]亚当·斯密 著

赵东旭 丁 毅 译

（三）

中国社会科学出版社

CHAPTER II

Of Money Considered As A Particular Branch Of The General Stock Of The Society, Or Of The Expence Of Maintainng The National Capital

<small>Prices are divided into three parts, wages, profits, and rent,</small>   It has been shewn in the first Book, that the price of the greater part of commodities resolves itself into three parts, of which one pays the wages of the labour, another the profits of the stock, and a third the rent of the land which had been employed in producing and bringing them to market: that there are, indeed, some commodities of which the price is made up of two of those parts only, the wages of labour, and the profits of stock: and a very few in which it consists altogether in one, the wages of labour: but that the price of every commodity necessarily resolves itself into some one, or other, or all of these three parts; every part of it which goes neither to rent nor to wages, being necessarily profit to somebody.

<small>and the whole annual produce is divided into the same three parts;</small>   Since this is the case, it has been observed, with regard to every particular commodity, taken separately; it must be so with regard to all the commodities which compose the whole annual produce of the land and labour of every country, taken complexly. The whole price or exchangeable value of that annual produce, must resolve itself into the same three parts, and be parcelled out among the different inhabitants of the country, either as the wages of their labour, the profits of their stock, or the rent of their land.

<small>but we may distinguish between gross and net revenue</small>   But though the whole value of the annual produce of the land and labour of every country is thus divided among and constitutes a revenue to its different inhabitants; yet as in the rent of a private estate we distinguish between the gross rent and the neat rent, so may we likewise in the revenue of all the inhabitants of a great country.

第二章　论作为社会总资财的一部分或作为维持国民资本的费用的货币

在第一篇里，我曾经指出：因为商品的生产和流通过程中，曾经使用劳动、资本与土地，所以大部分商品的价格都可分解为三个部分，其一为劳动工资，其二为资本利润，其三为土地地租。诚然，事实上有些商品的价格，只由两部分构成，即劳动工资和资本利润；甚至还有极少数商品的价格，仅仅由一部分构成，即劳动工资。但无论如何，商品价格终归成为上述那三个部分中的一个或全部。如果不是地租也不是工资的部分，那必定是利润部分。

价格可分成三部分，即工资、利润和租金，

就各个特殊商品分别论述，情形与上面所论述一样，就构成全国土地和劳动的年产物的全部商品而总括论述，情况也是一样。我在第一篇里讲过：一个国家年产出的总价格或总交换价值，也必分解为这三个部分进而分配给国内各居民。不是作为劳动工资，或者不是作为资本利润，那么就是作为土地地租。

年总产出也同样可以分成三部分；

一个国家土地和劳动的年产出的全部价值，虽然以这三种形式分归各个居民，并成为各居民的收入，但是，好像个人私有土地的地租可以分为总地租和纯地租一样，国内全部居民的收入也可分为总收入和纯收入。

但我们可以对总收入和纯收入进行区分，

Gross rent is the whole sum paid by the farmer; net rent what is left free to the landlord.

The gross rent of a private estate comprehends whatever is paid by the farmer; the neat rent, what remains free to the landlord, after deducting the expence of management, of repairs, and all other necessary charges; or what, without hurting his estate, he can afford to place in his stock reserved for immediate consumption, or to spend upon his table, equipage, the ornaments of his house and furniture, his private enjoyments and amusements. His real wealth is in proportion, not to his gross, but to his neat rent.

Gross revenue is the whole annual produce: net revenue what is left free after deducting the maintenance of fixed and circulating capital.

The gross revenue of all the inhabitants of a great country, comprehends the whole annual produce of their land and labour; the neat revenue, what remains free to them after deducting the expence of maintaining; first, their fixed; and, secondly, their circulating capital; or what, without encroaching upon their capital, they can place in their stock reserved for immediate consumption, or spend upon their subsistence, conveniencies, and amusements. Their real wealth too is in proportion, not to their gross, but to their neat revenue.

The whole expence of maintaining the fixed capital must be excluded,

The whole expence of maintaining the fixed capital, must evidently be excluded from the neat revenue of the society. Neither the materials necessary for supporting their useful machines and instruments of trade, their profitable buildings, &c. nor the produce of the labour necessary for fashioning those materials into the proper form, can ever make any part of it. The price of that labour may indeed make a part of it; as the workmen so employed may place the whole value of their wages in their stock reserved for immediate consumption. But in other sorts of labour, both the price and the produce go to this stock, the price to that of the workmen, the produce to that of other people, whose subsistence, conveniencies, and amusements, are augmented by the labour of those workmen.

The intention of the fixed capital is to increase the productive powers of labour, or to enable the same number of labourers to perform

个人私有土地的总地租,包括农场主所付出的一切;在总地租中减去管理、修缮和其他各种必要费用,剩余的留给地主支配的部分,称为纯地租。换言之,所谓纯地租,就是在不伤害其财产的条件下可留供地主目前消费的资财,或者说可用来购置衣食和修饰住宅,供私人享乐的资财。地主的实际财富,不取决于其总地租的多少,而取决于纯地租的多少。

> 总地租是农场主付出的总额,减去由地主支配的那部分叫做纯地租。

一个大国全体居民的总收入,包含他们土地和劳动的全部年产出。在总收入中减去维持固定资本和流动资本的费用,其余留给居民自由使用的部分便是纯收入。换言之,所谓纯收入,乃是以不侵蚀资本为条件,留供居民享用的资财。这种资财用作目前消费,或用来购置生活必需品、便利品和娱乐品等等。国民真实财富的大小,不取决于其总收入的大小,而取决于其纯收入的大小。

> 总收入是年产出;纯收入就是扣除维持固定资本和流动资本的费用后留给居民自由使用的那一部分。

很明显,补充固定资本的费用绝不能算在社会纯收入之内。有用的机器和营业上使用的工具,必须在修理以后才能工作;用来营利的房屋,必须在修缮以后才有利可图。这些修理所必须使用的材料与把这种材料制为成品所需要的劳动产品,也都不能算作社会上的纯收入。固然,这种劳动的价格也许会成为社会纯收入的一部分,因为从事此种劳动的工人,可能要把工资的全部价值作为目前消费的资财使用。但就其他种类的劳动来说,那就不仅把劳动的价格归入这种资财,而且把劳动的产品也归入这种资财;劳动的价格归入工人目前消费的资财,劳动的产品则成为别人目前消费的资财。别人的生活必需品、便利品和娱乐品,都随着工人的劳动而增加。

> 必须把固定资本的全部维持费扣除掉。

固定资本的目标在于增加劳动生产力,或者说在于使人数相

<small>since the only object of the fixed capital is to increase the productive powers of labour.</small> a much greater quantity of work. In a farm where all the necessary buildings, fences, drains, communications, &c. are in the most perfect good order, the same number of labourers and labouring cattle will raise a much greater produce, than in one of equal extent and equally good ground, but not furnished with equal conveniencies. In manufactures the same number of hands, assisted with the best machinery, will work up a much greater quantity of goods than with more imperfect instruments of trade. The expence which is properly laid out upon a fixed capital of any kind, is always repaid with great profit, and increases the annual produce by a much greater value than that of the support which such improvements require. This support, however, still requires a certain portion of that produce. A certain quantity of materials, and the labour of a certain number of workmen, both of <small>and any cheapening or simplification is regarded as good.</small> which might have been immediately employed to augment the food, clothing and lodging, the subsistence and conveniencies of the society, are thus diverted to another employment, highly advantageous indeed, but still different from this one. It is upon this account that all such improvements in mechanics, as enable the same number of workmen to perform an equal quantity of work with cheaper and simpler machinery than had been usual before, are always regarded as advantageous to every society. A certain quantity of materials, and the labour of a certain number of workmen, which had before been employed in supporting a more complex and expensive machinery, can afterwards be applied to augment the quantity of work which that or any other machinery is useful only for performing. The undertaker of some great manufactory who employs a thousand a-year in the maintenance of his machinery, if he can reduce this expence to five hundred, will naturally① employ the other five hundred in purchasing an additional quantity of materials to be wrought up by an additional number of workmen. The quantity of that work, therefore, which his machinery was useful only for performing, will naturally be augmented, and with it all the advantage and conveniency which the society <small>The cost of maintaining the fixed capital is like the cost of repairs on an estate,</small> can derive from that work.

<small>　</small>The expence of maintaining the fixed capital in a great country, may very properly be compared to that of repairs in a private estate. The expence of repairs may frequently be necessary for supporting the

---

① [There seems no reason whatever for supposing that this is necessarily the natural action.]

同的工人能够完成更多的工作。设施完善,有必要的建筑物、围墙、水沟、道路等等的农场,与没有这些设施的农场相比较,即使幅员大小相等,肥瘠相同,劳动人数相等,役畜数目相等,但所获得产物也一定多得多。有最精良机器设备的加工厂,和工具不这么完备的加工厂相比较,虽然所雇工人的人数相等,出产量也一定会大得多。适当地在固定资本上开支的任何费用,一定都能很快地并带回很大的利润,而且年产出价值由此而带来的增加,会比进行这类改造所必要的维持费用大得多。不过这种维持费用要使用这种年产出的一部分。原来可直接用来增加一定数量的食品、衣料、住宅以及各种必需品和便利品的材料和人工,就有一部分被改作他用。这种新的用途当然是很有利的,尽管与原来的用途不同。因此我们说,机械设备的更新改造,使同一数目的工人以较低廉和较简单的机器可以进行等量的工作,这确实被认为是社会的福利。从前比较昂贵复杂的机器,其修理维护常常必须要花费去一定数量的材料和人工。现在机器改良了,这些数量的材料和人工可以节省下来,再凭借某种机器的力量,用来增加产品的数量。比如,大制造厂主原来每年必须以 1000 镑作为机器修理费,现在如果能够把修理费用变成 500 镑,其余 500 镑[①]就可用来增加购买材料,增加雇佣工人。这样,机器产品的数量自然会增加起来。产品增加了,由此种产品而产生的社会福利也会跟着增加。

  一个大国的固定资本的维持费用,可以与私有土地的修理费用相比。保持土地产出,从而保持地主的总地租和纯地租的数

----

① 没有任何理由来假设这一定是"自然的行为"。

produce of the estate, and consequently both the gross and the neat rent of the landlord. When by a more proper direction, however, it can be diminished without occasioning any diminution of produce, the gross rent remains at least the same as before, and the neat rent is necessarily augmented.

but the expence of maintaining the last three parts of the circulating capital is not to be deducted. But though the whole expence of maintaining the fixed capital is thus necessarily excluded from the neat revenue of the society, it is not the same case with that of maintaining the circulating capital. Of the four parts of which this latter capital is composed, money, provisions, materials, and finished work, the three last, it has already been observed, are regularly withdrawn from it, and placed either in the fixed capital of the society, or in their stock reserved for immediate consumption. Whatever portion of those consumable goods is not employed in maintaining the former, goes all to the latter, and makes a part of the neat revenue of the society. The maintenance of those three parts of the circulating capital, therefore, withdraws no portion of the annual produce from the neat revenue of the society, besides what is necessary for maintaining the fixed capital.

the circulating capital of the society being different in this respect from that of an individual. The circulating capital of a society is in this respect different from that of an individual. That of an individual is totally excluded from making any part of his neat revenue, which must consist altogether in his profits. But though the circulating capital of every individual makes a part of that of the society to which he belongs, it is not upon that account totally excluded from making a part likewise of their neat revenue. Though the whole goods in a merchant's shop must by no means be placed in his own stock reserved for immediate consumption, they may in that of other people, who, from a revenue derived from other funds, may regularly replace their value to him, together with its profits, without occasioning any diminution either of his capital or of theirs. ①

The maintenance of the money alone must be deducted. Money, therefore, is the only part of the circulating capital of a

---

① [In this paragraph the capital or stock of goods is confused with the goods themselves. The goods of which the stock consists may become revenue, but the stock itself cannot. The maintenance of a stock, even of perishable and consumable goods, does form a charge on the labour of the society.]

额,都经常必须有修理费用。如果措施得当,修理费用就会减少,而产出并不减少时,则总地租至少与以前一样,而纯地租则一定会有所增加。

但是,固定资本的维持费用,虽然不能列在社会纯收入之内,但流动资本的维持费用却与固定资本不同。流动资本包含四个部分,即货币、食品、材料和制成品。正如我们所了解,后面三个部分常常从流动资本中分离出来,成为社会上的固定资本或留作目前消费的资财。凡没有变为固定资本的可消费品,就变作目前消费的资财,从而成为社会纯收入的一部分。所以,维持这个三部分流动资本,并没从社会纯收入中分离出来任何部分的年产物;只有维持固定资本时,才需要从社会纯收入中分离出来一部分年产物用来维持它。

<small>但维持流动资本后三部分所花费用不能列入纯收入以外</small>

就从这点来看,社会流动资本与个人流动资本有所不同。个人的流动资本绝不能算作个人的纯收入;个人的纯收入全由他的利润构成。尽管社会流动资本由社会内各个人的流动资本组成,但不能因此就说社会流动资本绝对不是社会纯收入的一部分。商店内储存的货物,虽然不是商人自己留作目前消费的资财,但可以是别人留作目前消费的资财。由其他资金渠道取得收入的其他人,可以经常用这些收入偿还商人的货物的价值和商人的利润,不会引起商人或社会的资本有所减少。①

<small>社会流动资本这方面个与人资本有所不同</small>

因此,社会流动资本中只有一部分,其维持所发生的费用会

<small>只是货币的维持费用必须排除在纯收入以外</small>

---

① 在本段里物品资本或物品存货与物品有所混淆。由存货组成的物品可能成为收入,但存货自己则不可能;存货的维持,甚至是易变质和消费的物品的维持,确实是对社会劳动形成的一种费用。

society, of which the maintenance can occasion any diminution in their neat revenue.

<small>The money resembles the fixed capital, since (1) the maintenance of the stock of money is part of the gross but not of the net revenue,</small>

The fixed capital, and that part of the circulating capital which consists in money, so far as they affect the revenue of the society, bear a very great resemblance to one another.

First, as those machines and instruments of trade, &c. require a certain expence, first to erect them, and afterwards to support them, both which expences, though they make a part of the gross, are deductions from the neat revenue of the society; so the stock of money which circulates in any country must require a certain expence, first to collect it, and afterwards to support it, both which expences, though they make a part of the gross, are, in the same manner, deductions from the neat revenue of the society. A certain quantity of very valuable materials, gold and silver, and of very curious labour, instead of augmenting the stock reserved for immediate consumption, the subsistence, conveniencies, and amusements of individuals, is employed in supporting that great but expensive instrument of commerce, by means of which every individual in the society has his subsistence, conveniencies, and amusements, regularly distributed to him in their proper proportion.

<small>and (2) the money itself forms no part of the net revenue.</small>

Secondly, as the machines and instruments of trade, &c. which compose the fixed capital either of an individual or of a society, make no part either of the gross or of the neat revenue of either; so money, by means of which the whole revenue of the society is regularly distributed among all its different members, makes itself no part of that revenue. The great wheel of circulation is altogether different from the goods which are circulated by means of it. The revenue of the society consists altogether in those goods, and not in the wheel which circulates them. In computing either the gross or the neat revenue of any society, we must always, from their whole annual circulation of money and goods, deduct the whole value of the money, of which not a single farthing can ever make any part of either. ①

---

① [If it were not for the use of the old-fashioned term 'circulation' instead of the newer 'produce,' the explanation which follows would be unnecessary. No one could be suspected of a desire to add all the money to the annual produce.]

减少社会纯收入;这一部分就是货币。

货币虽然是流动资本的一部分,但就它对社会收入的影响来说,它和固定资本是很相像的。

第一,营业上所使用的机器和工具是需要花费一定费用的,先是用在建造上,再用在维护上。这些费用虽然是社会总收入的一部分,但应该从社会纯收入中给予扣除。货币也是这样。一个国家流通领域里的货币收集与弥补,也需要支出一项费用,这种费用虽然是社会总收入的一部分,但也是要从社会纯收入中给予扣除。货币在商业领域里是数量很大的工具,有了它,社会上的生活必需品、便利品和娱乐品,才能够以适当的比例经常地分配给社会上的各个人;但它是非常昂贵的工具。这昂贵工具的维持必须使用社会上一定数量如金银价值贵重的材料和一定数量极其精巧的劳动,这样就不能够增加留作目前消费的资财,即不能用来增加人民的生活必需品、便利品和娱乐品。

第二,无论就个人说或就社会说,构成固定资本的营业上所使用的机器和工具,都不是总收入或纯收入的一部分。货币也是如此。社会的全部收入,虽然通过货币能够经常分配给社会各个成员,但货币不是社会总收入的一部分。货币只是货物进行流通的车轮,而与它所流通的货物大不相同。构成社会收入的只是货物,而不是流通货物的工具。在计算社会总收入或纯收入时,必须从每年流通的全部货币和全部货物中,减去货币的全部价值,一个铜板也不能计算在里面。①

傍注:货币与固定资本相似,因为:(1)货币资财的维持的费用是总收入的一部分,而不是纯收入一部分;(2)货币本身不构成纯收入的一部分。

---

① 如果不是使用新词汇"产出"替代旧词汇"流通"的话,接下来的解释就没有必要。没有人对一种把所有货币的价值都加到年产出中去的愿望产生怀疑。

国民财富的性质与原理

<small>It only appears to do so from the ambiguity of language, sums of money being often used to indicate the goods purchaseable as well as the coins themselves.</small>

It is the ambiguity of language only which can make this proposition appear either doubtful or paradoxical. When properly explained and understood, it is almost self-evident.

When we talk of any particular sum of money, we sometimes mean nothing but the metal pieces of which it is composed; and sometimes we include in our meaning some obscure reference to the goods which can be had in exchange for it, or to the power of purchasing which the possession of it conveys. Thus when we say, that the circulating money of England has been computed at eighteen millions, we mean only to express the amount of the metal pieces, which some writers have computed, or rather have supposed to circulate in that country. But when we say that a man is worth fifty or a hundred pounds a-year, we mean commonly to express not only the amount of

<small>We must not add both together.</small>

the metal pieces which are annually paid to him, but the value of the goods which he can annually purchase or consume. We mean commonly to ascertain what is or ought to be his way of living, or the quantity and quality of the necessaries and conveniencies of life in which he can with propriety indulge himself.

<small>If a man has a guinea a week he enjoys a guinea's worth of subsistence £ c.,</small>

When, by any particular sum of money, we mean not only to express the amount of the metal pieces of which it is composed, but to include in its signification some obscure reference to the goods which can be had in exchange for them, the wealth or revenue which it in this ease denotes, is equal only to one of the two values which are thus intimated somewhat ambiguously by the same word, and to the latter more properly than to the former, to the money's worth more properly than to the money.

<small>and his real revenue is that subsistence, &c.</small>

Thus if a guinea be the weekly pension of a particular person, he can in the course of the week purchase with it a certain quantity of subsistence, conveniencies, and amusements. In proportion as this quantity is great or small, so are his real riches, his real weekly revenue. His weekly revenue is certainly not equal both to the guinea, and to what can be purchased with it, but only to one or other of those two equal values; and to the latter more properly than to the former, to the guinea's worth rather than to the guinea.

If the pension of such a person was paid to him, not in gold, but in a weekly bill for a guinea, his revenue surely would not so properly consist in the piece of paper, as in what he could get for it. A guinea

这个言论会让人觉得有些诡辩或存在疑问,原因在于所使用的文字模棱两可;如果解释适当并理解正确,那几乎是不言自明的。

我们说一定数量货币时,有时指的仅仅是货币内含的金块,有时又暗暗地指这些货币所能够换得的货物或者由于占有这些货币而拥有的购买力。比如,我们说英国的通货共计 1800 万镑时,我们的意思不过是说,据某些作者计算或所设想的在英国现在流通金块的数量。但如果我们说某人年收入 50 镑或 100 镑时,我们通常所指的,不仅是他每年可收入的金块数量,而且是他每年可以购买或可以消费的货物的价值。我们通常用这句话来表明他是如何生活的或他应该怎样生活,或者说,他所能够享受的生活必需品和便利品,就数量和质量上来讲,该是怎样?

我们说到一定数量货币,意思不仅指的是这些数量货币内含的金块,而且还暗指这些数量的货币所能够换取的货物;所以,在这种情况下这些数量的货币所代表的财富或收入,绝不能同时等于这两种价值,却只能等于二者之一。与其说等于前者,不如说等于后者;与其说等于货币,不如说等于货币的价值。

如果某甲每星期领取养老金一个几尼,在一星期内他可以用这一个几尼去购买一定数量的生活必需品、便利品和娱乐品。他每星期的真实收入即他的真实财富,是和这个数量的大小成比例。他每星期的收入,绝不可能同时与一个几尼相等,又与这一个几尼所能购买的货物相等。它只能等于二者之一。事实上,与其说等于前者,不如说等于后者;与其说等于这一个几尼,不如说等于这一个几尼的价值。

如果这个人的养老金,不是以金块的形式获得,而是每星期可以获得一个几尼的纸质票据;很明显,他的收入与其说是这一

may be considered as a bill for a certain quantity of necessaries and conveniencies upon all the tradesmen in the neighbourhood. The revenue of the person to whom it is paid, does not so properly consist in the piece of gold, as in what he can get for it, or in what he can exchange it for. If it could be exchanged for nothing, it would, like a bill upon a bankrupt, be of no more value than the most useless piece of paper.

<small>The same is true of all the inhabitants of a country.</small>
Though the weekly or yearly revenue of all the different inhabitants of any country, in the same manner, may be, and in reality frequently is paid to them in money, their real riches, however, the real weekly or yearly revenue of all of them taken together, must always be great or small in proportion to the quantity of consumable goods which they can all of them purchase with this money. The whole revenue of all of them taken together is evidently not equal to both the money and the consumable goods; but only to one or other of those two values, and to the latter more properly than to the former.

Though we frequently, therefore, express a person's revenue by the metal pieces which are annually paid to him, it is because the amount of those pieces regulates the extent of his power of purchasing, or the value of the goods which he can annually afford to consume. We still consider his revenue as consisting in this power of purchasing or consuming, and not in the pieces which convey it.

<small>The coins annually paid to an individual often equal his revenue, but the stock of coin in a society is never equal to its whole revenue.</small>
But if this is sufficiently evident even with regard to an individual, it is still more so with regard to a society. The amount of the metal pieces which are annually paid to an individual, is often precisely equal to his revenue, and is upon that account the shortest and best expression of its value. But the amount of the metal pieces which circulate in a society, can never be equal to the revenue of all its members. As the same guinea which pays the weekly pension of one man to-day, may pay that of another to-morrow, and that of a third the day thereafter, the amount of the metal pieces which annually circulate in any country, must always be of much less value than the whole money pensions annually paid with them. But the power of purchasing, or the goods which can successively be bought with the whole of those money pensions as they are successively paid, must always be precis-

片纸质票据,不如说是这一片纸质票据所能够换得的物品。一个几尼,也可以看作一张票据。有了这张票据,可以向邻近各个商人购买一定数量必需品和便利品。取得这些物品的人的收入构成,与其说是金块,不如说是由于他占有这一个几尼而能够换得的货物。如果这一个几尼竟然不能换得什么物品,那么它的价值,就与破产者所开具的票据一样没有价值。

一国全体居民每星期或每年的收入,虽然都可以是而且实际上也是由货币支付;但无论如何,他们真实财富的大小,即他们全部每星期或每年的真实收入的大小,总是和他们全体用货币所能购买的消费品数量大小成比例。这样,他们全体总收入显然不能既等于这些数量货币,又等于这些消费品,而只能够等于这两个价值之一,与其说等于前一个价值量,不如说等于后一个价值。_{在一个国家里所有居民也如此。}

我们常用一个人每年领取的金块来表示这个人的收入。但之所以如此,只是因为这些金块可以支配一定的购买力,或者说,可以支配他每年所能够取得的消费品的价值。我们仍然认为,构成他收入的是这种购买能力或消费能力,而不是含有这种能力的金块。

如果就个人来说,情况已经十分明白;那么,就社会来说,情况还更加明白。一个人每年领取的金块,往往恰好等于他的收入;他所领取的金块,最能简捷明了表示他收入的价值。但在社会中流通的金块,绝不可能等于社会全体人员的收入。同一个几尼,今日支付给甲,就作为甲的养老金;明日可以支付给乙,就作为乙的养老金;后日又可以付给丙,作为丙的养老金。所以在任何国家里,年年流通的金块,与年年支付付出去的养老金相比较,价值都要小得多。但购买力或由陆续付出的全部养老金所陆续

ely of the same value with those pensions; as must likewise be the revenue of the different persons to whom they are paid. That revenue, therefore, cannot consist in those metal pieces, of which the amount is so much inferior to its value, but in the power of purchasing, in the goods which can successively be bought with them as they circulate from hand to hand.

<small>Money is therefore no part of the revenue of the society</small>

Money, therefore, the great wheel of circulation, the great instrument of commerce, like all other instruments of trade, though it makes a part and a very valuable part of the capital, makes no part of the revenue of the society to which it belongs; and though the metal pieces of which it is composed, in the course of their annual circulation, distribute to every man the revenue which properly belongs to him, they make themselves no part of that revenue.

<small>(3) Every saving in the cost of maintaining the stock of money is an improvement.</small>

Thirdly, and lastly, the machines and instruments of trade, &c. which compose the fixed capital, bear this further resemblance to that part of the circulating capital which consists in money; that as every saving in the expence of erecting and supporting those machines, which does not diminish the productive powers of labour, is an improvement of the neat revenue of the society; so every saving in the expence of collecting and supporting that part of the circulating capital which consists in money, is an improvement of exactly the same kind.

<small>The substitution of paper for gold money is an improvement.</small>

It is sufficiently obvious, and it has partly too been explained already, in what manner every saving in the expence of supporting the fixed capital is an improvement of the neat revenue of the society. The whole capital of the undertaker of every work is necessarily divided between his fixed and his circulating capital. While his whole capital remains the same, the smaller the one part, the greater must necessarily be the other. It is the circulating capital which furnishes the materials and wages of labour, and puts industry into motion. Every saving, therefore, in the expence of maintaining the fixed capital, which does not diminish the productive powers of labour, must increase the fund which puts industry into motion, and consequently the annual produce of land and labour, the real revenue of every society.

The substitution of paper in the room of gold and silver money, replaces a very expensive instrument of commerce with one much less costly, and sometimes equally convenient. Circulation comes to be carried on by a new wheel, which it costs less both to erect and to

买进的全部货物,与这全部养老金相比较,却总具有同样的价值;同样,全体领取养老金的人的收入,也必定与全部养老金具有同样的价值。构成社会收入的绝不是金块;社会上所有的金块,其数量比它的价值要小得多。构成社会收入的其实是购买力,是那些辗转在各个人手中流通的金块陆续所能够购买的货物。

货币是流通的大车轮,是商业上的重要工具。像一切其他行业上的工具一样,都是资本的一部分,并且还是极有价值的一部分,但不是社会收入的一部分。把收入分配给应得收入的人,固然是要通过铸币内含金块的流通,但那些金块绝不是社会收入的一部分。因此货币不是社会收入的一部分。

最后,构成固定资本的机器和工具,与货币组成的那一部分流动资本相类似。建造和维持机器的费用的节省,如果不减少劳动生产力,就是社会纯收入的改善。同样,收集和维持货币这一部分流动资本的费用的节省,也是社会纯收入的增进。(3)每一种维护货币财用的节约都是一种改进。

为什么固定资本维持费用的节省就是对社会纯收入的增进?这个问题十分明白,而且我们已经部分做出过解释。企业家的全部资本,必然会分为固定资本和流动资本。在资本总额不变的情况下,二者肯定会此消彼长。这部分越小,那部分就越大。提供材料、支付工资和推动产业发展的是流动资本。所以,固定资本维持费的节省,如果不减少劳动生产力,那么就一定会增加推动产业发展的基金,从而相应地增加土地和劳动的年产出,增加社会的真实收入。纸币代替金币是一种改进。

以纸代替金银币,可以说是用一种十分廉价的商业工具代替另一种极其昂贵的商业工具,但其便利程度有时几乎一样。有了纸币,流通领域里无异于使用了一个新的车轮,与过去的车轮相

— 643 —

maintain than the old one. But in what manner this operation is performed, and in what manner it tends to increase either the gross or the neat revenue of the society, is not altogether so obvious, and may therefore require some further explication.

Bank notes are the best sort of paper money.

There are several different sorts of paper money; but the circulating notes of banks and bankers are the species which is best known, and which seems best adapted for this purpose.

When the people of any particular country have such confidence in the fortune, probity, and prudence of a particular banker, as to believe that he is always ready to pay upon demand such of his promissory notes as are likely to be at any time presented to him; those notes come to have the same currency as gold and silver money, from the confidence that such money can at any time be had for them.

When a banker lends out £100,000 in notes and keeps in hand only £20,000 in gold and silver, £80,000 in gold and silver is spared from the circulation:

A particular banker lends among his customers his own promissory notes, to the extent, we shall suppose, of a hundred thousand pounds. As those notes serve all the purposes of money, his debtors pay him the same interest as if he had lent them so much money. This interest is the source of his gain. Though some of those notes are continually coming back upon him for payment, part of them continue to circulate for months and years together. Though he has generally in circulation, therefore, notes to the extent of a hundred thousand pounds, twenty thousand pounds in gold and silver may, frequently, be a sufficient provision for answering occasional demands. By this operation, therefore, twenty thousand pounds in gold and silver perform all the functions which a hundred thousand could otherwise have performed. The same exchanges may be made, the same quantity of consumable goods may be circulated and distributed to their proper consumers, by means of his promissory notes, to the value of a hundred thousand pounds, as by an equal value of gold and silver money. Eighty thousand pounds of gold and silver, therefore, can, in this manner, be spared from the circulation of the country; and if different operations of the same kind should, at the same time, be carried on by many different banks and bankers, the whole circulation may thus be conducted with a fifth part only of the gold and silver which would otherwise have been requisite.

Let us suppose, for example, that the whole circulating money of some particular country amounted, at a particular time, to one million sterling, that sum being then sufficient for circulating the whole annual produce of their land and labour. Let us suppose too, that some time thereafter, different banks and bankers issued promissory notes, payable to the bearer, to the extent of one million, reserving in their different coffers two hundred thousand pounds for answering occasion-

比,它的建立费用和维持费用都要轻微得多。但它如何充当流通领域的车轮工具,用哪一种方式来增加社会的总收入或纯收入,人们对此还不十分明了;所以,需要进一步的说明。

> 银行券是一种最佳的纸币。

纸币有好几种,各不相同;银行流通的银行券是最普通的,也是最适于使用的。

一个国家人民如果相信某银行家资产雄厚,行为正直,处事谨慎,相信他有能力随时可以兑换他所接到的自己发行的本票时,那么银行家所发行的票据,便可以在社会上流通使用,与金币银币一样没有区别。

我们假设某银行家,以面值10万镑期票借给他的顾客;这种期票由于和货币有同等作用,与借入货币一样,所以,债务人才愿意偿付同样的利息,与借入货币一样。这些利息就是银行家获利的来源。发出去的期票,尽管有一部分会不断回来要求兑现,但总有一部分会不断地在社会上流通。所以,他所发出去的期票,虽然是10万镑,但只需要有两万镑金银币,常常就足够应付不时之需。这样,这种期票的发行,使两万镑金银币可以行使10万镑金银币的作用。同一数量消费品的交换,同一数量消费品的周转和分配,可通过这10万镑期票而实现,与通过使用10万镑金银相同。因此,国内银行发行期票的这种方式,可以把8万镑金银从流通领域里节省下来。假设国内银行众多,都按照这种办法经营,那么,这时国内货物流通所需要的金银,就只不过等于没有期票时所需要的1/5了。

> 当一家银行用期票10万镑并在手备金两万镑,那么就从流通领域节省8万镑下来;

让我们假设,某个国家在某个时间的通货总共为一百万镑,这个数目已经足够国内流通全部土地和劳动的年产出。再让我们假定,后来由于银行众多,发行的期票总金额为100万镑,而他

and if many bankers do the same, four-fifths of the gold and silver previously circulating may be sent abroad,   al demands. There would remain, therefore, in circulation, eight hundred thousand pounds in gold and silver, and a million of bank notes, or eighteen hundred thousand pounds of paper and money together. But the annual produce of the land and labour of the country had before required only one million to circulate and distribute it to its proper consumers, and that annual produce cannot be immediately augmented by those operations of banking. One million, therefore, will be sufficient to circulate it after them. The goods to be bought and sold being precisely the same as before, the same quantity of money will be sufficient for buying and selling them. The channel of circulation, if I may be allowed such an expression, will remain precisely the same as before. One million we have supposed sufficient to fill that channel. Whatever, therefore, is poured into it beyond this sum, cannot run in it, but must overflow. One million eight hundred thousand pounds are poured into it. Eight hundred thousand pounds, therefore, must overflow, that sum being over and above what can be employed in the circulation of the country. But though this sum cannot be employed at home, it is too valuable to be allowed to lie idle. It will, therefore, be sent abroad, in order to seek that profitable employment which it cannot find at home. But the paper cannot go abroad; because at a distance from the banks which issue it, and from the country in which payment of it can be exacted by law, it will not

and exchanged for goods,   be received in common payments. Gold and silver, therefore, to the amount of eight hundred thousand pounds will be sent abroad, and the channel of home circulation will remain filled with a million of paper, instead of the million of those metals which filled it before.

either to supply the consumption of another country, in which case the profit will be an addition to the net revenue of the country.   But though so great a quantity of gold and silver is thus sent abroad, we must not imagine that it is sent abroad for nothing, or that its proprietors make a present of it to foreign nations. They will exchange it for foreign goods of some kind or another, in order to supply the consumption either of some other foreign country, or of their own.

If they employ it in purchasing goods in one foreign country in order to supply the consumption of another, or in what is called the carrying trade, whatever profit they make will be an addition to the neat revenue of their own country. It is like a new fund, created for

第二篇 第二章

们在金柜内保留20万镑以应对不时之需。这样,在流通领域就有了80万镑金银币和100万镑期票,总共为180万镑。但国内土地和劳动的年产出的流通、周转和分配,原来只需要100万镑;现在,银行的这些运作又不能马上增加国内年产出的数额;所以,在有银行运作以后,流通国内年产出,100万镑已经足够。等待买卖流通的货物量依然不变,用来买卖所使用的货币量也自然可以没有改变。流通的渠道——如果这个名称适当——肯定完全一样。100万镑就足以充满渠道了。超过这个限度,再投放下去,不能被渠道所吸纳而向其他地方溢出。现在,我们已经投入180万镑。80万镑定然会溢流出来,这些数额是国内流通领域所容纳不下的。但是,对国内不能容纳的数目弃之不用,又不免损失太大。因此,一定会把它送到外国去,寻求在本国寻求不到的有利用途。不过,纸币是不能送到外国去的,因为外国离发行银行远,距离那些可以使用法律强迫纸币兑现的国家远,所以,纸币在外国是不能流通使用的。送到外国去的一定是80万镑金银。国内流通的渠道,以前由100万镑金银充满,现在却将由纸币100万镑来充满了。

<small>如果银行都按照同样的方式运作的话,那么以前流通领域里80%的金银就会被输往国外,与外国交换进入本国,</small>

尽管如此庞大数量的金银被送往外国,我们绝对不要认为它们输往国外是无所作为的行为,或者是金银主人把它们当作礼物送给外国。它的流出,肯定会换进一些外国货物进来,供本国人消费或转卖给别国人民消费。

<small>要么是供应其他国人消费,这种情况带来的是本国纯收入增加;要么是供应本国人消费,这种情况带来利润增加国纯收入;</small>

假设运输金银的人是甲国人民,他们现在用这些金银购买乙国货物,供两个国家人民消费。他们所经营的就是所谓贩运贸易。通过贸易而获得的利润,当然是对甲国纯收入的增进。所以,这些巨额金银就像新设的基金一样,可用来开办新的事业。

^{or to supply home consumption (1) of luxuries. (2) of materials, tools and provisions wherewith industrious people are maintained and employed. If to supply luxuries, prodigality and consumption are increased; if to supply materials, &c., a permanent fund for supporting consumption is provided.}

carrying on a new trade; domestic business being now transacted by paper, and the gold and silver being converted into a fund for this new trade.

If they employ it in purchasing foreign goods for home consumption, they may either, first, purchase such goods as are likely to be consumed by idle people who produce nothing, such as foreign wines, foreign silks, &c. ; or, secondly, they may purchase an additional stock of materials, tools, and provisions, in order to maintain and employ an additional number of industrious people, who re-produce, with a profit, the value of their annual consumption.

So far as it is employed in the first way, it promotes prodigality, increases expence and consumption without increasing production, or establishing any permanent fund for supporting that expence, and is in every respect hurtful to the society.

So far as it is employed in the second way, it promotes industry; and though it increases the consumption of the society, it provides a permanent fund for supporting that consumption, the people who consume re-producing, with a profit, the whole value of their annual consumption. The gross revenue of the society, the annual produce of their land and labour, is increased by the whole value which the labour of those workmen adds to the materials upon which they are employed; and their neat revenue by what remains of this value, after deducting what is necessary for supporting the tools and instruments of their trade.

^{The greater part of the gold and silver sent abroad purchases materials, &c.}

That the greater part of the gold and silver which, being forced abroad by those operations of banking, is employed in purchasing foreign goods for home consumption, is and must be employed in purchasing those of this second kind, seems not only probable but almost unavoidable. Though some particular men may sometimes increase their expence very considerably though their revenue does not increase at all, we may be assured that no class or order of men ever does so; because, though the principles of common prudence do not always govern the conduct of every individual, they always influence that of the majority of every class or order. But the revenue of idle people, considered as a class or order, cannot, in the smallest degree, be increased by those operations of banking. Their expence in general, therefore, cannot be much increased by them, though that of a few in-

国内事业现由纸币经营,就可以把金银移转到这种新事业上来充当基金使用。

如果他们使用这些巨额金银购买外国货物,供本国消费,那些购买进来的货物,第一,就是供那些无所事事的懒惰阶级所消费的货品,如外国葡萄酒、外国绸缎等等。或是第二,购买额外的材料、工具和食料等,从而维持和雇用更多的勤劳人民;这些人民再生产出他们每年消费的价值和利润。

如果用于前一种途径,就无异于鼓励奢侈浪费,增加开支和消费,而又不增加生产,不增加维持这项消费的固定基金;无论就哪一点说,对社会都是有害的。

如果是用于后一种途径,却可以鼓励勤劳;尽管会增加社会上的消费,但也会提供维持这项消费的固定资金。消费者会把每年消费的价值全都再生产出来,同时提供利润。社会上的总收入或社会上土地和劳动的年产出,肯定会有所增加;其增加的数量等于工人对加工材料所增加的全部价值。社会的纯收入也必然增加,其增加的数量等于上述价值减去这些工人使用工具和机械所需要的维持费用后剩下的价值。

由于银行作用而被迫输往外国的金银,如果是用来购买本国消费的外国货物,就有大部分是而且一定是用来购买第二类货物;这不仅是可能的而且几乎是必然的。尽管也有这样的人,他们的收入虽然没有增加,但忽然大肆挥霍起来,我确信在世界上没有一个阶级全是这么做事。不能希望每一个人都谨慎从事,但至少在一个阶级中总有大多数人不奢侈浪费,不乱花钱;大多数人的行为总能奉行谨慎的原则。至于那些懒惰者,作为一个阶级他们的收入,既不能由于银行的运作而有丝毫增加,所以,除

dividuals among them may, and in reality sometimes is. The demand of idle people, therefore, for foreign goods, being the same, or very nearly the same, as before, a very small part of the money, which being forced abroad by those operations of banking, is employed in purchasing foreign goods for home consumption, is likely to be employed in purchasing those for their use. The greater part of it will naturally be destined for the employment of industry, and not for the maintenance of idleness.

<small>The quantity of industry which the circulating capital can employ is determined by the provisions, materials, and finished work, and not at all by the quantity of money.</small>
When we compute the quantity of industry which the circulating capital of any society can employ, we must always have regard to those parts of it only, which consist in provisions, materials, and finished work: the other, which consists in money, and which serves only to circulate those three, must always be deducted. In order to put industry into motion, three things are requisite; materials to work upon, tools to work with, and the wages or recompence for the sake of which the work is done. Money is neither a material to work upon, nor a tool to work with; and though the wages of the workman are commonly paid to him in money, his real revenue, like that of all other men, consists, not in the money, but in the money's worth; not in the metal pieces, but in what can be got for them.

The quantity of industry which any capital can employ, must, evidently, be equal to the number of workmen whom it can supply with materials, tools, and a maintenance suitable to the nature of the work. Money may be requisite for purchasing the materials and tools of the work, as well as the maintenance of the workmen. But the quantity of industry which the whole capital can employ, is certainly not equal both to the money which purchases, and to the materials, tools, and maintenance, which are purchased with it; but only to one or other of those two values, and to the latter more properly than to the former.

<small>The substitution of paper for gold and silver increases the materials, tools, and maintenance at the expense of the gold and silver money.</small>
When paper is substituted in the room of gold and silver money, the quantity of the materials, tools, and maintenance, which the whole circulating capital can supply, may be increased by the whole value of gold and silver which used to be employed in purchasing them. The whole value of the great wheel of circulation and distribution, is added to the goods which are circulated and distributed by means of it. The operation, in some measure, resembles that of the undertaker of some great work, who, in consequence of some improvement in mechanics, takes down his old machinery, and adds the

了少数实际的个别例外,他们这一个阶级的费用,也不能由于银行的运作而增加。懒惰阶级对外国货物的需求依旧不变或者大概不变。由于银行作用而被迫输往外国,用来购买外国货物以供本国消费的货币,也只有一极小部分是用来购买这些人需用的物品。其中大部分当然是指定用来兴办实业,而不是用来维持懒惰人群的奢华消费。

我们在计算社会流动资本所能推动的劳动量时,常须记住一件事情,那就是在社会流动资本中,可以只计算食品、材料和制成品三项。而由货币构成的、仅用来实现这三项流通的部分,必须从中减去。为了推动产业发展,需要三件物品,即材料、工具和工资。材料是工作的对象;工具是工作的手段;工资或报酬是工人工作的目的。货币既不是工作的材料,也不是工作的工具;虽然工资一般用货币支付,但工人的真实收入并非由货币或金块构成。构成工人真实收入的是货币的价值,或者说是金块所能换得的货物。

_{流动资本所能雇佣的劳动量取决于食品、材料和产品,一点也不取决于货币量。}

一定数量资本所能雇用的劳动量,显然必须等于资本能够供应材料、工具和适于工作性质的维持费用的工人数量。购买材料、工具和维持工人,尽管缺少不了货币,但全部资本所能雇佣的劳动量,无疑不能同时等于用来购买的货币量和用货币购买材料、工具和食品的数量。而只能等于这两个价值之一,与其说是等于前者,不如说等于后者。

以纸币代替金银币,全部流动资本所能提供的材料、食品和工具,必须按照纸币所代替金银的全部价值而增加。起流动和分配作用的车轮的全部价值,现在被加在本来依靠它而流通的货物价值上面。这件事有些像某个大工厂厂主的境况。由于机器的

_{在牺牲银币的情况下,纸币可以用来对金银币增加材料、工具和维持工人的费用购买。}

difference between its price and that of the new to his circulating capital, to the fund from which he furnishes materials and wages to his workmen.

<small>The quantity of money bears a small proportion to the whole produce, but a large one to that part destined to maintain industry.</small>

What is the proportion which the circulating money of any country bears to the whole value of the annual produce circulated by means of it, it is, perhaps, impossible to determine. It has been computed by different authors at a fifth, at a tenth, at a twentieth, and at a thirtieth part of that value. ① But how small soever the proportion which the circulating money may bear to the whole value of the annual produce, as but a part, and frequently but a small part, of that produce, is ever destined for the maintenance of industry, it must always bear a very considerable proportion to that part. When, therefore, by the substitution of paper, the gold and silver necessary for circulation is reduced to, perhaps, a fifth part of the former quantity, if the value of only the greater part of the other four-fifths be added to the funds which are destined for the maintenance of industry, it must make a very considerable addition to the quantity of that industry, and, conesquently, to the value of the annual produce of land and labour.

<small>An operation of this kind has been carried out in Scotland with excellent effects.</small>

An operation of this kind has, within these five-and-twenty or thirty years, been performed in Scotland, by the erection of new banking companies in almost every considerable town, and even in some country villages. The effects of it have been precisely those above described. The business of the country is almost entirely carried on by means of the paper of those different banking companies, with which purchases and payments of all kinds are commonly made. Silver very seldom appears except in the change of a twenty shillings bank note, and gold still seldomer. But though the conduct of all those different companies has not been unexceptionable, and has accordingly required an act of parliament to regulate it; the country. notwithstanding, has evidently derived great benefit from their trade. I have heard it asserted, that the trade of the city of Glasgow, doubled in about fifteen years after the first erection of the banks there; and that the trade of Scotland has more than quadrupled since the first erection of the two public banks at Edinburgh, of which the one, called The Bank of Scotland, was established by act of parliament in

---

① [Petty's estimate in *Verbum Sapienti* is £ 40,000,000 for the income and £ 6,000,000 for the coin. Gregory King's estimate is £ 43,500,000 for the income and no less than £ 11,500,000 for the coin, in Geo. Chalmers, *Estimate*, 1802, pp. 423, 427.]

进步,他舍弃旧机器不用,把新旧机器价格之间的差额加入流动资本,即加入作为购置材料和支付工资的基金。

一国流通的货币与依靠它而流通的年产出的全部价值之间,究竟保持什么样比例,也许不可能对此加以确定。有些作者说是全部价值的1/5,又有人说是1/10、1/20或1/30。① 但是,货币对年产出全部价值所保持的比例,无论多么小,尽管只有一部分而且常常是一小部分的年产出,被指定用作维持产业的基金,但货币对这一部分年产物所保持的比例总是有一个相当大的比例。如果通过纸币代替金银,流通中所需要的金银数量减少到原来的1/5,那么,如果把其余4/5中的大部分增加到被指定用来维持产业的基金上,当然会大大增加产业的数量,因而会大大增加土地和劳动的年产出的价值。

最近25~30年以来,苏格兰几乎所有大都市里都纷纷设立许多新的银行,甚至在那些穷乡僻壤地区有时也如此。银行的这种运作结果,正如上所述。国内经营业务几乎完全使用由不同银行发行的纸币进行周转;一切种类的购买和支付也都凭借纸币开展。除了兑现20先令的钞票以外,银币很少见到,金币尤其少见。尽管银行众多,难免良莠不齐,议院必须要通过立法加以规范,但国家依然从银行的设立和其业务经营中受益匪浅。我听说格拉斯格自银行创立以来,15年期间商业已经增加一倍。苏格兰的商业自从两家公立银行(一家为苏格兰银行,在1695年由议会

---

① 配第对收入的估计为4000万镑,对铸币的估计为600万镑;格雷戈里·金对收入的估计为4350万镑,而对铸币的估计则不低于1150万镑。见乔治·乔默斯(Chalmers):《大不列颠实力比较之估计》,第423、427页。

1695; the other, called The Royal Bank, by royal charter in 1727. ①
Whether the trade, either of Scotland in general, or of the city of
Glasgow in particular, has really increased in so great a proportion,
during so short a period, I do not pretend to know. If either of them
has increased in this proportion, it seems to be an effect too great to
be accounted for by the sole operation of this cause. That the trade
and industry of Scotland, however, have increased very considerably
during this period, and that the banks have contributed a good deal to
this increase, cannot be doubted.

<small>There was at the Union at least a million sterling of gold and silver money, and now there is not half a million.</small> The value of the silver money which circulated in Scotland before the union, in 1707, and which, immediately after it, was brought into the bank of Scotland in order to be re-coined, amounted to 411, 117*l*. 10*s*. 9*d*. sterling. No account has been got of the gold coin; but it appears from the ancient accounts of the mint of Scotland, that the value of the gold annually coined somewhat exceeded that of the silver. ② There were a good many people too upon this occasion, who, from a diffidence of repayment, did not bring their silver into the bank of Scotland: and there was, besides, some English coin, which was not called in. ③ The whole value of the gold and silver, therefore, which circulated in Scotland before the union, cannot be estimated at less than a million sterling. It seems to have constituted almost the whole circulation of that country; for though the circulation

---

① [Adam Anderson, Commerce, A. D. 1695.]

② See Ruddiman's Preface to Anderson's Diplomata, &c. Scotiae. [pp. 84, 85. See above, p. 212, note.]

③ ['The folly of a few misers or the fear that people might have of losing their money, or various other dangers and accidents, prevented very many of the old Scots coins from being brought in,' *op. cit.* p. 175. Ruddiman in a note *op. cit.* p. 231, says: 'The English coin was also ordained to be called in,' but does not include it in his estimate of not less than £ 900,000, p. 176.]

批准创立;一家叫皇家银行,由国王敕令批准设立于1727年)。①在爱丁堡创立以来,已经增加四倍以上。在这个短期内,无论是苏格兰一般情况下的商业,还是格拉斯哥特殊情况下的商业,是否增加这么高的比例,我不敢自作聪明,妄加判断。如果无论是谁真是取得如此巨大的进展,似乎也不能完全归功于银行的设立,也许还有其他原因。不过,就苏格兰在这个时期工商业进步迅速以及银行设立是促进它们取得进步的一个重要原因这一点来说,是毋庸置疑的。

这些在1707年英格兰和苏格兰合并以后不久拿到苏格兰银行重新铸造的银币,在合并以前在苏格兰境内流通的价值为411,117镑10先令9便士。至于金币则没有记录可供考证。但据苏格兰造币厂过去的账簿记录显示,似乎每年铸造的金币的价值,稍微比银币多一些。②当时有许多人担心银币一旦回流给苏格兰银行以后,就不可能再归属自己,所以有许多银币,始终没有拿回苏格兰银行;③此外,还有一些流通的英格兰铸币,也没有缴回银行。因此,在未合并以前,苏格兰通用的金银币价值,共计不少于100万镑。这个数额似乎构成当时苏格兰全部的通货,因为当时

（合并至金币而联国有银100镑,现在不到50万镑。王少万）

---

① 亚当·安德森:《商业起源的历史性考察和年序演绎》,1695年。
② 参阅鲁迪曼为安德森写的《苏格兰古文书》序言,第84、85页。
③ 那些人们害怕失去自己的货币或吝啬人的愚蠢行为,或者其他各种危险和事故可能阻止旧版苏格兰铸币的回收;前面引用的书,第175页。鲁迪曼在前面引用的书的第231页的一个注释里说,英国铸币也是被强令收回的,但在他的估计里并不包括不少于90万镑的铸币。

of the bank of Scotland, which had then no rival, was considerable, it seems to have made but a very small part of the whole. In the present times the whole circulation of Scotland cannot be estimated at less than two millions, of which that part which consists in gold and silver, most probably, does not amount to half a million. But though the circulating gold and silver of Scotland have suffered so great a diminution during this period, its real riches and prosperity do not appear to have suffered any. Its agriculture, manufactures, and trade, on the contrary, the annual produce of its land and labour, have evidently been augmented.

<small>Notes are ordinarily issued by discounting bills,</small>   It is chiefly by discounting bills of exchange, that is, by advancing money upon them before they are due, that the greater part of banks and bankers issue their promissory notes. They deduct always, upon whatever sum they advance, the legal interest till the bill shall become due. The payment of the bill, when it becomes due, replaces to the bank the value of what had been advanced, together with a clear profit of the interest. The banker who advances to the merchant whose bill he discounts, not gold and silver, but his own promissory notes, has the advantage of being able to discount to a greater amount by the whole value of his promissory notes, which he finds by experience, are commonly in circulation. He is thereby enabled to make his clear gain of interest on so much a larger sum.

<small>but the Scotch banks invented the system of cash accounts,</small>   The commerce of Scotland, which at present is not very great, was still more inconsiderable when the two first banking companies were established; and those companies would have had but little trade, had they confined their business to the discounting of bills of exchange. They invented, therefore, another method of issuing their promissory notes; by granting, what they called, cash accounts, that is by giving credit to the extent of a certain sum (two or three thousand pounds, for example), to any individual who could procure two persons of undoubted credit and good landed estate to become surety for him, that whatever money should be advanced to him, within the sum for which the credit had been given, should be repaid upon demand, together with the legal interest. Credits of this kind are, I believe, commonly granted by banks and bankers in all different parts of the world. But the easy terms upon which the Scotch banking companies accept of re-payment are, so far as I know, peculiar to them, and have, perhaps, been the principal cause, both of the great trade of those companies, and of the benefit which the country has received from it.

苏格兰银行虽然在流通领域没有竞争者,它的钞票发行不少,但在全部通货中也仅仅只占极小的一部分。现在苏格兰的全部通货估计少于200万镑,其中金银币大概不超过50万镑。但是,虽然在此期间苏格兰的金银币大大减少,它的真实财富和繁荣却丝毫没有遭受任何损害。反过来,农工商各个行业的发达以及土地和劳动的年产出的增加,已经得到显著地增加。

银行发行银行券的主要方法是通过贴现汇票的方法,也就是是预先垫付货币,购买未到期的汇票,从而发行货币。汇票在没有到期以前,就可以持有票据前往银行预先贷出现金。在银行方面,计算从现在至到期日应收的法定利息,并在全部贷款额中扣除利息。到期以后,汇票的兑付,既可以偿还银行预先贷出去的价值,还会带来利息形式的纯利润。银行贴现汇票是以本银行发行的银行券支付,并不是用金银进行支付。银行家可以根据以往经验,在可能范围内,尽量把银行券垫付出去;所以,他所能够贴现的汇票金额可以更多,他在利息方面所能够获得的纯利润也就自然增多。

银行券一般通过贴现的方法来发行,

苏格兰的商业,今天仍然不很繁荣;在上述两家银行创立时还微不足道。如果这两家银行仅仅经营汇票的贴现业务,业务肯定不多。所以,它们发明另外一种方法来发行信用票据,也就是所谓现金结算法。随便任何一个人,只要他找到两个信用良好并有真实地产的担保人进行担保,并在银行要求偿还借款时,就可以立即如数还清所借金额和法定利息,他就可以向银行借入一定数额的款项如2000镑或3000镑。我相信,这种放贷方法在世界各处银行都有。但据我所知,苏格兰各家银行所接受的还款条件特别便利宽松。这也许是他们银行营业兴旺、国家受益深厚的主

但是苏格兰银行发明了现金结算法,

which enable them to issue notes readily,

    Whoever has a credit of this kind with one of those companies, and borrows a thousand pounds upon it, for example, may repay this sum piece-meal, by twenty and thirty pounds at a time, the company discounting a proportionable part of the interest of the great sum from the day on which each of those small sums is paid in, till the whole be in this manner repaid. All merchants, therefore, and almost all men of business, find it convenient to keep such cash accounts with them, and are thereby interested to promote the trade of those companies, by readily receiving their notes in all payments, and by encouraging all those with whom they have any influence to do the same. The banks, when their customers apply to them for money, generally advance it to them in their own promissory notes. These the merchants pay away to the manufacturers for goods, the manufacturers to the farmers for materials and provisions, the farmers to their landlords for rent, the landlords repay them to the merchants for the conveniencies and luxuries with which they supply them, and the merchants again return them to the banks in order to balance their cash accounts, or to replace what they may have borrowed of them; and thus almost the whole money business of the country is transacted by means of them. Hence the great trade of those companies.

and make it possible for every merchant to carry on a greater trade than he otherwise could.

    By means of those cash accounts every merchant can, without imprudence, carry on a greater trade than he otherwise could do. If there are two merchants, one in London, and the other in Edinburgh, who employ equal stocks in the same branch of trade, the Edinburgh merchant can, without imprudence, carry on a greater trade, and give employment to a greater number of people than the London merchant. The London merchant must always keep by him a considerable sum of money, either in his own coffers, or in those of his banker, who gives him no interest for it, in order to answer the demands continually coming upon him for payment of the goods which he purchases upon credit. Let the ordinary amount of this sum be supposed five hundred pounds. The value of the goods in his warehouse must always be less by five hundred pounds than it would have been, had he not been obliged to keep such a sum unemployed. Let us suppose that he generally disposes of his whole stock upon hand, or of goods to the value of his whole stock upon hand, once in the year. By being obliged to keep so great a sum unemployed, he must sell in a year five hundred pounds worth less goods than he might otherwise have done. His annual profits must be less by all that he could have made by the sale of five hundred pounds worth more goods; and the number of people employed in preparing his goods for the market, must be less by all those that five hundred pounds more stock could have employed. The mer-

要原因。

在苏格兰,凡具有上述信用条件的人,就可以向银行按照这个方法借到比如说1000镑,他可以随时分期还款,有二三十镑就可以偿还一次。银行方面就以每次收回货款的日期算起,到全数偿清的日期为止,计算每次所收回的数额,并在全部金额的利息中减少相应数目的利息。各种商人和各种实业家,都觉得这种方法很便利,因而乐于促进银行业务发展;不仅在一切支付上都欣然接受银行钞票,并劝说其他人接受银行钞票。在顾客借入货币时,银行大部分用本银行的钞票支付。商人以钞票购买制造者的货物,制造者以钞票购买农业家的食品和材料,农场主以钞票向地主支付地租,地主以钞票向商人购买各种便利品和奢侈品,商人最后又把钞票还给银行来偿还借款。全国所有货币业务几乎都是使用这种方法;银行业务也就自然兴旺发达起来。

> 也使银行能够很容易地发行银行券。

依靠现金结算法,商人们才可以扩大经营业务。假设有两位商人,一位在伦敦,一位在爱丁堡,他们二者所经营的业务相同,所投入的资本也相等。爱丁堡商人由于有现金结算法,所以营业规模才能够发展壮大,能够雇用比较多的人员。伦敦商人则由于没有现金结算法,常常必须在自己金柜内或在银行金柜内(那自然没有利息)储备巨额货币,以应付因购货而借入的贷款被不断索要的要求。假如常常必须准备500镑,那么,和不需要常常保存现金500镑的准备金的情况相比较,货栈内货物的价值就会少500镑。假设商人保有的存货一般每年售完一次,这时候与不需要保有准备金的情况相比较,他就因为经常必须保有500镑准备金,所以销售的货物总共要少500镑的价值。在这种情况下,他每年的利润与他所能雇用来办理销售业务的工人人数,一定比他

> 并且使每一个商人比以前都扩大业务。

chant in Edinburgh, on the other hand, keeps no money unemployed for answering such occasional demands. When they actually come upon him, he satisfies them from his cash account with the bank, and gradually replaces the sum borrowed with the money or paper which comes in from the occasional sales of his goods. With the same stock, therefore, he can, without imprudence, have at all times in his warehouse a larger quantity of goods than the London merchant; and can thereby both make a greater profit himself, and give constant employment to a greater number of industrious people who prepare those goods for the market. Hence the great benefit which the country has derived from this trade.

<small>The Scotch banks can of course discount bills when required.</small> The facility of discounting bills of exchange, it may be thought indeed, gives the English merchants a convenieney equivalent to the cash accounts of the Scotch merchants. But the Scotch merchants, it must be remembered, can discount their bills of exchange as easily as the English merchants; and have, besides, the additional conveniency of their cash accounts.

<small>The whole of the paper money can never exceed the gold and silver which would have been required in its absence.</small> The whole paper money of every kind which can easily circulate in any country never can exceed the value of the gold and silver, of which it supplies the place, or which (the commerce being supposed the same) would circulate there, if there was no paper money. If twenty shilling notes, for example, are the lowest paper money current in Scotland, the whole of that currency which can easily circulate there cannot exceed the sum of gold and silver which would be necessary for transacting the annual exchanges of twenty shillings value and upwards usually transacted within that country. Should the circulating paper at any time exceed that sum, as the excess could neither be sent abroad nor be employed in the circulation of the country, it must immediately return upon the banks to be exchanged for gold and silver. Many people would immediately perceive that they had more of this paper than was necessary for transacting their business at home, and as they could not send it abroad, they would immediately demand payment of it from the banks. When this superfluous paper was converted into gold and silver, they could easily find a use for it by sending it abroad; but they could find none while it remained in the shape of paper. There would immediately, therefore, be a run upon the banks to the whole extent of this superfluous paper, and, if they shewed any difficulty or backwardness in payment, to a much greater extent; the alarm, which this would occasion, necessarily increasing the run.

能够多卖500镑货物的情况少。反之,爱丁堡商人不需要保有准备金来应付这种不时之需;万一遇到紧急情况需要,他可以使用现金结算法,向银行借钱来应对,以后用不断卖出货物而所得的货币或纸币,逐渐偿还银行借款。与伦敦商人比较,他可以使用等量资本,囤积较多数量货物。因此,他给自己赚取更多的利润,给那些为市场提供货物的劳动人民以更多的就业机会。所以国家也从中获利不小。

英格兰银行通过贴现汇票所给予英格兰商人的便利,与现金结算法所给予苏格兰商人的便利相同,但要记住的是,苏格兰商人也可以向银行申请贴现汇票,和英格兰商人一样容易。而除了贴现期票以外,苏格兰银行还有现金结算法,所以对商人更为便利。

<small>苏格兰商人当然可以根据需要请求贴现汇票。</small>

在任何国家里,各种纸币能够畅通无阻地到处流通的全部金额,不可能超过其所代替的金银的价值,或(在商业状况不变的条件下)在没有这些纸币的情况下所必需金银币的价值。例如,苏格兰通用的纸币,假设最低面值是20先令纸票,那么,能在全苏格兰流通的这种通货的总额,绝不可能超过国内每年交易20先令以及20先令以上价值的交易一般所需要的金银的数额。如果超过了这个总额,那些过剩的部分,既不能在国内使用,又不能输往国外;结果,必定会马上回到银行去兑换金银。获得钞票的人民立即觉得,他们所有的钞票超过国内交易的需要。他们既然不能把纸币送往外国,当然,马上会向银行申请兑现。因为,过剩的钞票一旦兑换成金银,就会输往国外,很容易就有用处;但是在钞票还是钞票的时候,钞票一点用处也没有。总之,过剩的数额将全数回到银行兑现,如果银行对兑现表现困难或迟缓,回到银行

<small>纸币来超过通里纸币所流通领域时,过剩的数量没有金银必需的数量。</small>

The peculiar expenses of a bank are (1) the keeping and (2) the replenishing of a stock of money with which to repay notes.	Over and above the expences which are common to every branch of trade; such as the expence of house-rent, the wages of servants, clerks, accountants, &c.; the expences peculiar to a bank consist chiefly in two articles: First, in the expence of keeping at all times in its coffers, for answering the occasional demands of the holders of its notes, a large sum of money, of which it loses the interest: And, secondly, in the expence of replenishing those coffers as fast as they are emptied by answering such occasional demands.
A bank which issues too much paper will increase both the first	A banking company, which issues more paper than can be employed in the circulation of the country, and of which the excess is continually returning upon them for payment, ought to increase the quantity of gold and silver, which they keep at all times in their coffers, not only in proportion to this excessive increase of their circulation, but in a much greater proportion; their notes returning upon them much faster than in proportion to the excess of their quantity. Such a company, therefore, ought to increase the first article of their expence, not only in proportion to this forced increase of their business, but in a much greater proportion.
and the second expense.	The coffers of such a company too, though they ought to be filled much fuller, yet must empty themselves much faster than if their business was confined within more reasonable bounds, and must require, not only a more violent, but a more constant and uninterrupted exertion of expence in order to replenish them. The coin too, which is thus continually drawn in such large quantities from their coffers, cannot be employed in the circulation of the country. It comes in place of a paper which is over and above what can be employed in that circulation, and is therefore over and above what can be employed in it too. But as that coin will not be allowed to lie idle, it must, in one shape or another, be sent abroad, in order to find that profitable employment which it cannot find at home; and this continual exportation of gold and silver, by enhancing the difficulty, must necessarily enhance still further the expence of the bank, in finding new gold and silver in order to replenish those coffers, which empty themselves so very rapidly. Such a company, therefore, must, in proportion to this forced increase of their business, increase the second article of their expence still more than the first.

Let us suppose that all the paper of a particular bank, which the circulation of the country can easily absorb and employ, amounts exactly to forty thousand pounds; and that for answering occasional de-

去的钞票还会更多。由此而引起的惊慌和猜疑,必然会使兑现要求更加紧张起来。

各种企业的经营都少不了经费。房租和佣人、办事员、会计员等的工资在各种企业中都是必不可少的。银行所特有的费用可分为两类:第一,在金柜内,经常必须储存没有利息可得的巨额货币,以应对持票兑现的不时要求。第二,因应对不时要求而将清空的金柜,必须时时补充。

如果银行发行纸币过多,超过国内流通的需要,不能流通的过剩货币量不断要求兑现,在这种情况下,银行的金柜不但要按照纸币过剩的比例增加储存的金银,而且要按更大的比例增加储存的金银,因为纸币的回笼,其速度比发行过剩数量的扩大要快得多。银行第一项特别费用的增加,不仅要按迫不得已的兑现所增加的比例而增加,而且要按更大的比例增加。

此外,这种发行过度的银行,尽管它应该有较充实的金柜,但其金柜的清空速度,却一定比在谨慎发行的情况下要快得多。因此,对于金柜的补充,常常必须作不断的和丝毫不懈怠的努力。但这样大量不断地由金柜流出来的铸币却不能在国内流通。这种铸币是为兑换超过流通所需要的纸币而流出的,所以也是流通所不需要的。按照常理,铸币是不会被弃之不用的,它在国内没有用处,就会以这种或那种形态输往外国,以寻求有利的用途。但金银这样的不断出口,会增加银行寻找新的金银来补充金柜的困难,从而进一步增加银行的费用。所以,像这样的银行,一定会由于兑现的迫不得已的增加,而增加它的第二项特别费用,并增加得比第一项还要多。

我们假设某银行发行的纸币为40,000镑,而这恰恰是国内

| as may be shown by an example. | mands, this bank is obliged to keep at all times in its coffers ten thousand pounds in gold and silver. Should this bank attempt to circulate forty-four thousand pounds, the four thousand pounds which are over and above what the circulation can easily absorb and employ, will return upon it almost as fast as they are issued. For answering occasional demands, therefore, this bank ought to keep at all times in its coffers, not eleven thousand pounds only, but fourteen thousand pounds. It will thus gain nothing by the interest of the four thousand pounds excessive circulation; and it will lose the whole expence of continually collecting four thousand pounds in gold and silver, which will be continually going out of its coffers as fast as they are brought into them. |

| Banks have sometimes not understood this, | Had every particular banking company always understood and attended to its own particular interest, the circulation never could have been overstocked with paper money. But every particular banking company has not always understood or attended to its own particular interest, and the circulation has frequently been overstocked with paper money. |

| e. g., the Bank of England, | By issuing too great a quantity of paper, of which the excess was continually returning, in order to be exchanged for gold and silver, the bank of England was for many years together obliged to coin gold to the extent of between eight hundred thousand pounds and a million a year; or at an average, about eight hundred and fifty thousand pounds. ① For this great coinage the bank (in consequence of the worn and degraded state into which the gold coin had fallen a few years ago) was frequently obliged to purchase gold bullion at the high price of four pounds an ounce, which it soon after issued in coin at $3l. \ 17s. \ 10\frac{1}{2}d.$ an ounce, losing in this manner between two and a half and three per cent. upon the coinage of so very large a sum. Though the bank therefore paid no seignorage, though the government was properly at the expence of the coinage, this liberality of government did not prevent altogether the expence of the bank. |

| and the Scotch banks. | The Scotch banks, in consequence of an excess of the same kind, were all obliged to employ constantly agents at London to collect money for them, at an expence which was seldom below one and a half or two per cent. This money was sent down by the waggon, and |

---

① [From 1766 to 1772 inclusive the coinage averaged about £ 810, 000 per annum. The amount for 'ten years together' is stated below, vol. ii., pp. 51, 56, to have been upwards of £ 800, 000 a year though the average for the ten years 1763-1772 was only £ 760, 000. But the inclusion of the large coinage of 1773, viz., £ 1, 317, 645 would raise these averages considerably. See the figures at the end of each year in Macpherson, *Annals of Commerce*.]

第二篇 第二章

流通所能容易吸收和使用的数目;为了应付不时之需,银行金柜必须经常储备有 10,000 镑金银。假使这家银行企图发行 44,000 镑,增加的 4000 镑,既是超过社会容易吸收和使用的数目,将一边发出去,一边又流回来。这样,为应付不时之需,银行金柜应该储存的款项就不止 11,000 镑,而为 14,000 镑。于是,4,000 镑过剩的纸币将毫无利益可得,而且,不仅无利,还有损失;因为这家银行还要负担不断收集 4,000 镑金银的费用,这些金银一边收进来,马上又要散发出去;不断收进,不断散出,所需费用不少。正如例子所阐述的那样。

如果所有银行都理解并关注自身利益,流通领域内就不可能有纸币过剩的现象。不幸的是,所有银行未必都理解本身的利益。流通领域里纸币过剩的现象也就常常发生了。银行有时没有理解这一点,

由于发行纸币量过大,剩余金额不断地回笼要求兑换金银,许多年来,英格兰银行每年都必须铸造金币,从 80 万镑至 100 万镑不等;平均计算,每年大约要铸造 85 万镑。① 几年以前,因为金币磨损破旧,质量低劣,银行大量铸造金币,常常必须以每盎司 4 镑的高价购买金块,铸成时每盎司却仅值 3 镑 17 先令 10 便士半,损失达 2.5% 至 3%。铸造的数额很大,所以损失不小。虽然银行免缴铸币税,造币一切费用全部由政府负担,但政府的慷慨也不能使银行免于损失。如英格兰银行,

苏格兰银行也由于发行纸币过多,不得不常常委托伦敦代理人代理他们收集货币,其费用很少低于 1.5% 或 2%。这样收集和苏格兰银行等。

---

① 从 1776 年到 1772 年每年铸造金币达 81 万镑。10 年的总金额在第二卷 55 页和第 56 页里所述,已经上升到 180 万镑,尽管在 1763 年至 1772 年仅为 76 万镑。但 1773 年全部铸币最大达 1317,645 镑,使得平均金额大幅增加;这些数字可在年终参见马克菲尔森所著的《商业年鉴》。

insured by the carriers at an additional expence of three quarters per cent. or fifteen shillings on the hundred pounds. Those agents were not always able to replenish the coffers of their employers so fast as they were emptied. In this case the resource of the banks was, to draw upon their correspondents in London bills of exchange to the extent of the sum which they wanted. When those correspondents afterwards drew upon them for the payment of this sum, together with the interest and a commission, some of those banks, from the distress into which their excessive circulation had thrown them, had sometimes no other means of satisfying this draught but by drawing a second set of bills either upon the same, or upon some other correspondents in London; and the same sum, or rather bills for the same sum, would in this manner make sometimes more than two or three journies: the debtor bank, paying always the interest and commission upon the whole accumulated sum. Even those Scotch banks which never distinguished themselves by their extreme imprudence, were sometimes obliged to employ this ruinous resource.

<small>The excessive circulation was caused by over trading.</small>

The gold coin which was paid out either by the bank of England, or by the Scotch banks, in exchange for that part of their paper which was over and above what could be employed in the circulation of the country, being likewise over and above what could be employed in that circulation, was sometimes sent abroad in the shape of coin, sometimes melted down and sent abroad in the shape of bullion, and sometimes melted down and sold to the bank of England at the high price of four pounds an ounce. It was the newest, the heaviest, and the best pieces only which were carefully picked out of the whole coin, and either sent abroad or melted down. At home, and while they remained in the shape of coin, those heavy pieces were of no more value than the light: But they were of more value abroad, or when melted down into bullion, at home. The bank of England, notwithstanding their great annual coinage, found to their astonishment, that there was every year the same scarcity of coin as there had been the year before; and that notwithstanding the great quantity of good and new coin which was every year issued from the bank, the state of the coin, instead of growing better and better, became every year worse and worse. Every year they found themselves under the necessity of coining nearly the same quantity of gold as they had coined the year before, and from the continual rise in the price of gold bullion, in consequence of the continual wearing and clipping of the coin, the expence of this great annual coinage became every year greater and

第二篇 第二章

的货币通常由马车送来,保险费每百镑为 15 先令,即 0.75%。但代理人所收集的货币,还往往不能及时补充本银行的金柜。金柜清空太快了。在这种情况下,苏格兰银行就必须向有来往的伦敦各家银行开具汇票来筹集所需数目;到期后伦敦银行再向它们开出汇票索取借款以及利息和佣金。一些苏格兰银行由于发行过剩,困难重重,常常苦于无法应对,不得不向原债权人或伦敦其他往来银行,开出第二批汇票。有时,相同金额或者说是相同金额的汇票,会在伦敦和爱丁堡之间往返两三次以上。这样累积的全部金额的利息和佣金,都必须由债务银行支付。有些苏格兰银行从来都是以谨慎经营而著名,有时也不得不使用这种自取灭亡的方法。

由于兑换过剩纸币而由英格兰银行或苏格兰银行付出的金币,也肯定与纸币一样成为过剩的一部分,为流通领域所不能吸纳和使用。结果,这种金币以铸币形式输往外国,或熔成金块后输往外国,或又熔化成金块,再以每盎司四镑的高价出售给英格兰银行。以金块输往外国的或熔化成金块的总是所有金币中最新的、最重的和最好的一种。因为留在国内保持铸币形态的铸币,并不区分轻重。轻的与重的铸币价值都一样。但在外国或在国内熔为金块时,重的铸币价值就较大。所以,英格兰银行尽管每年铸造大批新币,但年终仍不免大吃一惊,感叹今年铸币的缺乏程度和去年没有什么不同。而且,英格兰银行尽管每年发行许多崭新而且质地良好的铸币,而铸币的形状不是一天天地好起来,而是一天天地坏下去。今年铸造了这么多新币,明年感觉还有必要再铸造这么多新币。又因为铸币常常遭受磨损侵蚀,金块价格就不断上涨起来;因此,每年造币的费用也是一年超过一年。

流通是由过剩贸易造成的。超额的。

greater. The bank of England, it is to be observed, by supplying its own coffers with coin, is indirectly obliged to supply the whole kingdom, into which coin is continually flowing from those coffers in a great variety of ways. Whatever coin therefore was wanted to support this excessive circulation both of Scotch and English paper money, whatever vacuities this excessive circulation occasioned in the necessary coin of the kingdom, the bank of England was obliged to supply them. The Scotch banks, no doubt, paid all of them very dearly for their own imprudence and inattention. But the bank of England paid very dearly, not only for its own imprudence, but for the much greater imprudence of almost all the Scotch banks.

The over-trading of some bold projectors in both parts of the united kingdom, was the original cause of this excessive circulation of paper money.

A bank ought not to advance more than the amount which merchants would otherwise have to keep by them in cash. What a bank can with propriety advance to a merchant or undertaker of any kind, is not either the whole capital with which he trades, or even any considerable part of that capital; but that part of it only, which he would otherwise be obliged to keep by him unemployed, and in ready money for answering occasional demands. If the paper money which the bank advances never exceeds this value, it can never exceed the value of the gold and silver, which would necessarily circulate in the country if there was no paper money; it can never exceed the quantity which the circulation of the country can easily absorb and employ.

This limit is observed when only real bills of exchange are discounted. When a bank discounts to a merchant a real bill of exchange drawn by a real creditor upon a real debtor, and which, as soon as it becomes due, is really paid by that debtor; it only advances to him a part of the value which he would otherwise be obliged to keep by him unemployed and in ready money for answering occasional demands. The payment of the bill, when it becomes due, replaces to the bank the value of what it had advanced, together with the interest. The coffers of the bank, so far as its dealings are confined to such customers, resemble a water pond, from which, though a stream is continually running out, yet another is continually running in, fully equal to that

根据观察就可以知道,英格兰银行需要用铸币直接供给本银行的金柜,也需要用铸币间接供应全国。英格兰银行金柜内的铸币,会以各种方式不断流向全国各地。所有需要用来支持发行过剩的英格兰和苏格兰纸币的铸币,所有由于纸币造成的国内必须的铸币的缺乏,英格兰银行都得出来供应。无疑,苏格兰各银行必定因为自己不谨慎小心和未加谋划,吃亏不小。不过英格兰银行遭受损失更大。因为,不但它自己不小心谨慎使它吃亏;苏格兰各银行更不小心谨慎,而使它吃更大的亏。

英国两个地区的某些大胆计划冒险家们,他们不衡量自己的实力,业务经营过度,这是导致英国纸币如此过剩的最初原因。

商人或企业家经营的资本,既不可以全部向银行借贷,也不适宜大部分资本都向银行借贷。商人或企业家固然可以向银行借钱来应付不时之需,避免储备不用的准备金,但他的资本也只有这个部分适合向银行借贷。企业家向银行借钱应该局限于这个部分。如果银行借出纸币不超过这个限度的价值,那么发行出去的纸币金额,也绝不会超过国内没有纸币流通时所需的金银额,不会导致数量过剩,也不可能有一部分为国内流通界所不能吸纳和使用。

<small>银行向商人贷款提供的数量不应过该商人来应付不时之需的准备金量。</small>

银行给商人贴现的是由真实债权人向真实债务人开具的、在到期时后者会立即兑付的汇票,那么,银行所垫付的就只是这部分的价值,就是商人以前没有进行汇票业务以前,必须以现金形式保留以备不时之需的这部分价值。这种汇票,一经到期就会兑付,所以,银行垫付出去的价值和利息也一定可以收回。如果银行只和这类顾客进行业务来往,银行的金柜,就像一个水池,虽然有水不断流出,也有水不断流入,出入数量相等,因此,积水常常

<small>在贴现汇票对这种限制仅仅银行现时要加以关注。</small>

国民财富的性质与原理

which runs out; so that, without any further care or attention, the pond keeps always equally, or very near equally full. Little or no expence can ever be necessary for replenishing the coffers of such a bank.

<small>Cash accounts should be carefully watched to secure the same end,</small> A merchant, without over-trading, may frequently have occasion for a sum of ready money, even when he has no bills to discount. When a bank, besides discounting his bills, advances him likewise upon such occasions, such sums upon his cash account, and accepts of a piece meal repayment as the money comes in from the occasional sale of his goods, upon the easy terms of the banking companies of Scotland; it dispenses him entirely from the necessity of keeping any part of his stock by him unemployed and in ready money for answering occasional demands. When such demands actually come upon him, he can answer them sufficiently from his cash account. The bank, however, in dealing with such customers, ought to observe with great attention, whether in the course of some short period (of four, five, six, or eight months, for example) the sum of the repayments which it commonly receives from them, is, or is not, fully equal to that of the advances which it commonly makes to them. If, within the course of such short periods, the sum of the repayments from certain customers is, upon most occasions, fully equal to that of the advances, it may safely continue to deal with such customers. Though the stream which is in this case continually running out from its coffers may be very large, that which is continually running into them must be at least equally large; so that without any further care or attention those coffers are likely to be always equally or very near equally full; and scarce ever to require any extraordinary expence to replenish them. If, on the contrary, the sum of the repayments from certain other customers falls commonly very much short of the advances which it makes to them, it cannot with any safety continue to deal with such customers, at least if they continue to deal with it in this manner. The stream which is in this case continually running out from its coffers is necessarily much larger than that which is continually running in; so that, unless they are replenished by some great and continual effort of expence, those coffers must soon be exhausted altogether.

<small>as they were for a long time by the Scotch banks, which required frequent and regular operations,</small> The banking companies of Scotland, accordingly, were for a long time very careful to require frequent and regular repayments from all their customers, and did not care to deal with any person, whatever might be his fortune or credit, who did not make, what they called, frequent and regular operations with them. By this attention, besides saving almost entirely the extraordinary expence of replenishing their coffers, they gained two other very considerable advantages.

First, by this attention they were enabled to make some tolerable judgment concerning the thriving or declining circumstances of their debtors, without being obliged to look out for any other evidence be-

— 670 —

一样或几乎一样充满,无需时时刻刻留神关注。这种银行金柜的补充,并不需要多少费用,甚至完全不需要费用。

一个业务经营没有过度的商人,即使在没有期票要求银行贴现的情况下,也常有现金的要求。如果银行方面除了给他的汇票贴现以外,还允许按照苏格兰银行规定的简单条件,用现金结算法在他需要资金的时候贷出货币,而在他连续出售存货的时候,再陆续零星地偿还;这对商人就极其便利,他就不需要常常储备专款以应不时之急。而确实有需要时,他就可凭借现金结算法来应对。不过,银行对待这种顾客应该十分注意,看它在一个短时期之中(比方说4个月、5个月、6个月,或者8个月),从他们那里正常收回来的总额,是否等于通常贷给他们的总额。如果在这个短时期内,收入在大多数情况下能够等于贷出数量,就可以放心大胆地继续和这种顾客来往。像这样的来往,金柜的流出量固然很大,但流入量也很大;所以,无需进一步关注,金柜可以始终一样或几乎一样充实;补充这样的金柜用不着多大的费用。反之,如果顾客偿还的数额常常小于贷出的数额,那就不能继续放心和他来往,至少不能继续按照这种方式和他来往。在这种情况下,金柜的流出量必定远远大于流入量。除非不断地做出重大努力来花费巨额费用才能补充金柜,否则金柜就会很容易被清空。

因此,苏格兰各银行在长时期以来非常谨慎地要求一切顾客经常定期地归还贷款。如果他不能按上述要求照办,那么无论他有多么多的财富和多么好的信用,银行再也不可能向他贷出一分钱。由于如此谨慎,银行方面除了几乎完全不必要特别支出费用来补充金柜以外,还会获得其他两种很大的好处。

由于如此谨慎,银行方面除了自己账簿以外,不必另外去搜

and thus (1) were able to judge of the circumstances of their debtors.

sides what their own books afforded them; men being for the most part either regular or irregular in their repayments, according as their circumstances are either thriving or declining. A private man who lends out his money to perhaps half a dozen or a dozen of debtors, may, either by himself or his agents, observe and enquire both into the conduct and situation of each of them. But a banking company, which lends money to perhaps five hundred different people, and of which the attention is continually occupied by objects of a very different kind, can have no regular information concerning the conduct and circumstances of the greater part of its debtors beyond what its own books afford it. ① In requiring frequent and regular repayments from all their customers, the banking companies of Scotland had probably this advantage in view.

and (2) were secured against issuing too much paper.

Secondly, by this attention they secured themselves from the possibility of issuing more paper money than what the circulation of the country could easily absorb and employ. When they observed, that within moderate periods of time the repayments of a particular customer were upon most occasions fully equal to the advances which they had made to him, they might be assured that the paper money which they had advanced to him, had not at any time exceeded the quantity of gold and silver which he would otherwise have been obliged to keep by him for answering occasional demands; and that, consequently, the paper money, which they had circulated by his means, had not at any time exceeded the quantity of gold and silver which would have circulated in the country, had there been no paper money. The frequency, regularity and amounts of his repayments would sufficiently demonstrate that the amount of their advances had at no time exceeded that part of his capital which he would otherwise have been obliged to keep by him unemployed and in ready money for answering occasional demands; that is, for the purpose of keeping the rest of his capital in constant employment. It is this part of his capital only which, within moderate periods of time, is continually returning to every dealer in the shape of money, whether paper or coin, and continually going from him in the same shape. If the advances of the bank had commonly exceeded this part of his capital, the ordinary amount of his repayments could not, within moderate periods of time, have equalled the ordinary amount of its advances. The stream which,

① [But as Playfair (ed. of *Wealth of Nations*, vol. i., p. 472) points out, the more customers a bank has the more it is likely to know the transactions of each of them.]

集其他各种证据，也就能够相当准确地判断债务人的兴衰经营情况。债务人偿债情况是否正常，大部分取决于其业务的兴衰。私人借贷的债务人有数家或数十家，所以，委托一个经理人或经理人自己，连续并仔细地对债务人的行为和经济情况了解和调查就可以了。但银行放债的债务人达 500 家，而且还有许多其他事情要不断留心和注意，所以，除了自己账簿所提供的资料以外，它还需要有关于大部分债务人情况和行为的其他经常性报道。① 苏格兰各银行，所以要求债务人必须常常偿还贷款，也许因为他看到了这一点带来的好处。

一是能够对债务人的经营状况进行判断。

第二，由于如此谨慎，银行方面就不至于发行过剩的、为社会所不能吸纳和使用的纸币。在相当时间内，顾客偿还的数额在大多数情况下都等于贷出的数额，那么银行确信银行贷给他的纸币额，并没有超过他在没有银行借贷的情况下为应付不时之需所必须保留的金银量，从而使银行确信银行所发出去的纸币额，也没有超过国内在没有纸币的情况下所应流通的金银量。频繁和定期的偿还以及偿还款项的数量，充分表明银行方面贷出去的数额，并没有超过顾客在没有借贷时所必须以现金形式保留的、以应不时之需的那一部分资本，也就是说，并没有超过顾客在没有借贷时所必须以现金形式保留，使得他拥有其余资本可以继续不断使用的那一部分资本。在这种情况下，只有这一部分顾客的资本，在相当时期内，继续不断以铸币或纸币这两种货币形态时而收进、时而付出。银行借贷，如果超过这一部分，在相当时期内顾

二是可以防止纸币的过度发行。

---

① 但正如普雷法尔版的《国民财富》的第 1 卷第 472 页中所指出的那样，银行所拥有的客户越多，它就越有可能了解每一个客户的交易状况。

by means of his dealings, was continually running into the coffers of the bank, could not have been equal to the stream which, by means of the same dealings, was continually running out. The advances of the bank paper, by exceeding the quantity of gold and silver which, had there been no such advances, he would have been obliged to keep by him for answering occasional demands, might soon come to exceed the whole quantity of gold and silver which (the commerce being supposed the same) would have circulated in the country had there been no paper money; and consequently to exceed the quantity which the circulation of the country could easily absorb and employ; and the excess of this paper money would immediately have returned upon the bank in order to be exchanged for gold and silver. This second advantage, though equally real, was not perhaps so well understood by all the different banking companies of Scotland as the first.

<small>Bankers' loans ought to be only for moderate periods of time.</small> When, partly by the conveniency of discounting bills, and partly by that of cash accounts, the creditable traders of any country can be dispensed from the necessity of keeping any part of their stock by them unemployed and in ready money for answering occasional demands, they can reasonably expect no farther assistance from banks and bankers, who, when they have gone thus far, cannot, consistently with their own interest and safety, go farther. A bank cannot, consistently with its own interest, advance to a trader the whole or even the greater part of the circulating capital with which he trades; because, though that capital is continually returning to him in the shape of money, and going from him in the same shape, yet the whole of the returns is too distant from the whole of the outgoings, and the sum of his repayments could not equal the sum of its advances within such moderate periods of time as suit the conveniency of a bank. Still less could a bank afford to advance him any considerable part of his fixed capital; of the capital which the undertaker of an iron forge, for example, employs in erecting his forge and smelting-house, his workhouses and warehouses, the dwelling-houses of his workmen, &c. ; of the capital which the undertaker of a mine employs in sinking his shafts, in erecting engines for drawing out the water, in making roads and waggon-ways, &c. ; of the capital which the person who undertakes to improve land employs in clearing, draining, enclosing, manuring and ploughing waste and uncultivated fields, in building farm-houses, with all their necessary appendages of stables, granaries, &c. The returns of the fixed capital are in almost all cases much slower than those of the circulating capital; and such expences, even when laid out with the greatest prudence and judgment, very seldom return to the undertaker till after a period of many years, a period by far too distant to suit the conveniency of a bank. Traders and other undertakers may, no doubt, with great propriety, carry on a very considerable part of their projects with borrowed money. In justice to their

客偿还的数额,一定不能等于贷出的数额。就银行的金柜来说,同种交易方式的流入不可能等于同种方式的流出。纸币的发行,由于超过了在没有纸币发行时顾客所必须保有以应急需的金银量,也就马上超过了在没有纸币发行时国内流通领域所容纳的金银量,因而马上就会超过了在没有纸币发行时国内流通领域所容易容纳的数量。这些过剩的纸币,马上会转回来向银行兑换现金。这第二种好处与第一种好处相比较,是同样实在的。但对于第二种利益,苏格兰各银行似乎没有了解得那么清楚。

部分由于银行使用贴现汇票法和部分使用现金结算法带来的便利,使国内有信用的商人无需储备准备金,以应付不时之需,那就算是竭尽全力了,国内商人就不可再对银行有所更高的期盼。从银行本身的利益与安全考虑,它也只能做到这个地步,不能再做什么了。从银行本身利益考虑,商人的流动资本不能全部贷自银行,即使是大部分资本也不行。因为商人的流动资本,虽然继续以货币的形式,时收时支,但全部收入的时间距离全部付出的时间太远了,要在短期内适合于银行的利益,使偿还的数额等于贷出的数额,那是办不到的。至于固定资本,就更不应该大部分贷自银行了。比如说,钢铁业主建立铁厂、铁炉、工场、仓库、工人住宅等等资本,又比如说矿业主开掘矿井、排除积水、建筑道路车轨的资本,土地改良家开垦荒地、排泄积水、筑围墙、建农舍、厩舍、谷仓等必要建筑物的资本,这些都不适宜大部分贷自银行。固定资本的收回比流动资本收回速度要缓慢得多。固定资本一旦投入,即使投入的方法非常适当,也要经过许多年才能收回。这样长的时间当然不利于银行。固然,企业家可以很适当地使用借入的资本实施他的大部分计划,但要使债权人不吃亏,债务人

<small>银行贷款应该有合理期限。</small>

creditors, however, their own capital ought, in this case, to be sufficient to ensure, if I may say so, the capital of those creditors; or to render it extremely improbable that those creditors should incur any loss, even though the success of the project should fall very much short of the expectation of the projectors. Even with this precaution too, the money which is borrowed, and which it is meant should not be repaid till after a period of several years, ought not to be borrowed of a bank, but ought to be borrowed upon bond or mortgage, of such private people as propose to live upon the interest of their money, without taking the trouble themselves to employ the capital; and who are upon that account willing to lend that capital to such people of good credit as are likely to keep it for several years. A bank, indeed, which lends its money without the expence of stampt paper, or of attornies fees for drawing bonds and mortgages, and which accepts of repayment upon the easy terms of the banking companies of Scotland; would, no doubt, be a very convenient creditor to such traders and undertakers. But such traders and undertakers would, surely, be most inconvenient debtors to such a bank.

_{More than twenty-five years ago the proper amount of paper money had been reached in Scotland, but the traders were not content, and some of them resorted to drawing and redrawing,} It is now more than five-and-twenty years since the paper money issued by the different banking companies of Scotland was fully equal, or rather was somewhat more than fully equal, to what the circulation of the country could easily absorb and employ. Those companies, therefore, had so long ago given all the assistance to the traders and other undertakers of Scotland which it is possible for banks and bankers, consistently with their own interest, to give. They had even done somewhat more. They had over-traded a little, and had brought upon themselves that loss, or at least that diminution of profit, which in this particular business never fails to attend the smallest degree of overtrading. Those traders and other undertakers, having got so much assistance from banks and bankers, wished to get still more. The banks, they seem to have thought, could extend their credits to whatever sum might be wanted, without incurring any other expence besides that of a few reams of paper. They complained of the contracted views and dastardly spirit of the directors of those banks, which did not, they said, extend their credits in proportion to the extension of the trade of the country; meaning, no doubt, by the extension of that trade the extension of their own projects beyond what they could carry on, either with their own capital, or with what they had credit to borrow of private people in the usual way of bond or mortgage. The banks, they seem to have thought, were in honour bound to supply the deficiency, and to provide them with all the capital which they wanted to trade with. The banks, however, were of a different opinion, and upon their refusing to extend their credits, some of those

应该拥有充分的资本,足够保证(如果我可以这样说)债权人资本的安全,足够使债务人的营业计划即使在失败的情况下,也不会导致债权人蒙受损失,这样对债权人才算公平合理。然而,即使如此,如果数年以后才能还清的借款,仍然以不向银行借贷为上策。可以用最好的抵押品向那些专门依靠利息为生的私人借贷;因为他们自己不想投资经营,仅仅愿意把钱提供给有信用的人,数年不还也未尝不可。不收取抵押品,也无需印花费和律师费,就用货币贷于其他人,而偿还条件又像苏格兰银行所愿意接受的那么简单的银行一样,对于这样的商人和企业家来说,当然可说是最方便的债权人。不过,像这样的商人,对于这样的银行来说却是最不方便的债务人。

自从苏格兰各家银行所发行的纸币数量,恰好等于或稍微超过国内流通领域所能够容易吸纳和使用的数额,已经超过 25 年了。对于苏格兰各种产业来说,从银行自身利益角度考虑,银行对各种产业的帮助已经算是竭尽全力了。而且事实上,它们的经营已经稍微有些过度;因为这种过度致使银行方面已经吃亏不小,至少利润是减少了。在这种特殊的业务上,经营规模只要稍微有些过度,便不免有此结果。商人们和企业家们已经从银行那里得到很大的帮助,但他们仍然还认为不够,这是有点得陇望蜀味道;他们以为银行的信用业务可以任意扩大;除了增加少数纸张费用以外,扩大银行业务并不需要增加什么额外费用。他们埋怨银行董事先生们眼光狭小、态度畏缩不前。他们说,银行信用业务还没有扩充到与国内各种产业的扩充相适应的程度。他们所谓产业扩大,肯定是指把产业推广到超过他们自己的资本或能够凭借抵押品向私人借得的资本所能经营的范围。他们以为,对于他们短少

traders had recourse to an expedient which, for a time, served their purpose, though at a much greater expence, yet as effectually as the utmost extension of bank credits could have done. This expedient was no other than the well-known shift of drawing and re-drawing; the shift to which unfortunate traders have sometimes recourse when they are upon the brink of bankruptcy. The practice of raising money in this manner had been long known in England, and during the course of the late war, when the high profits of trade afforded a great temptation to over-trading, is said to have been carried on to a very great extent. From England it was brought into Scotland, where, in proportion to the very limited commerce, and to the very moderate capital of the country, it was soon carried on to a much greater extent than it ever had been in England.

<small>which shall be explained.</small> The practice of drawing and re-drawing is so well known to all men of business, that it may perhaps be thought unnecessary to give any account of it. But as this book may come into the hands of many people who are not men of business, and as the effects of this practice upon the banking trade are not perhaps generally understood even by men of business themselves, I shall endeavour to explain it as distinctly as I can.

<small>Bills of exchange have extraordinary legal privileges.</small> The customs of merchants, which were established when the barbarous laws of Europe did not enforce the performance of their contracts, and which during the course of the two last centuries have been adopted into the laws of all European nations, have given such extraordinary privileges to bills of exchange, that money is more readily advanced upon them, than upon any other species of obligation; especially when they are made payable within so short a period as two or three months after their date. If, when the bill becomes due, the acceptor does not pay it as soon as it is presented, he becomes from that moment a bankrupt. The bill is protested, and returns upon the drawer, who, if he docs not immediately pay it, becomes likewise a bankrupt. If, before it came to the person who presents it to the acceptor for payment, it had passed through the hands of several other persons, who had successively advanced to one another the contents of it either in money or goods, and who to express that each of them had in his turn received those contents, had all of them in their order endorsed, that is, written their names upon the back of the bill; each endorser becomes in his turn liable to the owner of the bill for those contents, and, if he fails to pay, he becomes too from that moment a bankrupt. Though the drawer, acceptor, and endorsers of the bill should, all of them, be persons of doubtful credit; yet still the short-

的资本,银行有设法供给的义务。他们觉得,他们所希望得到的全部资本是银行应当供给的。但银行方面有不同的意见。于是,在银行拒绝推广其信用的时候,有些企业家想出了一个办法。这个办法在一段时期内显得对他们很适用;尽管支出费用要大得多,但其有效性和大肆推广银行信用业务一样。这个办法正是大家知道的循环划汇方法。不幸的商人在濒临破产时往往利用这个办法。通过这个办法取得资金在英格兰已经有很长时间了。据说,上次战争期间,因为营业利润极大,商人们深受诱惑,就把产业进行过度扩张;于是这种循环划汇的办法就广泛流行开来。后来这个办法又由英格兰传入苏格兰。在苏格兰,由于商业和资本都很有限,所以这种办法在传入苏格兰以后,更加广泛流行。

  对于一般实业家来说,当然都很明白这种循环划汇的办法似乎没有说明的必要。但本书许多读者未必都是实业家,而且这种办法对于银行的影响,即使是一般实业家也似乎不大了解,所以,我将努力尽可能地把它阐述清楚。这将在下面进行说明。

  当欧洲野蛮法律还没有强迫商人履行契约的时候,在商人之间就形成一种习惯,在过去 200 多年里它已经变成所有欧洲国家的法律;它赋予汇票以特殊的权利,使得以汇票的方式,尤其是期限为两三个月的短期汇票,比用任何其他方式都容易取得借款。汇票到期以后,如果承兑人不能立即兑付,他立刻就算破产;于是持票人把汇票当作拒付证明,转向出票人索取款项。如果出票人也不能立即兑付,也算破产。如果汇票在没有到期以前,辗转流通,用来购买货物或用来借款,流经数人之手,这些人各在票据背面背书保证,这些人也就对这些汇票负完全责任;如果汇票到了自己面前,自己不能立即兑付,也马上被宣告破产。出票人、承兑汇票被法律赋予特殊的权利。

ness of the date gives some security to the owner of the bill. Though all of them may be very likely to become bankrupts; it is a chance if they all become so in so short a time. The house is crazy, says a weary traveller to himself, and will not stand very long; but it is a chance if it falls to-night, and I will venture, therefore, to sleep in it to-night.

<small>so two persons, one in London and one in Edinburgh, would draw bills on each other.</small>

The trader A in Edinburgh, we shall suppose, draws a bill upon B in London, payable two months after date. In reality B in London owes nothing to A in Edinburgh; but he agrees to accept of A's bill, upon condition that before the term of payment he shall redraw upon A in Edinburgh for the same sum, together with the interest and a commission, another bill, payable likewise two months after date. B accordingly, before the expiration of the first two months, re-draws this bill upon A in Edinburgh; who again, before the expiration of the second two months, draws a second bill upon B in London, payable likewise two months after date; and before the expiration of the third two months, B in London re-draws upon A in Edinburgh another bill, payable also two months after date. This practice has sometimes gone on, not only for several months, but for several years together, the bill always returning upon A in Edinburgh, with the accumulated interest and commission of all the former bills. The interest was five per cent. in the year, and the commission was never less than one half per cent. on each draught. This commission being repeated more than six times in the year, whatever money A might raise by this expedient must necessarily have cost him something more than eight per cent. in the year, and sometimes a great deal more; when either the price of the commission happened to rise, or when he was obliged to pay compound interest upon the interest and commission of former bills. This practice was called raising money by circulation.

<small>Much money was raised in this expensive way.</small>

In a country where the ordinary profits of stock in the greater part of mercantile projects are supposed to run between six and ten per cent, it must have been a very fortunate speculation of which the returns could not only repay the enormous expence at which the money was thus borrowed for carrying it on; but afford, besides, a good surplus profit to the projector. Many vast and extensive projects, however, were undertaken, and for several years carried on without any other fund to support them besides what was raised at this enormous expence. The projectors, no doubt, had in their golden dreams the most

人和背书人,即使信用存在问题,但由于汇票期限如此短暂,这多少对持票人也是一种保障;虽然他们都有破产的危险,但不一定在这么短促的时间内他们都会破产。房子已经倾斜,不能支撑很长时间,不一定今晚就会坍塌,我就算冒险住上一个晚上,这是疲劳不堪的旅行者的心中盘算,正好用来比喻汇票持有人的心理状态。

假设有爱丁堡商人甲向伦敦商人乙开具汇票,期限为两个月,到期以后要求乙兑付汇票。事实上,伦敦商人乙并没有对爱丁堡商人甲负债;他之所以愿意承兑商人甲的汇票,因为经过双方协商,在票据到期以前,乙也可以向甲出具一张汇票,数额相等,再加上利息和佣金,兑付期限也为两个月。所以,在两个月的期限未满以前,乙向甲出具一张汇票,甲又在这张汇票到期以前,再向乙第二次出具汇票。在这第二次汇票到期以前,乙再照样向甲出具汇票,都是两个月的期限。这样循环下去,可连续数月,甚至数年;不过,乙向甲开出的一切汇票,累积下来的利息和佣金,都要计算在内。利息率为每年5%,佣金每次至少为0.5%。如果每年来往超过6次,佣金就要增加6倍,所以依靠这种办法筹款的商人甲,每年费用就至少也在8%以上,有时会更多。如果佣金上涨,或要对以前汇票的利息和佣金支付复利,那么,费用就要更大。这就是所谓循环借款的办法。

假设国内大部分商业项目上的投资,正常利润率是在6%至10%之间。使用这样方法借得货币进行经营,如果除了偿还借钱的巨大费用以外,还能够提供可观的剩余利润,那非是一种非常幸运的投机才行。但是,近来有许多规模巨大的计划,在若干年中除了依靠这个花费巨额费用才借来资金的方法以外别无其他

distinct vision of this great profit. Upon their awaking, however, either at the end of their projects, or when they were no longer able to carry them on, they very seldom, I believe, had the good fortune to find it. ①

The bills which A in Edinburgh drew upon B in London, he regularly discounted two months before they were due with some bank or banker in Edinburgh; and the bills which B in London redrew upon A in Edinburgh, he as regularly discounted either with the bank of England, or with some other bankers in London. Whatever was advanced upon such circulating bills, was, in Edinburgh, advanced in the pa-

---

① The method described in the text was by no means either the most common or the most expensive one in which those adventurers sometimes raised money by circulation. It frequently happened that A in Edinburgh would enable B in London to pay the first bill of exchange by drawing, a few days before it became due, a second bill at three months date upon the same B in London. This bill, being payable to his own order, A sold in Edinburgh at par; and with its contents purchased bills upon London payable at sight to the order of B, to whom he sent them by the post. Towards the end of the late war, the exchange between Edinburgh and London was frequently three per cent. against Edinburgh, and those bills at sight must frequently have cost A that premium. This transaction therefore being repeated at least four times in the year, and being loaded with a commission of at least one half per cent. upon each repetition, must at that period have cost A at least fourteen per cent. in the year. At other times A would enable B to discharge the first bill of exchange by drawing, a few days before it became due, a second bill at two months date; not upon B, but upon some third person, C, for example, in London. This other bill was made payable to the order of B, who, upon its being accepted by C, discounted it with some banker in London; and A enabled C to discharge it by drawing, a few days before it became due, a third bill, likewise at two months date, sometimes upon his first correspondent B, and sometimes upon some fourth or fifth person, D or E, for example. This third bill was made payable to the order of C; who, as soon as it was accepted, discounted it in the same manner with some banker in London. Such operations being repeated at least six times in the year, and being loaded with a commission of at least one-half per cent. upon each repetition, together with the legal interest of five per cent. , this method of raising money, in the same manner as that described in the text, must have cost A something more than eight per cent. By saving, however, the exchange between Edinburgh and London it was less expensive than that mentioned in the foregoing part of this note; but then it required an established credit with more houses than one in London, an advantage which many of these adventurers could not always find it easy to procure. [This note appears first in ed. 2. Playfair observes that the calculation of the loss of 14 Per cent. by the first method is wrong, since if A at Edinburgh negotiated his bills on London at 3 per cent. loss, he would gain as much in purchasing bills on London with the money. —Ed, of *Wealth of Nations*, vol. i. , p. 483, note.]

资本。这些计划冒险家们在他们的黄粱美梦中看到了丰厚利润的景象。但是,当他们醒来时,或在他们经营结束时,或在他们无力再继续经营下去时,我相信没有几个运气好得能够实现他们所做黄粱美梦中的景象。①

爱丁堡的甲向伦敦的乙开出的汇票,经常由甲在到期以前两个月向爱丁堡银行申请贴现。伦敦的乙随后向甲开出的汇票,也照样地经常由乙向英格兰银行或伦敦的其他银行申请贴现。银

---

① 在文章中阐述的方法,绝不是那些计划冒险家们运用循环划汇方法,筹集资金所使用的最普通和最昂贵的方法;经常发生的是,爱丁堡的甲在汇票到期以前的几天,允许伦敦乙再开出期限为三个月的第二张汇票,使商人乙兑现第一张汇票;按照甲的要求,把这张汇票在爱丁堡以平价的价格卖出,从而兑付这张汇票;同时按照乙的要求,购进向伦敦开具见票即付的、由甲通过邮局寄给乙的汇票。在快到战争结束时,爱丁堡和伦敦之间的汇兑一般是百分之三,这些见票即付的汇票肯定让甲花费百分之三的额外费用。因此这种交易在一年里至少被重复四次以上,佣金至少百分之零点五;在这种不断重复情况下,甲每年必须支付费用至少在百分之十四以上;另外甲可以使乙在汇票到期以前,以开具汇票的方式兑付第一张汇票;甲两个月以后再开出第二张汇票;这次甲不是向乙开出汇票,而是其他人如伦敦丙的开具汇票;第二张汇票在丙承兑的前提下,按照乙的要求,可以向伦敦银行进行贴现而取得款项。甲也可以让丙在到期前几天,向最初的乙或其他第四个或第五个人开出一张期限为两个月的汇票;第三张汇票一旦被接受承兑,按照乙的要求,可以向伦敦银行进行贴现而取得款项。一年里重复操作至少六次以上,并带有百分之零点五的佣金;在每一次操作中还有5%的法定利息;正如下文所阐述的同样筹集资金的方式,必须要支付稍微高于百分之八的资金成本;然而,通过储蓄的方法,在爱丁堡和伦敦之间进行的汇兑比注释前半部分所提到的方法进行汇兑要便宜;不过另一方面比伦敦要多要求一个拥有更多房产的可靠信用,而对于冒险家来说,他们并不总是能发现他的优点,从而轻而易举地取得贷款。这个注释最先出现在第二版。普雷费厄注意到,通过使用第一种方法计算损失为14%是错误的,因为"如果爱丁堡商人甲在伦敦商定汇票损失为3%的话,他就会获得与用现金在伦敦购买汇票一样的收益。"——见《国民财富》第一卷483页注释。

国民财富的性质与原理

The bill on London would be discounted in Edinburgh, and the bill on Edinburgh discounted in London, and each was always replaced by another.

per of the Scotch banks, and in London, when they were discounted at the bank of England, in the paper of that bank. Though the bills upon which this paper had been advanced, were all of them re-paid in their turn as soon as they became due; yet the value which had been really advanced upon the first bill, was never really returned to the banks which advanced it; because, before each bill became due, another bill was always drawn to somewhat a greater amount than the bill which was soon to be paid; and the discounting of this other bill was essentially necessary towards the payment of that which was soon to be due. This payment, therefore, was altogether fictitious. The stream, which, by means of those circulating bills of exchange, had once been made to run out from the coffers of the banks, was never replaced by any stream which really run into them.

The amount thus advanced by the banks was in excess of the limit laid down above, but this was not perceived at first.

The paper which was issued upon those circulating bills of exchange, amounted, upon many occasions, to the whole fund destined for carrying on some vast and extensive project of agriculture, commerce, or manufactures; and not merely to that part of it which, had there been no paper money, the projector would have been obliged to keep by him, unemployed and in ready money for answering occasional demands. The greater part of this paper was, consequently, over and above the value of the gold and silver which would have circulated in the country, had there been no paper money. It was over and above, therefore, what the circulation of the country could easily absorb and employ, and upon that account immediately returned upon the banks in order to be exchanged for gold and silver, which they were to find as they could. It was a capital which those projectors had very artfully contrived to draw from those banks, not only without their knowledge or deliberate consent, but for some time, perhaps, without their having the most distant suspicion that they had really advanced it.

When the banks found it out they made difficulties about discounting, which alarmed and enraged the projectors;

When two people, who are continually drawing and re-drawing upon one another, discount their bills always with the same banker, he must immediately discover what they are about, and see clearly that they are trading, not with any capital of their own, but with the capital which he advances to them. But this discovery is not altogether so easy when they discount their bills sometimes with one banker, and sometimes with another, and when the same two persons do not constantly draw and re-draw upon one another, but occasionally run the round of a great circle of projectors, who find it for their interest to assist one another in this method of raising money, and to render it, upon that account, as difficult as possible to distinguish between a real

— 684 —

行贴现这些循环汇票所支付的大部分是钞票;在爱丁堡支付的是苏格兰银行的钞票;在伦敦支付的是英格兰银行的钞票。尽管已经是贴现的汇票,到期以后都可以兑付;不过,为贴现第一张汇票而实际付出去的价值,却永远没有实际归还给贴现它的银行。因为,在第一张汇票即将到期的时候,第二张汇票又开出了,数额还更大。没有这第二张汇票,第一张汇票就应该有进行兑付的可能。所以,第一张汇票的兑付全然是个名义。这种循环汇票的流转,使银行金柜在发生流出之后,一直没有流入来补还这项流出。

> 伦敦爱丁堡汇票在贴现,两者相互偿还。

银行因贴现这些循环汇票而发行的纸币,往往达到进行大规模农业、工业或商业计划所要使用的全部资金的数量,而不仅限于在没有纸币的情况下,企业家必须以现金形式保持在手中,以备不时之需的那部分资金的数量。所以,银行发出的这种纸币大部分是社会所不能容纳的,是超过国内在无纸币的情况下流通界应有的金银价值的。过剩的部分,马上会回到银行,要求兑换金银。银行必须尽其所能,设法寻求这项金银。这是这些计划冒险家们施用诡计向银行弄去的资本,不但没有经过银行知道或经过银行慎重考虑后的同意,甚至,银行在若干时间中,可能毫不觉得曾经贷给了他们这些资本。

> 贴现汇票银行发行数经已超过上述规定的限制,但这一点却最初没有被发觉。

设甲乙二人狼狈为奸,互相出具循环期票,并向同一家银行贴现。银行方面当然不久就能发现他们的行径,就能明白看出他们营业并没有使用自己的资本,而他们所使用的资本全部是它借给他们的。但是,假如他们不常在同一家银行贴现,时而在这家,时而在那家,而且两人并不一直互相彼此开具汇票,而是兜一个大圈子,经过许多其他计划冒险家,这些计划冒险家出于利益考虑,互相帮忙,最后由其中之一向他们开出汇票;那么,这就让银

> 当银行觉察发现贴现汇票取得贷款的方法比较困难时,这些计划冒险家们惊慌起来;使贴现获款方法困难,做计划冒险家们愤怒起来;

and a fictitious bill of exchange; between a bill drawn by a real creditor upon a real debtor, and a bill for which there was properly no real creditor but the bank which discounted it; nor any real debtor but the projector who made use of the money. When a banker had even made this discovery, he might sometimes make it too late, and might find that he had already discounted the bills of those projectors to so great an extent, that, by refusing to discount any more, he would necessarily make them all bankrupts, and thus, by ruining them, might perhaps ruin himself. For his own interest and safety, therefore, he might find it necessary, in this very perilous situation, to go on for some time, endeavouring, however, to withdraw gradually, and upon that account making every day greater and greater difficulties about discounting, in order to force those projectors by degrees to have recourse, either to other bankers, or to other methods of raising money; so as that he himself might, as soon as possible, get out of the circle. The difficulties, accordingly, which the bank of England, which the principal bankers in London, and which even the more prudent Scotch banks began, after a certain time, and when all of them had already gone too far, to make about discounting, not only alarmed, but enraged in the highest degree those projectors. Their own distress, of which this prudent and necessary reserve of the banks was, no doubt, the immediate occasion, they called the distress of the country; and this distress of the country, they said, was altogether owing to the ignorance, pusillanimity, and bad conduct of the banks, which did not give a sufficiently liberal aid to the spirited undertakings of those who exerted themselves in order to beautify, improve, and enrich the country. It was the duty of the banks, they seemed to think, to lend for as long a time, and to as great an extent as they might wish to borrow. The banks, however, by refusing in this manner to give more credit to those, to whom they had already given a great deal too much, took the only method by which it was now possible to save either their own credit, or the public credit of the country.

In the midst of this clamour and distress, a new bank[①] was es-

---

① [The index s. v. Bank gives the name, 'the Ayr bank'. Its head office was at Ayr, but it had branches at Edinburgh and Dumfries. A detailed history of it is to be found in *The Precipitation and Fall of Messrs. Douglas, Heron and Company, late Bankers in Air with the Causes of their Distress and Ruin investigated and considered by a Committee of Inquiry appointed by the Proprietors*, Edinburgh, 1778.

行很难辨认出哪一张是有真实债务人和真实债权人的真实汇票，哪一张是除了贴现汇票的银行别无真实债权人或者除了套取货币的计划冒险家别无真实债务人的虚假汇票；这时银行就不容易发现他们的所作所为。即使银行终于察觉了这一点，但可能已经太晚；这样的汇票已经贴现不少了。这时再拒绝他们，不再进行贴现，必然会使他们一齐破产，而他们破产可能使银行随着破产。出于自身利益与安全考虑，在这种危险情况中，银行方面也许只好再冒险继续贴现一段时间，企图慢慢把贷款收回；或者提高贴现条件，迫使他们逐渐转向其他方面或者其他银行，设法使自己尽快从这个圈套中摆脱出来。然而就在英格兰银行、伦敦各家主要银行以及比较慎重的苏格兰各家银行，陷入太深，都开始对贴现提出比较苛刻的条件时，这帮计划冒险家不仅惊慌起来，而且愤怒起来。他们自己的苦恼无疑是直接起因于银行方面这种慎重和必要的准备措施，但他们竟把自己的苦恼说成是全国的苦恼。他们说，这种全国的苦恼完全是由于银行方面见识短浅，举措失当；他们想努力使国家繁荣富裕起来，而银行却吝于帮助他们。他们似乎认为银行按照他们所希望的借款期限和借款利息借给他们资金，乃是银行的义务。然而就事实来说，要挽救银行自身的信用，要挽救国家的信用，银行拒绝对已经贷款过多的人继续按照这种方法贷给款项，是这个时候唯一可实行的办法。

再如：在嘈杂和困境之中，在苏格兰开设了一家新的银行，[①]

[①] 索引给出银行的名称叫"埃尔银行"。它的总部在埃尔(苏格兰西南部特区，在克莱德湾的艾尔河河口处，是一个旅游胜地和渔港)，但它分支机构遍布伦敦和度姆弗里。具体历史情况可以在 1778 年爱丁堡由银行股东任命的一个调查委员会所提供的报告里找到，报告名为《道格拉斯和海罗

国民财富的性质与原理

then the Ayr bank was established and advanced money very freely, but soon got into difficulties and was obliged to stop in two years. tablished in Scotland for the express purpose of relieving the distress of the country. The design was generous; but the execution was imprudent, and the nature and causes of the distress which it meant to relieve, were not, perhaps, well understood. This bank was more liberal than any other had ever been, both in granting cash accounts, and in discounting bills of exchange. With regard to the latter, it seems to have made scarce any distinction between real and circulating bills, but to have discounted all equally. It was the avowed principle of this bank to advance, upon any reasonable security, the whole capital which was to be employed in those improvements of which the returns are the most slow and distant, such as the improvements of land. To promote such improvements was even said to be the chief of the public spirited purposes for which it was instituted. By its liberality in granting cash accounts, and in discounting bills of exchange, it, no doubt, issued great quantities of its bank notes. But those bank notes being, the greater part of them, over and above what the circulation of the country could easily absorb and employ, returned upon it, in order to be exchanged for gold and silver, as fast as they were issued. Its coffers were never well filled. The capital which had been subscribed to this bank at two different subscriptions, amounted to one hundred and sixty thousand pounds, of which eighty per cent. only was paid up. This sum ought to have been paid in at several different instalments. A great part of the proprietors, when they paid in their first instalment, opened a cash account with the bank; and the directors, thinking themselves obliged to treat their own proprietors with the same liberality with which they treated all other men, allowed many of them to borrow upon this cash account what they paid in upon all their subsequent instalments. Such payments, therefore, only put into one coffer, what had the moment before been taken out of another. But had the coffers of this bank been

---

From this it appears that Smith's account of the proceedings of the bank is extremely accurate, a fact which is doubtless due to his old pupil, the Duke of Buccleuch, having been one of the principal shareholders. Writing to Pulteney on 5th September, 1772, Smith says,' though I have had no concern myself in the public calamities, some of the friends in whom I interest myself the most have been deeply concerned in them; and my attention has been a good deal occupied about the most proper method of extricating them'. The extrication was effected chiefly by the sale of redeemable annuities. See Rae, *Life of Adam Smith*, 1895, pp. 253-255; David Macpherson, Annals of Commerce, vol. iii. , pp. 525, 553; *House of Commons' Journals*, vol. xxxiv. , pp. 493-495, and the Act of Parliament, 14 Geo. III. , c. 21. The East India Company opposed the bill on the ground that the bonds to be issued would compete with theirs, but their opposition was defeated by a vote of 176 to 36 in the House of Commons, *Journals*, vol. xxxiv. , p. 601.]

第二篇 第二章

声称以拯救国难为立行宗旨。它立意慷慨,但措施欠缺谨慎,而且似乎对它所企图要解决的困难的性质和原因并不十分清楚。这家银行的信贷业务,无论是从现金结算法还是从贴现汇票来看,都比其他银行更加宽松。就后者说,它几乎不问汇票是真实汇票还是循环汇票,都一律予以贴现。这家银行曾经公开宣布其宗旨,说只要有合理的保证,即使是需要很长时间才能偿还(像改良土地用的)的资本,也全部可以向银行借取。甚至还说,促进这样的土地改良是银行之所以设立的爱国目标的核心。由于对现金结算和期票贴现采取宽松的政策,银行必然要发行大量钞票;其过剩的部分既然不容易被社会所吸纳和使用,当然一边发出一边又收回来兑换金银。银行金柜本来就不十分充实。它从两次招股募集到的资本虽号称 16 万镑,但实收资本金不到 80%,而且是分期缴纳。大部分股东于第一次缴入股本款后,立即就向银行用现金结算法借出款项。银行董事先生们,以为股东借款理所应当地享受与他人一样宽松的待遇,所以,有大部分股东在缴纳了第一期股本款以后,其余各期缴入的几乎全是在现金结算法下借出的款项。这样,他们后来的缴纳股本金,就不过是把先从银行

埃尔银行成立以后,向它贷款非常容易,但不久该银行就陷人困境,在两年后停止营业。

恩先生以及公司沉浮录——《最近风云银行家的失败和没落》。从这点来看,斯密先生对银行事件的描述极其准确,这肯定归因于他的较年长的学生布克勒齐公爵,他是该家银行的主要股东之一;斯密在 1772 年 9 月 5 日写给普滕尼的一封信里说,"尽管我自己与公共灾难并无关系,但我非常感兴趣的一些朋友却与这些灾难性事件密切相关;我所关注的是从这种事件中解脱出来找到最佳的方法来说是一件好事"。这种解脱主要受那些可赎回年金销售的影响;参见雷 1895 年所著《斯密年谱》一书第 253~255 页;大卫·马克菲尔森《商业年鉴》第 3 卷第 525 页和第 553 页;《国会下议院杂志》第 34 卷第 493~495 页;东印度公司反对这项提议的原因在于将要发行的债券与他们的债券产生竞争,但他们的反对在下议院以 176 票对 36 票而遭到失败。

filled ever so well, its excessive circulation must have emptied them faster than they could have been replenished by any other expedient but the ruinous one of drawing upon London, and when the bill became due, paying it, together with interest and commission, by another draught upon the same place. Its coffers having been filled so very ill, it is said to have been driven to this resource within a very few months after it began to do business. The estates of the proprietors of this bank were worth several millions, and by their subscription to the original bond or contract of the bank, were really pledged for answering all its engagements. ① By means of the great credit which so great a pledge necessarily gave it, it was, notwithstanding its too liberal conduct, enabled to carry on business for more than two years. When it was obliged to stop, it had in the circulation about two hundred thousand pounds in bank notes. In order to support the circulation of those notes, which were continually returning upon it as fast as they were issued, it had been constantly in the practice of drawing bills of exchange upon London, of which the number and value were continually increasing, and, when it stopt, amounted to upwards of six hundred thousand pounds. This bank, therefore, had, in little more than the course of two years, advanced to different people upwards of eight hundred thousand pounds at five per cent. Upon the two hundred thousand pounds which it circulated in bank notes, this five per cent. might, perhaps, be considered as clear gain, without any other deduction besides the expence of management. But upon upwards of six hundred thousand pounds, for which it was continually drawing bills of exchange upon London, it was paying, in the way of interest and commission, upwards of eight per cent, and was conesquently losing more than three per cent. upon more than three-fourths of all its dealings.

The operations of this bank seem to have produced effects quite opposite to those which were intended by the particular persons who planned and directed it. They seem to have intended to support the spirited undertakings, for as such they considered them, which were at that time carrying on in different parts of the country; and at the same time, by drawing the whole banking business to themselves,

---

① [Macpherson, op. cit. p. 525, says the partners were the Dukes of Buccleuch and Queensberry, the Earl of Dumfries, Mr. Douglas and many other gentlemen.]

某一金柜提出去的款项,再放入银行的另一金柜。所以,银行金柜即使原来很充实,但钞票过度的发行,也必定使银行金柜很快被清空,只好走上失败的途径;向伦敦银行开出汇票,期满时再开出汇票,加上利息和佣金的数额,从而兑付以前一期开出的汇票,除了这个办法以外,没有其他方法能够及时补充金柜的耗竭。这家银行的金柜,原来就不很充实;据说,营业不超过数月,就不得不求助于这个办法。① 幸运的是各股东的田产不低于数百万镑,在他们认购股份或契约时,实际上就等于把这些田产向银行提供保证;有如此充实的保证作为银行信用的后盾,所以,信贷政策尽管如此宽松,银行经营仍能够延续两年有余。到非停业不可时,发出的纸币额已近 20 万镑了。这种纸币,随时发出又随时收回,因为要支持这些纸币的流通,它屡屡向伦敦各银行开出汇票。累积下去,到了银行不得不倒闭的时候为止,汇票价值已在 60 万镑以上。这样,在两年多的时间里,这家银行借出去的也达 80 万镑以上,利息率为 5%。对用纸币借出的 20 万镑贷款所收取的 5% 的利息,也许可以视为纯利,因为除了管理费用外,再也没有其他扣除。但向伦敦出具汇票所借来的 60 多万镑,其利息佣金等却在 8% 以上。所以,两者对比,银行借出的款项,其中要吃亏 3% 以上的利息的超出 3/4 以上。

这家银行经营的结果,似乎正和它的创办人的本来意图相违背。他们的目的,似乎在于对国内那些他们认为有勇敢进取精神的企业给予支持,同时把苏格兰所有银行,尤其是那些在贴现业务方面被指责为过于胆小的、设于爱丁堡的各家银行排挤掉,从

---

① 马克菲尔森在第 525 页说银行经营伙伴有布克勒齐和昆斯伯里公爵、杜姆里伯爵、道格拉斯先生以及其他著名人物。

<small>Its action and failure increased the distress of projectors and the country generally, but relieved the other Scotch banks.</small> to supplant all the other Scotch banks; particularly those established at Edinburgh, whose backwardness in discounting bills of exchange had given some offence. This bank, no doubt, gave some temporary relief to those projectors, and enabled them to carry on their projects for about two years longer than they could otherwise have done. But it thereby only enabled them to get so much deeper into debt, so that when ruin came, it fell so much the heavier both upon them and upon their creditors. The operations of this bank, therefore, instead of relieving, in reality aggravated in the long-run the distress which those projectors had brought both upon themselves and upon their country. It would have been much better for themselves, their creditors and their country, had the greater part of them been obliged to stop two years sooner than they actually did. The temporary relief, however, which this bank afforded to those projectors, proved a real and permanent relief to the other Scotch banks. All the dealers in circulating bills of exchange, which those other banks had become so backward in discounting, had recourse to this new bank, where they were received with open arms. Those other banks, therefore, were euabled to get very easily out of that fatal circle, from which they could not otherwise have disengaged themselves without incurring a considerable loss, and perhaps too even some degree of discredit.

In the long-run, therefore, the operations of this bank increased the real distress of the country which it meant to relieve; and effectually relieved from a very great distress those rivals whom it meant to supplant.

<small>Another plan would nave been to raise money on the securities pledged by borrowers: this would have been a losing business,</small> At the first setting out of this bank, it was the opinion of some people, that how fast soever its coffers might be emptied, it might easily replenish them by raising money upon the securities of those to whom it had advanced its paper. Experience, I believe, soon convinced them that this method of raising money was by much too slow to answer their purpose; and that coffers which originally were so ill filled, and which emptied themselves so very fast, could be replenished by no other expedient but the ruinous one of drawing bills upon London, and when they became due, paying them by other draughts upon the same place with accumulated interest and commission. But

第二篇 第二章

而把整个银行业务集于一身。无疑这家银行曾经给各个计划冒险家以暂时的救济,使他们又多苟延残喘了两年左右。但这种做法最终只不过是使他们陷入程度更深的债务之中,因此到了失败的时候,他们的损失就更加严重,他们债权人的损失也更加严重。所以,对于这些计划冒险家们给他们自己和国家带来的困难,这家银行不但没有给予减轻,事实上反而加深了困难。如果要从他们本身、债权人以及国家本身利益考虑,他们大部分的业务不如早两年停止更好。不过这家银行所给予各计划冒险家暂时性的救济,结果成为对苏格兰其他银行永久性的救济。在苏格兰其他银行不肯贴现循环汇票的时候,这家新银行对出具循环汇票的人,却伸出双手欢迎。因此,其他各银行很容易就脱离了困境,否则它们就不可能摆脱困境,一定要遭受重大损失,甚至有可能名誉还要遭受一定程度的损失。

这家银行的经营方法最终加重了它原打算要减轻的国家困境;却使它原本要取而代之的竞争对手的困境有所减轻。

在这家银行刚刚成立时,有些人认为,尽管银行金柜很迅速地被清空,但通过把借贷纸币所提供的担保品拿来进行抵押担保,很容易地就可以获得金钱来补充金柜。但我认为,不久经验就会让他们确信,使用这个筹款方法来解决问题未免有点远水不解近渴。这样原本就不充实而又容易清空的金柜,除了走上一条穷途末路,即向伦敦银行开出一次汇票,在汇票满期时再开出一次汇票,依次递增下去,累积的利息和佣钱越来越多以外,简直没有第二个办法可以用来补充金柜。尽管这种办法能够使它在需

银行做失计划遭灾加重,苏格兰银行灾难却减轻了。

这家银行的做法使冒险家所受难深

另一种可以把借款供担保的用品进行抵押来补充金柜的方式逐渐成为已消失的做法;这种方式经资金式的做法

— 693 —

though they had been able by this method to raise money as fast as they wanted it; yet, instead of making a profit, they must have suffered a loss by every such operation; so that in the long-run they must have ruined themselves as a mercantile company, though, perhaps, not so soon as by the more expensive practice of drawing and re-drawing. They could still have made nothing by the interest of the paper, which, being over and above what the circulation of the country could absorb and employ, returned upon them, in order to be exchanged for gold and silver, as fast as they issued it; and for the payment of which they were themselves continually obliged to borrow money. On the contrary, the whole expence of this borrowing, of employing agents to look out for people who had money to lend, of negociating with those people, and of drawing the proper bond or assignment, must have fallen upon them, and have been so much clear loss upon the balance of their accounts. The project of replenishing their coffers in this manner may be compared to that of a man who had a water-pond from which a stream was continually running out, and into which no stream was continually running, but who proposed to keep it always equally full by employing a number of people to go continually with buckets to a well at some miles distance in order to bring water to replenish it.

and even if profitable would have been hurtful to the Country.
But though this operation had proved, not only practicable, but profitable to the bank as a mercantile company; yet the country could have derived no benefit from it; but, on the contrary, must have suffered a very considerable loss by it. This operation could not augment in the smallest degree the quantity of money to be lent. It could only have erected this bank into a sort of general loan office for the whole country. Those who wanted to borrow, must have applied to this bank, instead of applying to the private persons who had lent it their money. But a bank which lends money, perhaps, to five hundred different people, the greater part of whom its directors can know very little about, is not likely to be more judicious in the choice of its debtors, than a private person who lends out his money among a few people whom he knows, and in whose sober and frugal conduct he thinks he has good reason to confide. The debtors of such a bank, as that whose conduct I have been giving some account of, were likely, the greater part of them, to be chimerical projectors, the drawers and re-drawers of circulating bills of exchange, who would employ the money in extravagant undertakings, which, with all the assistance that could be given them, they would probably never be able to complete, and which, if they should be completed, would never repay the expence

要款项的时候能立即借到款项,但结果不仅无利可图,而且肯定每一次都遭受损失;这样最终会导致一个营利性的公司一败涂地;尽管灭亡的过程没有采取一再出具汇票这种费用比较昂贵的筹款方法那么快。它仍然不能从所发行纸币的利息中取得利润,因为纸币既是超过国内流通领域所能吸收和使用的数量,必然会一边发现而一边又收回来换取金银;而为了兑换,银行方面须不断地借债,借债的全部用费、雇人了解谁有钱出借、与有钱的人磋商、签发债券和订立协议等所需全部费用,都落在银行身上负担。收入和支出相比较,显然对银行有损而无益。用这种方法来补充金柜,好比让人提水桶到远处水井打水,来补充只有流出而没有流入的水池,这注定是要失败的。

  这种办法,虽然对作为营利机构的银行,不但适用而且有利,但对于国家不仅没有好处且还会遭受很大的损失。这种办法,丝毫不能增加国内可贷出的货币量,只能使全国的借贷业务都集中在这家银行身上,从而使它成为全国总借贷机关而已。要借钱的将不再向有钱的私人进行借贷,而必定都来向这家银行申请贷款。私人借贷一般不超过数人或数十人,债务人的行为谨慎与否,诚实勤俭与否,都为债权人所熟悉,并有选择甄别的余地;而和银行来往的动辄数百家,其中大多数债务人的情况,往往不为董事先生所熟悉,当然选择甄别也就很难达到;因此,比较而言,银行在贷出资金上当然不如私人审慎。事实上,和这样一个银行来往的,本来大部分就是充满幻想的计划家,就是一再开出循环汇票的出票人。他们把资金投在奢侈浪费的事业上,这些事业,即使得到一切可能的帮助,也未必能够成功;即使能够成功,也不

即使有盈利,也会对国家带来损害。

which they had really cost, would never afford a fund capable of maintaining a quantity of labour equal to that which had been employed about them. The sober and frugal debtors of private persons, on the contrary, would be more likely to employ the money borrowed in sober undertakings which were proportioned to their capitals, and which, though they might have less of the grand and the marvellous, would have more of the solid and the profitable, which would repay with a large profit whatever had been laid out upon them, and which would thus afford a fund capable of maintaining a much greater quantity of labour than that which had been employed about them. The success of this operation, therefore, without increaseing in the smallest degree the capital of the country, would only have transferred a great part of it from prudent and profitable, to imprudent and unprofitable undertakings.

<small>Law's scheme has been sufficiently explained by Du Verney and Du Tot.</small>   That the industry of Scotland languished for want of money to employ it, was the opinion of the famous Mr. Law By establishing a bank of a particular kind, which he seems to have imagined might issue paper to the amount of the whole value of all the lands in the country, he proposed to remedy this want of money. The parliament of Scotland, when he first proposed his project, did not think proper to adopt it. ① It was afterwards adopted, with some variations, by the duke of Orleans, at that time regent of France. The idea of the possibility of multiplying paper money to almost any extent, was the real foundation of what is called the Mississippi scheme, the most extravagant project both of banking and stock-jobbing that, perhaps, the world ever saw. The different operations of this scheme are explained so fully, so clearly, and with so much order and distinctness, by Mr. Du Verney, in his Examination of the Political Reflections upon Commerce and Finances of Mr. Du Tot, that I shall not give any account of them. ② The principles upon which it was founded are explained by Mr. Law himself, in a discourse concerning money and trade, which

---

① [*Lectures*, p. 211. The bookseller's preface to the and ed. of *Money and Trade*(below, p. 301, note 3) says the work consists of 'some heads of a scheme which Mr. Law proposed to the Parliament of Scotland in the year 1705'.]

② [In *Lectures* there is an account, apparently derived from Du Verney, which extends over eight pages, 211-218.]

可能偿还所需费用。它们也绝不能拿出足够的基金,维持事业所需雇用的那么多的劳动。反之,私人借贷就没有这种情况,诚实简朴的私人债务人,总是用借入的资本,经营与他们自己的资本额相称的事业。这些事业,也许没有那么宏大,那么惊人,但更稳健和更有利,一定能偿还投下的资本并提供高额的利润,一定能提供一笔基金,足以雇用比它们原先雇用的多得多的劳动。所以,即使新银行的计划成功,结果也丝毫不能增加国内的资本,只能使大部分资本没有投在谨慎和有效益的事业上去,而改投到不谨慎的和无效益的事业上去。

有名的劳先生面对苏格兰产业受困于缺少经营所需要的货币的情况,他提议设立一个特别银行,使该银行所发行纸币等于全国土地的总价值。他认为这是解决货币缺少的好办法。在他最初提出这个计划的时候,苏格兰议会也认为不可以采纳这个建议。① 后来奥林斯公爵摄政法兰西时,却在他原有建议的基础上略加修改以后又加以实施。可以任意增加纸币数量的观念,就成为所谓密西西比计划的实在依据。这个计划,就银行业和就买卖股票生意来说,这个计划其狂妄程度在世界上都是空前的。杜浮纳先生在其《对杜托特<关于商业与财政的政治观察>一书的评论》中,曾经全面和详细条理清楚地说明了这个计划的内容,在这里不再赘述。② 这个计划所依据的原理,在劳氏所著关于货币与

<small>杜浮纳对杜托特已经对劳先生的计划进行充分地说明。</small>

---

① 见《关于法律、警察、岁入及军备的演讲》第211页。在《货币与贸易》(见301页的注释3)第二版里在售书商所做的序言中说,在1705年由劳先生向苏格兰议会提出的计划里的某些见解组成了该理论内容。

② 在《关于法律、警察、岁入及军备的演讲》里有一个说明,很明显出自杜浮纳先生,它占了211页到218页整整8页的篇幅。

he published in Scotland when he first proposed his project. ① The splendid, but visionary ideas which are set forth in that and some other works upon the same principles, still continue to make an impression upon many people, and have, perhaps, in part, contributed to that excess of banking, which has of late been complained of both in Scotland and in other places.

<small>The bank of England was established in 1694,</small> The bank of England is the greatest bank of circulation in Europe. It was incorporated, in pursuance of an act of parliament, by a charter under the great seal, dated the 27th of July, 1694. It at that time advanced to government the sum of one million two hundred thousand pounds, for an annuity of one hundred thousand pounds; or for 96, 000l a year interest, at the rate of eight per cent. , and 4, 000l. a year for the expence of management. The credit of the new government, established by the Revolution, we may believe, must have been very low, when it was obliged to borrow at so high an interest.

<small>enlarged its stock in 1697</small> In 1697 the bank was allowed to enlarge its capital stock by an ingraftment of 1, 001, 171l. 10s. Its whole capital stock, therefore, amounted at this time to 2, 201, 171l. 10s. This engraftment is said to have been for the support of public credit. In 1696, tallies had been at forty, and fifty, and sixty per cent. discount, and bank notes at twenty per cent. ② During the great recoinage of the silver, which was going on at this time, the bank had thought proper to discontinue the payment of its notes, which necessarily occasioned their discredit.

<small>in 1708,</small> In pursuance of the 7th Anne, c. vii. the bank advanced and paid into the exchequer, the sum of 400, 000l. ; making in all the sum of 1, 600, 000l. which it had advanced upon its original annuity of 96, 000l. interest and 4, 000l. for expence of management. In 1708, therefore, the credit of government was as good as that of private persons, since it could borrow at six per cent. interest, the common legal and market rate of those times. In pursuance of the same

---

① [*Money and Trade Considered, with a Proposal for Supplying the Nation with Money,* 1705.]

② James Postlethwaite's History of the Public Revenue, page 301. [*History of the Public Revenue from* 1688 *to* 1753, *with an Appendix to* 1758, by James Postlethwayt, F. R. S. , 1759; see also below, vol. ii. , p. 397]

贸易的一篇论文(在他最初提出这个计划时,①就在苏格兰发表了)中也有说明。在这篇论文以及其他依据同一原理的著作中所提出的那些宏伟而空幻的理论,至今还在许多人头脑中留有很深刻的印象。最近由于经营上毫无节制而遭受攻击的苏格兰及其他各地银行,恐怕也多少受了这个理论的影响。

英格兰银行在欧洲是最大的银行,它是1694年7月27日由国会立法以敕令形式设立的。当时它借给政府的金额,共计120万镑,每年可向政府支取10万镑;其中,96,000镑作为利息(年利8%),4,000镑作为管理费用。我们可以认为大革命建立起来的新政府的信用一定还很差,否则借款不会有这样高的利息。英格兰银行成立于1694年,

在1697年,银行资本增加了1,001,171镑10先令。因此,这时其总资本达2,201,171镑10先令。这次增加资本金,据说旨在维护国家信用。在1696年,国库券要进行四成、五成或六成折扣,银行纸币要进行两成折扣。② 这时,正在大量进行重新铸造银币,银行认为应该暂时停止纸币兑现,而这必然会对银行信用产生不利的影响。在1697年扩大资本金,

根据安妮女王七年第7号法令,银行以40万镑贷给国库,加上原来借给政府的120万镑,贷给政府的钱总计达到了160万镑。因此,在1708年,政府信用已经和私人一样,因为政府能够以6%的利息率借到款项,而这正是当时市场上普通的利息率。1780年

---

① 《对货币和贸易的考察——对向国家供应货币的一个建议》1705年出版。

② 詹姆斯·普斯斯怀特所著《政府收入史》第301页。(他在1759年所著《从1688年到1753年的政府收入史以及1758年补充》;也可以参见第2卷397页。)

国民财富的性质与原理

act, the bank cancelled exchequer bills to the amount of 1,775,027*l*. 17*s*. 10 $\frac{1}{2}$*d*. at six per cent. interest, and was at the same time allowed to take in subscriptions for doubling its capital. In 1708, therefore, the capital of the bank amounted to 4,402,343*l*.; and it had advanced to government the sum of 3,375,027*l*. 17*s*. 10 $\frac{1}{2}$*d*.

<small>in 1709 and 1710,</small> By a call of fifteen per cent. in 1709, there was paid in and made stock 656,204*l*. 1*s*. 9*d*.; and by another of ten per cent. in 1710, 501,448*l*. 12*s*. 11*d*. In consequence of those two calls, therefore, the bank capital amounted to 5,559,995*l*. 14*s*. 8*d*.

<small>in 1717, and later.</small> In pursuance of the 3d George I. c. 8. the bank delivered up two millions of exchequer bills to be cancelled. It had at this time, therefore, advanced to government 5,375,027*l*. 17*s*. 10*d*. [1] In pursuance of the 8th George I. c. 21. the bank purchased of the South Sea Company, stock to the amount of 4,000,000*l*.; and in 1722, in conesquence of the subscriptions which it had taken in for enabling it to make this purchase, its capital stock was increased by 3,4400,000*l*. At this time, therefore, the bank had advanced to the public 9,375,027*l*. 17*s*. 10 $\frac{1}{2}$*d*.; and its capital stock amounted only to 8,959,995*l*. 14*s*. 8*d*. It was upon this occasion that the sum which the bank had advanced to the public, and for which it received interest, began first to exceed its capital stock, or the sum for which it paid a dividend to the proprietors of bank stock; or, in other words, that the bank began to have an undivided capital, over and above its divided one. It has continued to have an undivided capital of the same kind ever since. In 1746, the bank had, upon different occasions, advanced to the public 11,686,800*l*. and its divided capital had been raised by different calls and subscriptions to 10,780,000*l*. [2] The state of those two sums has continued to be the same ever since. In pursuance of the 4th of George III. c. 25. the bank agreed to pay to government for the renewal of its charter 110,000*l*. without interest

---

① [These three lines are not in ed. 1.]

② [From 'it was incorporated,' on p. 301, to this point is an abstract of the 'Historical State of the Bank of England,' in Postlethwayt's *History of the Public Revenue*, pp. 301-310. The totals are taken from the bottom of Postlethwayt's pages.]

按照同一法令,银行又购买了利息为 6% 的财政部国库券 1,775,027 镑 17 先令 10.5 便士。银行资本被批准再增加一倍。所以,在 1708 年,银行资本就达到 4,402,343 镑,贷给政府的款项总额就等于 3,375,027 镑 17 先令 10.5 便士。

在 1709 年,英格兰银行按 15% 的比例催收股本款,收入为 656,204 镑 1 先令 9 便士。在 1710 年,又按 10% 的比例催收股本款,又收入 501,448 镑 12 先令 11 便士。两次催收的结果,银行资本达到 5,559,995 镑 14 先令 8 便士。_{1709 年、1710 年}

按照乔治一世三年第 8 号法令,英格兰银行又购进财政部国库券 200 万镑,所以,这时银行贷给政府的金额已达 5,375,027 镑 17 先令 10 便士。① 按照乔治一世八年第 21 号法令,银行购买南海公司 400 万镑股票。因为要认购这只股票,银行不得不再募集资本金 340 万镑。这时总共计算下来,银行贷给政府的金额为 9,375,027 镑 17 先令 10.5 便士。但其资本总额却不过 8,959,995 镑 14 先令 8 便士。两者相比,银行贷给政府的有息贷款已经比资本金多,或者说,已多于其要对股东进行分派红利的资金了。换句话说,银行已开始有不分红利的资本,而这种资本已经多于分红的资本了。这种情况一直继续至现在。在 1746 年,银行陆续贷给政府 11,686,800 镑,银行陆续募集的分红派息资本也达 1,078 万镑。② 从那时一直到现在,这两个数目都没有改变。遵照乔治三世四年 25 号法令,为了延续银行经营许可,银行同意向_{1717 年以及后来}

---

① 这三行在第一版里没有。

② 前面论述的,是对普斯斯怀特所著《政府收入史》(301~310 页)里"英格兰银行历史情况"的摘要。全部内容摘自普斯斯怀特的页尾部分。

or repayment. This sum, therefore, did not increase either of those two other sums.

<small>The rate of interest received by it from the public has been reduced from 8 to 3 per cent. and its dividend has lately been 5 $\frac{1}{2}$ per cent. It acts as a great engine of state.</small>
The dividend of the bank has varied according to the variations in the rate of the interest which it has, at different times, received for the money it had advanced to the public, as well as according to other circumstances. This rate of interest has gradually been reduced from eight to three per cent. For some years past the bank dividend has been at five and a half per cent.

The stability of the bank of England is equal to that of the British government. All that it has advanced to the public must be lost before its creditors can sustain any loss. No other banking company in England can be established by act of parliament, or can consist of more than six members. It acts, not only as an ordinary bank, but as a great engine of state. It receives and pays the greater part of the annuities which are due to the creditors of the public, it circulates exchequer bills, and it advances to government the annual amount of the land and malt taxes, which are frequently not paid up till some years thereafter. In those different operations, its duty to the public may

<small>The operations of banking turn dead stock into productive capital.</small>
sometimes have obliged it, without any fault of its directors, to overstock the circulation with paper money. It likewise discounts merchants bills, and has. upon several different occasions, supported the credit of the principal houses, not only of England, but of Hamburgh and Holland. Upon one occasion, in 1763, it is said to have advanced for this purpose, in one week, about 1, 600, 000*l*. ; a great part of it in bullion. I do not, however, pretend to warrant either the greatness of the sum, or the shortness of the time. Upon other occasions, this great company has been reduced to the necessity of paying in sixpences. ①

It is not by augmenting the capital of the country, but by rendering a greater part of that capital active and productive than would otherwise be so, that the most judicious operations of banking can increase the industry of the country. That part of his capital which a dealer is obliged to keep by him unemployed, and in ready money for answering occasional demands, is so much dead stock, which, so long

---

① [In 1745. Magens *Universal Merchant*, p. 31, suggests that there may have been suspicions that the money was being drawn out for the support of the rebellion.]

政府缴纳 11 万镑,不收取利息,也不需要政府偿还;所以,这并不增加银行贷款金额和银行资本金。

　　银行红利的高低水平视各时期银行对政府贷款的利息水平的高低以及其他情况而有所变化。贷款利息率已由 8% 逐渐降到 3%。过去几年里,银行红利常为 5.5%。对政府贷款的利率水平由 8% 降到 3%,银行红利最近为 5.5%。

　　英政府稳定,英格兰银行也随之稳定。贷给政府的金额没有遭受损失,银行债权人也不会有所损失。英格兰不能有第二个银行由国会通过立法设立或由 6 人以上的股东组成的银行。所以英格兰银行已不是普通银行可比,它是一个大的国家机构。每年公债利息的大部分是由它收付;财政部国库券由它流通。土地税、麦芽税的征收额往往是由它先垫付。这些税收的税款,纳税人往往逾期好几年不到国库缴纳。在这种情况下,即使董事们明白,但由于要对国家负责,也不免过度发行纸币。它也贴现商人汇票。有时,不仅英格兰,就连汉堡、荷兰的巨商,也向它申请借贷。据说,在 1763 年,有一次英格兰银行在一个星期之内就贷出了将近 160 万镑,其中大部分还是金块。对数额庞大,借贷过程的时间是否短促,我不敢妄下断言。但英格兰银行却有时真是迫不得已,竟以六便士的银币来应付各种支出。①英格兰银行扮演了一个政府机构的角色。

　　审慎的银行活动可以促进一个国家产业的发展。但是,促进产业进步的方法不在于增加一国资本,而在于使本来没有使用的资本大部分有用,使本来并不产生效益的资本大部分产生效益。商人不得不储存用来应急的准备金全成为死的财货,对商人自己

---

　　① 在 1745 年版马根斯的《环球商人》第 31 页里,他对把货币正在被撤离出来用作支持战争的做法表示怀疑。

_{but make commerce and industry somewhat less secure.} as it remains in this situation, produces nothing either to him or to his country. The judicious operations of banking enable him to convert this dead stock into active and productive stock; into materials to work upon, into tools to work with, and into provisions and subsistence to work for; into stock which produces something both to himself and to his country. The gold and silver money which circulates in any country, and by means of which the produce of its land and labour is annually circulated and distributed to the proper consumers, is, in the same manner as the ready money of the dealer, all dead stock. It is a very valuable part of the capital of the country, which produces nothing to the country. The judicious operations of banking, by substituting paper in the room of a great part of this gold and silver, enables the country to convert a great part of this dead stock into active and productive stock; into stock which produces something to the country. The gold and silver money which circulates in any country may very properly be compared to a highway, which, while it circulates and carries to market all the grass and corn of the country, produces itself not a single pile of either. The judicious operations of banking, by providing, if I may be allowed so violent a metaphor, a sort of waggon-way through the air; enable the country to convert, as it were, a great part of its highways into good pastures and cornfields, and thereby to increase very considerably the annual produce of its land and labour. The commerce and industry of the country, however, it must be acknowledged, though they may be somewhat augmented, cannot be altogether so secure, when they are thus, as it were, suspended upon the Daedalian wings of paper money, as when they travel about upon the solid ground of gold and silver. Over and above the accidents to which they are exposed from the unskilfulness of the conductors of this paper money, they are liable to several others, from which no prudence or skill of those conductors can guard them.

_{Precautions should be taken to prevent the greater part of the circulation being filled with paper.} An unsuccessful war, for example, in which the enemy got possession of the capital, and consequently of that treasure which supported the credit of the paper money, would occasion a much greater confusion in a country where the whole circulation was carried on by paper, than in one where the greater part of it was carried on by gold and silver. The usual instrument of commerce having lost its value, no exchanges could be made but either by barter or upon credit. All taxes having been usually paid in paper money, the prince would not have wherewithal either to pay his troops, or to furnish his magazines; and the state of the country would be much more irretrievable than if the greater part of its circulation had consisted in gold and silver. A

第二篇 第二章

和他所在的国家都没有好处。审慎的银行活动，可以使这种死的财货变为活的财货，或者换句话说，变成工作所需要的材料、工具和食品，既有利于自己，又有利于国家。在国内流通即国内土地和劳动的生产物所依靠年年流通和年年分配给真正消费者的金银币，与在商人手上的准备金一样，也是死的财货。这种死财货在一国资本中虽然是极有价值的一部分，但不能为国家生产任何物品。慎重的银行活动，以纸币代替大部分的这类金银，使国家能把大部分这类死的财货，变成富有活力的财货，变成有利于国家的财货。似乎可以把流通国内的金币银币比喻为通衢大道；这个通衢大道能使稻谷小麦流转运输到国内各个市场，但它本身却不能够生产稻谷小麦。审慎的银行活动，以纸币代替金银，比喻得过分一点，简直有些像变天空为交通走廊一样，使过去的大多数通衢大道，化为良好的牧场和稻田，从而大大增加土地和劳动的年产物。但是，我们又必须承认，有了这种设施，国内工商业固然略有增进，但用比喻来说，与足踏金银铺成的实地相比，飞翔的纸币悬挂在空中是不能保证安全的。管理纸币，如果不很熟练，情况不用多说；即使管理纸币能力熟练慎重，恐怕仍然会发生无法控制的灾祸。

比如说，战争失败，敌军占领首都，用来支持纸币信用的金库也陷入敌手。在这种情况下，国内流通全靠纸币进行的国家，比起大部分依靠金银来流通的国家，当然要困难得多。一般交易手段全部失去价值，除了物物交换和赊账交易以外，就不能再进行交换活动。由于一切税收一般用纸币缴纳，所以君主也就无法支付军饷，也没有财力来充实武器库。在这种情况下，全用纸币的国家比那些大部分使用金银流通的国家更加难以恢复原状。因

银行的活动可以使死货资产业变些什么营可僵产但业的会有成的化财产变化资产那不变成的财产那有成生财产资产变化资产。

采防纸取预止币防流里措通泛施域到滥。

— 705 —

prince, anxious to maintain his dominions at all times in the state in which he can most easily defend them, ought, upon this account, to guard, not only against that excessive multiplication of paper money which ruins the very banks which issue it; but even against that multiplication of it, which enables them to fill the greater part of the circulation of the country with it.

<small>Circulation may be divided into that between dealers and that between dealers and consumers.</small>

The circulation of every country may be considered as divided into two different branches; the circulation of the dealers with one another, and the circulation between the dealers and the consumers. Though the same pieces of money, whether paper or metal, may be employed sometimes in the one circulation and sometimes in the other; yet as both are constantly going on at the same time, each requires a certain stock of money of one kind or another, to carry it on. The value of the goods circulated between the different dealers, never can exceed the value of those circulated between the dealers and the consumers; whatever is bought by the dealers, being ultimately destined to be sold to the consumers. The circulation between the dealers, as it is carried on by wholesale, requires generally a pretty large sum for every particular transaction. That between the dealers and the consumers, on the contrary, as it is generally carried on by retail, frequently requires but very small ones, a shilling, or even a halfpenny, being often sufficient. But small sums circulate much faster than large ones. A shilling changes masters more frequently than a guinea, and a halfpenny more frequently than a shilling Though the annual purchases of all the consumers, therefore, are at least equal in value to those of all the dealers, they can generally be transacted with a much smaller quantity of money; the same pieces, by a more rapid circulation, serving as the instrument of many more purchases of the one kind than of the other.

<small>The circulation of paper may be confined to the former by not allowing notes for small sums.</small>

Paper money may be so regulated, as either to confine itself very much to the circulation between the different dealers, or to extend itself likewise to a great part of that between the dealers and the consumers. Where no bank notes are circulated under ten pounds value, as in London, [1] paper money confines itself very much to the circulation between the dealers. When a ten pound bank note comes into the hands of a consumer, he is generally obliged to change it at the first

---

① [The Bank of England issued none under £ 20 till 1759, when £ 15 and £ 10 notes were introduced. —Anderson, *Commerce*, A. D. 1759.]

此,一国君主,要把他的领土随时都保持在易于防守的状态,就不仅要防止那种能导致发币银行破产的纸币发行过剩现象,而且还要设法使银行所发纸币不在国内流通领域里占较大的部分。

国内货物的流通,可以分为两类:一是商人彼此之间的流通;二是商人与消费者之间的流通。同一货币,无论它是一张纸币或一枚铸币,可能有时用于前一种流通,有时用于后一种流通,但由于这两种流通是同时不断进行的,所以,各自需要一定数量的货币来经营。商人彼此之间流通的货物价值,肯定不能超过商人和消费者之间流通的货物价值。商人所购买的一切,最终必须再卖给消费者。商人彼此之间的交易,往往是批发,所以每次都必须有大量货币。商人和消费者之间的交易,往往是零售,所以每次有小量货币(如一先令或甚至半便士)就够了。但小量货币流通速度比大量货币要快得多。一个先令比一个几尼要流转得快,半个便士又比一个先令流转得快。因此,以年为单位计算,全部消费者所购买的价值,虽然至少应该等于全部商人所购买的价值,但消费者每年购买物品所需要的货币量,却要小得多。由于流通速度较快,同一枚货币作为消费者购买手段所流通的次数,比作为商人购买手段所流通的次数要多得多。

对纸币可以施加管制,要求它要么仅仅在商人之间流通,要么扩大到商人与消费者之间的交易,使该领域也大部分使用纸币交易。如果没有面额在 10 镑以下的钞票,与在伦敦情况一样,[①]那么,纸币的流通一定局限于商人彼此之间。消费者手中有一张

---

① 英格兰银行一直到 1759 年才发行面值在 20 镑以下的钞票,发行的是面值为 15 镑和 10 镑——安德森:《商业》,1759 年版。

shop where he has occasion to purchase five shillings worth of goods; so that it often returns into the hands of a dealer, before the consumer has spent the fortieth part of the money. Where bank notes are issued for so small sums as twenty shillings, as in Scotland, paper money extends itself to a considerable part of the circulation between dealers and consumers. Before the act of parliament, which put a stop to the circulation of ten and five shilling notes,① it filled a still greater part of that circulation. In the currencies of North America, paper was commonly issued for so small a sum as a shilling, and filled almost the whole of that circulation. In some paper currencies of Yorkshire, it was issued even for so small a sum as a sixpence.

The issue of such notes enables mean people to become bankers.

Where the issuing of bank notes for such very small sums is allowed and commonly practised, many mean people are both enabled and encouraged to become bankers. A person whose promissory note for five pounds, or even for twenty shillings, would be rejected by every body, will get it to be received without scruple when it is issued for so small a sum as a sixpence. But the frequent bankruptcies to which such beggarly bankers must be liable, may occasion a very considerable inconveniency, and sometimes even a very great calamity, to many poor people who had received their notes in payment.

None for less than £5 should be issued.

It were better, perhaps, that no bank notes were issued in any part of the kingdom for a smaller sum than five pounds. Paper money would then, probably, confine itself, in every part of the kingdom, to the circulation between the different dealers, as much as it does at present in London, where no bank notes are issued under ten pounds value; five pounds being, in most parts of the kingdom, a sum which, though it will purchase, perhaps, little more than half the quantity of goods, is as much considered, and is as seldom spent all at once, as ten pounds are amidst the profuse expence of London.

---

① [5 Geo. III. . c. 49.]

面额 10 镑的钞票,在第一次购买东西的时候就必须兑换这张钞票,即使他所要购买的物品仅值 5 先令。① 所以在消费者把这张钞票用去 1/40 以前,钞票早已回到商人手中去了。苏格兰各银行所发行的钞票面额却有小至 20 先令的,在这种情况下,纸币的流通范围就自然得到扩大,使商人与消费者之间的交易,大部分也使用纸币进行交易。在国会通过决议禁止流通中使用 10 先令和 5 先令的钞票以前,消费者在购物时便常常使用小额纸币。北美洲那里发出的纸币,竟还有小至一个先令的,结果消费者在购物时几乎都用钞票。至于约克郡,有些纸币仅值六便士,结果如何就更不用说了。

发行这样的小额纸币,如果得到批准而且普遍实施,这无异于鼓励许多普通人去开银行,并还要使他们有能力成为银行家。普通人所发出的 5 镑甚至 1 镑的期票,大家会拒绝不用;但他发出的 6 便士期票,大家却不会拒绝。这些乞丐一样的银行家肯定很容易会破产,结果对于接受他们小额面值钞票的穷人,这可能引起很大的困难,甚至会带来极大的灾难。 <small>这种小额钞票的发行能够使很多平庸的人成为银行家。</small>

把全国各地银行钞票的最低面额限定为 5 镑,也许是较好的办法。这样,英国各地银行所发行的钞票,大部分就会只在商人彼此之间流通,与在伦敦的情况一样。在伦敦银行所发行的钞票面值不得小于 10 镑。5 镑所能购买的货物,虽然仅仅等于 10 镑的一半,但在英国其他各个地方,人们对 5 镑正如奢华的伦敦人那样对 10 镑重视,而且一次花掉 5 镑,也与伦敦人一次花掉 10 镑一样并不常见。 <small>禁止发行面值小于五镑的钞票。</small>

---

① 乔治三世五年,第 49 号法令。

| 国民财富的性质与原理

<small>This would secure the circulation of plenty of gold and silver,</small>   Where paper money, it is to be observed, is pretty much confined to the circulation between dealers and dealers, as at London, there is always plenty of gold and silver. Where it extends itself to a considerable part of the circulation between dealers and consumers, as in Scotland, and still more in North America, it banishes gold and silver almost entirely from the country; almost all the ordinary transactions of its interior commerce being thus carried on by paper. The suppression of ten and five shilling bank notes, somewhat relieved the scarcity of gold and silver in Scotland; and the suppression of twenty shilling notes, would probably relieve it still more. Those metals are said to have become more abundant in America, since the suppression of some of their paper currencies. They are said, likewise, to have been more abundant before the institution of those currencies.

<small>and would not prevent banks from giving sufficient assistance to traders.</small>   Though paper money should be pretty much confined to the circulation between dealers and dealers, yet banks and bankers might still be able to give nearly the same assistance to the industry and commerce of the country, as they had done when paper money filled almost the whole circulation. The ready money which a dealer is obliged to keep by him, for answering occasional demands, is destined altogether for the circulation between himself and other dealers, of whom he buys goods. He has no occasion to keep any by him for the circulation between himself and the consumers, who are his customers, and who bring ready money to him, instead of taking any from him. Though no paper money, therefore, was allowed to be issued, but for such sums as would confine it pretty much to the circulation between dealers and dealers; yet, partly by discounting real bills of exchange, and partly by lending upon cash accounts, banks and bankers might still be able to relieve the greater part of those dealers from the necessity of keeping any considerable part of their stock by them, unemployed and in ready money, for answering occasional demands. They might still be able to give the utmost assistance which banks and bankers can, with propriety, give to traders of every kind.

<small>A law against small notes would be a violation of natural liberty necessary for the security of the society,</small>   To restrain private people, it may be said, from receiving in payment the promissory notes of a banker, for any sum whether great or small, when they themselves are willing to receive them; or, to restrain a banker from issuing such notes, when all his neighbours are willing to accept of them, is a manifest violation of that natural liberty which it is the proper business of law, not to infringe, but to support. Such regulations may, no doubt, be considered as in some respect a violation of natural liberty. But those exertions of the natural liberty of a few individuals, which might endanger the security of the whole society, are, and ought to be, restrained by the laws of all governments;

— 710 —

如果纸币像在伦敦那样,主要在商人间流通,市面上的金银数量足够流通使用。如果像在苏格兰,尤其是像在北美洲那样,纸币的流通推广到商人与消费者之间的大部分交易,那么市面上的金银就会全部被驱逐出流通领域,国内商业流通只用纸币进行。苏格兰禁止发行10先令、5先令的钞票,对市面上金银缺乏的状况稍微有所缓解;如果再禁止发行20先令的钞票,那么效果会更加明显。据说美洲自从禁止发行若干种纸币以来,金银已经更加充裕了。在纸币还没有发行以前,听说美洲的金银还更充裕。

<small>可证这样以保证充足的金银流通,</small>

虽然纸币应当主要限制在商人之间的流通,但银行和银行家在这种情况下仍然能够帮助国内工商业,几乎与在货币流通几乎全部由纸币完成的情况一样。因为商人为了应付不时之需而必须储存的现金,本来就只在商人之间流通使用。在商人与消费者的交易上,商人没有储存准备金的必要。在这种交易上,商人只有钱收进来而没有钱支出去。所以,虽然银行钞票的发行只限于在商人之间流通所使用的数量,但银行通过贴现真实汇票和现金结算的办法,依然能够使大部分商人不必储备那么多的现金,专门用来应付不时之需。银行依然能够对各种商人提供它们所能提供的最大贡献。

<small>但不能阻止银行对商人提供足够的帮助。</small>

银行钞票无论面值大小,只要他们自己或同行愿意接受使用它,就应该再允许发行和使用它。政府限制纸币用于清偿债务,或取缔纸币发行,这种做法实在是侵犯天然的自由,不是法律应有的含义;因为法律不应该妨害天然的自由,而应该给以支持。从某种观点来说,这种限制肯定是侵犯天然的自由,但这种自由是少数人的天然自由,它会危害整个社会的安全;所以要受到而

<small>面值小的钞票法律是必安全所然要限制过的钞票法律可能会对社会所需要的一种侵犯。</small>

— 711 —

of the most free, as well as of the most despotical. The obligation of building party walls, in order to prevent the communication of fire, is a violation of natural liberty, exactly of the same kind with the regulations of the banking trade which are here proposed.

<small>Paper-money payable on demand is equal to gold and silver,</small>   A paper money consisting in bank notes, issued by people of undoubted credit, payable upon demand without any condition, and in fact always readily paid as soon as presented, is, in every respect, equal in value to gold and silver money; since gold and silver money can at any time be had for it. Whatever is either bought or sold for such paper, must necessarily be bought or sold as cheap as it could have been for gold and silver.

<small>and does not raise prices;</small>   The increase of paper money, it has been said, by augmenting the quantity, and consequently diminishing the value of the whole currency, necessarily augments the money price of commodities. But as the quantity of gold and silver, which is taken from the currency, is always equal to the quantity of paper which is added to it, paper money does not necessarily increase the quantity of the whole currency. From the beginning of the last century to the present time, provisions never were cheaper in Scotland than in 1759, though, from the circulation of ten and five shilling bank notes, there was then more paper money in the country than at present. The proportion between the price of provisions in Scotland and that in England, is the same now as before the great multiplication of banking companies in Scotland. Corn is, upon most occasions, fully as cheap in England as in France; though there is a great deal of paper money in England, and scarce any in France. In 1751 and in 1752, when Mr. Hume published his Political Discourses,① and soon after the great multiplication of paper money in Scotland, there was a very sensible rise in the price of provisions, owing, probably, to the badness of the seasons, and not to the multiplication of paper money.

---

① [The reference is *probably* to the passages in the ' *Discourse of Money*, and the ' Discourse of the *Balance of Trade*,' where Hume censures paper money as *the cause of a rise of prices*. —*Political Discourses*, 1752, pp. 43-45, 89-91; cp. *Lectures*, p. 197.]

第二篇 第二章

且应该受到一切政府的法律制裁,无论政府是最民主的政府或者是最专制的政府。法律强迫人民建筑隔离墙来预防火灾蔓延,这种强制也是侵犯天然的自由,这恰恰与我们这里主张的用法律限制银行活动一样。

由银行钞票构成的纸币,如果由信用良好的人发行,能够保证无条件的、见票随时都能兑现,那无论从哪一个方面来说,它的价值都等于金币银币的价值,因为它随时都可以兑换金银。无论用这种纸币买进还是卖出任何货物,其价格一定与用金银买卖货物一样便宜。〔如果纸币能够无条件兑换,那么它的价值与金银一样,〕

有人说,由于增加通货总量,从而会降低全部通货价值,所以,纸币的增加必定会提高商品的货币价格。这种说法不一定可靠,因为有多少纸币增加进来,就有多少金银会改作其他用途不再作为通货使用,所以,通货的总量不一定会有所增加。一个世纪以来,苏格兰粮食价格数 1759 年最为低廉。但那时却有十先令、五先令银行钞票的发行,纸币数量比现在要多出很多。再者,尽管现在苏格兰银行业规模急剧增加,但现在苏格兰粮食价格和英格兰粮食价格的比例,却与以前没有两样。尽管英格兰的纸币数量大而法兰西的纸币数量很小,但两国谷物价格却在大多情况下都是一样的便宜。在休谟发表《政治论文集》的 1751 年和 1752 年间,①以及在苏格兰增发纸币之后,粮食价格就极其明显地上涨起来,但其原因与其说是纸币增加,不如说是天时不好。〔不会提高价格。〕

---

① 这种推断可能与"论货币论文集"和"论贸易平衡"的内容有关;在这里休谟指责货币为引起价格上升的罪魁祸首——见 1752 年版的《政治论文集》第 43～45 和 89～91 页;见《关于法律、警察、岁入及军备的演讲》第 197 页。

| 国民财富的性质与原理

but paper not repayable on demand would fall below gold and silver,

It would be otherwise, indeed, with a paper money consisting in promissory notes, of which the immediate payment depended, in any respect, either upon the good will of those who issued them; or upon a condition which the holder of the notes might not always have it in his power to fulfil; or of which the payment was not exigible till after a certain number of years, and which in the mean time bore no interest. Such a paper money would, no doubt, fall more or less below the value of gold and silver, according as the difficulty or uncertainty of obtaining immediate payment was supposed to be greater or less; or according to the greater or less distance of time at which payment was exigible.

as happened in Scotland during the prevalence of the Optional Clause,

Some years ago the different banking companies of Scotland were in the practice of inserting into their bank notes, what they called an Optional Clause, by which they promised payment to the bearer, either as soon as the note should be presented, or, in the option of the directors, six months after such presentment, together with the legal interest for the said six months. The directors of some of those banks sometimes took advantage of this optional clause, and sometimes threatened those who demanded gold and silver in exchange for a considerable number of their notes, that they would take advantage of it, unless such demanders would content themselves with a part of what they demanded. The promissory notes of those banking companies constituted at that time the far greater part of the currency of Scotland, which this uncertainty of payment necessarily degraded below the value of gold and silver money. During the continuance of this abuse (which prevailed chiefly in 1762, 1763, and 1764), while the exchange between London and Carlisle was at par, that between London and Dumfries would sometimes be four per cent. against Dumfries, though this town is not thirty miles distant from Carlisle. But at Carlisle, bills were paid in gold and silver; whereas at Dumfries they were paid in Scotch bank notes, and the uncertainty of getting those bank notes exchanged for gold and silver coin had thus degraded them four per cent. below the value of that coin. The same act of parliament which suppressed ten and five shilling bank notes, suppressed likewise this optional clause,① and thereby restored the exchange between England and Scotland to its natural rate, or to what the course of trade and remittances might happen to make it.

and must have happened in regard to the Yorkshire currencies when small sums were repayable in guineas.

In the paper currencies of Yorkshire, the payment of so small a sum as a sixpence sometimes depended upon the condition that the holder of the note should bring the change of a guinea to the person

---

① [5 Geo. Ⅲ., c. 49; referred to above, p. 305.]

但如果构成纸币的银行券能否立即兑现,还必须取决于发行人有无诚意,或者取决于持券人未必有能力满足的某种条件,或者银行券要在若干年以后才能兑现,而且在此期间不支付任何利息,那么情况就不同了。这样的纸币,当然要依据能够立即兑现的困难度或不确定性程度情况,或者依据兑现时间的长短情况,或多或少地跌在金银价值之下。

不能兑现的纸币价值将会低于金银的价值。

数年以前,苏格兰各银行常常在所发行钞票上加印选择权条款。按照这些条款,凡持票提请要求兑现者,见票即兑,或见票提请 6 个月以后兑现但要附带 6 个月的法定利息,这也由银行董事决定。有些银行的董事先生有时会利用这个条款,有时威胁持有大批钞票要求兑现者,要求他们满足于部分兑现钞票的条件,否则就要利用这些条款。那时候,苏格兰的通货几乎大部分是这些银行发行的钞券。能否兑现存在着很大程度的不确定性,其价值当然就会低于金银的价值。在这个弊端没有消除时(尤其是在 1762 年、1763 年和 1764 年)以前,卡莱尔对伦敦实行平价汇兑,达弗里斯距卡莱尔不到 30 英里,但对伦敦的汇兑却往往贴水 4%。很明显,这是因为卡莱尔用金银来兑付汇票,达弗里斯则以苏格兰银行钞票来兑付汇票。这些钞票要兑换金银的不确定性,就使其价值下跌了 4%。后来,国会颁布禁止发行 5 先令、10 先令钞票的命令,又规定钞票不得附加选择性条款,①英格兰对苏格兰的汇兑才恢复自然汇兑,即顺应于贸易情况和汇兑情况的汇率。

苏格兰选择条款使纸币价值会在金银的价值以下。

约克郡纸币面值竟有小至六便士的,但持票人按规定要保存纸币到一个几尼才可以要求兑现。这个条件,在持票人方面,往

只有到值累到几尼以后,约克郡纸币才可要求兑现。

———————
① 乔治三世五年第 49 号法令。

国民财富的性质与原理

who issued it; a condition, which the holders of such notes might frequently find it very difficult to fulfil, and which must have degraded this currency below the value of gold and silver money. An act of parliament, accordingly, declared all such clauses unlawful, and suppressed, in the same manner as in Scotland, all promissory notes, payable to the bearer, under twenty shillings value. ①

The North American paper currencies consisted of government notes repayable at a distant date, and depreciated the currency to a great degree. The paper currencies of North America consisted, not in bank notes payable to the bearer on demand, but in a government paper, of which the payment was not exigible till several years after it was issued: And though the colony governments paid no interest to the holders of this paper, they declared it to be, and in fact rendered it, a legal tender of payment for the full value for which it was issued. But allowing the colony security to be perfectly good, a hundred pounds payable fifteen years hence, for example, in a country where interest is at six per cent. is worth little more than forty pounds ready money. To oblige a creditor, therefore, to accept of this as full payment for a debt of a hundred pounds actually paid down in ready money, was an act of such violent injustice, as has scarce, perhaps, been attempted by the government of any other country which pretended to be free. It bears the evident marks of having originally been, what the honest and downright Doctor Douglas assures us it was, a scheme of fraudulent debtors to cheat their creditors. ② The government of Pensylvania, indeed, pretended, upon their first emission of paper money, in 1722, to render their paper of equal value with gold and silver, by enacting penalties against all those who made any difference in the price of their goods when they sold them for a colony paper, and when they sold them for gold and silver; a regulation equally tyrannical, but much less effectual than that which it was meant to support. A positive law may render a shilling a legal tender for a guinea; because it may direct the courts of justice to discharge the debtor who has made that tender. But no positive law can oblige a person who sells goods, and who is at liberty to sell or not to sell, as he pleases, to accept of a shilling as equivalent to a guinea in the price of them.

① [15, Geo. III. , C. 51.]

② ['A knavish device of fraudulent debtors of the loan money to pay off their loans at a very depreciated value. William Douglass, M. D. , *Summary, Historical and Political, of the First Planting, Progressive Improvements, and Present State of the British Settlements in North America*, 1760, vol. ii. , p. 107. The author uses strong language in many places about what he calls this accursed affair of plantation paper currencies, vol. ii. , p. 13, note (s); cp. vol. i. , pp. 310, 359; vol. ii. , pp. 254-255, 334-335.]

往难于办到;所以其价值也在金银货币价值之下。后来,国会通过立法废止这种规定,认为它不合法,并且与苏格兰一样,禁止发行 20 先令以下的钞券。①

北美洲纸币并不是由银行发行,也不能随时兑现。它是由政府发行的,不经过数年以后是不能兑现的。殖民地政府虽然不向持票人支付任何利息,但曾经宣布纸币为法定货币,必须按票面价值接受其清偿债务。但是,即使殖民地政府非常稳健,在一般年利率为 6% 的地方,15 年后才能支付的 100 镑钞票,其价值和 40 镑现金差不了多少。所以,强迫债权人接受 100 镑纸币清偿其 100 镑现金债务,这是极其不公正的行为,任何以自由相标榜的政府大概都没有尝试这样做过。这显然像诚实坦率的道格拉斯博士所说,是不诚实的债务人欺骗债权人的一种阴谋。② 在 1772 年,宾夕法尼亚政府第一次发行纸币,声称纸币与金银在价值上相等,严禁人们以纸币出售货物时索取比以金银出售货物较高的价格。这个法令言语专横,与其本意所要支持的法令没有区别;这个法令言语的作用则远远低于其本意所要支持的法令要求。法律可以使一个先令在法律上等于一个几尼,因为它可以指导法庭解除这样拿出一个先令的债务人的义务。但是,销售货物与否,卖者各自拥有自由买卖的权利。法令不能够强迫卖者把一个

> 北美洲纸币是由政府发行的,兑现期限比较长,并且贬值幅度比较大。

---

① 乔治三世十五年第 51 号法令。
② 债务人利用阴谋欺骗债权人,在货币贬值幅度很大的情况下归还贷款。威廉·道格拉斯在 1760 年出版《不列颠北美殖民地的最初种植、后续改良和现状的历史和政治概述》的第二卷 107 页。该作者在多处使用激烈的言辞,称这种状况为"可恨的殖民地纸币"。见第 2 卷,第 13 页注解。第 1 卷,第 310、359 页。第 2 卷,第 254~255、334~335 页。

国民财富的性质与原理

Notwithstanding any regulation of this kind, it appeared by the course of exchange with Great Britain, that a hundred pounds sterling was occasionally considered as equivalent, in some of the colonies, to a hundred and thirty pounds, and in others to so great a sum as eleven hundred pounds currency; this difference in the value arising from the difference in the quantity of paper emitted in the different colonies, and in the distance and probability of the term of its final discharge and redemption.

They were therefore justly prohibited. No law, therefore, could be more equitable than the act of parliament, so unjustly complained of in the colonies, which declared that no paper currency to be emitted there in time coming, should be a legal tender of payment. ①

Pennsylvania was moderate in its issues, and its currency never went below the real par. Pensylvania was always more moderate in its emissions of paper money than any other of our colonies. Its paper currency accordingly is said never to have sunk below the value of the gold and silver which was current in the colony before the first emission of its paper money. Before that emission, the colony had raised the denomination of its coin, and had, by act of assembly, ordered five shillings sterling to pass in the colony for six and three-pence, and afterwards for six and eight-pence. A pound colony currency, therefore, even when that currency was gold and silver, was more than thirty per cent. below the value of a pound sterling, and when that currency was turned into paper, it was seldom much more than thirty per cent. below that value. The pretence for raising the denomination of the coin, was to prevent the exportation of gold and silver, by making equal quantities of those metals pass for greater sums in the colony than they did in the mother country. It was found, however, that the price of all goods from the mother country rose exactly in proportion as they raised the denomination of their coin, so that their gold and silver were exported as fast as ever.

The colonial paper was somewhat supported by being received in payment of taxes. The paper of each colony being received in the payment of the provincial taxes, for the full value for which it had been issued, it necessarily derived from this use some additional value, over and above what it would have had, from the real or supposed distance of the term of its final discharge and redemption. This additional value was greater or less, according as the quantity of paper issued was more or less above what could be employed in the payment of the taxes of the particular colony which issued it. It was in all the colonies very much above what could be employed in this manner.

---

① [4 Geo. Ⅲ., c. 34.]

先令看作为一个几尼。尽管如此,但有时英国法令还规定对一些殖民地的汇兑是以100镑等于130镑,而对另一些殖民地繁荣汇兑则以100镑甚至可以等于1,100镑。价值差异很大的原因在于,各殖民地发行出去的纸币数量、纸币兑现期限和可能性等方面存在巨大差异。

这样看来,国会立法规定殖民地以后发行的纸币都不得定为法币,是最恰当不过的。为什么各殖民地都不赞成这个议决案呢?① _{因此殖民地的这种应受到法律的禁止。}

与我国其他殖民地相比较,宾夕法尼亚对发行纸币往往比较慎重。那里发行的纸币价值,据说从来没有低落到没有发行纸币以前的金银价值以下。但在纸币第一次发行以前,宾夕法尼亚已经提高了殖民地铸币单位,并且由议会表决通过,英国5先令的铸币在殖民地境内流通,可以当作6先令3便士,后来又提高到6先令8便士。所以,殖民地一镑货币,即使在通货是金银币的时候,和英国货币1镑比较,价值已低30%以上,在通货是纸币时,其价值低于英国货币1镑的价值很少有超过30%以上。以为这样提高铸币单位的做法,就能够使等量金银在殖民地比在母国当作更大的数目使用,可以防止金银出口;却不知道殖民地铸币单位提高以后,由母国运来的货物的价格也必须按比例提高,结果金银出口还是与以前一样迅速。_{宾夕法尼亚发行纸币比较慎重,其纸币价值从来没有跌到金银币价以下。}

每个殖民地纸币允许人民按其面额缴纳本州各种税收,不折不扣。所以,即使纸币真的或被认为要在很久以后才可以兑现,那么其价值也一定可以多少增加一些。不过这种增加价值,要看本州发行的纸币数量超过本州缴纳税收所能使用的纸币数量的多少而定。各州纸币发行数量都大大超过本州缴纳税收所能使_{殖民地的纸币受到缴纳税收功能的支持}

---

① 乔治三世四年,第34号法令。

| 国民财富的性质与原理

<small>A requirement that certain taxes should be paid in particular paper money might give that paper a certain value even if it was irredeemable.</small>　　A prince, who should enact that a certain proportion of his taxes should be paid in a paper money of a certain kind, might thereby give a certain value to this paper money; even though the term of its final discharge and redemption should depend altogether upon the will of the prince. If the bank which issued this paper was careful to keep the quantity of it always somewhat below what could easily be employed in this manner, the demand for it might be such as to make it even bear a premium, or sell for somewhat more in the market than the quantity of gold or silver currency for which it was issued. Some people account in this manner for what is called the Agio of the bank of Amsterdam, or for the superiority of bank money over current money; though this bank money, as they pretend, cannot be taken out of the bank at the will of the owner. The greater part of foreign bills of exchange must be paid in bank money, that is, by a transfer in the books of the bank; and the directors of the bank, they allege, are careful to keep the whole quantity of bank money always below what this use occasions a demand for. It is upon this account, they say, that bank money sells for a premium, or bears an agio of four or five per cent. above the same nominal sum of the gold and silver currency of the country. This account of the bank of Amsterdam, however, it will appear hereafter, ① is in a great measure chimerical. ②

<small>A paper currency depreciated below the value of the coin does not sink the value of gold and silver.</small>　　A paper currency which falls below the value of gold and silver coin, does not thereby sink the value of those metals, or occasion equal quantities of them to exchange for a smaller quantity of goods of any other kind. The proportion between the value of gold and silver and that of goods of any other kind, depends in all cases, not upon the nature or quantity of any particular paper money, which may be current in any particular country, but upon the richness or poverty of the mines, which happen at any particular time to supply the great market of the commercial world with those metals. It depends upon the proportion between the quantity of labour which is necessary in order to bring a certain quantity of gold and silver to market, and that which is necessary in order to bring thither a certain quantity of any other sort of goods.

---

　　① [Ed. I reads'This account of the bank of Amsterdam, however, I have reason to believe is altogether chimerical. ']

　　② [Ed. I read 'sink the value of gold and silver, or occasion equal quantities of those metals. ']

— 720 —

用的纸币数量。

一国君主如果规定一定比例的税收必须用纸币缴纳,那么,即使纸币兑现和清偿的条件完全取决于国王的意志,这也能够多多少少提高纸币的价值。如果发行纸币的银行故意把纸币发行数量控制在纳税所需要的数量以下,常常使纸币不能满足纳税人的需求,那么纸币价值也将高于它的面值;或者说,纸币在市场上所能购买的金银币数量会多过它票面价值数量。但有些人就根据这点来说明所谓阿姆斯特丹银行纸币的升水问题,即说明它的价值为什么会高于通用货币的价值;虽然据他们说,这种纸币不能凭其所有者的意志随便拿到银行以外去。他们说,大部分外国汇票必须用银行纸币进行兑付;换句话说,必须在银行账上进行转账使用;该银行理事先生声称他们故意使银行纸币额数量常常不能满足这种用途的需要。他们说,这就是阿姆斯特丹银行纸币常常比金银币价值高出4%甚至5%的理由。但我们将在后面看到,这种说明是很不确实的。①

虽然纸币价值可以落在金银铸币价值以下,但金银价值不会因为纸币价值下降而下降。金银所能交换的其他货物的数量不会因此而减少。② 金银价值对其他货物价值的比例,无论在什么情况下,都不取决于国内通用纸币的性质与数量,而取决于当时向商业世界大市场提供金银金属的矿山的丰裕或稀缺程度;取决于一定数量金银上市所需要的劳动量与一定数量其他货物上市

---

① 第一版说,"阿姆斯特丹银行的历史说明,然而,我绝对有理由认为这种说明是不真实的"。

② 第一版说,"降低金银的价值或引起等量铸币换去的货物减少"。

> The only restrictions on banking which are necessary are the prohibition of small bank notes and the requirement that all notes shall be repaid on demand.

If bankers are restrained from issuing any circulating bank notes, or notes payable to the bearer, for less than a certain sum; and if they are subjected to the obligation of an immediate and unconditional payment of such bank notes as soon as presented, their trade may, with safety to the public, be rendered in all other respects perfectly free. The late multiplication of banking companies in both parts of the united kingdom, an event by which many people have been much alarmed, instead of diminishing, increases the security of the public. It obliges all of them to be more circumspect in their conduct, and, by not extending their currency beyond its due proportion to their cash, to guard themselves against those malicious runs, which the rivalship of so many competitors is always ready to bring upon them. It restrains the circulation of each particular company within a narrower circle, and reduces their circulating notes to a smaller number. By dividing the whole circulation into a greater number of parts, the failure of any one company, an accident which, in the course of things, must sometimes happen, becomes of less consequence to the public. This free competition too obliges all bankers to be more liberal in their dealings with their customers, lest their rivals should carry them away. In general, if any branch of trade, or any division of labour, be advantageous to the public, the freer and more general the competition, it will always be the more so.

第二篇　第二章

所需要的劳动量之间的比例。

如果对银行可流通的银行券或持有者可支付汇票的发行数量限制在一定额度之内,而且银行对提交的银行券必须无条件进行随时兑现,那么银行的业务对公众来说是安全的,而银行的其他方面的业务就可以任其自由发展。在英格兰和苏格兰两地近年来银行林立,许多人对此深感忧虑。但银行的设立对社会公众的安全感不是降低了,而是增加了人们的安全感。银行林立,竞争者众多,为提防同业进行恶意的挤兑,迫使各个银行的营业行为更加慎重,他们各自所发行的纸币与现金数量保持适当的比例。这种竞争可以使各银行的纸币在较狭窄范围内流通;可以把各银行在流通领域中的纸币数量降低到一个较小的规模上。通过把全部纸币划分在更多的区域内流通,一个银行的经营失败这种经常发生的事情,对于公众的影响会变得较小。同时,这种自由竞争又使银行对于顾客的营业条件必须更为宽大热情,否则将被同业排挤出银行业。总之,任何一种行业或劳动分工只要是对社会有益,就应当任其更加自由地发展;竞争越自由和越普遍,那么行业也就越有利于社会的进步。

CHAPTER III

Of The Accumulation Of Capital, Or Of Productive And Unproductive Labour

There are two sorts of labour. productive and unproductive.

There is one sort of labour which adds to the value of the subject upon which it is bestowed: there is another which has no such effect. The former, as it produces a value, may be called productive; the latter, unproductive① labour. Thus the labour of a manufacturer adds, generally, to the value of the materials which he works upon, that of his own maintenance, and of his master's.profit. The labour of a menial servant, on the contrary, adds to the value of nothing. Though the manufacturer has his wages advanced to him by his master, he, in reality, costs him no expence, the value of those wages being generally restored, together with a profit, in the improved value of the subject upon which his labour is bestowed. But the maintenance of a menial servant never is restored. A man grows rich by employing a multitude of manufacturers: he grows poor, by maintaining a multitude of menial servants. ② The labour of the latter, however, has its value, and deserves its reward as well as that of the former.

---

① Some French authors of great learning and ingenuity have used those words in a different sense. In the last chapter of the fourth book I shall endeavour to show that their sense is an improper one.

② [In the argument which follows in the text the fact is overlooked that this is only true when the manufacturers are employed to produce commodities for sale and when the menial servants are employed merely for the comfort of the employer. A man may and often does grow poor by employing people to make 'particular subjects or vendible commodities' for his own consumption, and an innkeeper may and often does grow rich by employing menial servants.]

第三章 论资本积累,并论生产性和非生产性劳动

有一种劳动作用在对象物上,能够增加对象物的价值;另一种劳动却没有这种功能。前者因为可以生产价值,称为生产性劳动,后者可以称为非生产性劳动。① 制造业工人的劳动,通常会把维持自身生活所需的价值并向雇主提供利润的价值,加在所加工的原材料的价值上。反之,家庭佣人的劳动却不能增加什么价值。制造业工人的工资虽然由雇主事先垫付,但事实上雇主什么也没有花费。制造业工人把劳动投在对象物上,对象物的价值便会增加。这样增加的价值,通常可以补偿工资的价值并提供利润。家庭佣人的维持费用却是不能收回的。雇用许多工人是致富的方法;维持供养许多家庭佣人是导致贫困的途径。② 但家庭佣人的劳动也有它本身的价值,与工人的劳动一样,应该得到报

> 有两种劳动,即生产性劳动和非生产性劳动。

---

① 有些学富五车又赋有天分的法国作者以不同的含义来使用这些词语。我在第四篇最后一章里将努力表明他们所给予这些的含义是不恰当的。

② 在下面讨论过程中,有一个被忽略的事实就是:当雇佣制造业工人生产物品以供出售时,以及当雇佣仆人仅仅用于雇主的安逸享受时,这种情况才是真的;一个人如果雇佣人是为了特殊目的或自己消费,他就常常变成穷人;而一个客栈所有者就可以通过雇佣客栈服务员来发家致富。

But the labour of the manufacturer fixes and realizes itself in some particular subject or vendible commodity, which lasts for some time at least after that labour is past. It is, as it were, a certain quantity of labour stocked and stored up to be employed, if necessary, upon some other occasion. That subject, or what is the same thing, the price of that subject, can afterwards, if necessary, put into motion a quantity of labour equal to that which had originally produced it. The labour of the menial servant, on the contrary, does not fix or realize itself in any particular subject or vendible commodity. His services generally perish in the very instant of their performance, and seldom leave any trace or value behind them, for which an equal quantity of service could afterwards be procured.

<small>Many kinds of labour besides menial service are unproductive.</small>

The labour of some of the most respectable orders in the society is, like that of menial servants, unproductive of any value, and does not fix or realize itself in any permanent subject, or vendible commodity, which endures after that labour is past, and for which an equal quantity of labour could afterwards be procured. The sovereign, for example, with all the officers both of justice and war who serve under him, the whole army and navy, are unproductive labourers. They are the servants of the public, and are maintained by a part of the annual produce of the industry of other people. Their service, how honourable, how useful, or how necessary soever, produces nothing for which an equal quantity of service can afterwards be procured. The protection, security, and defence of the commonwealth, the effect of their labour this year, will not purchase its protection, security, and defence for the year to come. In the same class must be ranked, some both of the gravest and most important, and some of the most frivolous professions: churchmen, lawyers, physicians, men of letters of all kinds; players, buffoons, musicians, opera-singers, opera-dancers, &c. The labour of the meanest of these has a certain value, regulated by the very same principles which regulate that of every other sort of labour; and that of the noblest and most useful, produces nothing which could afterwards purchase or procure an equal quantity of labour. Like the declamation of the actor, the harangue of the orator, or the tune of the musician, the work of all of them perishes in the very instant of its production.

Both productive and unproductive labourers, and those who do not labour at all, are all equally maintained by the annual produce of the land and labour of the country. This produce, how great soever,

酬。不过，制造业工人的劳动可以固定并且实现在某些特殊物品或可供出售的商品上；可以经历一段时间，不会立即消失掉。似乎是把一部分劳动贮存起来，如有需要再提出来使用。那种物品或者说那种物品的价格，以后在必要时还可用来雇用与原先生产这种物品而投下的劳动量相等的劳动量。反之，家庭佣人的劳动却不固定也不实现在特殊物品或可供出售的商品上。家庭佣人的劳动随生随灭，要把它的价值保存起来供以后雇用等量劳动来使用，是很困难的。

有些社会上层人士的劳动，与家仆的劳动一样，不生产价值，既不固定或实现在耐久物品或可供出售的商品上，也不能储藏起来供以后雇用等量劳动使用。例如，君主及其他的官吏和海陆军都是不生产的劳动者。他们是公仆，其生活由其他人劳动年产物的一部分来维持。他们的职务，无论是怎样高贵，怎样有用，如何必要，但终究是随生随灭，不能保留起来供以后取得同级别职务使用。他们治理国事，捍卫国家，功劳当然不小，但今年的政绩买不到明年的政绩；今年的安全买不到明年的安全。在这一类上层人士当中，当然包含着各种职业，有些是很尊贵和很重要的，有些却可说是最不重要的。前者如牧师、律师、医生和文人；后者如演员、歌手和舞蹈家。在这一类劳动中，即使是最低级的，也有一定的价值，支配这种劳动价值的原则就是支配所有其他劳动价值的原则。但在这一类劳动中，就连最尊贵的也不能生产什么东西供以后购买等量劳动使用。像演员的对白、雄辩家的演说和音乐家的歌唱，他们所有这些人的工作都是随生随灭的。

生产性劳动者、非生产性劳动者和不参加劳动者，同样依靠土地和劳动的年产物来生活。这些生产物的数量无论怎么大，也

除家庭佣人以外的许多劳动都是非生产性劳动。

The proportion of the produce employed in maintaining productive hands determines the next year's produce. can never be infinite, but must have certain limits. According, therefore, as a smaller or greater proportion of it is in any one year employed in maintaining unproductive hands, the more in the one case and the less in the other will remain for the productive, and the next year's produce will be greater or smaller accordingly; the whole annual produce, if we except the spontaneous productions of the earth, being the effect of productive labour.

Part of the produce replaces capital, part constitutes profit and rent. Though the whole annual produce of the land and labour of every country, is, no doubt, ultimately destined for supplying the consumption of its inhabitants, and for procuring a revenue to them; yet when it first comes either from the ground, or from the hands of the productive labourers, it naturally divides itself into two parts. One of them, and frequently the largest, is, in the first place, destined for replacing a capital, or for renewing the provisions, materials, and finished work, which had been withdrawn from a capital; the other for constituting a revenue either to the owner of this capital, as the profit of his stock; or to some other person, as the rent of his land. Thus, of the produce of land, one part replaces the capital of the farmer; the other pays his profit and the rent of the landlord; and thus constitutes a revenue both to the owner of this capital, as the profits of his stock; and to some other person, as the rent of his land. Of the produce of a great manufactory, in the same manner, one part, and that always the largest, replaces the capital of the undertaker of the work; the other pays his profit, and thus constitutes a revenue to the owner of this capital. ①

That which replaces capital employs none but productive hands. That part of the annual produce of the land and labour of any country which replaces a capital, never is immediately employed to maintain any but productive hands. It pays the wages of productive labour only. That which is immediately destined for constituting a revenue either as profit or as rent, may maintain indifferently either productive or unproductive hands.

Whatever part of his stock a man employs as a capital, he always expects is to be replaced to him with a profit. He employs it, therefore, in maintaining productive hands only; and after having served in

---

① [It must be observed that in this paragraph produce is not used in the ordinary economic sense of income or net produce, but as including all products, e. g. , the oil used in weaving machinery as well as the cloth.]

第二篇 第三章

不是无限的,而是有限的。因此,用来维持非生产性人口的部分越大,那么用来维持生产性人口的部分必定越小,从而下一年度的生产物也必定更少。反之,用来维持非生产性人口的部分越小,那么用来维持生产性人口的部分必定越大,从而下一年度的生产物肯定会越多。除了土地上天然生产的物品以外,一切年产出都是生产性劳动的结果。

> 用来维持生产性劳动者的比例决定下一年度产出。

尽管无论在哪一个国家里,土地和劳动的年产出都是用来供给国内居民消费,给国内居民提供收入;但无论是出自土地或出自生产性劳动者之手,它们都是一经生产出来就自然分成两个部分。一部分(往往是最大的一部分)是用来补偿资本,补充资本所购买回来的食品、材料和制成品;另一部分则以利润的形式作为资本所有者的收入,或者以地租的形式作为地主的收入。就土地的生产物来说,一部分是用来补偿农场主的资本,另一部分用来支付作为资本所有者收入的利润,或支付作为地主的收入的地租。就大工厂的生产物来说,一部分(往往是最大的一部分)是用以补偿厂商的资本,另一部分则用来支付作为资本所有者收入的利润。①

> 产出的一部分用补偿资本,一部分形成利润和租金。

用来补偿资本的那一部分年产物,从来没有立即用来维持非生产性劳动者的生活,而是用来维持生产性劳动者的生活。至于一开始就被指定用作利润或地租收入的部分,则可能用来维持生产性劳动者,也可能用来维持非生产性劳动者。

> 补偿资本的那一部分产出仅仅维持生产性劳动者。

把财货一部分当作资本而投入的人,没有不希望收回资本并

---

① 必须注意的是,本段中产出不是用作一般经济意义上所说的收入或净产出;它不仅包括所有产品,如用于织布机的石油,而且还包括布匹。

the function of a capital to him, it constitutes a revenue to them. Whenever he employs any part of it in maintaining unproductive hands of any kind, that part is, from that moment, withdrawn from his capital, and placed in his stock reserved for immediate consumption.

while unproductive hands and those who do not labour are supported by revenue.

Unproductive labourers, and those who do not labour at all, are all maintained by revenue; either, first, by that part of the annual produce which is originally destined for constituting a revenue to some particular persons, either as the rent of land or as the profits of stock; or, secondly, by that part which, though originally destined for replacing a capital and for maintaining productive labourers only, yet when it comes into their hands, whatever part of it is over and above their necessary subsistence, may be employed in maintaining indifferently either productive or unproductive hands. Thus, not only the great landlord or the rich merchant, but even the common workman, if his wages are considerable, may maintain a menial servant; or he may sometimes go to a play or a puppet-show, and so contribute his share towards maintaining one set of unproductive labourers; or he may pay some taxes, and thus help to maintain another set, more honourable and useful, indeed, but equally unproductive. No part of the annual produce, however, which had been originally destined to replace a capital, is ever directed towards maintaining unproductive hands, still after it has put into motion its full complement of productive labour, or all that it could put into motion in the way in which it was employed. The workman must have earned his wages by work done, before he can employ any part of them in this manner. That part too is generally but a small one. It is his spare revenue only, of which productive labourers have seldom a great deal. They generally have some, however; and in the payment of taxes the greatness of their number may compensate, in some measure, the smallness of their contribution. The rent of land and the profits of stock are everywhere, therefore, the principal sources from which unproductive hands derive their subsistence. These are the two sorts of revenue of

赚回利润。因此,他仅仅把资本用来雇用生产性劳动者。这些财货,首先对其所有者提供资本的作用,以后又构成生产性劳动者的收入。至于他用来维持非生产性劳动者的那一部分财货,从这样使用的时候开始,就从他的资本中撤离出来,放在供他直接消费的财货之中。

非生产性劳动者和不参加劳动者,必须完全依靠收入来生活。这里所谓收入,可分为两项:一是有一部分年产物,一开始就被指定用作某些人的地租收入或利润收入;二是在年产物中又有一部分,原是用来补偿资本和雇用生产性劳动者的,但在回归到获得它的人们手中之后,除维持他们衣食以外,他们往往不加区别地用来维持生产性劳动者和非生产性劳动者的生活。例如,不仅是大地主和富商,就连普通工人在工资丰厚的情况下,也常常雇用个把家庭佣人或看一回木偶戏。这样,他就拿一部分收入来维持非生产性劳动者的生活,而且他也许还要交纳一些税收。这时,他所维持的那些人,虽然地位尊贵得多,但同样是不生产的。不过按照正常情况,原想用来补偿资本的那部分年产物,在还没有用以雇用原先准备雇用的足够的生产性劳动者来推动他们工作以前,也不可能挪用于维持非生产性劳动者。劳动者在没有劳动获得工资以前,要想用一部分工资来维持非生产性劳动者也是绝不可能的。而且那部分工资往往不多,这只是他节省下来的收入;就生产性劳动者的情况来说,无论怎样也节省不了许多,不过他们总会有一些。就税收来说,因为他们这一阶层的人数很多很多,所以,他们虽然每个人所缴纳的税收金额很有限,但他们这一阶层所缴纳的总金额却很可观。地租和财货的利润,无论在什么地方都是非生产性劳动者生活所依赖的主要资源。这两种收入

> 那些非生产劳动者和不参加劳动人依靠收入来生活。然而生产劳动者和参加劳动者也靠收入来生活。

which the owners have generally most to spare. They might both maintain indifferently either productive or unproductive hands. They seem, however, to have some predilection for the latter. The expence of a great lord feeds generally more idle than industrious people. The rich merchant, though with his capital he maintains industrious people only, yet by his expence, that is, by the employment of his revenue, he feeds commonly the very same sort as the great lord.

The proportion, therefore, between the productive and unproductive hands, depends very much in every country upon the proportion between that part of the annual produce, which, as soon as it comes either from the ground or from the hands of the productive labourers, is destined for replacing a capital, and that which is destined for constituting a revenue, either as rent, or as profit. This proportion is very different in rich from what it is in poor countries.

<small>So the proportion of productive bands depends on the proportion between profit with rent and the part of produce which replaces capital. Rent anciently formed a larger proportion of the produce of agriculture than now.</small>

Thus, at present, in the opulent countries of Europe, a very large, frequently the largest portion of the produce of the land, is destined for replacing the capital of the rich and independent farmer; the other for paying his profits, and the rent of the landlord. But anciently, during the prevalency of the feudal government, a very small portion of the produce was sufficient to replace the capital employed in cultivation. It consisted commonly in a few wretched cattle, maintained altogether by the spontaneous produce of uncultivated land, and which might, therefore, be considered as a part of that spontaneous produce. It generally too belonged to the landlord, and was by him advanced to the occupiers of the land. All the rest of the produce properly belonged to him too, either as rent for his land, or as profit upon this paultry capital. The occupiers of land were generally bondmen, whose persons and effects were equally his property. Those who were not bondmen were tenants at will, and though the rent which they paid was often nominally little more than a quit-rent, it really amounted to the whole produce of the land. Their lord could at all times command their labour in peace, and their service in war. Though they lived at a distance from his house, they were equally dependent upon him as his retainers who lived in it. But the whole produce of the land undoubtedly belongs to him, who can dispose of the labour and service of all those whom it maintains. In the present state of Europe, the share of the landlord seldom exceeds a third, sometimes not a fourth part of the whole produce of the land. The rent of land,

最容易节省。它们的所有者可以用来雇用生产者，也同样可以用来雇用不参加生产者。但是，大体上他们似乎特别喜欢用在后一个方面。大领主的费用，通常用于供养懒惰人群的居多，用于供养勤劳人民的少。富商的资本虽只用来雇用勤劳人民，但也与大领主一样，他的收入也大都用来豢养那些不生产的人们。

我们说过，由土地或由生产性劳动者生产出来的年产出，一经生产出来，就有一部分被指定用作补偿资本的基金；还有一部分用作地租或利润的收入。我们现在又知道，无论在哪一个国家，生产者与不参加生产者之间的比例，在很大程度上取决于这两个部分的比例。而且，这个比例在贫国和富国又极不相同。

<small>所以生产性劳动者的取用比例决于利润和租金与补偿资本之间的比例。</small>

现在欧洲各个富国，往往使用土地生产物的极大部分来补偿自由富农的资本，剩余部分则用来支付他的利润与地主的地租。但在过去封建政府林立的时候，年产物的极小部分已经足够补偿耕种的资本。因为那时候耕种所需的资本，不过是几头老牛劣马而已，而它们的食物就是荒地上的天然产物；因此，也可以把它们看作天然产物的一部分。这些牲畜一般也是属于地主的，而由地主借给土地耕种者使用。土地的其余产物也归地主所有，或作为土地的地租或作为价值很小的资本的利润。耕种者大都是地主的奴仆，他们的身家财产都同样是地主的财产。那些不是奴仆的耕种者，是可以随意退租的佃户。他们所缴纳的地租，常常名义上和免役地租一样，但事实上依然等于全部土地生产物。而且，在和平的时候地主可以随时征用他们的劳役；在战争的时候，他们又必须去服兵役。他们虽然住得离地主的家远一些，但他们隶属于地主，与住在地主家里的家奴没有多大区别。他们的劳役既然都必须听从地主支配，土地生产物当然是全部属于地主。现在

<small>过去地租占年产出的比例比现在大。</small>

however, in all the improved parts of the country, has been tripled and quadrupled since those ancient times; and this third or fourth part of the annual produce is, it seems, three or four times greater than the whole had been before. In the progress of improvement, rent, though it increases in proportion to the extent, diminishes in proportion to the produce of the land.

<small>Profits were anciently a larger share of the produce of manufactures,</small>

In the opulent countries of Europe, great capitals are at present employed in trade and manufactures. In the ancient state, the little trade that was stirring, and the few homely and coarse manufactures that were carried on, required but very small capitals. These, however, must have yielded very large profits. The rate of interest was nowhere less than ten per cent., and their profits must have been sufficient to afford this great interest. At present the rate of interest, in the improved parts of Europe, is no-where higher than six per cent., and in some of the most improved it is so low as four, three, and two per cent., Though that part of the revenue of the inhabitants which is derived from the profits of stock is always much greater in rich than in poor countries, it is because the stock is much greater: in proportion to the stock the profits are generally much less. ①

<small>so the proportion of produce required for replacing capital is greater than it was.</small>

That part of the annual produce, therefore, which, as soon as it comes either from the ground, or from the hands of the productive labourers, is destined for replacing a capital, is not only much greater in rich than in poor countries, but bears a much greater proportion to that which is immediately destined for constituting a revenue either as rent or as profit. The funds destined for the maintenance of productive labour, are not only much greater in the former than in the latter, but bear a much greater proportion to those which, though they may be employed to maintain either productive or unproductive hands, have generally a predilection for the latter.

---

① [The question first propounded, whether profits form a larger proportion of the produce, is wholly lost sight of. With a stock larger in proportion to the produce, a lower rate of profit may give a larger proportion of the produce.]

欧洲情况却大不同了。在全部土地生产物中,地租所占的比例很少超过1/3,有时还不到1/4。但以数量计算,改良土地所缴纳的地租却大部分已经是过去的三倍或四倍;当今在年生产物中要拿出1/3或1/4,这和过去年产物的全部比较,似乎就有三倍或四倍之多。在农业日益进步的时代,就数量来说,地租虽然与日俱增,但对土地生产物的比例却是逐渐下降。

就欧洲各个富国来说,大部分资本现在都投在商业和制造业上。古代贸易很少,制造业又简单,它们所需资本极少。可是它们所能够产生的利润一定很大。古时候利息率很少在10%以下。这就可以证明他们的利润水平必定能够满足支付这么高的利息要求。现在,欧洲各个发达国家的利息率很少在6%以上;最进步国家的利息率有时低于4%、3%甚至2%。因为富国的资本比贫国多得多,所以富国居民通过资本利润而得到的收入也比贫国多出许多;但就利润与资本的比例来说,一般情况下那就要少很多。①

与贫国相比,富国用来补偿资本的那部分土地和劳动的年产出,当然要大得多。但不仅如此,与直接形成地租和利润的部分相比较,它在年产物中所占比例也大得多。此外,与贫国相比,富国雇用生产性劳动的基金当然也要多得多。一国的年产物,尽管一部分既可以用来雇用生产性劳动,也可以用来雇用非生产性劳动;但通常是用在后一种用途上。与贫国比较,富国雇用生产性劳动的基金在年产物中所占比例,也要多得多。

---

① 首先提出的问题就是,没有完全看到利润与产出的比例更高的情况。随着存货与产出的比例增加,利润率会降低,并引起产出上升。

国民财富的性质与原理

The proportion between the funds determines whether the inhabitants of the country shall be industrious or idle.

The proportion between those different funds necessarily determines in every country the general character of the inhabitants as to industry or idleness. We are more industrious than our forefathers; because in the present times the funds destined for the maintenance of industry, are much greater in proportion to those which are likely to be employed in the maintenance of idleness, than they were two or three centuries ago. Our ancestors were idle for want of a sufficient encouragement to industry. It is better, says the proverb, to play for nothing, than to work for nothing. In mercantile and manufacturing towns, where the inferior ranks of people are chiefly maintained by the employment of capital, they are in general industrious, sober, and thriving; as in many English, and in most Dutch towns. In those towns which are principally supported by the constant or occasional residence of a court, and in which the inferior ranks of people are chiefly maintained by the spending of revenue, they are in general idle, dissolute, and poor; as at Rome, Versailles, Compiegne, and Fontainbleau. If you except Rouen and Bourdeaux, there is little trade or industry in any of the parliament towns of France; and the inferior ranks of people, being chiefly maintained by the expence of the members of the courts of justice, and of those who come to plead before them, are in general idle and poor. The great trade of Rouen and Bourdeaux seems to be altogether the effect of their situation. Rouen is necessarily the entrepot of almost all the goods which are brought either from foreign countries, or from the maritime provinces of France, for the consumption of the great city of Paris. Bourdeaux is in the same manner the entrepot of the wines which grow upon the banks of the Garonne, and of the rivers which run into it, one of the richest wine countries in the world, and which seems to produce the wine fittest for exportation, or best suited to the taste of foreign nations. Such advantageous situations necessarily attract a great capital by the great employment which they afford it; and the employment of this capital is the cause of the industry of those two cities. In the other parliament towns of France, very little more capital seems to be employed than what is necessary for supplying their own consumption; that is, little more than the smallest capital which can be employed in them. The same thing may be said of Paris, Madrid, and Vienna. Of those three cities, Paris is by far the most industrious: but Paris itself is the principal market of all the manufactures established at Paris, and its own consumption is the principal object of all the trade which it carries on. London, Lisbon, and Copenhagen, are, perhaps, the only three

这两种基金的比例,在任何国家都必然会决定一国人民的性格是勤劳还是懒惰。和我们祖先相比较,我们是更勤劳的,这是因为,和二三百年前比较,我们用来维持勤劳人民的基金,在比例上比用来维持懒惰人民的基金要大得多。我们祖先由于没有受到勤劳的充分奖励,所以就懒惰了。俗话说:劳而无功,不如戏而无益。在下等居民大部分依靠资本使用而生活的工商业城市里,这些城市的居民大都是勤劳、认真和朝气蓬勃。英国和荷兰的大城市便是很好的例证。在主要依靠君主经常或临时驻节来维持的都市,人民的生计主要依靠收入的花费,这些人民大都是懒惰、堕落和贫穷。罗马、凡尔赛、贡比列、枫丹白露也是很好的例证。讲到法国,除了里昂、波尔多两个城市以外,其他各议会城市的工商业毫不足道。一般下等人民,由于大都依靠法院人员以及前来打官司的人的费用来维持,所以大都是懒惰和贫穷的人群。里昂和波尔多两市,则由于地理位置关系,商业比较发达。里昂必然是巴黎所需物品的集散地,无论物品是由外国进口或由沿海各地运来。波尔多则为加龙流域所产葡萄酒的集散地,这些地方产酒丰富,世界闻名,外国人都喜欢饮用,所以出口很多。这样好的地理位置当然会吸引资本投资到这里来。因为这样,这两个城市的工业才蒸蒸日上。其他各议会城市的情况便大不相同;人们投下资本,都只是为了维持本市的消费;换言之,投下的资本为数有限,绝不可能超过本市所能够使用的限度。巴黎、马德里、维也纳的情况也都是这样。在这三个城市中,巴黎要算最勤劳的了,但巴黎就是巴黎本市制造品的主要销售市场;巴黎本城的消费的就是一切营业的主要对象。既是王公大臣驻节所在地又是工商云集的地方,既为本市消费而营业又为外地和外国消费而营业的城

cities in Europe, which are both the constant residence of a court, and can at the same time be considered as trading cities, or as cities which trade not only for their own consumption, but for that of other cities and countries. The situation of all the three is extremely advantageous, and naturally fits them to be the entrep ts of a great part of the goods destined for the consumption of distant places. In a city where a great revenue is spent, to employ with advantage a capital for any other purpose than for supplying the consumption of that city, is probably more difficult than in one in which the inferior ranks of people have no other maintenance but what they derive from the employment of such a capital. The idleness of the greater part of the people who are maintained by the expence of revenue, corrupts, it is probable, the industry of those who ought to be maintained by the employment of capital, and renders it less advantageous to employ a capital there than in other places. There was little trade or industry in Edinburgh before the Union. When the Scotch parliament was no longer to be assembled in it, when it ceased to be the necessary residence of the principal nobility and gentry of Scotland, it became a city of some trade and industry. It still continues, however, to be the residence of the principal courts of justice in Scotland, of the boards of customs and excise, &c. A considerable revenue, therefore, still continues to be spent in it. In trade and industry it is much inferior to Glasgow, of which the inhabitants are chiefly maintained by the employment of capital. ① The inhabitants of a large village, it has sometimes been observed, after having made considerable progress in manufactures, have become idle and poor, in consequence of a great lord's having taken up his residence in their neighbourhood.

<small>Increase or diminution of the capital of a country consequently increases or diminishes its annual produce.</small> The proportion between capital and revenue, therefore, seems everywhere to regulate the proportion between industry and idleness. Wherever capital predominates, industry prevails; wherever revenue, idleness. Every increase or diminution of capital, therefore, naturally tends to increase or diminish the real quantity of industry, the number of productive hands, and consequently the exchangeable value of the annual produce of the land and labour of the country, the real wealth and revenue of all its inhabitants.

Capitals are increased by parsimony, and diminished by prodi-

---

① [In *Lectures*, pp. 154-156, the idleness of Edinburgh and such like places compared with Glasgow is attributed simply to the want of independence in the inhabitants. The introduction of revenue and capital is the fruit of study of the physiocratic doctrines.]

市,在欧洲只有伦敦、里斯本和哥本哈根。这三个城市所处的地理位置都很有利,适合于作为大部分远方消费物品的集散地。但那些既把资本用于供应本地的消费又想使用资本赚取利润的、要花费收入城市,就不如在下等人民生计专门依靠资本的使用来维持的工商大城市那么容易。靠花费收入来维持生活的大部分人们都游手好闲惯了,使得一些应该勤劳干事的人,也不免被他们这些懒惰人群所同化。所以,在这个地方使用资本自然比在其他地方不利。英格兰和苏格兰在没有合并以前,爱丁堡的工商业很不发达。后来,随着苏格兰议会的迁移,王公贵族不一定要住在那里了,那里的工商业才慢慢振兴起来。但苏格兰的大理院、税务机关等还没有迁移走,所以仍然有不少收入是在那里花费的。因此,就工商业来说,爱丁堡远远不如格拉斯哥。格拉斯哥居民的生计大都依靠资本的运用①来维持。再者,我们有时会看到,在制造业方面取得相当进展的大乡村的居民,往往由于公侯贵族杂居其间从而变得懒惰和贫困。

所以,无论在什么地方,资本与收入的比例似乎都支配勤劳与懒惰的比例。资本占优势的地方,多勤劳;收入占优势的地方,懒惰的人比例高。资本的增减自然会增减真实劳动量和增减生产性劳动者的人数,因而增减一个国家土地和劳动的年产物的交换价值,会增减一个国家人民的真实财富与收入。

一个国家的资本增加或减少应相应地增加或减少该国的产出水平。

资本增加在于节俭;资本减少是由于奢侈浪费与行为不正。

---

① 在《关于法律、警察、岁入及军备的演讲》第 154~156 页里,与格拉斯哥相对比,爱丁堡和与之相类似的城市居民懒惰的原因在于缺乏独立性。收入和资本的引入是自立信仰的成果。

<small>Capitals are increased by parsimony or saving.</small> gality and misconduct. Whatever a person saves from his revenue he adds to his capital, and either employs it himself in maintaining an additional number of productive hands, or enables some other person to do so, by lending it to him for an interest, that is, for a share of the profits. As the capital of an individual can be increased only by what he saves from his annual revenue or his annual gains, so the capital of a society, which is the same with that of all the individuals who compose it, can be increased only in the same manner.

Parsimony, and not industry, is the immediate cause of the increase of capital. Industry, indeed, provides the subject which parsimony accumulates. But whatever industry might acquire, if parsimony did not save and store up, the capital would never be the greater.

Parsimony, by increasing the fund which is destined for the maintenance of productive hands, tends to increase the number of those hands whose labour adds to the value of the subject upon which it is bestowed. It tends therefore to increase the exchangeable value of the annual produce of the land and labour of the country. It puts into motion an additional quantity of industry, which gives an additional value to the annual produce.

<small>What is saved is consumed by productive hands.</small> What is annually saved is as regularly consumed as what is annually spent, and nearly in the same time too; ① but it is consumed by a different set of people. That portion of his revenue which a rich man annually spends, is in most cases consumed by idle guests, and menial servants, who leave nothing behind them in return for their consumption. That portion which he annually saves, as for the sake of the profit it is immediately employed as a capital, is consumed in the same manner, and nearly in the same time too, but by a different set of people, by labourers, manufacturers, and artificers, who re-produce with a profit the value of their annual consumption. His revenue, we shall suppose, is paid him in money. Had he spent the whole, the food, clothing, and lodging, which the whole could have purchased, would have been distributed among the former set of people.

---

① [This paradox is arrived at through a confusion between the remuneration of the labourers who produce the additions to the capital and the additions themselves. What is really saved is the additions to the capital, and these are not consumed.]

一个人节省了多少收入，就增加了多少资本。这个增多的资本，他可以亲自投下来雇用更多的生产性劳动者，也可以带有利息地借给别人，使其能雇用更多的生产性劳动者。个人的资本，既然只能由节省每年收入或每年利得而增加，由个人构成的社会资本，也只能由这个方法来增加。

资本要增加，要么是通过节俭，要么是通过储蓄增加。

资本增加的直接原因是节俭而不是勤劳。实际上，在没有节俭以前，必须先有勤劳；节俭所积累的产出物都是由勤劳得来。但是如果只有勤劳，没有勤俭节约，只有收获而没有积蓄，资本就不可能增加。

勤俭节约可以增加维持生产性劳动者的基金，从而增加生产性劳动者的人数。他们的劳动既然可以增加工作对象的价值，所以，节俭可能增加一个国家土地和劳动的年产物的交换价值。勤俭节约可以推动更大的劳动量来增加年产物的价值。

每年节省的东西与每年花费的一样，一般都被消费掉，而且几乎是同时被消费掉，①但消费的人不同。富人每年花费的收入部分，大部分被懒惰的客人和家用的佣人所消费掉，这些人消费完了就算完了，没有带来什么报酬。至于由于追求利润而直接转为资本的每年节省下来的部分，几乎同时以同样的方式被消费掉，但消费的人是劳动者、制造者和技工。他们会再生产他们每年消费掉的价值并提供利润。现在假定他的收入都是货币，如果他把它全部花掉，他用全部收入所购买的食品、衣服和住宅，就是

节省下来的收入被生产性劳动者消费掉。

---

① 生产者为资本提供增加值，还为自己劳动提供增加值并得到报酬，由于把两个报酬混淆起来，就产生了这个似是而非的观点。实际节省下来的东西是使资本增加价值，并且这一部分还不被消费掉。

By saving a part of it, as that part is for the sake of the profit immediately employed as a capital either by himself or by some other person, the food, clothing, and lodging, which may be purchased with it, are necessarily reserved for the latter. The consumption is the same, but the consumers are different.

<small>The frugal man establishes a perpetual fund for the employment of productive hands.</small>

By what a frugal man annually saves, he not only affords maintenance to an additional number of productive hands, for that or the ensuing year, but, like the founder of a public workhouse, he establishes as it were a perpetual fund for the maintenance of an equal number in all times to come. The perpetual allotment and destination of this fund, indeed, is not always guarded by any positive law, by any trustright or deed of mortmain. It is always guarded, however, by a very powerful principle, the plain and evident interest of every individual to whom any share of it shall ever belong. No part of it can ever afterwards be employed to maintain any but productive hands, without an evident loss to the person who thus perverts it from its proper destination.

<small>The prodigal perverts such funds to other uses.</small>

The prodigal perverts it in this manner. By not confining his expence within his income, he encroaches upon his capital. Like him who perverts the revenues of some pious foundation to profane purposes, he pays the wages of idleness with those funds which the frugality of his forefathers had, as it were, consecrated to the maintenance of industry. By diminishing the funds destined for the employment of productive labour, he necessarily diminishes, so far as it depends upon him, the quantity of that labour which adds a value to the subject upon which it is bestowed, and, consequently, the value of the annual produce of the land and labour of the whole country, the real wealth and revenue of its inhabitants. If the prodigality of some was not compensated by the frugality of others, the conduct of every prodigal, by feeding the idle with the bread of the industrious, tends not only to beggar himself, but to impoverish his country.

<small>Whether he spends on home or foreign commodities makes no difference.</small>

Though the expence of the prodigal should be altogether in home-made, and no part of it in foreign commodities, its effect upon the productive funds of the society would still be the same. Every year there would still be a certain quantity of food and clothing, which ought to have maintained productive, employed in maintaining unproductive hands. Every year, therefore, there would still be some dimi-

分配给前一种人。如果节省的一部分，为追求利润而直接转作资本，亲自使用或借给别人使用，那么，他用这节省部分所购买的食品、衣料和住宅，就将分配给后一种人。消费是一样的，但消费者不同。

节俭的人通过每年所节省的收入，不但可以在今年或明年供养若干更多的生产性劳动者，而且他好像工厂的创办人一样，建立一种永久性基金，将来随便在什么时候，都可维持同样多的生产性劳动者。这种基金将如何分派和将用到什么地方，固然没有法律予以保障，没有信托契约或永远营业证书加以规定，但有一个强有力的原则保护其安全，那就是所有者个人的利益关系。如果把这些基金的任何部分，用于维持非生产性劳动者，这样不按照原来指定用途而滥用该基金的人，一定要吃亏不可。

奢侈者就是这样滥用资本：不以量入为出为原则，结果就侵占蚕食了资本。正如把一种用于敬神的基金收入被挪作用来亵渎神灵的人一样，他把父兄节省下来准备干点事业的金钱，却豢养着许多游手好闲的人。由于雇用生产性劳动的基金减少，基金所雇用的、能够增加物品价值的劳动量也减少了，因此全国的土地和劳动的年生产物价值也会减少，全国居民的真实财富和收入也随之减少。奢侈浪费者夺走勤劳者的面包，把它用来豢养游手好闲者。如果另一部分人的节俭不足抵偿这一部分人的奢侈浪费，奢侈者所作所为不但会使他自身陷于贫穷，而且将使全国陷于物质匮乏的境地。

尽管奢侈者所耗费的物品全部是国产商品，没有一点是外国货，结果也将同样影响社会的生产基金。每年总有一定数量的食品和衣服，本来应该用来维持供养生产性劳动者的，却被用来维

节俭的人可以形成维持生产性劳动者就业的永久基金。

浪费会滥用资金于其他用途。

无论他用钱购买货物者货物，两者并没有区别。

nution in what would otherwise have been the value of the annual produce of the land and labour of the country.

If he had not spent there would have been just as much money in the country and the goods produced by productive hands as well.

This expence, it may be said indeed, not being in foreign goods, and not occasioning any exportation of gold and silver, the same quantity of money would remain in the country as before. But if the quantity of food and clothing, which were thus consumed by unproductive, had been distributed among productive hands, they would have re-produced, together with a profit, the full value of their consumption. The same quantity of money would in this case equally have remained in the country, and there would besides have been a reproduction of an equal value of consumable goods. There would have been two values instead of one.

Besides, when the annual produce diminishes, money will go abroad;

The same quantity of money, besides, cannot long remain in any country in which the value of the annual produce diminishes. The sole use of money is to circulate consumable goods. By means of it, provisions, materials, and finished work, are bought and sold, and distributed to their proper consumers. The quantity of money, therefore, which can be annually employed in any country, must be determined by the value of the consumable goods annually circulated within it. These must consist either in the immediate produce of the land and labour of the country itself, or in something which had been purchased with some part of that produce. Their value, therefore, must diminish as the value of that produce diminishes, and along with it the quantity of money which can be employed in circulating them. But the money which by this annual diminution of produce is annually thrown out of domestic circulation, will not be allowed to lie idle. The interest of whoever possesses it, requires that it should be employed. But having no employment at home, it will, in spite of all laws and prohibitions, be sent abroad, and employed in purchasing consumable goods which may be of some use at home. Its annual exportation will in this manner continue for some time to add something to the annual consumption of the country beyond the value of its own annual produce. What in the days of its prosperity had been saved from that annual produce, and employed in purchasing gold and silver, will contribute for some little time to support its consumption in adversity. The exportation of gold and silver is, in this case, not the cause, but the effect of its declension, and may even, for some little time, alleviate the misery of

持非生产性劳动者。因此,每年一国生产物的价值则总不免会程度不同地低于本来应有的价值。

有人会说,这种花费不是用来购买外国货物,不会引起金银往外出口,国内货币是不会减少的。但是,如果这一定数量的食品和衣服,不被不参加劳动的生产者所消费,而是分配给生产者,他们就不仅可以再生产他们消费的全部价值,而且还可以提供利润。等量的货币将依然留在国内,却又再生产了一个价值相等的消费物品,所以结果将有两个价值,而不仅只有一个价值。

另外,年生产物价值逐渐减少的国家,绝不可能保留与以前数量相同的货币。货币的唯一用途是用来周转消费品。通过使用货币,食品、材料与制成品才可以进行买卖而分配给适当的消费者。一个国家每年所能够使用流通的货币量,取决于每年在国内流通的消费品的价值。每年在国内流通的消费品,不是本国土地和劳动的直接生产物,就是用本国生产物购买进来的物品。如果国内生产物的价值减少了,每年在国内流通的消费品的价值必定减少,因此,国内每年所能够流通使用的货币量也肯定随之减少。但是由于生产物年年减少而被逐出国内流通领域以外的货币,肯定不可能弃之不用。货币所有者由于利益关系,无论如何也不愿意把自己的货币放在一边不加使用。如果国内没有用途,他就会不顾法律和禁令,把货币送往国外,用来购买国内有用的各种消费物品。货币每年的出口将在一定时期内继续不断,这样会使国内人民每年的消费额超过他们本国年产物的价值。繁荣时期积累下来的年产物所购买的金银,在这种困境中可以支持他们一段时间。但在这种情况下,金银的出口不是民生凋敝的原因,而是民生凋敝的结果。实际上,这种出口甚至还可以暂时减

that declension.

and on the other hand money will come in when the annual produce increses.   The quantity of money, on the contrary, must in every country naturally increase as the value of the annual produce increases. The value of the consumable goods annually circulated within the society being greater, will require a greater quantity of money to circulate them. A part of the increased produce, therefore, will naturally be employed in purchasing, wherever it is to be had, the additional quantity of gold and silver necessary for circulating the rest. The increase of those metals will in this case be the effect, not the cause, of the public prosperity. Gold and silver are purchased every-where in the same manner. The food, clothing, and lodging, the revenue and maintenance of all those whose labour or stock is employed in bringing them from the mine to the market, is the price paid for them in Peru as well as in England, The country which has this price to pay, will never be long without the quantity of those metals which it has occasion for; and no country will ever long retain a quantity which it has no occasion for.

So even if the real wealth of a country consisted of its money, the prodigal would be a public enemy.   Whatever, therefore, we may imagine the real wealth and revenue of a country to consist in, whether in the value of the annual produce of its land and labour, as plain reason seems to dictate; or in the quantity of the precious metals which circulate within it, as vulgar prejudices suppose; in either view of the matter, every prodigal appears to be a public enemy, and every frugal man a public benefactor.

The effects of misconduct are often the same as those of prodigality. Every injudicious and unsuccessful project in agriculture, mines, *Injudicious employment of capital has the same effect as prodigality.* fisheries, trade, or manufactures, tends in the same manner to diminish the funds destined for the maintenance of productive labour. In every such project, though the capital is consumed by productive hands only, yet, as by the injudicious manner in which they are employed, they do not reproduce the full value of their consumption, there must always be some diminution in what would otherwise have *Frugality and prudence predominate.* been the productive funds of the society.

It can seldom happen, indeed, that the circumstances of a great nation can be much affected either by the prodigality or misconduct

轻民生凋敝带来的痛苦。

反过来,随着一个国家年产物价值的增加,货币量也一定自然增加。每年在国内流通的消费品价值的增加,将需要更多的货币量来流通。因此,有一部分增加的产出物必定会走向四方,在有金银的地方购买必要增加的金银。但在这种情况下,金银增加是社会繁荣的结果,而不是社会繁荣的原因。购买金银的条件到处一样的、没有区别。把金银从矿山挖掘出来,再运输到市场上,总需要使用一定数量的劳动或资本。为这些事业而提供劳动和投资的人,总需要衣食住的收入和供养。这些数量的供养和收入就是购买金银的价格。在英格兰购买金银是这样,在秘鲁购买金银也是这样。需要金银的国家只要支付得起这个价格,就用不着担心所需要的金银会长久稀缺。而不需要的金银也不会长时间留在国内。

<small>另一方面,随着年产出的增加,货币也会随之增加。</small>

所以,无论是根据明白合理的说法,即构成一个国家真实财富与收入的是一个国家劳动和土地的年产物的价值;还是依据世俗偏见,即构成一个国家真实财富与收入的是国内流通的贵金属量;无论从哪一个观点来说,奢侈浪费都是公众的敌人,勤俭节约的人都是社会的恩人。

<small>即使一个国家的财富由货币组成,但这种浪费者也是公众的敌人。</small>

谈到行为不正者,行为不端的结果常常和奢侈者一样。在农业、矿业、渔业、商业和工业领域,一切不谨慎和没有成功希望的计划,都有使雇用生产性劳动的基金减少的可能趋势。固然,投在这类每一种计划上的资本,也仅仅由生产性劳动者消费,但由于使用不当,所以,他们消费的价值不能充分再生产出来,与使用适当的情况相比较,总不免会减少社会上的生产基金。

<small>行为不端与奢侈带来的后果是一样的。</small>

实际上就大国的情况来说,个人奢侈和不当的行为发生的情

<small>节俭和谨慎行为占主导地位。</small>

of individuals; the profusion or imprudence of some, being always more than compensated by the frugality and good conduct of others.

<small>Prodigality is more intermittent than the desire to better our condition.</small> With regard to profusion, the principle which prompts to expence, is the passion for present enjoyment; which, though sometimes violent and very difficult to be restrained, is in general only momentary and occasional. But the principle which prompts to save, is the desire of bettering our condition, a desire which, though generally calm and dispassionate, comes with us from the womb, and never leaves us till we go into the grave. In the whole interval which separates those two moments, there is scarce perhaps a single instant in which any man is so perfectly and completely satisfied with his situation, as to be without any wish of alteration or improvement of any kind. An augmentation of fortune is the means by which the greater part of men propose and wish to better their condition. It is the means the most vulgar and the most obvious; and the most likely way of augmenting their fortune, is to save and accumulate some part of what they acquire, either regularly and annually, or upon some extraordinary occasions. Though the principle of expence, therefore, prevails in almost all men upon some occasions, and in some men upon almost all occasions, yet in the greater part of men, taking the whole course of their life at an average, the principle of frugality seems not only to predominate, but to predominate very greatly.

<small>Imprudent undertakings are small in number compared to prudent ones.</small> With regard to misconduct, the number of prudent and successful undertakings is every-where much greater than that of injudicious and unsuccessful ones. After all our complaints of the frequency of bankruptcies, the unhappy men who fall into this misfortune make but a very small part of the whole number engaged in trade, and all other sorts of business; not much more perhaps than one in a thousand. Bankruptcy is perhaps the greatest and most humiliating calamity which can befal an innocent man. The greater part of men, therefore, are sufficiently careful to avoid it. Some, indeed, do not avoid it; as some do not avoid the gallows.

况并不常见。另一部分人的俭朴慎重总能够补偿这一部分人的奢侈和行为不当而绰绰有余。

谈到奢侈浪费,一个人之所以会浪费,当然因为他有现在及时享乐的欲望。这种欲望之强烈,有时简直难于抑制,但一般说来,那仅仅是暂时和偶然的。再说勤俭节约,一个人之所以会节俭,当然因为他有改变自身状况的愿望。这种愿望虽然是冷静和沉着的,但我们从出生一直到死亡,从来没有一时一刻放弃过这种愿望。我们从出生一直到死亡,对于自身地位,几乎没有一个人会有哪一时刻觉得完全满意,不求进步,不想有所改善。但是大部分人都觉得增加财产是必要的手段,这手段最通俗,最明显。增加财产的最可能的方法,就是在常年或特殊的收入中,节省一部分并把它储蓄起来。所以,虽然每个人都不免有时有浪费的欲望,并且,有一种人,是时时刻刻都有这种欲望,但一般平均说来,在我们人类生命的过程中,节俭的心理不仅常占优势而且大占优势。

奢侈行为比改善现状的愿望要更短暂。

关于行为不端,无论在哪里,慎重和成功的事业总占极大多数。不慎重、不成功的事业,总占极少数。我们虽然常常看见陷于破产的失意者,但在无数的经营商业的人中,失败的总是全数中的极小部分。1000个之中不会超过一例。破产这种灾祸,尤其是降临到一个清白的人身上的破产事件,实在是极大和极其痛苦的灾难。绝大多数人都对它十分留意。当然不知道避免它的人,就与那些不知道规避绞刑台的人一样,也并非没有这样的人。

慎重与事件相比出事要少许多,不谨慎事件要多。

地大物博的国家,虽然不会因为私人奢侈和行为不正而贫

| 国民财富的性质与原理

Public prodigality and imprudence are more to be feared than private,

    Great nations are never impoverished① by private, though they sometimes are by public prodigality and misconduct. The whole, or almost the whole public revenue, is in most countries employed in maintaining unproductive hands. Such are the people who compose a numerous and splendid court, a great ecclesiastical establishment, great fleets and armies, who in time of peace produce nothing, and in time of war acquire nothing which can compensate the expence of maintaining them, even while the war lasts. Such people, as they themselves produce nothing, are all maintained by the produce of other men's labour. When multiplied, therefore, to an unnecessary number, they may in a particular year consume so great a share of this produce, as not to leave a sufficiency for maintaining the productive labourers, who should reproduce it next year. The next year's produce, therefore, will be less than that of the foregoing, and if the same disorder should continue, that of the third year will be still less than that of the second. Those unproductive hands, who should be maintained by a part only of the spare revenue of the people, may consume so great a share of their whole revenue, and thereby oblige so great a number to encroach upon their capitals, upon the funds destined for the maintenance of productive labour, that all the frugality and good conduct of individuals may not be able to compensate the waste and degradation of produce occasioned by this violent and forced encroachment.

but are counteracted by private frugality and prudence.

    This frugality and good conduct, however, is upon most occasions, it appears from experience, sufficient to compensate, not only the private prodigality and misconduct of individuals, but the public extravagance of government. The uniform, constant, and uninterrupted effort of every man to better his condition, the principle from which public and national, as well as private opulence is originally derived, is frequently powerful enough to maintain the natural progress of things toward improvement, in spite both of the extravagance of government, and of the greatest errors of administration. Like the unknown principle of animal life, it frequently restores health and vigour to the constitution, in spite, not only of the disease, but of the absurd prescriptions of the doctor.

---

    ① ['Impoverished' is here equivalent to 'made poor,' i. e., ruined, not merely to 'made poorer'.]

穷,①但政府的奢侈浪费和行为不当,却有时可以使国家陷于穷困的境地。在许多国家中,全部或几乎全部的公众收入都是用来维持非生产者。朝廷上的王公大臣和教会中的牧师神父,就是这一类人。又如海陆军人,他们在和平时期既不生产,在战争时期又不能有所收获来补偿他们的维持费用,甚至在战争持续进行期间,也是如此。这些人,因为他们不能生产,不得不依靠别人劳动的产物来生活。如果他们人数增加到不应该有的数量,他们可能在某一年消费掉这么多的上述产物,结果导致没有足够剩余数量来维持能在下一个年度进行再生产的生产性劳动者。于是下一个年度的再生产,一定不如上一年。如果这种不好的状况继续下去,那么第三年的再生产又一定不如第二年。那些只应该拿走人民的一部分剩余收入来维持非生产者,他们可能实际上消费了人民全部收入中很大的一部分,使得这么多人民不得不侵蚀他们的资本,侵占维持生产性劳动的基金,以致不论个人多么节俭和慎重,都不能补偿这样大的浪费。

【政府的奢侈浪费行为比私人的奢侈浪费行为则更加可怕,】

然而,从经验就可以知道,在大多数情况下,个人的节俭慎重又似乎不仅可以补偿个人的奢侈和行为不当,而且可以补偿政府的浪费。每个人改善自身境况所进行的一致的、经常和不断的努力是社会、国民和私人的财富所赖以产生的重大因素。这种努力常常有力而坚强,足以补偿政府的浪费和挽救行政的重大错误,使事情不断向好的方向发展。比如,人间虽然不仅有疾病,而且还有庸医,但人身上总似有一种莫名其妙的力量,可以突破一切

【但却被私人的节俭慎行为所抵消。】

---

① "贫困"在这里就等于"致贫"、败落等,不仅仅指"变得更加贫困"。

| 国民财富的性质与原理

To increase the produce of a nation an inorease of capital is necessary The annual produce of the land and labour of any nation can be increased in its value by no other means, but by increasing either the number of its productive labourers, or the productive powers of those labourers who had before been employed. The number of its productive labourers, it is evident, can never be much increased, but in consequence of an increase of capital, or of the funds destined for maintaining them. The productive powers of the same number of labourers cannot be increased, but in consequence either of some addition and improvement to those machines and instruments which facilitate and abridge labour; or of a more proper division and distribution of employment. In either case an additional capital is almost always required. It is by means of an additional capital only, that the undertaker of any work can either provide his workmen with better machinery, or make a more proper distribution of employment among them. When the work to be done consists of a number of parts, to keep every man constantly employed in one way, requires a much greater capital than where every man is occasionally employed in every different part of the work. When we compare, therefore, the state of a nation at two different periods, and find, that the annual produce of its land and labour is evidently greater at the latter than at the former, that its lands are better cultivated, its manufactures more numerous and more flourishing, and its trade more extensive, we may be assured that its capital must have increased during the interval between those two periods, and that more must have been added to it by the good conduct of some, than had been taken from it either by the private misconduct of others, or by the public extravagance of government. But we shall find this to have been the case of almost all nations, in all tolerably quiet and peaceable times, even of those who have not enjoyed the most prudent and parsimonious governments. To form a right judgment of it, indeed, we must compare the state of the country at periods somewhat distant from one another. The progress is frequently so gradual, that, at near periods, the improvement is not only not sensible, but from the declension either of certain branches of industry, or of certain districts of the country, things which sometimes happen though the country in general be in great prosperity, there frequently arises a suspicion, that the riches and industry of the whole are decaying.

Marginal notes: *To increase the produce of a nation an inorease of capital is necessary.* *If, therefore the produce has increased, we may be sure the capital has increased.* *This has been the case of almost all nations in peaceable times.* *England for example from 1660 to 1776.*

    The annual produce of the land and labour of England, for example, is certainly much greater than it was, a little more than a century ago, at the restoration of Charles Ⅱ. Though, at present, few people, I believe, doubt of this, yet during this period, five years have seldom passed away in which some book or pamphlet has not been published, written too with such abilities as to gain some authority

难关,恢复原来的健康和活力。

  要增加一个国家土地和劳动的年产物的价值,只有两个方法,一个是增加生产性劳动者的数量,一个是提高雇佣劳动者的生产力。很明显,要增加生产性劳动者的数量,必须先增加资本,增加维持生产性劳动者的基金。要增加雇佣等量劳动者的生产力,只有增加那些便利劳动和增加缩减劳动的机械和工具,或对它们进行改良。也就是让工作的分配更加适当。但无论如何,都有增加资本的必要。要改良机器,少不了增加资本;要改进工作的分配,也少不了增加资本。把工作分成许多部分,使每个工人一直专门做一种工作,比由一个人兼任各种工作,肯定要增加不少资本。因此,我们如果比较同一个国家的前代和后代,就发现那里的土地和劳动的年产物,后代比前代多,其土地耕种状况取得进步,工业得到扩大和繁荣,商业逐步推广;我们可以断言,在这两个时代之间,这个国家的资本必定增加了不少。那里一部分人民的节俭慎重资本增加的数量,一定要多于另一部分人民的行为不端和政府的浪费所侵占了的资本的数量。说到这里,我应该声明一句,只要国泰民安,即使政府不是节约慎重的政府,国家情况也有可能取得这种进步。不过,我们要正确判定这种进步,不应该比较两个时间距离太近的时代。进步是逐渐取得的,时代太近了,不但看不出它的进步,有时即使国家已经取得进步,但我们往往因为只看到某种产业的萎缩或某一地方的衰落,便怀疑地认为全国的财富与产业都在退步。

  和一百年前查理二世复辟时期相比较,现在英格兰土地和劳动的年产物当然要多得多。现在怀疑英国年产物增加的人,固然不多,但在这 100 年的时间内,几乎每隔五年,就有几本写得很好

with the public, and pretending to demonstrate that the wealth of the nation was fast declining, that the country was depopulated, agriculture neglected, manufactures decaying, and trade undone. Nor have these publications been all party pamphlets, the wretched offspring of falsehood and venality. Many of them have been written by very candid and very intelligent people; who wrote nothing but what they believed, and for no other reason but because they believed it.

<small>or from 1558 to 1660,</small> The annual produce of the land and labour of England again, was certainly much greater at the restoration, than we can suppose it to have been about an hundred years before, at the accession of Elizabeth. At this period too, we have all reason to believe, the country was much more advanced in improvement, than it had been about a century before, towards the close of the dissensions between the houses of York and Lancaster. Even then it was, probably, in a better condition than it had been at the Norman conquest, and at the Norman conquest, than during the confusion of the Saxon Heptarchy. Even at this early period, it was certainly a more improved country than at the invasion of Julius Cesar, when its inhabitants were nearly in the same state with the savages in North America.

<small>though there was much public and private profuaion, and many other disorders and misfortunes occurred.</small> In each of those periods, however, there was, not only much private and public profusion, many expensive and unnecessary wars, great perversion of the annual produce from maintaining productive to maintain unproductive hands; but sometimes, in the confusion of civil discord, such absolute waste and destruction of stock, as might be supposed, not only to retard, as it certainly did, the natural accumulation of riches, but to have left the country, at the end of the period,

第二篇　第三章

又让人动听的书或小册子,说英格兰的国家财富正在锐减,人口正在减少,并且还说那里是农业退步,工业凋零,商业衰落。而且这类书籍不一定全都是党派的宣传品,全部是欺诈和见利忘义的产物。我知道它们里面有许多是极诚实和极聪明的作家所写的。这些人所叙述的内容没有不是他们自己相信的东西。

再者,和 200 年前伊丽莎白即位时期相比较,查理二世复辟时代英格兰土地和劳动的年产物,必定要多得多。和 300 年前约克与兰克斯特争胜时代末期相比较,伊丽莎白时代的英格兰年产物,肯定又要多出许多。再往前推理,约克与兰开斯特[1]时代当然要胜过诺尔曼征服的时代;诺尔曼征服的时代当然又强于撒克逊七国[2]统治的时代。在撒克逊七国统治的时代,英国当然不能说是一个进步的国家,但与朱利阿·恺撒侵略时代(这时英格兰居民的状况和北美野蛮人相差不远)相比较,又算进步很多。

或从 1558 年到 1660 年,

然而,在这各个时期中,私人有很多浪费,政府也有很多浪费,而且发生了许多次费用浩大又不必要的战争,原用来维持生产者的年产物,有许多被挪用来维持非生产者。有时,在内讧激烈的时候,浪费的浩大,资本的破坏,在任何人看来都会感觉这不但会妨碍财富的自然蓄积(实际上确是如此),而且会使国家在这个时期结束时陷于更为贫困的地位。查理二世复辟以后,英国境

尽管存在许多公共和著各种浪费、混乱和不幸现象的发生。

---

〔1〕　兰开斯特王朝(Lancaster)从 1399 年至 1461 年的英格兰王朝,产生过英格兰三个国王:亨利四世、亨利五世和亨利六世。在蔷薇战争期间它的标志是一朵红蔷薇。

〔2〕　常作 Heptarchy 七王国:从 5 世纪到 9 世纪盎格鲁·撒克逊王国的非正式联盟,由肯特、南撒西克斯、西撒西克斯、东撒西克斯、诺森布里亚、东英格兰和麦西亚组成。

poorer than at the beginning. Thus, in the happiest and most fortunate period of them all, that which has passed since the restoration, how many disorders and misfortunes have occurred, which, could they have been foreseen, not only the impoverishment, but the total ruin of the country would have been expected from them ? The fire and the plague of London, the two Dutch wars, the disorders of the revolution, the war in Ireland, the four expensive French wars of 1688, 1702, 1742, and 1756, together with the two rebellions of 1715 and 1745. In the course of the four French wars, the nation has contracted more than a hundred and forty-five millions of debt, over and above all the other extraordinary annual expence which they occasioned, so that the whole cannot be computed at less than two hundred millions. So great a share of the annual produce of the land and labour of the country, has, since the revolution, been employed upon different occasions, in maintaining an extraordinary number of unproductive hands. But had not those wars given this particular direction to so large a capital, the greater part of it would naturally have been employed in maintaining productive hands, whose labour would have replaced, with a profit, the whole value of their consumption. The value of the annual produce of the land and labour of the country, would have been considerably increased by it every year, and every year's increase would have augmented still more that of the following year. More houses would have been built, more lands would have been improved, and those which had been improved before would have been better cultivated, more manufactures would have been established, and those which had been established before would have been more extended; and to what height the real wealth and revenue of the country might, by this time, have been raised, it is not perhaps very easy even to imagine.

<small>Private frugality and prudence have silently counteracted these circumstances.</small>   But though the profusion of government must, undoubtedly, have retarded the natural progress of England towards wealth and improvement, it has not been able to stop it. The annual produce of its land and labour is, undoubtedly, much greater at present than it was either at the restoration or at the revolution. The capital, therefore, annually employed in cultivating this land, and in maintaining this labour, must likewise be much greater. In the midst of all the exactions of government, this capital has been silently and gradually accumulated by the private frugality and good conduct of individuals, by their universal, continual, and uninterrupted effort to better their own condition. It is this effort, protected by law and allowed by liberty to exert itself in the manner that is most advantageous, which has maintained the progress of England towards opulence and improvement in almost

况是最幸福最富裕的了,但那时又有多少紊乱与不幸事件发生呢?如果我们是生在那个时代,我们一定会担心英格兰的前途,说它不仅要陷于贫困,怕还会全部毁灭吧。你想想看,伦敦大火以后,继以大疫,又加上英荷之间两次战后的革命骚扰,对爱尔兰战争,1688年、1702年、1742年和1756年四次对法耗费巨大的大战,再有1715年和1745年二次叛乱。不说别的,单就达四次英法大战的结果来说,英国欠下来的债务,就在14,500万镑以上,加上战争所引起的各种特殊支出,恐怕总共少于2亿镑。自革命以来,我国年产出,就常有这样大的部分用来维持非常多的不参加生产者。假使当时没有战争,那么当时用作战争费用的资本,其中定有一大部分会改变用途来雇用生产性劳动者。生产性劳动者既能再生产他们消费的全价值,并提供利润,那么,我国土地和劳动的年产出的价值年年增加,而且每一年的增加又必能使下一年的增加更多。如果当时没有战争,建造起来的房屋一定更多;改良了的土地一定更广大;已改良土地的耕种一定更加完善;制造业一定增多,已有的制造业又一定推广;至于国民真实财富与收入将要如何增加起来,我们也许难于想象。

  政府的浪费,虽然无疑曾经阻碍英格兰在财富与进步方面的自然发展,但不能使它停止发展。与复辟时代相比,现在英格兰土地和劳动的年生产物要多出许多;与革命时代相比较,也是要多得多。英格兰每年用来耕种土地和维持农业劳动的资本,也一定比过去多得多。一方面虽有政府的诉求,但另一方面,却有无数个人在那里普遍地和不断地努力改进自己的境况,节省、慎重,他们不动声色地、一步一步地把资本累积起来。正是这种努力,受着法律保障,能在最有利情况下自由发展,使英格兰几乎在过

<small>但私人节俭和谨慎悄悄地对这些情况进行抵消。</small>

all former times, and which, it is to be hoped, will do so in all future times. England, however, as it has never been blessed with a very parsimonious government, so parsimony has at no time been the characteristical virtue of its inhabitants. It is the highest impertinence and presumption, therefore, in kings and ministers, to pretend to watch over the economy of private people, and to restrain their expence, either by sumptuary laws, or by prohibiting the importation of foreign luxuries. They are themselves always, and without any exception, the greatest spendthrifts in the society. Let them look well after their own expence, and they may safely trust private people with theirs. If their own extravagance does not ruin the state, that of their subjects never will.

Apart from increase or diminution of capital different kinds of expense may be distinguished.   As frugality increases, and prodigality diminishes the public capital, so the conduct of those whose expence just equals their revenue, with. out either accumulating or encroaching, neither increases nor diminishes it. Some modes of expence, however, seem to contribute more to the growth of public opulence than others.

An individual who spends on durable commodities will be richer than one who spends on perishable ones.   The revenue of an individual may be spent, either in things which are consumed immediately, and in which one day's expence can neither alleviate nor support that of another; or it may be spent in things more durable, which can therefore be accumulated, and in which every day's expence may, as he chuses, either alleviate or support and heighten the effect of that of the following day. A man of fortune, for example, may either spend his revenue in a profuse and sumptuous table, and in maintaining a great number of menial servants, and a multitude of dogs and horses; or contenting himself with a frugal table and few attendants, he may lay out the greater part of it in adorning his house or his country villa, in useful or ornamental buildings, in useful or ornamental furniture, in collecting books, statues, pictures; or in things more frivolous, jewels, baubles, ingenious trinkets of different kinds; or, what is most trifling of all, in amassing a great wardrobe of fine clothes, like the favourite and minister of a great prince who died a few years ago. Were two men of equal fortune to spend their revenue, the one chiefly in the one way, the other in the other, the magnificence of the person whose expence had been chiefly in durable commodities, would be continually increasing, every day's expence contributing something to support and heighten the

去一切时代,都能日趋富裕,日趋改良。而且,将来永远照此进行下去,亦不是没有希望的事体。可是,英格兰从来没有过很节俭的政府,所以,居民亦没有节俭的特性。由此可见,英格兰王公大臣没有自我反省,颁布节俭法令,甚至也没有禁止外国奢侈品进口,倡言要监督私人经济、节制铺张浪费,实在是最放肆、最专横的行为啊。他们不知道,他们自己始终无例外的是社会上最浪费的阶级。他们好好注意自己的费用就行了,人民的费用,可以任凭人民自己去管。如果他们的浪费,不会使国家灭亡,那么人民的浪费更无从谈起。

节俭可以增加社会资本,奢侈可以减少社会资本。所以,支出等于收入的人不蓄积资本,也不侵占资本;既不增加资本,也不减少资本。不过,在各种支出方法之中,有些方法是比其他方法更能够促进国家财富的增长。除了可以增加或减少资本外,其支出类型还可以进行划分的方法。

个人的收入,有的用来购买及时享用的物品,这样的及时享用,会使今天的支出对未来的日子于事无补。有的用来购买比较耐久的、可以蓄积起来的物品,今日的购买就可以减少明日的费用,或者改进和促进明日费用的效果。例如,有些富翁生活上简直就是事事使奴唤仆,名犬好马成群,常常山珍海味大宴宾朋。有些人宁愿在吃用上勤俭节约,使用奴婢很少,却把钱花在修饰庄园,整理别墅,不断大兴土木,大量购置有用的或专门作为装饰使用的家具、书籍藏画等等。有些人却把钱财用来购买奇珍异宝,家里四处珠光宝气。还有些人,例如前些年逝世的某大王的宠臣,衣服满箱,锦绣满床。设有甲乙两位富翁,财产相等,甲把他大部分收入购买比较耐久的商品,乙则把他大部分收入购买及时享用的物品。后来甲的境况肯定一天好过一天,今日的费用多把钱用于耐久物品的人会比把钱用于及时享用的物品的人更富裕。财产耐用品将比财用于及时享用的物品加更多。

国民财富的性质与原理

effect of that of the following day: that of the other, on the contrary, would be no greater at the end of the period than at the beginning. The former too would, at the end of the period, be the richer man of the two. He would have a stock of goods of some kind or other, which, though it might not be worth all that it cost, would always be worth something. No trace or vestige of the expence of the latter would remain, and the effects of ten or twenty years profusion would be as completely annihilated as if they had never existed.

<small>The same thing is true of a nation.</small> As the one mode of expence is more favourable than the other to the opulence of an individual, so is it likewise to that of a nation. The houses, the furniture, the clothing of the rich, in a little time, become useful to the inferior and middling ranks of people. They are able to purchase them when their superiors grow weary of them, and the general accommodation of the whole people is thus gradually improved, when this mode of expence becomes universal among men of fortune. In countries which have long been rich, you will frequently find the inferior ranks of people in possession both of houses and furniture perfectly good and entire, but of which neither the one could have been built, nor the other have been made for their use. What was formerly a seat of the family of Seymour, is now an inn upon the Bath road. ① The marriage-bed of James the First of Great Britain, which his Queen brought with her from Denmark, as a present fit for a sovereign to make to a sovereign, was, a few years ago, the ornament of an ale-house at Dunfermline. ② In some ancient cities, which either have been long stationary, or have gone somewhat to decay, you will sometimes scarce find a single house which could have been built for its present inhabitants. If you go into those houses too, you will frequently find many excellent, tnough antiquated pieces of furniture, which are still very fit for use, and which could as little have been made for them. Noble palaces, magnificent villas, great collections of books, statues, pictures, and other curiosities, are frequently both an ornament and an honour, not only to the neighbourhood, but to the whole country to which they belong. Versailles is an ornament and an

---

① [This was the Castle Inn at Marlborough, which ceased to be an inn and became Marlborough College in 1843, thus undergoing another vicissitude.]

② [The innkeeper, Mrs. Walker, a zealous Jacobite, refused an offer of fifty guineas for the bed, but presented it about 1764 to the Earl of Elgin (John Fernie, *History of the Town* and *Parish of Dunfermline*, 1815, p. 71), and its remains now form a mantel-piece in the dining-room at Broomhall, near Dunfermline.]

多少少可以增加和促进明日费用的效果。乙的境况肯定不会比原先更好。最后，甲一定比乙富裕。甲还有一些存货，虽然存货的价值当时所花费的数量少，但总还是有些价值。乙所花费的就连一点痕迹也没保留下来，10年或20年浪费的结果好像是什么都没有发生一样。

对个人财富比较有好处的消费方法，对国民财富也比较有利。富人的房屋、家具和衣服，转瞬之间变成对中下等人民有用的物品。当上等阶级对这些物品厌烦时，中下层阶级的人民可以把它们买来使用；所以，在富人一般都是这样使用钱财的时候，全体人民的一般生活状况就逐步得到改善。在一个富裕已久的国家，下等人民虽然自己不能够出资建造大厦，但往往占有大厦；虽然自己不能定制上等家具，但往往能够使用上等家具。昔日的西穆尔邸宅，现如今已经成为巴斯道上的客栈；①詹姆士一世的婚床是皇后从丹麦带来的嫁妆，是邻国通婚的礼物；几年前已经陈列在敦弗林的酒店里。② 在有些没有进步也没有退步或已稍显没落的古城里，我们有时可以发现几乎没有一所房屋是目前占有人所能够盖得起的。如果你走进里面去看看，还可以见到许多还可使用的、非常讲究但已经是老式的家具。这些家具绝不可能是目前使用者花钱定制的。王宫别墅、书籍、雕像以及各种珍奇物品，常常既是光荣又是装饰，不但对其所在的本地方如此，对其所属国

<small>对于国家道理也是一样。</small>

---

① 这就是位于大楼的城堡客栈；在1843年客栈停止使用，成为大楼学院，又经历了另一种变迁。

② 客栈管理者沃克夫人，一个热心的雅各宾派人士，拒绝以50几尼出售这张床；后来又在1764年呈转给额尔金伯爵；现在它的遗存在靠近的敦弗林的布鲁姆豪的餐厅里，变成一面壁炉。

honour to France, Stowe and Wilton to England. Italy still continues to command some sort of veneration by the number of monuments of this kind which it possesses, though the wealth which produced them has decayed, and though the genius which planned them seems to be extinguished, perhaps from not having the same employment.

<small>The former expense is easier to bring to an end,</small>   The expence too, which is laid out in durable commodities, is favourable, not only to accumulation, but to frugality. If a person should at any time exceed in it, he can easily reform without exposing himself to the censure of the public. To reduce very much the number of his servants, to reform his table from great profusion to great frugality, to lay down his equipage after he has once set it up, are changes which cannot escape the observation of his neighbours, and which are supposed to imply some acknowledgment of preceding bad conduct. Few, therefore, of those who have once been so unfortunate as to launch out too far into this sort of expence, have afterwards the courage to reform, till ruin and bankruptcy oblige them. But if a person has, at any time, been at too great an expence in building, in furniture, in books or pictures, no imprudence can be inferred from his changing his conduct. These are things in which further expence is frequently rendered unnecessary by former expence; and when a person stops short, he appears to do so, not because he has exceeded his fortune, but because he has satisfied his fancy.

<small>and gives maintenance to more people.</small>   The expence, besides, that is laid out in durable commodities, gives maintenance, commonly, to a greater number of people, than that which is employed in the most profuse hospitality. Of two or three hundred weight of provisions, which may sometimes be served up at a great festival, one-half, perhaps, is thrown to the dunghill, and there is always a great deal wasted and abused. But if the expence of this entertainment had been employed in setting to work masons, carpenters, upholsterers, mechanics, &c. a quantity of provisions, of equal value, would have been distributed among a still greater number of people, who would have bought them in penny-worths and pound weights, and not have lost or thrown away a single ounce of them. In the one way, besides, this expence maintains productive, in the other unproductive hands. In the one way, therefore, it increases, in the other, it does not increase, the exchangeable value of the annual produce of the land and labour of the country.

家也是如此。凡尔赛宫是法兰西的装饰和光荣,斯托威和威尔登是英格兰的装饰和光荣。意大利创造名胜古迹的财富,虽然是陨落了,创造名胜古迹的大天才(也许因为没有用处)虽然似乎是被埋没了,但那里的名胜古迹,却仍然博得世人的赞赏。

　　把收入花费在比较耐久的物品上,那不仅更加有利于蓄积,而且也比较容易养成俭朴的风尚。如果一个人在这方面花费得过多,他可幡然醒悟而改过自新,而不致遭受社会人士的批评指责。如果原来是仆役成群,现在骤然减少;如果原来是豪华盛宴款待宾朋,现如今要突然俭省下来;如果原来是家庭陈设富丽堂皇,现在突然要简洁适用,就不免被左邻右舍全部看见,而且似乎是意味着自己承认过去行为的错误。所以,像这样挥霍大度的人,不是迫于破产,很少有改变不良习惯的勇气。反之,如果他原来喜欢用钱添置房屋、家具、书籍或图画,以后如果自己感觉财力不够,他就可以幡然改正过来,人们也就对此不在表示怀疑。因为这类物品先前已经被购置,无需源源不断地进行购置。在别人看来,他改变习性的原因似乎不是财力不足,而是对他自己目前的状况已经心满意足了。

　　何况,把钱财花在耐久物品上,能够供养的人一般比较多;把钱财用于款待宾客上,所能够供养的人就比较少。一次盛大宴会所耗费的物品价值为二三百斤粮食,其中也许有一半被倒进粪堆,损失浪费严重。但是如果把大宴宾客的支出用来雇用泥木工、技师等等,虽然所花费粮食的价值相等,但所供养的人数会增加很多。工人们将一个便士一个便士、一镑一镑地购买这些粮食,一镑也不会浪费。一个方面是用来维持生产者,能够增加一个国家土地和劳动的年产物的交换价值,一个方面是用来维持非

把钱花在前者上面,会容易花光钱财,

可以维持供养更多的人。

I would not, however, by all this be understood to mean, that the one species of expence always betokens a more liberal or generous spirit than the other. When a man of fortune spends his revenue chiefly in hospitality, he shares the greater part of it with his friends and companions; but when he employs it in purchasing such durable commodities, he often spends the whole upon his own person, and gives nothing to any body without an equivalent. The latter species of expence, therefore, especially when directed towards frivolous objects, the little ornaments of dress and furniture, jewels, trinkets, gewgaws, frequently indicates, not only a trifling, but a base and selfish disposition. All that I mean is, that the one sort of expence, as it always occasions some accumulation of valuable commodities, as it is more favourable to private frugality, and, consequently, to the increase of the public capital, and as it maintains productive, rather than unproductive hands, conduces more than the other to the growth of public opulence.

> It does not follow that it betokens a more generous spirit.

生产者，虽然不能增加一个国家土地和劳动的年产物的交换价值。

　　读者不要认为，把钱财花在耐久物品上，就是良好的行为，把钱财花在款待宾客上，全部都是不好的行为。一个富有的人把他的收入主要用于款待宾客时，也就是把收入的大部分与朋友共享。如果他把收入用来购买耐久物品，好处则仅仅局限于他自己本人，除非是等价交换，否则是不允许其他人进行分享。因此，后一种的花费，特别是花在购买珠宝、衣饰等等这些琐细东西，常常不仅表示一种轻浮倾向，而且还表示卑微和自私自利的倾向。我上面的意思不过是说，把钱财花在耐久物品上的支出方式，由于导致有价商品的蓄积，也更有利于私人形成节俭习惯，所以也有利于社会资本的增加；由于所维持供养的是生产者而不是非生产者，所以更有利于国家财富的增长。

<small>据此不能推此把花在买耐久物品就具有慷慨精神</small>

CHAPTER IV

Of Stock Lent At Interest

<small>Stock lent at interest is a capital to the lender, but may or may not be so to the borrower.</small> The stock which is lent at interest is always considered as a capital by the lender. He expects that in due time it is to be restored to him, and that in the mean time the borrower is to pay him a certain annual rent for the use of it. The borrower may use it either as a capital, or as a stock reserved for immediate consumption. If he uses it as a capital, he employs it in the maintenance of productive labourers, who reproduce the value with a profit. He can, in this case, both restore the capital and pay the interest without alienating or encroaching upon any other source of revenue. If he uses it as a stock reserved for immediate consumption, he acts the part of a prodigal, and dissipates in the maintenance of the idle, what was destined for the support of the industrious. He can, in this case, neither restore the capital nor pay the interest, without either alienating or encroaching upon some other source of revenue, such as the property or the rent of land.

<small>Generally it is so to the borrower,</small> The stock which is lent at interest is, no doubt, occasionally employed in both these ways, but in the former much more frequently than in the latter. The man who borrows in order to spend will soon be ruined, and he who lends to him will generally have occasion to repent of his folly. To borrow or to lend for such a purpose, therefore, is in all cases, where gross usury is out of the question, contrary to the interest of both parties; and though it no doubt happens sometimes that people do both the one and the other; yet, from the regard that all men have for their own interest, we may be assured, that it cannot happen so very frequently as we are sometimes apt to imagine. Ask any rich man of common prudence, to which of the two sorts of people he has lent the greater part of his stock, to those who, he thinks, will employ it profitably, or to those who will spend it idly, and he will laugh at you for proposing the question. Even among bor-

第四章 论贷出取息的财货

出借人总是把贷出取息的财货看作是资本。出借人总希望借贷到期后，财货重新回到自己手中，而在借贷期间借入者由于曾经使用这笔财货，也要向他支付年租若干。这种财货在借用人手里可用作资本，也可以用作目前消费的财货。如果用作资本，就是用来维持生产性劳动者，可以再生产价值并提供利润。在这种情况下，他无须割让或侵占任何其他收入的资源便能够偿还资本本金和利息。如果用作目前消费的资财，他就成为浪费者，他夺走了维持勤劳阶级的基金来维持懒惰阶级。在这种情况下，除非他侵占某种收入的资源如土地产权或地租，他就无法偿还资本并支付利息。

贷出取息的财货，无疑有时会同时用在这两种用途上，但用在前一用途的较多，用在后一用途的较少。借钱挥霍的人，肯定难以持久，借钱给他的人常常要后悔自己愚不可及，不应该借钱给他们。除了高利贷盘剥者以外，像这样的借贷行为对双方都毫无利益可言。社会上固然难免有这样借贷的事件发生，但由于各自出于自己利益考虑，所以，可以肯定它不会像我们所想象的那样经常发生。任何比较谨慎的富人，如果问他是愿意以大部分财货贷放给用于谋利的人呢还是浪费的人呢，他听后怕只会发笑，

（贷出财货者对于借者说来是资本；借出者则当作使用来资而人说一是资用。）

（一般来讲出借贷货的财对于借者当作资本使用。）

rowers, therefore, not the people in the world most famous for frugality, the number of the frugal and industrious surpasses considerably that of the prodigal and idle.

<small>except in case of mortgages effected by country gentlemen.</small> The only people to whom stock is commonly lent, without their being expected to make any very profitable use of it, are country gentlemen who borrow upon mortgage. Even they scarce ever borrow merely to spend. What they borrow, one may say, is commonly spent before they borrow it. They have generally consumed so great a quantity of goods, advanced to them upon credit by shopkeepers and tradesmen, that they find it necessary to borrow at interest in order to pay the debt. The capital borrowed replaces the capitals of those shopkeepers and tradesmen, which the country gentlemen could not have replaced from the rents of their estates. It is not properly borrowed in order to be spent, but in order to replace a capital which had been spent before.

<small>Loans are made in money, but what the borrower wants and gets is goods.</small> Almost all loans at interest are made in money, either of paper, or of gold and silver. But what the borrower really wants, and what the lender really supplies him with, is not the money, but the money's worth, or the goods which it can purchase. If he wants it as a stock for immediate consumption, it is those goods only which he can place in that stock. If he wants it as a capital for employing industry, it is from those goods only that the industrious can be furnished with the tools, materials, and maintenance, necessary for carrying on their work. By means of the loan, the lender, as it were, assigns to the borrower his right to a certain portion of the annual produce of the land and labour of the country, to be employed as the borrower pleases. ①

The quantity of stock, therefore, or, as it is commonly expressed, of money which can be lent at interest in any country, is not regulated by the value of the money, whether paper or coin, which serves as the instrument of the different loans made in that country, but by the value of that part of the annual produce which, as soon as it comes either from the ground, or from the hands of the productive

---

① [*Lectures*, p. 220.]

笑你会提出这样不成问题的问题。借用人虽然不是世上很有名的节俭家，但在他们之中节俭的人终究一定比奢侈的人要多，勤劳的人终究要比懒惰的人多出许多。

除了那些乡绅大佬通过抵押借贷以偿还欠款。

把借款仅仅用于自己挥霍的人只有是乡绅。乡绅借款，通常有财产作为抵押，这种借款常常不是用于有利的用途。但即使是乡绅，他们借钱也并不全部用于消费。他们借贷来的钱，常常早在没有借以前就已经花光。他们日常享用的东西多数向商店老板赊购，并且往往赊购很多，必须用有息借款来还清账目，乡绅们所借的资本实是补偿商店老板的资本；他们所收的地租不够偿还借款，所以还要向别人借款来偿还。这时他借钱并不是为了要花费，只是为了要补偿先前已经花掉了的资本。

贷款以货币的形式贷出，但借用人想要的和得到的是货物。

有息贷款大部分是以钞票或金银的货币形式借出。但借用人所需要的和出借人所供给的实际上都不是货币，而是货币的价值，换句话说，它是货币所能购买的货物。如果他所要求的是及时享用的资财，那么，他所借贷的便是能够立即享用的货物。如果他所要求的是兴办产业的资本，那么，他所借贷的便是劳动者工作所必需的工具、材料与食品。借贷这件事情实际上就是出借人把自己一定部分土地和劳动的年产物的使用权让与借用人，由他随意支配使用。①

货币总是国内各种借贷的手段，不论其为钞票或为铸币。一个国家能够有多少资财在收取利息的方式下借贷，或者像一般人所说，能有多少货币在收取利息的方式下出借，这些并不受货币价值的支配，而受特定部分年产出价值的支配。这些特定部分年

① 《关于法律、警察、岁入及军备的演讲》，第220页。

国民财富的性质与原理

<small>So the quantity of stock which can be lent is determined by the value of that part of the produce which replaces the owner does not himself employ.</small> labourers, is destined not only for replacing a capital, but such a capital as the owner does not care to be at the trouble of employing himself. As such capitals are commonly lent out and paid back in money, they constitute what is called the monied interest. It is distinct, not only from the landed, but from the trading and manufacturing interests, as in these last the owners themselves employ their own capitals. Even in the monied interest, however, the money is, as it were, but the deed of assignment, which conveys from one hand to another those capitals which the owners do not care to employ themselves. Those capitals may be greater in almost any proportion, than the amount of the money which serves as the instrument of their conveyance; the same pieces of money successively serving for many different loans, as well as for many different purchases. A, for example, lends to W athousand pounds, with which W immediately purchases of B a thousand pounds worth of goods. B having no occasion for the money himself, lends the identical pieces to X, with which X immediately purchases of C another thousand pounds worth of goods. C in the same manner, and for the same reason, lends them to Y, who again purchases goods with them of D. In this manner the same pieces, either of coin or of paper, may, in the course of a few days, serve as the instrument of three different loans, and of three different purchases, each of which is, in value, equal to the whole amount of those pieces. What the three monied men A, B, and C, assign to the three borrowers, W, X, Y, is the power of making those purchases. In this power consist both the value and the use of the loans. The stock lent by the three monied men, is equal to the value of the goods which can be purchased with it, and is three times greater than that of the money with which the purchases are made. Those loans, however, may be all perfectly well secured, the goods purchased by the different debtors being so employed, as, in due time, to bring back, with a profit, an equal value either of coin or of paper. And as the same pieces of money can thus serve as the instrument of different loans to three, or for the same reason, to thirty times their value, so they may likewise successively serve as the instrument of repayment.

第二篇 第四章

产出从土地生产出来或由生产的工人制造完工以后,就被指定作为资本使用,同时所有者又无意亲自使用,因此只有借给别人使用。因为这种资本的出借与偿还,都是使用货币来完成,所以被称为金钱上的利益关系。这不仅不同于农业上的利益关系,而且也不同于工商业上的利益关系,因为工商业的资本所有者是自己使用自己的资本。但我们应该知道,即使在金钱上的利益关系方面,货币也不过是与一张转让契约一样,甲把无意亲自使用的资本转让给乙。这种转让的资本量,与作为转让手段的货币的数量相比,不知要大多少倍。同一枚铸币或同一张纸币,可以用作许多次的购买,也可以连续用作许多次的借贷。例如,A 以 1,000 镑借给 B,B 立即用来向 C 购买 1,000 镑的货物。C 由于不需要货币,就把这 1,000 镑借给 D,D 又立即用来向 E 购买 1,000 镑货物。E 也因为不需要货币,同样地把这 1,000 镑借给 F,F 再立即向 G 购买 1,000 镑货物。所以货币还是原来那几枚铸币或几张纸币,但不用几天时间,借贷就已进行三次,购买也已进行三次了。每一次在价值上都与货币总额相等。A、C、E 是有钱出借的人,B、D、F 是要借钱的人。他们所借贷的其实只是购买那些货物的能力。借贷的价值与效用都在于这种购买力身上。这三个有钱人所借出的资财,等于这笔货币所能购买的货物的价值,所以,这三次借贷所借出的资财是购买货物所使用的货币价值的三倍。如果债务人所购买的货物使用得当,能够在借贷到期时用纸币或铸币的形式,偿还原先借入的价值和利息,那么这种借贷就十分可靠。而且,这笔货币既可用作三倍于借贷价值的手段,或基于同一种理由也可用作借贷 30 倍其价值的手段,所以,同样也可以连续用作偿还债务的手段。

用借贷取得所自愿自用的财产出借的价值小。可以借贷所能使货币实际比它所使用年数大。可作偿还的财产数决于借贷者不意亲自使用它。

| 国民财富的性质与原理

<small>This may be much greater than the actual money employed.</small>   A capital lent at interest may, in this manner, be considered as an assignment from the lender to the borrower of a certain considerable portion of the annual produce; upon condition that the borrower in return shall, during the continuance of the loan, annually assign to the lender a smaller portion, called the interest; and at the end of it, a portion equally considerable with that which had originally been assigned to him, called the repayment. Though money, either coin or paper, serves generally as the deed of assignment both to the smaller, and to the more considerable portion, it is itself altogether different from what is assigned by it.

<small>The money is altogether different from what is actually assigned either as principal or interest.</small>   In proportion as that share of the annual produce which, as soon as it comes either from the ground, or from the hands of the productive labourers, is destined for replacing a capital, increases in any country, what is called the monied interest naturally increases with it. The increase of those particular capitals from which the owners wish to derive a revenue, without being at the trouble of employing them themselves, naturally accompanies the general increase of capitals; or, in other words, as stock increases, the quantity of stock to be lent at interest grows gradually greater and greater.

<small>Interest falls as the quantity of stock to be lent increases,</small>   As the quantity of stock to be lent at interest increases, the interest, or the price which must be paid for the use of that stock, necessarily diminishes, not only from those general causes which make the market price of things commonly diminish as their quantity increases, but from other causes which are peculiar to this particular case.

<small>because profits diminish as it becomes more difficult to find a profitable method of employing new capital.</small>   As capitals increase in any country, the profits which can be made by employing them necessarily diminish. It becomes gradually more and more difficult to find within the country a profitable method of employing any new capital. There arises in consequence a competition between different capitals, the owner of one endeavouring to get possession of that employment which is occupied by another. But upon most occasions he can hope to justle that other out of this employment, by no other means but by dealing upon more reasonable terms. He must not only sell what he deals in somewhat cheaper, but in order to get it to sell, he must sometimes too buy it dearer. The demand for productive labour, by the increase of the funds which are destined for maintaining it, grows every day greater and greater. Labourers easily find employment, but the owners of capitals find it difficult to get labourers to employ. Their competition raises the wages of labour, and sinks the profits of stock. But when the profits which can be made by the use of a capital are in this manner diminished, as it were, at both ends,

同样,把资本借贷被别人并收取利息,实际上与出借人把一部分的年产物让渡与借用人没有差别。但作为对这种让与的回报,借用人必须在借用期间每年从较小部分的年生产物,向出借人转让,这就叫做支付利息;在借贷期满以后,又以在价值上与原来出借人转让给他的那部分年产物相等的数量,再让渡出借人,称作偿还本金。在转让这些较小部分和较大部分的情况中,作为纸币或铸币的货币虽然都作为转让契约,但与其所转让的东西完全不同。

_{货币用作本利息时,两者所起的作用完全不同。}

一旦从土地生产或由生产性劳动者制造出来,就被指定用作补偿资本使用的那一部分年产物;如果增加了,则所谓金钱上的利益关系也自然随之而增加。资本一般增加了,所有者无意亲自使用但希望从中取得一份收入的资本也必定增加。或者说,财货增加了,贷出用来生息的资财也必须逐渐增加。

_{随着整个财货数量的增加,贷出来收息的货财也很自然地随之增加。}

随着贷出生息的资财增加,使用这种资财所必须支付的价格即利息率必然下降。那种物品市场价格随着物品数量增加而降低的一般因果关系,固然是利息率降低的一个原因,但除了这个原因以外,我们还可以找出几个特殊的原因:第一,如果一个国家的资本增加,投资的利润就必定减少。要是在国内为新资本找到有利的投资方法,将逐渐困难起来。于是就发生了资本之间的竞争,资本所有者常互相争斗倾轧,努力把原投资人排挤出去。但要排挤原投资人,只有把自己的要求条件放宽一些。他不仅要贱卖,而且有时因为要出售,还不得不高价购进。第二,维持生产性劳动的基金增加了,对生产性劳动的需求也必定逐渐增加。因此,劳动者并不担心无人雇用,资本家反而担心无人可雇。资本家之间的竞争提高了劳动的工资水平,降低了资本的利润水平。

_{随着可借贷的财货数量的增加而下降。由于越难找到一个以获丰厚利润的使用资本方法,利润就下降,以水平。}

国民财富的性质与原理

the price which can be paid for the use of it, that is, the rate of interest, must necessarily be diminished with them.

<small>The notion that it was the discovery of the West Indies which lowered interest has been refuted by Hume.</small>   Mr. Locke, Mr. Law, and Mr. Montesquieu, as well as many other writers,① seem to have imagined that the increase of the quantity of gold and silver, in consequence of the discovery of the Spanish West Indies, was the real cause of the lowering of the rate of interest through the greater part of Europe. Those metals, they say, having become of less value themselves, the use of any particular portion of them necessarily became of less value too, and consequently the price which could be paid for it. This notion, which at first sight seems so plausible, has been so fully exposed by Mr. Hume,② that it is, perhaps, unnecessary to say any thing more about it. The following very short and plain argument, however, may serve to explain more distinctly the fallacy which seems to have misled those gentlemen.

<small>If £ 100 are now required to purchase what £ 50 would have purchased then, £ 10 must now be required to purchase what £ 5 would have purchased then.</small>   Before the discovery of the Spanish West Indies, ten per cent. seems to have been the common rate of interest through the greater part of Europe. It has since that time in different countries sunk to six, five, four, and three per cent. Let us suppose that in every particular country the value of silver has sunk precisely in the same proportion as the rate of interest; and that in those countries, for example, where interest has been reduced from ten to five per cent., the same quantity of silver can now purchase just half the quantity of goods which it could have purchased before. This supposition will not, I believe, be found any-where agreeable to the truth; but it is the most favourable to the opinion which we are going to examine; and even upon this supposition it is utterly impossible that the lowering of the value of silver could have the smallest tendency to lower the

---

① [Locke, *Some Considerations*, ed. of 1696, pp. 6, 10, 11, 81; Law, Money and Trade, 2nd ed., 1720, p. 17; Montesquieu, *Esprit des Lois*, liv. xxii., ch. vi. Locke and Law suppose that the rate rises and falls with the quantity of money, and Montesquieu specifically attributes the historical fall to the discovery of the American mines. Cantillon disapproves of the common and received idea that an increase of effective money diminishes the rate of interest. —*Essai*, pp. 282-285; see *Lectures*, pp. 219, 220.]

② [In his essay, 'Of Interest', in *Political Discourses*, 1752.]

第二篇 第四章

因为使用资本而造成的利润既然减少了,为使用资本而付给的代价即利息率,也要随之降低不可。

洛克、劳氏、孟德斯鸠以及还有许多其他的作家①都认为,因为西属西印度的发现而导致金银数量的增加,才是大部分欧洲利息率水平降低的真实原因。他们说,由于两种金属本身的价值降低,所以,它们特定部分的使用也只有较小的价值,因而使用它们时支付购买的价格也较小。这个观念乍看来似乎很有道理,但其实是错误的。这个错误已经被休谟②充分揭露,我们也许没有再进行阐述的必要。但下面非常简明的议论也许可以进一步说明迷惑这几位先生的谬见。

在西属西印度尚未发现以前,大部分欧洲的普通利息率大致为10%。从西属西印度发现开始,各国的普通利息率,也已经降为6%、5%、4%,甚至3%。假设某国银价降低的比例恰恰等于利息率降低的比例。例如,在利息率由10%降至5%的地方,现在等量的银所能购买的货物量,只等于从前的一半。这种假设真与事实符合吗?我相信,事实并不如此,但这种假设对于我现今要研究的那种学说却很有利。而且,就是根据这个假设,我们也不能完全就说,银的价值的降低有一点点降低利息率的趋势。因

> 由属西印度的发现导致利率水平降低的观点已经被休谟所驳倒。
> 有关西印度的发现而利率水平降低的观点已经被休谟驳倒。
> 如果现在100镑的价值等于过去的50镑价值的话,那么现在10镑的价值也就只等于过去的5镑的价值。

---

① 洛克1696年出版的《关于降低利率、提高货币价值后果的一些思考》的第6、10、11、81页;劳1720年再版的《货币与商业》第17页;孟德斯鸠:《法的精神》liv. xxii,第4章。洛克和劳认为利息率随着货币数量而升降;孟德斯鸠则把利息率的下降归因于美洲矿产的发现;肯提伦对有效货币的增加会降低利息率——这个一般和被大家已经接受的观点表示不同意。——《论文集》第282~285页;见《关于法律、警察、岁入及军备的演讲》,第219、220页。

② 在休谟1752年出版的《政治演讲录》里"论利息"一文。

<small>An increase in the quantity of silver could only diminish its value.</small> rate of interest. If a hundred pounds are in those countries now of no more value than fifty pounds were then, ten pounds must now be of no more value than five pounds were then. Whatever were the causes which lowered the value of the capital, the same must necessarily have lowered that of the interest, and exactly in the same proportion. The proportion between the value of the capital and that of the interest, must have remained the same, though the rate had never been altered. By altering the rate, on the contrary, the proportion between those two values is necessarily altered. If a hundred pounds now are worth no more than fifty were then, five pounds now can be worth no more than two pounds ten shillings were then. By reducing the rate of interest, therefore, from ten to five per cent. , we give for the use of a capital, which is supposed to be equal to one-half of its former value, an interest which is equal to one-fourth only of the value of the former interest.

<small>Nominal wages would be greater, but real wages the same; profits would be the same nominally and really.</small> Any increase in the quantity of silver, while that of the commodities circulated by means of it remained the same, could have no other effect than to diminish the value of that metal. The nominal value of all sorts of goods would be greater, but their real value would be precisely the same as before. They would be exchanged for a greater number of pieces of silver; but the quantity of labour which they could command, the number of people whom they could maintain and employ, would be precisely the same. The capital of the country would be the same, though a greater number of pieces might be requisite for conveying any equal portion of it from one hand to another. The deeds of assignment, like the conveyances of a verbose attorney, would be more cumbersome, but the thing assigned would be precisely the same as before, and could produce only the same effects. The funds for maintaining productive labour being the same, the demand for it would be the same. Its price or wages, therefore, though nominally greater, would really be the same. They would be paid in a greater number of pieces of silver; but they would purchase only the same quantity of goods. The profits of stock would be the same both nominally and really. The wages of labour are commonly computed by the quantity of silver which is paid to the labourer. When that is increased, therefore, his wages appear to be increased, though they may sometimes be no greater than before. But the profits of stock are not computed by the number of pieces of silver with which they are paid, but by the proportion which those pieces bear to the whole capital employed. Thus in a particular country five shillings a week are

为,假若现今 100 镑的价值仅等于过去 50 镑的价值,那现今 10 镑的价值也就只等于过去 5 镑的价值。无论降低资本价值的原因如何,这也必然会按相同比例降低利息的价值。资本价值与利息价值的比例必然不变,因为利息率并未改变。如果利息率真是发生改变,这两个价值之间的比例就非改变不可。如果现今 100 镑的价值,只等于过去 50 镑的价值,那么,现在 5 镑的价值,也只等于过去 2.5 镑的价值。所以,在资本价值减半的时候,把利息率由 10% 降至 5%,那对使用资本所支付的利息的价值,也就只等于昔时利息价值的 1/4 了。

> 白银数量增加仅减少它自己的价值。

在依靠白银流通的商品数量还没有增加时,白银数量增加只会降低白银的价值。这时的各种货品的名义价值都会增加,但他们的真实价值,却依然没有改变。它们可以换回较多的白银,但它们所能支配的劳动量与所能维持和雇用的劳动者人数,必定依然不变。转移等量资本由甲向乙所需要的白银数量可能增加,但资本却没有增加。那些转让契约与冗长的委托书一样累赘多余;但所转让的物品,却依然没有改变,而只能产生同样的效果。维持生产性劳动的基金依然如旧,对生产性劳动的需求自然也没有改变。所以,生产性劳动的价格或工资,名义上虽然是增大了,但实际上却是没有改变。按照所支付的白银数量计算,工资或劳动价格虽然是有所增加,但按照所能购买的货物量计算,工资却是依然如旧。资本利润,无论是从名义上还是从实际上来说,都没有变动。劳动的工资,因为常常按照所支付的白银数量计算,所以在所支付白银数量增加时,有时工资虽然与以前一样,表面上却似乎已经增加。资本的利润却不是这样。资本利润不按照所得白银数量的多少计算。在计算利润的时候,我们只计算

> 名义工资可能增加,但实际工资没有改变;无论是名义利润还是实际利润都没有变化。

said to be the common wages of labour, and ten per cent. the common profits of stock. But the whole capital of the country being the same as before, the competition between the different capitals of individuals into which it was divided would likewise be the same. They would all trade with the same advantages and disadvantages. The common proportion between capital and profit, therefore, would be the same, and consequently the common interest of money; what can commonly be given for the use of money being necessarily regulated by what can commonly be made by the use of it.

<small>An increase in the goods annually circulated would cause a fall of profits and consequently of interest.</small>　Any increase in the quantity of commodities annually circulated within the country, while that of the money which circulated them remained the same, would, on the contrary, produce many other important effects, besides that of raising the value of the money. The capital of the country, though it might nominally be the same, would really be augmented. It might continue to be expressed by the same quantity of money, but it would command a greater quantity of labour. The quantity of productive labour which it could maintain and employ would be increased, and consequently the demand for that labour. Its wages would naturally rise with the demand, and yet might appear to sink. They might be paid with a smaller quantity of money, but that smaller quantity might purchase a greater quantity of goods than a greater had done before. The profits of stock would be diminished both really and in appearance. The whole capital of the country being augmented, the competition between the different capitals of which it was composed, would naturally be augmented along with it. The owners of those particular capitals would be obliged to content themselves with a smaller proportion of the produce of that labour which their respective capitals employed. The interest of money, keeping pace always with the profits of stock, might, in this manner, be greatly diminished, though the value of money, or the quantity of goods which any particular sum could purchase, was greatly augmented.

　In some countries the interest of money has been prohibited by law. But as something can every-where be made by the use of money, something ought every-where to be paid for the use of it. This regula-

所得白银数量与所投入资本的比例。比如，我们说到工资，常常说这个国家的普通工资是每星期 5 先令；我们说到利润，常常说这个国家的普通利润是 10%。但国内所有的资本和以前一样没有改变，把全部资本划分为国内各个人的资本的竞争，也一定和以前一样。他们做交易时所享受的便利和从前一样，所遇到的困难也和从前一样。因此，资本对利润的普通比例依然不变，而货币的普通利息也没有改变。使用货币一般所能支付的利息，必须受使用货币一般能够取得的利润来支配。

在国内流通领域的货币数量不变的情况下，国内每年流通的商品量的增加，除了发生货币价值提高的结果以外，还会引起许多其他的重要结果。这时的一国资本名义上虽然没有改变，实际上却已经增加；它可能仍然继续由等量货币表示，但能够支配较大的劳动量。随着它所能维持和雇用的生产性劳动量的增加，劳动的需求也相应地随之增加。工资将伴随劳动需求的增加而提高；但从表面上看却可能似乎在下跌。这时劳动者所获得作为工资的货币量，可能比以前少，但现在这些较少的货币所能够购买的物品量，却比从前较多货币所能购买的物品数量还要多。但无论在实际上和名义上，资本的利润都会减少。随着国内所有的资本总量的增加，资本之间的竞争，当然会随之增加。资本家各自投资的结果，即使所获取的回报在各自资本所雇劳动的生产物品中所占比例比以前小，他们也只有自认时运不佳。货币的利息总是与资本的利润共增减，所以，货币的价值虽然大幅度增加，或者说，一定数量货币所能购买的物品量虽然大幅度增加，但货币的利息仍然可能大幅度减少。

有些国家的法律禁止货币的利息。但由于在任何地方使用

国内流通领域商品数量的增加将会引起利润以及利率的下降。

国民财富的性质与原理

The pr-ohibition of interest is wrong, and increases the evil of usury. tion, instead of preventing, has been found from experience to increase the evil of usury; the debtor being obliged to pay, not only for the use of the money, but for the risk which his creditor runs by accepting a compensation for that use. He is obliged, if one may say so, to insure his creditor from the penalties of usury.

Where a maximum rate is fixed, this should be somewhat above the market rate on good security, In countries where interest is permitted, the law, in order to prevent the extortion of usury, generally fixes the highest rate which can be taken without incurring a penalty. This rate ought always to be somewhat above the lowest market price, or the price which is commonly paid for the use of money by those who can give the most undoubted security. If this legal rate should be fixed below the lowest market rate, the effects of this fixation must be nearly the same as those of a total prohibition of interest. The creditor will not lend his money for less than the use of it is worth, and the debtor must pay him for the risk which he runs by accepting the full value of that use. If it is fixed precisely at the lowest market price, it ruins with honest people, who respect the laws of their country, the credit of all those who cannot give the very best security, and obliges them to have recourse to exorbitant usurers. In a country, such as Great Britain, where money is lent to government at three per cent. and to private people upon good security at four, and four and a half, the present legal rate, five per cent., is perhaps, as proper as any.

but not much above, or the greater part of loans would be to prodigals and prolectors. The legal rate, it is to be observed, though it ought to be somewhat above, ought not to be much above the lowest market rate. If the legal rate of interest in Great Britain, for example, was fixed so high as eight or ten per cent., the greater part of the money which was to be lent, would be lent to prodigals and projectors, who alone would be willing to give this high interest. Sober people, who will give for the use of money no more than a part of what they are likely to make by the use of it, would not venture into the competition. A great part of the capital of the country would thus be kept out of the hands which were most likely to make a profitable and advantageous use of it, and thrown into those which were most likely to waste and destroy it. Where the legal rate of interest, on the contrary, is fixed but a very

资本都会取得利润,所以在任何地方使用资本都应该把利息作为报酬进行支付。经验告诉我们,这种法律,不但禁止不了高利贷盘剥的罪恶,反会使盘剥程度加大;因为,债务人不但要支付使用货币的报酬,而且要对出借人冒险接受这种报酬支付一笔费用。或者说要给出借人保险,使他不会遭受对高利贷盘剥所处的刑罚。

<small>对货币收息禁行,并不会实际上禁止取利行为,只会增大遭受高利贷盘剥的程度。</small>

在那些允许放债取利的国家里,为了禁止高利贷盘剥,法律往往规定合法的最高利息率。这个最高利息率总应稍稍高于最低市场利息率,后者就是那些能够提供绝对可靠担保品的借款人借用货币时通常所支付的价格。这个法定利息率若低于最低市场利息率,其结果将无异于全面禁止放债取利的行为。如果取得的报酬少于货币使用的价值,则债权人便不肯借钱出去,所以债务人必须为债权人冒险接受货币使用全部价值而支付一笔费用。如果法定利息率恰恰等于最低市场利息率,则一般没有稳当担保品的人便不能从遵守国家法律的诚实人那里借到钱,而只好求助于高利贷者任其盘剥。现在英国,把货币贷给政府,年息为3%;贷给有质量优良担保品的私人,则年息为4%或4.5%,所以,像英国这样的国家,规定5%的法定利息率,也许再适当不过。

<small>规定的法定利息率应该微微高于有可靠担保品的市场利率,</small>

必须注意的是,法定利息率虽然应略高于最低市场利息率,但也不应高得太多。比如说,如果英国法定利息率规定为8%或10%,那么,就有大部分等待借出的货币会被浪费者和投机家借到手中,因为只有他们这一类人才愿意出这样高的利息。诚实人只能以使用货币所获取利润的一部分作为使用货币的报酬,所以,不敢和他们竞争。这样,一个国家的资本将有大部分离开诚实人,而转到浪费者手里,不用在有利的用途上,却用在浪费资

<small>如果不市利那大落者家手但场率大货到这手中。利,借危中;</small>

little above the lowest market rate, sober people are universally preferred, as borrowers, to prodigals and projectors. The person who lends money gets nearly as much interest from the former as he dares to take from the latter, and his money is much safer in the hands of the one set of people, than in those of the other. A great part of the capital of the country is thus thrown into the hands in which it is most likely to be employed with advantage.

<small>No law can reduce interest below the market rate.</small> No law can reduce the common rate of interest below the lowest ordinary market rate at the time when that law is made. Notwithstanding the edict of 1766, by which the French king attempted to reduce the rate of interest from five to four per cent. , money continued to be lent in France at five per cent. , the law being evaded in several different ways.

<small>The number of years' purchase commonly paid for land depends on the rate of interest.</small> The ordinary market price of land, it is to be observed, depends every-where upon the ordinary market rate of interest. ① The person who has a capital from which he wishes to derive a revenue, without taking the trouble to employ it himself, deliberates whether he should buy land with it, or lend it out at interest, The superior security of land, together with some other advantages which almost every-where attend upon this species of property, will generally dispose him to content himself with a smaller revenue from land, than what he might have by lending out his money at interest. These advantages are sufficient to compensate a certain difference of revenue; but they will compensate a certain difference only; and if the rent of land should fall short of the interest of money by a greater difference, nobody would buy land, which would soon reduce its ordinary price. On the contrary, if the advantages should much more than compensate the difference, every body would buy land, which again would soon raise its ordinary price. When interest was at ten per cent. , land was commonly sold for ten and twelve years purchase. As interest sunk to

---

① [This seems obvious, but it was distinctly denied by Locke, *Some Considerations*, pp. 83, 84.]

本和破坏资本的用途上。反之,在法定利息率仅略高于最低市场利息率的情况下,有钱并愿意出借的人都愿意借给诚实人,而不愿借给浪费者和投机家。因为借给诚实人所得的利息和借给浪费者所收取的利息几乎相同,而钱在诚实人手上要稳妥得多。这样,一个国家的大部分资本在诚实人手中,而在这些人手中的资本极有可能都使用得很好。

没有任何法律能把利息降低到当时最低普通市场利息率以下。在 1766 年,尽管法国国王企图颁布法令把利息率由 5% 降至 4%,但其结果是人民用种种方法逃避该项法律,民间借贷利息率仍为 5%。

没有任何法律可以把利率降低到市场利率以下。

应该指出的是,土地的普通市场价格取决于普通市场利息率。① 那些不愿亲自使用但想从资本中取得收入的人,对于究竟把资本用来购买土地好,还是把它借出收取利息好,通常总是要仔细斟酌的。土地财产是极其稳健可靠的,除此以外,大都还有其他几种利益。比较起来,把钱贷给别人收取利息,所得虽然会更多,但他通常却宁愿购买土地而获得较小收入。这些利益可以足够补偿收入上一定的差额,但也只能补偿收入上一定的差额。如果土地地租远远低于货币利息,那么谁也就不愿意购买土地,土地的普通价格必定因此而下跌。反之,如果这些利益在补偿这些差额以后还有许多剩余,那么谁都愿意购买土地,土地普通价格就会提高。在利息率为 10% 时,土地售价常常为年租的 10 倍或 12 倍。利息率降至 6%、5%、4% 时,土地售价就上升到年租的

土地年租金的数量大小取决于利息率的大小。

---

① 这似乎很明白,但在洛克所著的《关于降低利率、提高货币价值后果的一些思考》第 83 和 84 页很清楚地否认了这一点。

six, five, and four per cent., the price of land rose to twenty, five and twenty, and thirty years purchase. The market rate of interest is higher in France than in England; and the common price of land is lower. In England it commonly sells at thirty; in France at twenty years purchase.

20倍、25倍,甚至30倍。法国市场利息率高于英国;法国土地的普通价格低于英国。英国土地售价常常为年租的30倍;法国土地售价常为年租的20倍。

CHAPTER V

Of The Different Employment Of Capitals

The quantity of labour put in motion and the value added to the annual produce by capitals vary with their employment.

Though all capitals are destined for the maintenance of productive labour only, yet the quantity of that labour, which equal capitals are capable of putting into motion, varies extremely according to the diversity of their employment; as does likewise the value which that employment adds to the annual produce of the land and labour of the country.

There are four different ways of employing capital,

A capital may be employed in four different ways: either, first, in procuring the rude produce annually required for the use and consumption of the society; or, secondly, in manufacturing and preparing that rude produce for immediate use and consumption; or, thirdly, in transporting either the rude or manufactured produce from the places where they abound to those where they are wanted; or, lastly, in dividing particular portions of either into such small parcels as suit the occasional demands of those who want them. In the first way are employed the capitals of all those who undertake the improvement or cultivation of lands, mines, or fisheries; in the second, those of all master manufacturers; in the third, those of all wholesale merchants; and in the fourth, those of all retailers. It is difficult to conceive that *all of which are necessary:* a capital should be employed in any way which may not be classed under some one or other of those four.

Each of those four methods of employing a capital is essentially *(1) procuring rude produce,* necessary either to the existence or extension of the other three, or to the general conveniency of the society.

— 786 —

第五章 论资本的各种用途

虽然一切资本都被指定用于维持生产性劳动,但等量资本所能够推动的生产性劳动量会随用途的不同而极不相同,从而对一国土地和劳动的年产物所能增加的价值也极不相同。

> 资本所推动的劳动数量和年产出的价值会由于资本用途的不同而不同。

资本有四种不同用途。第一,用来获取社会上每年必须使用和消费的原生产物;第二,用以制造原生产物,使这些物品适合于眼前的使用和消费;第三,用来运输原生产物或制造品,从多余的地方运往缺乏的地方;第四,把一定部分的原生产物或制造品分成较小的部分,使他们适合于需要者的临时需要。第一种用法是农场主、矿业家和渔业家的用法;第二种用法是制造者的用法;第三种用法是批发商人的用法;第四种用法是零售商人的用法。我以为,这四种用法已经包括了一切投资的方法。

> 有四种不同的资本用途。

这四种投资方法,有相互密切关系,少了一种,其他不能独立存在;即使能够独立生存下来,也不能够发展。从为全社会谋福利的角度来看,也是缺一不可的。

> 他们都是社会所必需的:

假设没有资本用来提供相当丰富的原生产物,制造业和商业恐怕都不能存在。原生产物有一部分往往需要加工制造以后,才适于使用或消费。

> 一是获取原生产物,

假设没有资本投在制造业中来对它进行加工,那么这些原生

国民财富的性质与原理

(2) manufacturing. Unless a capital was employed in furnishing rude produce to a certain degree of abundance, neither manufactures nor trade of any kind could exist.

Unless a capital was employed in manufacturing that part of the rude produce which requires a good deal of preparation before it can be fit for use and consumption, it either would never be produced, because there could be no demand for it; or if it was produced spontaneously, it would be of no value in exchange, and could add nothing to the wealth of the society.

(3) transportation. Unless a capital was employed in transporting, either the rude or manufactured produce, from the places where it abounds to those where it is wanted, no more of either could be produced than was necessary for the consumption of the neighbourhood. The capital of the merchant exchanges the surplus produce of one place for that of another, and thus encourages the industry and increases the enjoyments of both.

and (4) distribution. Unless a capital was employed in breaking and dividing certain portions either of the rude or manufactured produce, into such small parcels as suit the occasional demands of those who want them, every man would be obliged to purchase a greater quantity of the goods he wanted, than his immediate occasions required. If there was no such trade as a butcher, for example, every man would be obliged to purchase a whole ox or a whole sheep at a time. This would generally be inconvenient to the rich, and much more so to the poor. If a poor workman was obliged to purchase a month's or six months provisions at a time, a great part of the stock which he employs as a capital in the instruments of his trade, or in the furniture of his shop, and which yields him a revenue, he would be forced to place in that part of his stock which is reserved for immediate consumption, and which yields him no revenue. Nothing can be more convenient for such a person than to be able to purchase his subsistence from day to day, or even from hour to hour, as he wants it. He is thereby enabled to employ almost his whole stock as a capital. He is thus enabled to furnish work to a greater value, and the profit, which he makes by it in this way, much more than compensates the additional price which the profit of the retailer imposes upon the goods. The prejudices of some political writers against shopkeepers and tradesmen, are altogether without foundation. So far is it from being necessary, either to tax them, or to restrict their numbers, that they can never be multiplied so as to hurt the publick, though they may so as to hurt one another. The quantity of grocery goods, for example, which can be sold in a particular town, is limited by the demand of that town and its neighbourhood. The capital, therefore, which can be employed in the grocery trade cannot exceed what is sufficient to purchase that quantity.

产物将永远不会被生产出来,因为没有对它的需求;或如果它是天然生长的,它就没有交换价值,不能增加社会财富。

原生产物和制造品丰富的地方,必须把它从剩余的地方运往缺乏的地方;假设没有资本投在运输业中,这种运输便不可能。于是它们的生产量便不能超过本地消费所需要的数量。批发商人的资本使这个地方的剩余生产物交换其他地方的剩余生产物,这样既可以促进产业发展,又可以增加这两个地方的享用。

假设没有资本投在零售商业中,没有把大批原生产物和制造品分成较小的部分,使他们适应需要者的临时需要,那么,一切人对于所需的货品都得大批买进来,这样购进的物品会超过目前的需要数量。假设社会上没有屠户,我们大家都必须一次购买一头整牛或一只全羊不可。这对富人也一定是不方便的,对贫民将更为不便。贫穷劳动者如果要勉强一次购买一个月或半年的粮食,那么他的资本一定有一大部分不得不改作留给目前消费的财货,一定有一部分本来能提供收入的财货,不得不改作不能提供收入的财货。职业上的工具或店铺内的家具,也要减少不可。对这种人来说,最方便的办法是在他需要生活品的时候,能够逐日、逐时地购买。这样,他可以把几乎全部财货用作资本。于是他所能提供的工作的价值扩大了,而他由此所获得的利润,将足够补偿零售商的利润对货物价格所增加的数目而且还有剩余。有些政论家对商店老板的成见是完全没有根据的。小商贩众多,虽然他们相互之间也许有妨害,但对整个社会毫无害处。所以,不需要对他们课税或限制他们的人数。例如,某城市及其邻近地带对于杂货的需求限制着该市所能够售出的杂货量,因此可以投资在杂货商业上的资本,绝不可能超过足以购买这些杂货数量所必须的数

If this capital is divided between two different grocers, their competition will tend to make both of them sell cheaper, than if it were in the hands of one only; and if it were divided among twenty, their competition would be just so much the greater, and the chance of their combining together, in order to raise the price, just so much the less. Their competition might perhaps ruin some of themselves; but to take care of this is the business of the parties concerned, and it may safely be trusted to their discretion. It can never hurt either the consumer, or the producer; on the contrary, it must tend to make the retailers both sell cheaper and buy dearer, than if the whole trade was monopolized by one or two persons. Some of them, perhaps, may sometimes decoy a weak customer to buy what he has no occasion for. This evil, however, is of too little importance to deserve the publick attention, nor would it necessarily be prevented by restricting their numbers. It is not the multitude of ale-houses, to give the most suspicious example, that occasions a general disposition to drunkenness among the common people; but that disposition arising from other causes necessarily gives employment to a multitude of ale-houses.

<small>The employers of such capitals are productive labourers:</small> The persons whose capitals are employed in any of those four ways are themselves productive labourers. Their labour, when properly directed, fixes and realizes itself in the subject or vendible commodity upon which it is bestowed, and generally adds to its price the value at least of their own maintenance and consumption. The profits of the farmer, of the manufacturer, of the merchant, and retailer, are all drawn from the price of the goods which the two first produce, and the two last buy and sell. Equal capitals, however, employed in each of those four different ways, will immediately put into motion very different quantities of productive labour, and augment too in very different proportions the value of the annual produce of the land and labour of the society to which they belong.

<small>the capital of the retailer employs only himself;</small> The capital of the retailer replaces, together with its profits, that of the merchant of whom he purchases goods, and thereby enables him to continue his business. The retailer himself is the only produc-

额。这种有限的资本,如果分给两个杂货商人经营,这两人之间的竞争,会使双方都把售价降低得比一个人独自经营的情况下便宜。如果分为20个杂货商人经营,他们之间的竞争会更激烈,而他们结合起来抬高价格的可能性会变得更小。他们之间的竞争,也许会导致他们中的一些人破产,但我们不必过问这种事情,当事人应该自己小心。他们的竞争既不会对消费者不利,也不会有损于生产者。比其市场由一个人或两个人独占经营,那只能使零售商人以更高的价格购进而以较低的价格卖出。零售商人多了,其中也许有坏分子,诱骗软弱顾客购买自己并不需要的货品。不过,这种小弊端不值得国家去关注,再者说,国家通过限制零售商的方式也不能够防止这种事情的发生。举一个很明白的例子,如不是因为市场上有许多酒店,我们社会上才有饮酒的风尚;而是社会上由于其他种种原因而产生了喜好饮酒的风尚,才使市场上有许多酒店。

把资本投在这四种用途上的人,都是生产性劳动者,他们的劳动,如果使用得当,就可固定而且实现在劳动对象或可出售的物品身上;至少也可把维持他们自身和自身消费的价值,添加在劳动对象或可卖出物品的价格上。农场主、制造者、批发商人和零售商人的利润,都是来自于前两者所生产以及后两者所卖出货品的价格。但是,各自投在这四种用途的资本即使相等,但由于用途不同,等量资本所直接推动的生产性劳动量却也不相同,从而对于所属社会土地和劳动的年产物所增加的价值的比例,也不相同。

投资在这四种用途上的资本使用者都是生产性劳动者:

向批发商人购买货物的零售商人所使用的资本,补偿并提供批发商人的资本和利润,使其营业得以继续。零售商的资本只是

零售商只雇佣他自己;

tive labourer whom it immediately employs. In his profits, consists the whole value which its employment adds to the annual produce of the land and labour of the society.

the capital of the merchant employs sailors and carriers
The capital of the wholesale merchant replaces, together with their profits, the capitals of the farmers and manufacturers of whom he purchases the rude and manufactured produce which he deals in, and thereby enables them to continue their respective trades. It is by this service chiefly that he contributes indirectly to support the productive labour of the society, and to increase the value of its annual produce. His capital employs too the sailors and carriers who transport his goods from one place to another, and it augments the price of those goods by the value, not only of his profits, but of their wages. This is all the productive labour which it immediately puts into motion, and all the value which it immediately adds to the annual produce. Its operation in both these respects is a good deal superior to that of the capital of the retailer.

the capital of the manufacturer employs his workmen;
Part of the capital of the master manufacturer is employed as a fixed capital in the instruments of his trade, and replaces, together with its profits, that of some other artificer of whom he purchases them. Part of his circulating capital is employed in purchasing materials, and replaces, with their profits, the capitals of the farmers and miners of whom he purchases them. But a great part of it is always, either annually, or in a much shorter period, distributed among the different workmen whom he employs. It augments the value of those materials by their wages, and by their masters profits upon the whole stock of wages, materials, and instruments of trade employed in the business. It puts immediately into motion, therefore, a much greater quantity of productive labour, and adds a much greater value to the annual produce of the land and labour of the society, than an equal capital in the hands of any wholesale merchant.

No equal capital puts into motion a greater quantity of productive labour than that of the farmer. Not only his labouring servants, but his labouring cattle, are productive labourers. In agriculture too nature labours along with man; and though her labour costs no expence, its produce has its value, as well as that of the most expensive work-

直接雇用了他自己,他自己就是受雇佣的唯一的生产性劳动者。这种资本的使用对社会的土地和劳动的年产物所增加的价值,仅仅是他自己的利润而已。

向农场主购买原生产物、向制造者购买制造品的批发商人的资本,补偿并提供农业家和制造者的资本和利润,使其营业得以继续。这就是批发商间接维持社会上生产性劳动和增加社会年产物价值的主要方法。他的资本也雇用了运输货物的水手脚夫。所以它对于这种货物的价格所增加的价值不仅等于批发商自己利润的价值,而且还包括向水手脚夫支付工资的价值。这就是它所直接雇用的生产性劳动和它所直接增加年产物的价值。但批发商人的资本在这两个方面的作用要比零售商人的资本要大得多。

<small>商人资本雇佣水手和脚夫;</small>

制造者的资本,有一部分用作固定资本,投在他的生意所需要的工具上,补偿销售这些工具的其他制造者的资本并给他们提供利润;其余就是流动资本。在流动资本中,有一部分是用来购买原材料,这一部分用来补偿生产这些材料的农场主和矿商的资本并给他们提供利润。但其中大部分资本,是一年一次地或在比一年短得多的时间内分配给他所雇用的工人的。所以,他的资本对他所加工的材料所增加的价值,包括雇工的工资与雇主投资支付工资和购买材料工具而应得的利润。所以,与批发商人的等量资本相比较,他的资本所直接推动的生产性劳动量要多得多;对于社会的土地和劳动的年产物所增加的价值,也要多出许多。

<small>制造者资本雇佣工人;</small>

农场主资本所能够推动的生产性劳动量最大。他的工人是生产性劳动者,他的牲畜也是生产性劳动者。在农业上,自然也和人一起劳动;自然的劳动,虽然不用花费任何代价,但它的生产

| 国民财富的性质与原理

the capital of the farm er employs his servants and his cattle, and adds a much greater value to the annual produce than other capital.

men. The most important operations of agriculture seem intended, not so much to increase, though they do that too, as to direct the fertility of nature towards the production of the plants most profitable to man. A field overgrown with briars and brambles may frequently produce as great a quantity of vegetables as the best cultivated vineyard or corn field. Planting and tillage frequently regulate more than they animate the active fertility of nature; and after all their labour, a great part of the work always remains to be done by her. The labourers and labouring cattle, therefore, employed in agriculture, not only occasion, like the workmen in manufactures, the reproduction of a value equal to their own consumption, or to the capital which employs them, together with its owners profits; but of a much greater value. Over and above the capital of the farmer and all its profits, they regularly occasion the reproduction of the rent of the landlord. This rent may be considered as the produce of those powers of nature, the use of which the landlord lends to the farmer. It is greater or smaller according to the supposed extent of those powers, or in other words, according to the supposed natural or improved fertility of the land. It is the work of nature which remains after deducting or compensating every thing which can be regarded as the work of man. It is seldom less than a fourth, and frequently more than a third of the whole produce. No. equal quantity of productive labour employed in manufactures can ever occasion so great a reproduction. In them nature does nothing; man does all; and the reproduction must always be in proportion to the strength of the agents that occasion it. The capital employed in agriculture, therefore, not only puts into motion a greater quantity of productive labour than any equal capital employed in manufactures, but in proportion too to the quantity of productive labour which it employs, it adds a much greater value to the annual produce of the land

Capitals employed in agriculture and retail trade must reside within the country;

and labour of the country, to the real wealth and revenue of its inhabitants. Of all the ways in which a capital can be employed, it is by far the most advantageous to the society.

The capitals employed in the agriculture and in the retail trade of any society, must always reside within that society. Their employment is confined almost to a precise spot, to the farm, and to the shop of the retailer. They must generally too, though there are some excep-

第二篇　第五章

物却和最昂贵的工人生产物一样,也有它的价值。农业的最重要的任务,与其说是增加自然的产出能力,不如说是指引自然的产出能力,使生产最有利于人类的植物,虽然它也增加自然的产出能力。长满野草荆棘的田地可能生产的植物,常常不比耕种最好的葡萄园或谷田所能生产的少。耕耘与其说是增加自然的产出能力,不如说是支配自然的产出能力。除人工以外,尚有大部分工作必须依赖自然力不可。所以,农业上雇用的工人与牲畜,不仅与制造业工人一样再生产他们消费掉的价值(或者说,再生产雇用他们的资本)和资本家的利润,而且还生产更大的价值。他们除了再生产农业家的资本和利润以外,通常还要再生产地主的地租。这种地租,可以看作是地主借给农业家使用的自然力的产物。地租的大小取决于想象上的自然力的大小,换言之,取决于想象上的土地的自然产出力或土地的改进产出力的大小。扣减或补偿一切人的劳动之后,所剩余的便是自然的劳动成果。它在全部生产物中很少占 1/4 以下,通常占 1/3 以上。用在制造业上的任何等量的生产性劳动,都不能产生这样大的再生产劳动。在制造业上,自然没做什么,人做了一切;再生产的大小总是和导致再生产因素的力量大小成比例。所以,和投在制造业上的等量资本相比较,投在农业上的资本不仅推动较大的生产性劳动量,而且按照它所雇用的生产性劳动的数量来说,它对一国土地和劳动的年产物所增加的价值以及对国内居民的真实财富与收入所增加的价值,都要大得多。在各种资本用途中,在农业上投资最有利于社会。

农业雇用的工人和牲畜,所带来年产物价值其资本和利润比两资本多多。

投在农业上和零售业上的资本总是留在本社会内。它们的使用有一定地点,在农业上是农场;在零售业上是商店。而且,它

农业上和零售业上的资本必须留在本国内;

— 795 —

tions to this, belong to resident members of the society.

<small>the capital of the merchant may reside anywhere;</small> The capital of a wholesale merchant, on the contrary, seems to have no fixed or necessary residence anywhere, but may wander about from place to place, according as it can either buy cheap or sell dear.

<small>the capital of the manufacturer must be where the manufacture is, but that is not necessarily determined.</small> The capital of the manufacturer must no doubt reside where the manufacture is carried on; but where this shall be is not always necessarily determined. It may frequently be at a great distance both from the place where the materials grow, and from that where the complete manufacture is consumed. Lyons is very distant both from the places which afford the materials of its manufactures, and from those which consume them. The people of fashion in Sicily are cloathed in silks made in other countries, from the materials which their own produces. Part of the wool of Spain is manufactured in Great Britain, and some part of that cloth is afterwards sent back to Spain.

<small>Whether the merchant who exports belongs to the country or not makes little difference.</small> Whether the merchant whose capital exports the surplus produce of any society be a native or a foreigner, is of very little importance. If he is a foreigner, the number of their productive labourers is necessarily less than if he had been a native by one man only; and the value of their annual produce, by the profits of that one man. The sailors or carriers whom he employs may still belong indifferently either to his country, or to their country, or to some third country, in the same manner as if he had been a native. The capital of a foreigner gives a value to their surplus produce equally with that of a native, by exchanging it for something for which there is a demand at home. It as effectually replaces the capital of the person who produces that surplus, and as effectually enables him to continue his business; the service by which the capital of a wholesale merchant chiefly contributes to support the productive labour, and to augment the value of the annual produce of the society to which he belongs.

It is of more consequence that the capital of the manufacturer should reside within the country. It necessarily puts into motion a greater quantity of productive labour, and adds a greater value to the

们的所有者大部分都是本社会内的居民。当然,有时也有例外。

批发商人的资本却似乎不固定或停留在什么地方,而且也没有必要固定或停留在什么地方。因为要低价买进高价卖出,所以他们的资本才往往周游遍布各个地方。

> 批发商人资本可以停留在任何地方；

制造者的资本当然要停留在生产制造的场所。但具体在什么地方制造,却似乎没有确定的必要。有时制造业的场所不仅距离材料出产地很远,而且离制成品销售地也很远。里昂制造业的材料从很远的地方运来,那里的产成品也要运到远处才有人消费。西西里时尚人士的衣料是由其他国家制造的丝绸；丝绸的材料却又是西西里的产物。有一部分西班牙的羊毛在英国加工制造,但英国织成的毛织产品却有一部分后来又送还西班牙出售。

> 制造者的资本必须留在生产的所,但在地方什么却没有确定的必要。

投资于国内运输剩余生产物业务的人,无论是我们本国人或是外国人,都无关紧要。如果是外国人,我国受雇的生产性劳动者人数与从事该项业务的本国人相比,肯定比较少,但仅仅只少一个；我国的年产物价值肯定也比较少,但也仅仅只少这一个人的利润数量。至于所雇用的水手脚夫是不是本国人,那与他是否是本国人无关,他是本国人,也可以雇用外国的水手脚夫。运输人虽然在国籍上有差别,但投入资本以出口国内剩余生产物来交换国内所需要的物品,无论是外国人或是本国人的资本,对这些剩余生产物所给予的价值总是一样的。批发商人是本国人也好,不是本国人也好,他的资本同样有效地使生产这些剩余生产物的人的资本得以偿还,同样还有效地使生产这些剩余生产物的人的营业得以继续经营下去。这就是批发商人资本对维持本国生产性劳动和对增加本国年产物价值所提供的主要作用。

> 投资于国内运输的人是不是本国人则无关紧要。

更为重要的是,制造者的资本应该留在国内。因为有这种资

The capital of the manufacturer will put into motion more native labour if it resides within the country, but may be useful even if outside it.	annual produce of the land and labour of the society. It may, however, be very useful to the country, though it should not reside within it. The capitals of the British manufacturers who work up the flax and hemp annually imported from the coasts of the Baltic, are surely very useful to the countries which produce them. Those materials are a part of the surplus produce of those countries which, unless it was annually exchanged for something which is in demand there, would be of no value, and would soon cease to be produced. The merchants who export it, replace the capitals of the people who produce it, and thereby encourage them to continue the production; and the British manufacturers replace the capitals of those merchants.
Particular countries often have not enough capital for cultivation, manufactures, and transportation.	A particular country, in the same manner as a particular person, may frequently not have capital sufficient both to improve and cultivate all its lands, to manufacture and prepare their whole rude produce for immediate use and consumption, and to transport the surplus part either of the rude or manufactured produce to those distant markets where it can be exchanged for something for which there is a demand at home. The inhabitants of many different parts of Great Britain have not capital sufficient to improve and cultivate all their lands. The wool of the southern counties of Scotland is, a great part of it, after a long land carriage through very bad roads, manufactured in Yorkshire, for want of a capital to manufacture it at home. There are many little manufacturing towns in Great Britain, of which the inhabitants have not capital sufficient to transport the produce of their own industry to those distant markets where there is demand and consumption for it. If there are any merchants among them, they are properly only the agents of wealthier merchants who reside in some of the greater commercial cities.
In such cases the larger the proportion employed in agriculture, the larger will be the annual produce.	When the capital of any country is not sufficient for all those three purposes, in proportion as a greater share of it is employed in agriculture, the greater will be the quantity of productive labour which it puts into motion within the country; as will likewise be the value which its employment adds to the annual produce of the land and labour of the society. After agriculture, the capital employed in manufactures puts into motion the greatest quantity of productive labour, and adds the greatest value to the annual produce. That which is employed in the trade of exportation, has the least effect of any of the three.

第二篇 第五章

本留在国内，本国所能推动的生产性劳动数量肯定比较大，本国土地和劳动的年产物所能够增加的价值也肯定比较大。但不在本国境内使用的制造者资本也对本国很有效用。比如，英国亚麻制造者年年对从波罗的海沿岸各地进口的亚麻和大麻进行加工所投入的资本，虽非产麻国所有，但很明显对产麻国也有利。这些亚麻只是产麻国家的一部分剩余生产物，如果年年不把他们输往国外，用来交换本地所需要的各种物品，那么他们也就没有什么价值可言，其生产将立即停止下来。从事出口亚麻业务的商人可偿还亚麻生产人的资本，从而鼓励他们继续生产；英国制造者又可以偿还这种商人的资本，使他们继续从事运输业务。

> 如果制造业资本留在国内，那么它所能够推动的国内劳动更多，但即使在国外，也是有用的。

与个人一样，一个国家往往没有足够资本，既对一切土地进行改良和耕种，又对全部原生产物进行加工，使它们适合于直接的消费和使用，又把剩余的原生产物及制造品运往远方的市场换取国内需要的物品。不列颠许多地方的居民，没有足够资本来改良和耕种他们所有的全部土地。苏格兰南部的羊毛的大部分就因为当地缺乏资本，不得不经过极不平坦的道路，用车远运到约克郡去加工。英国有许多小工业城市，其人民没有足够资本把产品运到需要它们的远方的市场上去销售。他们当中，即使有个把商人，也只能说是大富商的经理人。这种大富商往往住在比较大的商业城市里。

> 没有一个国家同时能够拥有耕种、制造业和运输业所需要的充足资本。

一国资本要是不能够满足同时经营这三种产业，那么，我们就可以说，投在农业上的资本部分越多，它所推动的国内生产性劳动的数量也就越大；同时，对社会土地和劳动的年产物所增加的价值也越大。除了农业以外，就数制造业在这两个方面的作用最大。在三种产业之中，投在出口贸易上的资本所产生效果是最

> 在这种情况下，投在农业上本领域的资本越多，那么年产物就会更多。

— 799 —

| 国民财富的性质与原理

The quickest way to make the capital sufficient for all these purposes is to begin with the most profitable.

  The country, indeed, which has not capital sufficient for all those three purposes, has not arrived at that degree of opulence for which it seems naturally destined. To attempt, however, prematurely and with an insufficient capital, to do all the three, is certainly not the shortest way for a society, no more than it would be for an individual, to acquire a sufficient one. The capital of all the individuals of a nation, has its limits in the same manner as that of a single individual, and is capable of executing only certain purposes. The capital of all the individuals of a nation is increased in the same manner as that of a single individual, by their continually accumulating and adding to it whatever they save out of their revenue. It is likely to increase the fastest, therefore, when it is employed in the way that affords the greatest revenue to all the inhabitants of the country, as they will thus be enabled to make the greatest savings. But the revenue of all the inhabitants of the country is necessarily in proportion to the value of the annual produce of their land and labour.

That they have done so is the principal cause of the progress of the American colonies.

  It has been the principal cause of the rapid progress of our American colonies towards wealth and greatness, that almost their whole capitals have hitherto been employed in agriculture. They have no manufactures, those houshold and coarser manufactures excepted which necessarily accompany the progress of agriculture, and which are the work of the women and children in every private family. The greater part both of the exportation and coasting trade of America, is carried on by the capitals of merchants who reside in Great Britain. Even the stores and warehouses from which goods are retailed in some provinces, particularly in Virginia and Maryland, belong many of them to merchants who reside in the mother country, and afford one of the few instances of the retail trade of a society being carried on by the capitals of those who are not resident members of it. Were the Americans, either by combination or by any other sort of violence, to stop the importation of European manufactures, and, by thus giving a monopoly to such of their own countrymen as could manufacture the like goods, divert any considerable part of their capital into this employment, they would retard instead of accelerating the further increase in the value of their annual produce, and would obstruct instead of promoting the progress of their country towards real wealth and greatness. This would be still more the case, were they to attempt, in the same manner, to monopolize to themselves their whole exportation trade.

— 800 —

小的。

在所有资本还不能够满足经营这三种产业的国家里,就其富裕的程度来说,实际上还没有达到自然所允许达到的富裕水平。无论是个人或社会,企图用不充足的资本在时机未成熟的时候经营这三种产业,都不是取得充足资本的最佳捷径。正像一个人的资本有一定的限度一样,国内全体人民的资本也有一定的限度,只能够用于某几个方面。要增加个人资本,必须从收入内节省而不断积累;要增加国民资本,也必须从收入内节省而不断积累。因此,资本的用途如果能够给国内全体居民提供最大的收入,从而使全体居民都能够有最大的积蓄,则国民资本大概就会极其迅速地增加起来。但国内全体居民收入的大小,必定与国民土地和劳动的年产物的大小成比例。

英属美洲殖民地几乎把所有的资本都投在农业上。在那里也就主要是由于这个原因,才很迅速地日趋富强起来。在那里,除了家庭制造业和粗糙制造业(这种制造业,一定会随着农业的进步而产生,每个家庭的妇女儿童都能经营这种工作),就没有制造业。至于出口业和航运业,则大部分由住在英国的商人投资经营。甚至有些省份,特别是弗吉里亚和马里兰,甚至经营零售生意的店铺和货栈也为居住在母国的商人所有。零售业不由本地商人资本经营的事例不多,这就是其中之一。假使美洲人联合起来或使用其他过激的手段,阻止欧洲制造品进口,使能制造同种物品的本地人独占享有市场的机会,而使本地大部分资本转投到制造业上来,结果将不仅不能进一步增加他们年产物的价值,恐怕还会有不利于这种结果的情况发生;不但不能使其国家逐渐富强起来,恐怕还会带来阻碍作用。同样,如果他们要设法垄断整

> 能够以最快的速度满足所有的目的就能来收带最大的资途用始着
> 方法是从最大的资本开始手。

> 英属美洲殖民地把资本都投在农业上的做法是他们取得进步的主要原因。

国民财富的性质与原理

<small>Great countries have scarcely ever acquired sufficient capital for all those purposes.</small>   The course of human prosperity, indeed, seems scarce ever to have been of so long continuance as to enable any great country to acquire capital sufficient for all those three purposes; unless, perhaps, we give credit to the wonderful accounts of the wealth and cultivation of China, of those of antient Egypt, and of the antient state of Indostan. Even those three countries, the wealthiest, according to all accounts, that ever were in the world, are chiefly renowned for their superiority in agriculture and manufactures. They do not appear to have been eminent for foreign trade. The antient Egyptians had a superstitious antipathy to the sea; a superstition nearly of the same kind prevails among the Indians; and the Chinese have never excelled in foreign commerce. The greater part of the surplus produce of all those three countries seems to have been always exported by foreigners, who gave in exchange for it something else for which they found a demand there, frequently gold and silver.

<small>Different kinds of wholesale trade employ different quantities of productive labour and add different amounts to the annual produce.</small>   It is thus that the same capital will in any country put into motion a greater or smaller quantity of productive labour, and add a greater or smaller value to the annual produce of its land and labour, according to the different proportions in which it is employed in agriculture, manufactures, and wholesale trade. The difference too is very great, according to the different sorts of wholesale trade in which any part of it is employed.

<small>There are three different kinds of trade: home, foreign and carrying.</small>   All wholesale trade, all buying in order to sell again by wholesale, may be reduced to three different sorts. The home trade, the foreign trade of consumption, and the carrying trade. The home trade is employed in purchasing in one part of the same country, and selling in another, the produce of the industry of that country. It comprehends both the inland and the coasting trade. The foreign trade of consumption is employed in purchasing foreign goods for home consumption. The carrying trade is employed in transacting the commerce of foreign countries, or in carrying the surplus produce of one to another.

<small>Capital employed in buying in one part of the country to sell in another replaces two domestic capitals.</small>   The capital which is employed in purchasing in one part of the country in order to sell in another the produce of the industry of that country, generally replaces by every such operation two distinct capitals that had both been employed in the agriculture or manufactures of that country, and thereby enables them to continue that employment. When it sends out from the residence of the merchant a certain value of commodities, it generally brings back in return at least an equal value of other commodities. When both are the produce of domestick industry, it necessarily replaces by every such operation two distinct

个运输业,结果也许情况会更加糟糕。

实际上人类繁荣的过程似乎从来没有延续这么长的时间,使得任何一个大国可以获得足够的资本来经营这三种产业,除非我们对有关中国、古埃及、古印度的富裕和农业耕种情况的那些奇异记载表示认可。然而,依据这些记载而被认为是世界上最富裕的这三个国家,也仅仅主要擅长农业和制造业。他们的国外贸易并不繁荣。古埃及人对于海洋有一种迷信的敬畏心理;印度人也常有这种迷信;至于中国的对外通商向来就不发达。这三个国家的剩余生产物似乎大部分都是由外国人运到外国去,换回它们所需要的其他东西常常是金银。

> 有拥有足够资本经营三种产业的大国很少有足够的资本来同时经营三种产业的目标。

这样,同一资本在国内所能够推动的劳动量有多有少,所增加的土地和劳动的年产物价值也有大有小,要看它投在农业、工业和批发商业上的比例不同而不同。而且,同是批发商业,投资结果也将因所经营批发商业的种类不同而很不相同。

> 不同的贸易方式雇佣同样性质和数量的生产劳动,提供同样的年产物。

一切批发贸易或一切大批买进以便大批再卖出去的贸易,可分为三类,即国内贸易、消费品的国外贸易和贩运贸易。国内贸易是从国内某个地方买国产货物进来,再在国内另一个地方把它卖出去,包括内陆贸易和沿海贸易。消费品的国外贸易是购买外国货物供给本国消费。贩运贸易是在各个外国之间从事的贸易,即把甲国的剩余产物运往乙国。

> 有三种贸易方式,即国内贸易、国外贸易和贩运贸易。

投资在国内贸易上,购买国内甲地产物运往乙地销售,往返一次,一般可以偿还投在本国农业或制造业上的两个不同资本,使本国的农业和制造业能够持续经营下去。运用这些资本从商人店里把一定价值的商品运出去,结果至少可以换回一个等量价值的其他商品。当交换的双方全是本国产业的产物时,当然国内

> 在国内一个地方购买国内另一个地方销售,一个往返可以偿还两个国内资本。

— 803 —

capitals, which had both been employed in supporting productive labour, and thereby enables them to continue that support. The capital which sends Scotch manufactures to London, and brings back English corn and manufactures to Edinburgh, necessarily replaces, by every such operation, two British capitals which had both been employed in the agriculture or manufactures of Great Britain.

<small>Capital employed in importation replaces one domestic and one foreign capital.</small> The capital employed in purchasing foreign goods for home-consumption, when this purchase is made with the produce of domestick industry, replaces too, by every such operation, two distinct capitals; but one of them only is employed in supporting domestick industry. The capital which sends British goods to Portugal, and brings back Portuguese goods to Great Britain, replaces by every such operation only one British capital. The other is a Portuguese one. Though the returns, therefore, of the foreign trade of consumption should be as quick as those of the home-trade, the capital employed in it will give but one-half the encouragement to the industry or productive labour of the country.

<small>Its returns are not so quick as those of home trade.</small> But the returns of the foreign trade of consumption are very seldom so quick as those of the home-trade. The returns of the home-trade generally come in before the end of the year, and sometimes three or four times in the year. The returns of the foreign trade of consumption seldom come in before the end of the year, and sometimes not till after two or three years. A capital, therefore, employed in the home-trade will sometimes make twelve operations, or be sent out and returned twelve times, before a capital employed in the foreign trade of consumption has made one. If the capitals are equal, therefore, the one will give four and twenty times more encouragement and support to the industry of the country than the other. ①

The foreign goods for home-consumption may sometimes be purchased, not with the produce of domestick industry, but with some

---

① [If this doctrine as to the advantage of quick returns had been applied earlier in the chapter, it would have made havoc of the argument as to the superiority of agriculture.]

贸易可以偿还本国两个用来维持生产性劳动的资本,使之能够继续用来维持生产性劳动。比如,把苏格兰制造品运到伦敦,再把英格兰谷物或制造品运到爱丁堡的资本,往返一次,无疑可以换回两个投在英国制造业或农业上的资本。

国内消费的外国货物如果是用本国产业的产物来购买,那么,每往返一次,投在这种贸易上的资本也能换回两个不同的资本;不过其中只有一个是用来维持本国产业的。例如,把英国货物运到葡萄牙,再把葡萄牙货物运到英国的资本,往返一次,补偿只有一个是英国资本,另一个补偿的却是葡萄牙的资本。所以,即使此种贸易能像国内贸易那样迅速地赚回本利,但与投在这种贸易上的资本比较起来,也只能带动半数的本国产业和鼓励半数的本国生产性劳动。_{在对外贸易上的资本可以偿还本国一个资本和一个外国资本。}

但是,此种贸易很少能够像国内贸易那么迅速地赚回本利。国内贸易的本利,大都每年能赚回一次,甚至三四次。这种贸易的本利每年赚回一次,已经算是难能可贵,两三年赚回一次,也很常见。因此投在国内贸易上的资本有时已经使用了 12 次,即付出而又收回了 12 次,而投在这种对外贸易上的资本才运用一次。所以,如果两个资本数量相等,投在国内贸易上的资本与投在对外贸易上的资本相比,结果前者对于本国产业往往可提供 24 倍于后者的鼓励与扶持。①_{对外贸易方式收回的速度没有国内贸易迅速。}

国内消费的外国货物,有时不是用本国产物来购买,而是用第二个其他国家货品交换购买。但这第二个其他国家的货品,并

---

① 如果有关迅速收回益处的信条在本章更早加以运用的话,那么就有关农业优先发展的讨论将会产生混乱的状况。

<small>Roundabout foreign trade has the same effect as direct.</small> other foreign goods. These last, however, must have been purchased either immediately with the produce of domestick industry, or with something else that had been purchased with it; for the case of war and conquest excepted, foreign goods can never be acquired, but in exchange for something that had been produced at home, either immediately, or after two or more different exchanges. The effects, therefore, of a capital employed in such a round-about foreign trade of consumption, are, in every respect, the same as those of one employed in the most direct trade of the same kind, except that the final returns are likely to be still more distant, as they must depend upon the returns of two or three distinct foreign trades. If the flax and hemp of Riga are purchased with the tobacco of Virginia, which had been purchased with British manufactures, the merchant must wait for the returns of two distinct foreign trades before he can employ the same capital in re-purchasing a like quantity of British manufactures. If the tobacco of Virginia had been purchased, not with British manufactures, but with the sugar and rum of Jamaica which had been purchased with those manufactures, he must wait for the returns of three. If those two or three distinct foreign trades should happen to be carried on by two or three distinct merchants, of whom the second buys the goods imported by the first, and the third buys those imported by the second, in order to export them again, each merchant indeed will in this case receive the returns of his own capital more quickly; but the final returns of the whole capital employed in the trade will be just as slow as ever. Whether the whole capital employed in such a round-about trade belong to one merchant or to three, can make no difference with regard to the country, though it may with regard to the particular merchants. Three times a greater capital must in both cases be employed, in order to exchange a certain value of British manufactures for a certain quantity of flax and hemp, than would have been necessary, had the manufactures and the flax and hemp been directly exchanged for one another. The whole capital employed, therefore, in such a round-about foreign trade of consumption,

不直接与本国产品交换而购买,必须间接地与本国产品交换购买,也就是用本国产物购买第三个其他国家的货品,再用第三个其他国家的物品来购买第二个其他国家的货品,因为除了在战争和征服的情况下,外国货品只有用本国产品直接交换购买而得,或用本国产品经过两三次不同交易间接交换购买而得,此外没有其他方法可以获得外国货品。所以,使用这样间接迂回的消费品国外贸易方式的资本,与使用最直接的消费品国外贸易方式的资本相比较,除了前者必须依靠两三次不同对外贸易的资本的收回,所需用时间较长一点才能最终收回资本以外,无论就哪一点来说,两者都有相同的效果。如果商人用英国制造品交换购买弗吉尼亚的烟草,再用弗吉尼亚的烟草交换购买里加的亚麻和大麻,那么,容易国不经过两次对外贸易,资本就不能够返还到商人手中用来购买等量的英国制造品。再假设用来购买弗吉尼亚烟草的不是英国制造品,而是牙买加的砂糖;牙买加的砂糖正是与英国的制造品进行交换购买而得,那就要等候三次对外贸易资本的收回,这才能使商人再次使用同一资本购买等量的英国制造品。又假设经营这两次或三次对外贸易的是两三个不同的商人。第一个商人进口的货品,由第二个买走并出口;第二个进口的货品,又有第三个买走并出口;那么就各个商人来说,各自资本的收回的确是比较迅速;但投在贸易上全部资本的最后收回却是一样缓慢。投在这种间接迂回贸易上的资本,究竟是为一人所有还是为三人所有,对个别商人虽有关系,但对国家却毫无关系。无论是为一人所有还是为三人所有,间接地使用一定价值的英国制造品来交换一定量的亚麻和大麻,与英国制造品和亚麻、大麻直接互相交换的情况相比较,所需要资本总要大三倍。所以,和比较直

> 间接迂回的国外贸易方式与直接国外贸易方式所产生的效果相同。

will generally give less encouragement and support to the productive labour of the country, than an equal capital employed in a more direct trade of the same kind.

<small>Foreign trade carried on by means of gold and silver is in no way different from the rest.</small> Whatever be the foreign commodity with which the foreign goods for home-consumption are purchased, it can occasion no essential difference either in the nature of the trade, or in the encouragement and support which it can give to the productive labour of the country from which it is carried on. If they are purchased with the gold of Brazil, for example, or with the silver of Peru, this gold and silver, like the tobacco of Virginia, must have been purchased with something that either was the produce of the industry of the country, or that had been purchased with something else that was so. So far, therefore, as the productive labour of the country is concerned, the foreign trade ot consumption which is carried on by means of gold and silver, has all the advantages and all the inconveniencies of any other equally roundabout foreign trade of consumption, and will replace just as fast or just as slow the capital which is immediately employed in supporting that productive labour. It seems even to have one advantage over any other equally round-about foreign trade. The transportation of those metals from one place to another, on account of their small bulk and great value, is less expensive than that of almost any other foreign goods of equal value. Their freight is much less, and their insurance not greater; and no goods, besides, are less liable to suffer by the carriage. ① An equal quantity of foreign goods, therefore, may frequently be purchased with a smaller quantity of the produce of domestick industry, by the intervention of gold and silver, than by that of any other foreign goods. The demand of the country may frequently, in this manner, be supplied more completely and at a smaller expence than in any other. Whether, by the continual exportation of those metals, a trade of this kind is likely to impoverish the country from which it is carried on, in any other way, I shall have occasion to examine at great length hereafter. ②

That part of the capital of any country which is employed in the

---

① [The second part of this sentence is not in Ed. ,r.]
② [Bk, iv.]

接的消费品国外贸易方式相比较，投在迂回的消费品国外贸易方式上的资本，虽然数量相等，但它对本国生产性劳动所能够提供的鼓励与支持却往往要少一些。

无论购买什么样的外国货品用于国内消费，都不能改变贸易的性质，也不能增减它对本国生产性劳动所能提供的鼓励与支持。如果用的是巴西的金或者秘鲁的银，这些金银的购买就与弗吉尼亚烟草的购买一样，当然少不了要用某种本国产业的产物，或由本国产物所交换购买的某种物品。所以，就本国的生产性劳动来说，无论在有利一面还是在不利一面，在偿还直接用来维持该生产性劳动的资本的快慢上，以金银为手段的消费品的国外贸易都和任何其他同样使用迂回的消费品国外贸易方式一样，没有任何区别。比较起来，以金银为购买手段的消费品的国外贸易方式，似乎还有一个好处；以金银作为购买手段，可以具有体积小、价值大的特点，所以与价值相等的其他货品相比较，运输费用比较少，保险费也未必就比较多。此外，金银在运输过程中较不容易遭受破损。① 所以，用金银为交换媒介，与用其他外国货物为交换媒介比较起来，我们往往可用较小数量的本国货物购得等量的外国货品。所以，比较起来，用其他外国货物为交换媒介，不如用金银为交换媒介，因为国内的需求可以得到更充分的供应，而所花费又比较少。至于不断出口金银来购买本国所需要的外国货物，能否使国家陷于贫困的问题，对此我们以后再详细讨论。②

投在运送贸易上的资本全是从本国抽调出来，并不用来维持

---

① 该句的第二部分在第一版里没有。
② 第四篇中讨论。

carrying trade, is altogether withdrawn from supporting the productive labour of that particular country, to support that of some foreign countries. Though it may replace by every operation two distinct capitals, yet neither of them belongs to that particular country. The capital of the Dutch merchant, which carries the corn of Poland to Portugal, and brings back the fruits and wines of Portugal to Poland, replaces by every such operation two capitals, neither of which had been employed in supporting the productive labour of Holland; but one of them in supporting that of Poland, and the other that of Portugal. The profits only return regularly to Holland, and constitute the whole addition which this trade necessarily makes to the annual produce of the land and labour of that country. When, indeed, the carrying trade of any particular country is carried on with the ships and sailors of that country, that part of the capital employed in it which pays the freight, is distributed among, and puts into motion, a certain number of productive labourers of that country. Almost all nations that have had any considerable share of the carrying trade have, in fact, carried it on in this manner. The trade itself has probably derived its name from it, the people of such countries being the carriers to other countries. It does not, however, seem essential to the nature of the trade that it should be so. A Dutch merchant may, for example, employ his capital in transacting the commerce of Poland and Portugal, by carrying part of the surplus produce of the one to the other, not in Dutch, but in British bottoms. It may be presumed, that he actually does so upon some particular occasions. It is upon this account, however, that the carrying trade has been supposed peculiarly advantageous to such a country as Great Britain, of which the defence and security depend upon the number of its sailors and shipping. But the same capital may employ as many sailors and shipping, either in the foreign trade of consumption, or even in the home-trade, when carried on by coasting vessels, as it could in the carrying trade. The number of sailors and shipping which any particular capital can employ, does not depend upon the nature of the trade, but partly upon the bulk of the goods in proportion to their value, and partly upon the distance of the ports between which they are to be carried; chiefly upon the former of those two circumstances. The coal-trade from Newcastle to London, for example, employs more shipping than all the carrying trade of England,

第二篇 第五章

本国的生产性劳动,却转用来维持外国的生产性劳动;这种贸易经营一次,虽然可以偿还两个资本,但资本都不是本国所有。荷兰商人从波兰运送谷物到葡萄牙、再把葡萄牙水果和葡萄酒运到波兰,这样每一次运作的确偿还了两个资本,但全都不是用来维持荷兰的生产性劳动。其中的一个是用来维持波兰的生产性劳动,另一个是用来维持葡萄牙的生产性劳动,回到荷兰去的只是荷兰商人的利润。有了这种贸易,荷兰土地和劳动的年产物并不是没有增加,但所增加的仅限于此。诚然,如果运送贸易所用的船舶与水手是本国的船舶与水手,那么,为支付运费而使用的那一部分资本,是用来推动和雇佣本国的生产性劳动的。事实上,运送贸易繁荣的国家几乎都是这样进行的。运送贸易的名词,也许就是由此而来,因为这些国家的人民对于外国人来说常常是运送者。但运输所需要的船舶与水手不一定为本国所有。比如说,经营波兰与葡萄牙之间运送贸易的荷兰商人,不一定要使用荷兰船舶,用英国船舶也未尝不可。我们可以说,在某些时候他的确是这样做的;就是因为这个原因,人们认为,运送贸易特别有利于像英国这种国家,它的国防与安全取决于船舶与水手的数量。但是,在消费品的国外贸易方面,甚至在国内贸易方面,等量的资本可以照样雇用那么多的船舶与水手;如果所必需的运输是用近海航船来进行的话。一定数量的资本究竟能雇用多少船舶与水手,不取决于贸易的性质,而是一部分取决于货物体积与货物价值的比例,一部分取决于运输海港之间的距离。在这两个条件中,前者尤为重要。纽卡斯尔与伦敦之间的煤炭贸易,虽然两个海港相距甚近,但所雇用的船舶与水手比英格兰全部运送贸易都更多。所以,以过分奖励的方式,强迫一国资本不按照自然发展的用途

though the ports are at no great distance. To force, therefore, by extraordinary encouragements, a larger share of the capital of any country into the carrying trade, than what would naturally go to it, will not always necessarily increase the shipping of that country.

The capital, therefore, employed in the home-trade of any country will generally give encouragement and support to a greater quantity of productive labour in that country, and increase the value of its annual produce more than an equal capital employed in the foreign trade of consumption: and the capital employed in this latter trade has in both these respects a still greater advantage over an equal capital employed in the carrying trade. The riches, and so far as power depends upon riches, the power of every country, must always be in proportion to the value of its annual produce, the fund from which all taxes must ultimately be paid. But the great object of the political oeconomy of every country, is to increase the riches and power of that country. It ought, therefore, to give no preference nor superior encouragement to the foreign trade of consumption above the home-trade, nor to the carrying trade above either of the other two. It ought neither to force nor to allure into either of those two channels, a greater share of the capital of the country than what would naturally flow into them of its own accord.

Each of those different branches of trade, however, is not only advantageous, but necessary and unavoidable, when the course of things, without any constraint or violence, naturally introduces it.

When the produce of any particular branch of industry exceeds what the demand of the country requires, the surplus must be sent abroad, and exchanged for something for which there is a demand at home. Without such exportation, a part of the productive labour of the country must cease,① and the value of its annual produce

---

① [But why may not the labour be diverted to the production of 'something for which there is a demand at home'? The 'corn, woollens and hardware' immediately below perhaps suggest that it is supposed the country has certain physical characteristics which compel its inhabitants to produce particular commodities.]

来使用,而把大部分资本投在运送贸易上,这样做却未必能够促进一国航运业的发展。

这样,与投在消费品国外贸易上的等量资本相比较,投在国内贸易上的资本所维持和鼓励的本国生产性劳动数量,一般比较大,所增加的本国年生产物价值一般也比较大。但投在消费品国外贸易上的资本与投在运送贸易上的等量资本相比较,在这两个方面却能够提供更大的利益。在拥有财富就意味着强大的今天,一国的富强一定和其年产物价值,即和其一切赋税最终所能提供的资金相一致。政治经济学的大目标就是促进本国的富强,所以,与其奖励消费品国外贸易,不如奖励国内贸易;与其奖励运送贸易,不如奖励消费品国外贸易或国内贸易。不应强制也不应诱使大部分资本违反自然发展规律,投入到消费品国外贸易或运送贸易方面去。

但是,如果这三种贸易是顺应事物发展的趋势而自然发展起来,没有受到拘束,没有遭遇压力;那么,无论是其中的那一种,都是有利的、必须的和不可避免的贸易方式。

在特定工业部门的产品超过本国需要的情况下,其剩余部分就必然被送往国外以交换国内所需要的物品。如果没有这种出口,国内生产性劳动一定有一部分会停止下来,①因而会减少国内年产出的价值。英国出产的谷物、呢绒和金属制品,常常超过国内市场的需要。因此,剩余部分必须被送往国外以交换英国所

---

① 但是为什么劳动不可以转向"生产那些国内需要的产品"上面去? 下面所说的"谷物、呢绒和金属制品"大概表明,假设一个国家具有某些自然特点,迫使这个国家的居民生产特殊的物品。

diminish. The land and labour of Great Britain produce generally more corn, woollens, and hard ware, than the demand of the home-market requires. The surplus part of them, therefore, must be sent abroad, and exchanged for something for which there is a demand at home. It is only by means of such exportation, that this surplus can acquire a value sufficient to compensate the labour and expence of producing it. The neighbourhood of the sea coast, and the banks of all navigable rivers are advantageous situations for industry, only because they facilitate the exportation and exchange of such surplus produce for something else which is more in demand there.

<small>Foreign goods obtained in exchange must often be re-exported.</small> When the foreign goods which are thus purchased with the surplus produce of domestic industry exceed the demand of the home-market, the surplus part of them must be sent abroad again, and exchanged for something more in demand at home. About ninety-six thousand hogsheads of tobacco are annually purchased in Virginia and Maryland, with a part of the surplus produce of British industry. But the demand of Great Britain does not require, perhaps, more than fourteen thousand. ① If the remaining eighty-two thousand, therefore, could not be sent abroad and exchanged for something more in demand at home, the importation of them must cease immediately, and with it the productive labour of all those inhabitants of Great Britain, who are at present employed in preparing the goods with which these eighty-two thousand hogsheads are annually purchased. Those goods, which are part of the produce of the land and labour of Great Britain,

<small>When the other employments are full, the surplus capital disgorges itself into the carrying trade, which is a symptom rather than a cause of great national wealth.</small> having no market at home, and being deprived of that which they had abroad, must cease to be produced. The most round-about foreign trade of consumption, therefore, may, upon some occasions, be as necessary for supporting the productive labour of the country, and the value of its annual produce, as the most direct.

When the capital stock of any country is increased to such a degree, that it cannot be all employed in supplying the consumption, and supporting the productive labour of that particular country, the surplus part of it naturally disgorges itself into the carrying trade, and is employed in performing the same offices to other countries. The carrying trade is the natural effect and symptom of great national wealth; but it does not seem to be the natural cause of it. Those statesmen who have been disposed to favour it with particular encouragements, seem to have mistaken the effect and symptom for the

---

① [Below, vol. ii., p. 2. The figures 96,000 and 13,500 are given in the continuation of Anderson's *Commerce*, A. D. 1775, ed. of 1801, vol. iv., p. 187.]

需要的物品。没有这种出口,这些剩余部分将不能获得充足的价格来补偿生产它时所花费的劳动与费用。沿海沿江一带之所以适合于兴办产业,就是因为剩余产物容易出口,也容易换回本地所需要的物品。

用本国剩余产物所购得的外国货品,如果比国内市场所需要的数量要多,则其剩余部分必须运往国外,以交换国内需要的其他货品。英国出口本国剩余产物的一部分,每年在弗吉尼亚、马里兰两地购买烟草约96,000桶。但英国每年所需要的数量也许不过14,000桶。① 所以,其余82,000桶,若不能送往国外以交换国内需要品,这个82,000桶的进口就会立刻停顿下来。每年用来购买这82,000桶而制造的货品,原来不是为了本国的需要,现在又没有出口的渠道,当然就会停止生产,而为制造这种货品而被雇的那一部分英国人,也将失去工作。所以,最迂回的消费品国外贸易方式,有时和最直接的消费品国外贸易方式一样,也是扶持本国生产劳动、维持本国年产物价值所必要的手段。

如果一国积累的资本,不能全部用来供给本国消费,全部用来维持本国的生产性劳动,则其剩余部分自然会流入运送贸易渠道,供给他国消费,维持他国的生产性劳动。运送贸易是国民巨额财富的自然结果与标志,但不是国民巨额财富的自然原因。赞成这种贸易而给予特殊奖励的政治家,似乎把结果与标志误认为原因。就土地面积和居民数量来衡量,荷兰是欧洲最富裕的国家,所以,荷兰就占有了欧洲运送贸易的最大部分。英格兰是仅

---

① 在第二卷第2页下面。96000桶和13500桶这两个数字在安德森1775年出版的《商业》的1801年再版第4卷187页里有记载。

cause. Holland, in proportion to the extent of the land and the number of its inhabitants, by far the richest country in Europe, has, accordingly, the greatest share of the carrying trade of Europe. England, perhaps the second richest country of Europe, is likewise supposed to have a considerable share of it; though what commonly passes for the carrying trade of England, will frequently, perhaps, be found to be no more than a round-about foreign trade of consumption. Such are, in a great measure, the trades which carry the goods of the East and West Indies, and of America, to different European markets. Those goods are generally purchased either immediately with the produce of British industry, or with something else which had been purchased with that produce, and the final returns of those trades are generally used or consumed in Great Britain. The trade which is carried on in British bottoms between the different ports of the Mediterranean, and some trade of the same kind carried on by British merchants between the different ports of India, make, perhaps, the principal branches of what is properly the carrying trade of Great Britain.

The possible extent of the carrying trade is much the greatest.   The extent of the home-trade and of the capital which can be employed in it, is necessarily limited by the value of the surplus produce of all those distant places within the country which have occasion to exchange their respective productions with one another. That of the foreign trade of consumption, by the value of the surplus produce of the whole country and of what can be purchased with it. That of the carrying trade, by the value of the surplus produce of all the different countries in the world. Its possible extent, therefore, is in a manner infinite in comparison of that of the other two, and is capable of absorbing the greatest capitals.

Agriculture does not yield sufficient profit to attract all the capital which it might absorb. The reason will be explained in the next two books.   The consideration of his own private profit, is the sole motive which determines the owner of any capital to employ it either in agriculture, in manufactures, or in some particular branch of the wholesale or retail trade. The different quantities of productive labour which it may put into motion, and the different values which it may add to the annual produce of the land and labour of the society, according as it is employed in one or other of those different ways, never enter into his thoughts. In countries, therefore, where agriculture is the most profitable of all employments, and farming and improving the most direct roads to a splendid fortune, the capitals of individuals will naturally be employed in the manner most advantageous to the whole society. The profits of agriculture, however, seem to have no superiority over those of other employments in any part of Europe. Projectors, indeed, in every corner of it, have within these few years amused the public with most magnificent accounts of the profits to be made by the

次于荷兰的欧洲富裕国家,也有不少运送贸易。不过,在多数情况下,英格兰的运送贸易不如称为间接的消费品国外贸易多。我们把来自东方的、西印度的和美洲的货物运到欧洲各市场去的贸易,大半就是这种性质的贸易。购买这种货物的手段,一般即使不是英国的产物,也是用英国产物购来的物品,而且这些贸易最后所带回的物品,又大都在英国消费或在英国使用。只有由英国轮船装运地中海各港口之间的贸易与由英国商人经营的印度沿海各港口之间的贸易,才是英国的真正运送贸易。

因为国内各地都有相互交换剩余生产物的必要,所以才有国内贸易;国内贸易的范围和投在国内贸易上的资本量,必须受国内各地剩余生产物价值的限制。消费品的国外贸易范围,必定受本国全部剩余生产物价值以及能由这些价值所购买的物品的价值限制。运送贸易所交换的是全世界各国的剩余生产物。所以,运送贸易范围必受全世界各国剩余生产物的价值的限制。与以上两种贸易相比较,它可能有的范围,简直没有止境,它所能吸引的资本也最大。

私人出于利润的考虑是决定资本用途的唯一动机。是投在农业上或投在工业上,还是投在批发商业上或投在零售商业上呢?那要看哪一种用途带来的利润最大。至于什么用途所能推动的生产性劳动量最大,什么用途所能增加的社会的土地和劳动的年产出价值最多,他从来不会想到这些。所以,在农业最有利润、耕种最容易致富的国家里,个人的资本自然就会投在对社会最有利的农业用途上。可是在欧洲,投资于农业所获利润并不一定比其他产业更为丰厚。的确,这几年来欧洲各地有许多计划创业家盛赞土地改良和农业深耕细作带来的利润,但不必仔细对他

cultivation and improvement -of land. Without entering into any particular discussion of their calculations, a very simple observation may satisfy us that the result of them must be false. We see every day the most splendid fortunes that have been acquired in the course of a single life by trade and manufactures, frequently from a very small capital, sometimes from no capital. A single instance of such a fortune acquired by agriculture in the same time, and from such a capital, has not, perhaps, occurred in Europe during the course of the present century. In all the great countries of Europe, however, much good land still remains uncultivated, and the greater part of what is cultivated, is far from being improved to the degree of which it is capable. Agriculture, therefore, is almost every-where capable of absorbing a much greater capital than has ever yet been employed in it. What circumstances in the policy of Europe have given the trades which are carried on in towns so great an advantage over that which is carried on in the country, that private persons frequently find it more for their advantage to employ their capitals in the most distant carrying trades of Asia and America, than in the improvement and cultivation of the most fertile fields in their own neighbourhood, I shall endeavour to explain at full length in the two following books.

们的估算进行讨论,只要稍微观察一下,就知道他们的结论是完全错误的。我们常常看到一些白手起家的人,他们从小小的资本,甚至没有资本,只要经营制造业或商业,便可成为一个富翁。然而一个世纪以来,用少量资本经营农业而发财的事例在欧洲几乎没有一个。欧洲各大国仍有许多无人耕种的优良土地;即使已经被人耕种的土地,也还没有进行充分改良。所以,现今随便什么地方的农业,都还可以容纳许多资本。欧洲各国的政策环境使得在都市经营产业的利益,远远超过在农村经营农业的利益,从而往往使私人宁愿对远方(如亚洲美洲)的运送贸易进行投资,而不愿投资耕种靠近自己的最丰沃土地,关于这一点,我将在下一篇再详细讨论。

BOOK III

Of The Different Progress Of Opulence In Different Nations

CHAPTER I

Of The Natural Progress Of Opulence

<small>The great commerce is that between town and country, which is obviously advantageous to both.</small> The great commerce of every civilized society, is that carried on between the inhabitants of the town and those of the country. It consists in the exchange of rude for manufactured produce, either immediately, or by the intervention of money, or of some sort of paper which represents money. The country supplies the town with the means of subsistence, and the materials of manufacture. The town repays this supply by sending back a part of the manufactured produce to the inhabitants of the country. The town, in which there neither is nor can be any reproduction of substances,①may very properly be said to gain its whole wealth and subsistence from the country. We must not, however, upon this account, imagine that the gain of the town is the loss of the country. The gains of both are mutual and reciprocal, and the division of labour is in this, as in all other cases, advantageous to all the different persons employed in the various occupations into which it is subdivided. The inhabitants of the country purchase of the town a greater quantity of manufactured goods, with the produce of a much smaller quantity of their own labour, than they must have employed had they attempted to prepare them themselves. The town affords a market

---

① [The error that agriculture produces substances and manufacture only alters them is doubtless at the bottom of much of the support gained by the theory of productive and unproductive labour.]

第三篇 论不同国家财富的不同途径

第一章 论财富的自然增长

所有社会最大的商业就是城镇居民与农村居民之间的通商。这种商业有的是以天然物品与制成品直接进行交换,有的是以货币或某种充当货币的纸币作交换的媒介。农村为城镇提供生活资料和制造业所需的原料,而城镇则以一部分制造品作为回报提供给农村居民。城市不再生产而且也无法再生产生活资料①,可以非常恰当地说城市的全部财富和生活资料都是从农村中获得的。但我们不能因此就设想,城镇的收益就是农村的损失。他们的收益是共同的和相互的。这里的劳动分工和所有其他情况下的其他分工一样,对双方从事各种不同分工的居民来说都是有利的。农村居民不必自己去制造,可以通过交换,用他们较少量的自身劳动来购买到较多量的制造品。城镇为那些用不完自己制

要重视城乡之间的商业,它对于双方来说都是有利的。很大的商业就是城乡之间的通商。

---

① 这种农业生产生活资料,制造业只改造生活资料的错误,毫无疑问是生产性劳动和非生产性劳动理论获得大量支持的基础。

for the surplus produce of the country, or what is over and above the maintenance of the cultivators, and it is there that the inhabitants of the country exchange it for something else which is in demand among them. The greater the number and revenue of the inhabitants of the town, the more extensive is the market which it affords to those of the country; and the more extensive that market, it is always the more advantageous to a great number. The corn which grows within a mile of the town, sells there for the same price with that which comes from twenty miles distance. But the price of the latter must generally, not only pay the expence of raising and bringing it to market, but afford too the ordinary profits of agriculture to the farmer. The proprietors and cultivators of the country, therefore, which lies in the neighbourhood of the town, over and above the ordinary profits of agriculture, gain, in the price of what they sell, the whole value of the carriage of the like produce that is brought from more distant parts, and they save, besides, the whole value of this carriage in the price of what they buy. Compare the cultivation of the lands in the neighbourhood of any considerable town, with that of those which lie at some distance from it, and you will easily satisfy yourself how much the country is benefited by the commerce of the town. Among all the absurd speculations that have been propagated concerning the balance of trade, it has never been pretended that either the country loses by its commerce with the town, or the town by that with the country which maintains it.

The cultivation of the country must be prior to the increase of the town, though the town may sometimes be distant from the country from which it derives its subsistence. As subsistence is, in the nature of things, prior to conveniency and luxury, so the industry which procures the former, must necessarily be prior to that which ministers to the latter. The cultivation and improvement of the country, therefore, which affords subsistence, must, necessarily, be prior to the increase of the town, which furnishes only the means of conveniency and luxury. It is the surplus produce of the country only, or what is over and above the maintenance of the cultivators, that constitutes the subsistence of the town, which can therefore increase only with the increase of this surplus produce. The town, indeed, may not always derive its whole subsistence from the country in its neighbourhood, or even from the territory to which it belongs, but from very distant countries; and this, though it forms no exception from the general rule, has occasioned considerable variations in the progress of opulence in different ages and nations.

That order of things which necessity imposes in general, though

造产品的农场主提供了市场,农村居民可以在城镇用生产品交换得到他们需要的产品。城镇的居民人数越多收入越大,为农村剩余产物提供的市场也就越宽广。这种市场越加宽广,对于大多数人来说也越加有利。距离城镇一英里的地方生产的谷物,在市上的售价和距离城镇二十英里处生产的谷物是一样的。但通常来说在后者销售的价格中,不仅要补偿其种植费用和送到市场上的费用,而且还要为农业劳动者提供一般的农业利润。因此,城镇附近的乡村地主和耕种者,在其所售谷物的价格中,不仅获得了将谷物从远地运入城市的费用的全部价值,还得到了从城市购回货物运费的全部价值。比较一下在任何大城市附近郊区的耕地和远离城镇的耕地,就可以看到农村是多么的受益于城镇商业。在一切有关贸易差额的荒谬言论中,从来没有人认为,乡村和城市进行贸易使自己利益受到损害,也不敢说城乡通商对城市或对乡村来说是有害的。

按照事物的性质,生活资料要优先于便利品和奢侈品。因此,生产前者的产业也就必然要优先于生产后者的产业;提供生活资料的农村的耕种和改良,也必须优先于那些只提供便利品和奢侈品的城镇的增加。正是那些农村的剩余产品,或者超出了农村劳动者维持生活资料之外的产品,才能用于供应城镇居民。因此,必须先增加农村产品的剩余,才能增加城镇农产品的供应。不过,城镇居民的生活资料,不一定总是来自于附近的农村,甚至不一定都非要来自于所属领土内的农村,可以从远方的国家运来。所以,这虽然从一般原则来讲并不特殊,但却使各个时期各个国家富裕的过程产生了很大的差异。

农村先于城镇的这种顺序在一般国家是由必要性造成的,即

国民财富的性质与原理

This order of things is favoured by the natural preference of man for agriculture. not in every particular country, is, in every particular country, promoted by the natural inclinations of man. If human institutions had never thwarted those natural inclinations, the towns could no-where have increased beyond what the improvement and cultivation of the territory in which they were situated could support; till such time, at least, as the whole of that territory was completely cultivated and improved. Upon equal, or nearly equal profits, most men will chuse to employ their capitals rather in the improvement and cultivation of land, than either in manufactures or in foreign trade. The man who employs his capital in land, has it more under his view and command, and his fortune is much less liable to accidents, than that of the trader, who is obliged frequently to commit it, not only to the winds and the waves, but to the more uncertain elements of human folly and injustice, by giving great credits in distant countries to men, with whose character and situation he can seldom be thoroughly acquainted. The capital of the landlord, on the contrary, which is fixed in the improvement of his land, seems to be as well secured as the nature of human affairs can admit of. The beauty of the country besides, the pleasures of a country life, the tranquillity of mind which it promises, and wherever the injustice of human laws does not disturb it, the independency which it really affords, have charms that more or less attract every body; and as to cultivate the ground was the original destination of man, so in every stage of his existence he seems to retain a predilection for this primitive employment.

Cultivators require the assistance of artificers, who settle together and form a village, and their employment augments with the improvement of the country. Without the assistance of some artificers, indeed, the cultivation of land cannot be carried on, but with great inconveniency and continual interruption. Smiths, carpenters, wheel-wrights, and plough-wrights, masons, and bricklayers, tanners, shoemakers, and taylors, are people, whose service the farmer has frequent occasion for. Such artificers too stand, occasionally, in need of the assistance of one another; and as their residence is not, like that of the farmer, necessarily tied down to a precise spot, they naturally settle in the neighbourhood of one another, and thus form a small town or village. The butcher, the brewer, and the baker, soon join them, together with many other artificers and retailers, necessary or useful for supplying their occasional wants, and who contribute still further to augment the town. The inhabitants of the town and those of the country

便不是在每个国家都这样;但在所有国家,人类的天性也促其使然。如果人类制度没有阻碍人类的这种天性,则直到所在的全部地区得到完全改良和耕种的时候,城镇的发展都不能超过农村的耕种情况和改良情况所能支持的限度。在利润相等或大致相等的情况下,多数人会选择投资以改良土地开垦土地,而不是投资于制造业和对外贸易。将自己的资本投在土地上的人,能对资本进行支配和更直接的监察;与商人资本比较,他的财产遭遇意外事故的影响较少。商人的财产往往是冒着狂风巨浪的风险得来的,因为商人不得不对风俗情况都不熟悉的遥远国家的人们贷给信用,还要冒着更不可靠的人类愚蠢和不公正行为风险。反之,地主的资本固定在土地上,其安全的程度达到了人类事物性质所允许的极限。而且,乡村风景秀丽、生活愉悦、心情恬静,在这里不受到人类法律的不公正干扰,为地主提供了独立性。这些魅力都或多或少吸引每一个人。由于耕地是人的最初使命,所以,在有人类存在的一切阶段,人类似乎都保留了对这个原始职业的永远喜爱。

当然,没有工匠的帮助,农耕便不可能顺利进行,会遭受巨大的不便和经常的干扰。农场主需要的一些服务常常是由铁匠、木匠、车轮匠、犁匠、泥水匠、砖匠、皮革匠、鞋匠和缝匠提供的。这类工匠偶尔也需要互相帮助,由于他们不必要像农场主那样必须固定在一个地点,所以他们自然而然地聚居一地,结果就形成了一种小市镇或小村落。屠户、酒家、面包师后来也参加进来,以及许其他工匠及零售商人也加入进来,这些人都是满足他们的不时之需的必要或有用的人们,于是使得市镇进一步发展起来。乡村的居民和城市的居民是彼此相互的服务者。城市是一个经常的

are mutually the servants of one another. The town is a continual fair or market, to which the inhabitants of the country resort, in order to exchange their rude for manufactured produce. ①It is this commerce which supplies the inhabitants of the town both with the materials of their work, and the means of their subsistence. The quantity of the finished work which they sell to the inhabitants of the country, necessarily regulates the quantity of the materials and provisions which they buy. Neither their employment nor subsistence, therefore, can augment, but in proportion to the augmentation of the demand from the country for finished work; and this demand can augment only in proportion to the extension of improvement and cultivation. Had human institutions, therefore, never disturbed the natural course of things, the progressive wealth and increase of the towns would, in every political society, be consequential, and in proportion to the improvement and cultivation of the territory or country.

In the American colonies an artificer who has acquired sufficient stock becomes a planter instead of manufacturing for distant sale,
 In our North American colonies, where uncultivated land is still to be had upon easy terms, no manufactures for distant sale have ever yet been established in any of their towns. When an artificer has acquired a little more stock than is necessary for carrying on his own business in supplying the neighbouring country, he does not, in North America, attempt to establish with it a manufacture for more distant sale, but employs it in the purchase and improvement of uncultivated land. From artificer he becomes planter, and neither the large wages nor the easy subsistence which that country affords to artificers, can bribe him rather to work for other people than for himself. He feels that an artificer is the servant of his customers, from whom he derives his subsistence; but that a planter who cultivates his own land, and derives his necessary subsistence from the labour of his own family, is really a master, and independent of all the world.

as in countries where no uncultivated land can be procured.
 In countries, on the contrary, where there is either no uncultivated land, or none that can be had upon easy terms, every artificer who has acquired more stock than he can employ in the occasional jobs of the neighbourhood, endeavours to prepare work for more distant sale.

① [This passage, from the beginning of the paragraph, may well have been suggested by Cantillon, *Essai*, pp. 11-22.]

市集或市场,乡民常常到那里,用天然物产交换制成品①。正是这种商业的交换,为城镇居民提供了工作的原材料和他们的生活资料。他们售给乡村居民的制成品的数量,必然决定着他们所购回的原料及食物的数量。所以,城市居民所购回的原料及食物数量的增加,只能按照乡村居民对制成品需要增加的比例而增加,而这种需要,又只能按照改良和耕种的扩大比例而发展。所以,如果人为制度从来没有干扰事物的自然进程,那就无论在什么政治社会里,城镇财富的增长与规模的扩大,都是乡村耕种及改良事业发展的结果,而且按照乡村耕种及改良事业发展的比例而增长扩大。

在我国的北美殖民地,那里仍然非常容易购买到尚未开垦的荒地,在所有城市中都还没有建立为远方的销售而建立的制造业。如果工匠获得的资金,超过他为供应临近乡村而经营的生意所必需的供给时,他会去购买或改良未开垦的土地,而不会再想着用来建立一种为在远方销售的制造业。这样他就从一个工匠转变成了农场主,当地为工匠提供的高额工资所带来的舒适生活,都不能吸引他们为别人工作,他们更愿意为自己工作。他们总是认为工匠仅是顾主的仆人,他从雇主那里获得自己的生活资料;而农场主则耕种自己的土地,从自己家庭的劳动力劳动中获取的生活必需品,这是一个真正的主人,独立于世界中。

与之相反,在没有荒地或者较难购买到耕地的国家,如果工匠所获得的资金超过了投资于附近地区的事业中时,他们就会扩

---

① 这一段,从开始到这里,很可能是受到肯提伦的影响,见《论一般商业的性质》,第 11~22 页。

The smith erects some sort of iron, the weaver some sort of linen or woollen manufactory. Those different manufactures come, in process of time, to be gradually subdivided, and thereby improved and refined in a great variety of ways, which may easily be conceived, and which it is therefore unnecessary to explain any further.

<small>Manufactures are naturally preferred to foreign commerce.</small>

In seeking for employment to a capital, manufactures are, upon equal or nearly equal profits, naturally preferred to foreign commerce, for the same reason that agriculture is naturally preferred to manufactures. As the capital of the landlord or farmer is more secure than that of the manufacturer, so the capital of the manufacturer, being at all times more within his view and command, is more secure than that of the foreign merchant. In every period, indeed, of every society, the surplus part both of the rude and manufactured produce, or that for which there is no demand at home, must be sent abroad in order to be exchanged for something for which there is some demand at home. But whether the capital, which carries this surplus produce abroad, be a foreign or a domestic one, is of very little importance. If the society has not acquired sufficient capital both to cultivate all its lands, and to manufacture in the completest manner the whole of its rude produce, there is even a considerable advantage that that rude produce should be exported by a foreign capital, in order that the whole stock of the society may be employed in more useful purposes. The wealth of ancient Egypt, that of China and Indostan, sufficiently demonstrate that a nation may attain a very high degree of opulence, though the greater part of its exportation trade be carried on by foreigners. The progress of our North American and West Indian colonies would have been much less rapid, had no capital but what belonged to themselves been employed in exporting their surplus produce.

<small>So the natural course of things is first agriculture, then manufactures, and finally foreign commerce.</small>

According to the natural course of things, therefore, the greater part of the capital of every growing society is, first, directed to agriculture, afterwards to manufactures, and last of all to foreign commerce. This order of things is so very natural, that in every society that had any territory, it has always, I believe, been in some degree observed. Some of their lands must have been cultivated before any considerable towns could be established, and some sort of coarse industry of the manufacturing kind must have been carried on in those towns, before they

张营业而为到远方的销售做准备工作。这样,铁匠将会建立制铁厂,织匠将会建立某麻织厂或毛织厂。这些制造业随着时间的推移将逐渐地实现分工,从而在各方面得到改进和完善。这是很容易理解的,因此没有必要进一步去说明。

在选择资本的用途时,在利润相等或者几乎相等的情况下,制造业自然优于对外贸易。其原因正如农业优于制造业一样。因为相对于制造商的资本,地主或农业家的资本更为安全。同样制造商的资本相对于对外贸易的资本就更为安全,因为随时都在他们的监控和支配之下。当然,每个社会的任何时期,天然产物和制造品的剩余部分,或在国内没有需求的部分,都必须送往外国以换取国内所需要的物品。但不管运送这些剩余产物到国外的资本,是本国资本还是外国资本,却都是无关紧要的。如果一国没有足够的资本,去耕种它所有的土地和用最完全的方式制造它全部的天然产物,那么利用外国资本来出口本国剩余产物,对本国而言还有一点是非常有利的:本国的全部资本就可以投入最有用的目的上。古埃及、中国、印度的富裕程度,就充分证明了,虽然一个国家的大部分出口贸易由外国人经营,该国仍可以达到很高的富裕程度。北美殖民地、西印度殖民地如果只使用本地自己的资本来出口他们的剩余产物,那么他们的进步就不会那么快了。

> 制造业自然优于对外贸易。

所以,按照事物发展的自然进程,每个成长中的社会的大部分资本,首先投在农业上,然后投在制造业上,最后才投在对外贸易上。这种顺序是极其自然的,所以在每一个拥有领土的社会,我相信某种程度上资本总是遵循这种顺序来投入。首先开垦一些土地来建立城市;在城市里总是先建立某种粗糙的制造业,然

> 所以事物的自然进程是:首先是农业,然后是制造业,最后是对外贸易。

could well think of employing themselves in foreign commerce.

<small>But this order has been in many respects inverted.</small> But though this natural order of things must have taken place in some degree in every such society, it has, in all the modern states of Europe, been, in many respects, entirely inverted. The foreign commerce of some of their cities has introduced all their finer manufactures, or such as were fit for distant sale; and manufactures and foreign commerce together, have given birth to the principal improvements of agriculture. The manners and customs which the nature of their original government introduced, and which remained after that government was greatly altered, necessarily forced them into this unnatural and retrograde order.

后才可以去考虑从事对外贸易。

　　然而,这个自然顺序必定会在每一个社会里都在某种程度上发生,但在现在的欧洲各国,许多方面这个顺序却完全颠倒了。欧洲一些城市里的对外贸易采用了比较精细的制造业,也就是适于供给远方销售产品的制造业。而制造业和对外贸易也一并促进了农业的主要改良。这些城市原来统治的性质形成的风俗习惯,在这种统治大大改变之后,却仍然保留了下来,迫使他们采取了这种非自然的退步的顺序。

> 但是这种顺序却颠倒在许多方面被了。

CHAPTER II

Of The Discouragement Of Agriculture In The Ancient State Of Europe After The Fall Of The Roman Empire

After the fall of the Roman Empire all the land of Western Europe was engrossed, chiefly by large proprietors.

When the German and Scythian nations over-ran the western provinces of the Roman empire, the confusions which followed so great a revolution lasted for several centuries. The rapine and violence which the barbarians exercised against the ancient inhabitants, interrupted the commerce between the towns and the country. The towns were deserted, and the country was left uncultivated, and the western provinces of Europe, which had enjoyed a considerable degree of opulence under the Roman empire, sunk into the lowest state of poverty and barbarism. During the continuance of those confusions, the chiefs and principal leaders of those nations, acquired or usurped to themselves the greater part of the lands of those countries. A great part of them was uncultivated; but no part of them, whether cultivated or uncultivated, was left without a proprietor. All of them were engrossed, and the greater part by a few great proprietors.

Primogeniture and entails prevented the great estates being divided.

This original engrossing of uncultivated lands, though a great, might have been but a transitory evil. They might soon have been divided again, and broke into small parcels either by succession or by alienation. The law of primogeniture hindered them from being divid-

— 832 —

第二章　论罗马帝国衰落后农业在欧洲过去状态下受到的压制

当日耳曼民族和塞西亚民族[1]侵占了罗马帝国西部各省之后,这样一个剧烈的变革引发了持续了几个世纪的一场动乱。城乡之间的贸易被这些野蛮民族对于古代居民的掠夺和迫害而中断了。城市变得无人居住,乡村土地也没有人耕种。欧洲西部各省曾在罗马帝国统治时期,非常地富裕,现在却变得极为贫穷和野蛮。在持续不断的动乱中,这些国家的大部分土地都被这些民族的头目和主要领导人据为己有了。大部分土地都是荒芜的,然而无论是已被开垦的土地还是没有被开垦的土地,均有所属。所有的土地都被吞并了,并且大部分土地集中于少数大地主手中。罗马帝国没落后欧洲西部全部基本地上土地都被大地主独占。

最初这种吞并对开垦土地的危害尽管很大,但也可能仅仅是暂时的危害。可能不久这些土地就会通过继承或分割把它们分割成许多小块。但长子继承法阻止了通过继承造成的分割:限定长子继承制和限定继承权阻止了土地的分割。

---

〔1〕 塞西亚(Scythian),欧亚大陆的一地区,从黑海的多瑙河口一直到咸海的东部地区。这个地区的游牧民从公元前 8 世纪到公元前 4 世纪很繁荣,但到了公元前 2 世纪被萨尔马西亚人征服后,就很快地被融合入其他的民族中去了。

ed by succession: the introduction of entails prevented their being broke into small parcels by alienation. ①

Primogeniture was introduced because every great landlord, w-as a petty prince.

When land, like moveables, is considered as the means only of subsistence and enjoyment, the natural law of succession divides it, like them, among all the children of the family; of all of whom the subsistence and enjoyment may be supposed equally dear to the father. This natural law of succession accordingly took place among the Romans, who made no more distinction between elder and younger, between male and female, in the inheritance of lands, than we do in the distribution of moveables. But when land was considered as the means, not of subsistence merely, but of power and protection, it was thought better that it should descend undivided to one. In those disorderly times, every great landlord was a sort of petty prince. His tenants were his subjects. He was their judge, and in some respects their legislator in peace, and their leader in war. He made war according to his own discretion, frequently against his neighbours, and sometimes against his sovereign. The security of a landed estate, therefore, the protection which its owner could afford to those who dwelt on it, depended upon its greatness. To divide it was to ruin it, and to expose every part of it to be oppressed and swallowed up by the incursions of its neighbours. The law of primogeniture, therefore, came to take place, not immediately, indeed, but in process of time, in the succession of landed estates, for the same reason that it has generally taken place in that of monarchies, though not always at their first institution. That the power, and consequently the security of the monarchy, may not be weakened by division, it must descend entire to one of the children. To which of them so important a preference shall be given, must be determined by some general rule, founded not upon the doubtful distinctions of personal merit, but upon some plain and evident difference which can admit of no dispute. Among the children of the same family, there can be no indisputable difference but that of

---

① [Primogeniture and entails are censured as inimical to agriculture in *Lectures*, pp. 120, 124, 228.]

继承权就阻碍了通过转让把土地分割成许多小块。①

如果我们只是把土地看作像动产一样的谋生享乐手段,那么按照自然继承法,土地就被分给一个家庭所有的子女。因为他们的父亲同样关心每一个子女的生活和享受。所以,自然继承法就是这样在罗马人之中产生的,在他们之中,无论长幼、无论男女,都可以像我们处理动产一样继承得到自己的土地。不过,当土地不仅仅被看作是谋生的手段,而且是权力和保卫能力时,土地就被认为最好传给一人更为恰当。在那些动乱的时代,每个大地主都是一个小君主。他的佃户就是他的子民。他是他们的裁判官。某种程度上他就是和平时期的立法者,战争时期的领导人。他可以根据自己的意愿发动战争,常常是对邻国的战争,有时是对国王的战争。因此,一个地产是否安全,在这个地产上居住的居民有无保障,就取决于这份地产的大小。所以将一个地产分割的话就意味着将它破坏,这样使它的每一部分都容易遭受邻人入侵、压迫和吞并。所以,长子继承法在地产继承方面慢慢地而非立刻的随着时间的推移产生了,尽管在初建之时并不总是如此,正如通常的君主政体那样。从一个国家的权利和君主权力的安危考虑,为了不让因为分裂而国力削弱,必须完全的选择一个人来单独继承权利。那样将权力授予谁这样重大的事情,当然必须要有一个普通的规例来确定,使得不是以个人资质好坏这个不可靠的标准来确定,而是以某种明确的无可争议的标准来确定。在同一个家庭的子女中,除了性别与年龄,再没有其他无可争议的标准

> 长嗣继承制是因为每个大地主都是一个小君主。采用长子继承制。

---

① 长嗣继承权和限定继承权在《关于法律、警察、岁入及军备的演讲》第120、124、228页中被指责为对农业不利。

sex, and that of age. The male sex is universally preferred to the female; and when all other things are equal, the elder every-where takes place of the younger. Hence the origin of the right of primogeniture, and of what is called lineal succession. ①

<small>It is now unreasonable, but supports the pride of family distinctions.</small> Laws frequently continue in force long after the circumstances, which first gave occasion to them, and which could alone render them reasonable, are no more. In the present state of Europe, the proprietor of a single acre of land is as perfectly secure of his possession as the proprietor of a hundred thousand. The right of primogeniture, however, still continues to be respected, and as of all institutions it is the fittest to support the pride of family distinctions, it is still likely to endure for many centuries. In every other respect, nothing can be more contrary to the real interest of a numerous family, than a right which in order to enrich one, beggars all the rest of the children.

<small>Entails have the same origin,</small> Entails are the natural consequences of the law of primogeniture. They were introduced to preserve a certain lineal succession, of which the law of primogeniture first gave the idea, and to hinder any part of the original estate from being carried out of the proposed line either by gift, or devise, or alienation; either by the folly, or by the misfortune of any of its successive owners. They were altogether unknown to the Romans. Neither their substitutions nor fideicommisses bear any resemblance to entails, though some French lawyers have thought proper to dress the modern institution in the language and garb of those antient ones. ②

<small>and are now absurd.</small> When great landed estates were a sort of principalities, entails might not be unreasonable. Like what are called the fundamental laws of some monarchies, they might frequently hinder the security of thousands from being endangered by the caprice or extravagance of one man. But in the present state of Europe, when small as well as great estates derive their security from the laws of their country, nothing

---

① [*Lectures*, pp. 117-118.]

② [In *Lectures* p. 123, the Roman origin of entails appears to be accepted.]

了。一般来说大家倾向于认为,男性优于女性,在其他条件相同的情况下,年长者优于年幼者。所以长子继承权就这样产生了,所谓的直系继承也这样产生了。①

一部法律刚建立起来时,都是当时的一些情况使然,也因此使其合理。但我们经常发现当产生这个法律的环境已经改变后,这个法律却仍在生效。如今的欧洲,仅拥有一英亩地的小地主与拥有10万英亩地的大地主的所有权一样的安全。现在长子继承仍然继续受到尊重,因为在各种制度中它最适于保持家族显赫的尊严,所以极可能它还要再持续很多世纪。但事实上除了这方面外,长子继承权完全违背了一个大家庭的实际利益,因为它虽然使得一个人富裕,但却使得其他子女沦为贫穷。除了维持家族显赫外,现在长子继承制并不合理。

限定继承权是长子继承法施行的自然结果。采用限定继承权,旨在保持由长子继承法导引出来的直系继承,阻止原始地产由于继承人的不羁或遭逢不幸,而使部分的原始地产在赠与、遗赠或割让中落入直系之外人手。罗马人完全不知道这种法律。虽然法国某些法律家认为古代的制度和条款仍然可以适用于现代的法制,但是,罗马人的所谓预定继承人或嘱托指定遗赠人,都与限定继承法毫不相似。②限定继承法的起源相同,

在大土地财产是一种大公国时,限嗣继承或许是合理的办法。如同某些所谓君主国的根本法律一样,可以避免许许多多人的安全因为某一个人的随心所欲或轻举妄动而遭受威胁。但现现在看来它是荒谬的。

---

① 《关于法律、警察、岁入及军备的演讲》,第 117~118 页。
② 《关于法律、警察、岁入及军备的演讲》,第 123 页,人们似乎接受限定继承制起源于罗马。

can be more completely absurd. They are founded upon the most absurd of all suppositions, the supposition that every successive generation of men have not an equal right to the earth, and to all that it possesses; but that the property of the present generation should be restrained and regulated according to the fancy of those who died perhaps five hundred years ago. ① Entails, however, are still respected through the greater part of Europe, in those countries particularly in which noble birth is a necessary qualification for the enjoyment either of civil or military honours. Entails are thought necessary for maintaining this exclusive privilege of the nobility to the great offices and honours of their country; and that order having usurped one unjust advantage over the rest of their fellow-citizens, lest their poverty should render it ridiculous, it is thought reasonable that they should have another. The common law of England, indeed, is said to abhor perpetuities, and they are accordingly more restricted there than in any other European monarchy; though even England is not altogether without them. In Scotland more than one-fifth, perhaps more than one-third part of the whole lands of the country, are at present supposed to be under strict entail.

<small>Great proprietors are seldom great improvers.</small> Great tracts of uncultivated land were, in this manner, not only engrossed by particular families, but the possibility of their being divided again was as much as possible precluded for ever. It seldom happens, however, that a great proprietor is a great improver. In the disorderly times which gave birth to those barbarous institutions, the great proprietor was sufficiently employed in defending his own territories, or in extending his jurisdiction and authority over those of his neighbours. He had no leisure to attend to the cultivation and improvement of land. When the establishment of law and order afforded him this leisure, he often wanted the inclination, and almost always the requisite abilities. If the expence of his house and person either equalled or exceeded his revenue, as it did very frequently, he had no stock to employ in this manner. If he was an economist, he generally found it more profitable to employ his annual savings in new purcha-

---

① [This passage follows *Lectures*, p. 124, rather closely, reproducing even the repetition of ' absurd'.]

在的欧洲各国,大小地产同样都受到法律的保护,这种情况下的法律就变得非常荒谬了。限定继承权的制定建立在一个最荒谬的假定上:人类的每一个后代没有同等的权利来享受所有土地及其他一切所有物,但是当代人的财产却要受到500年前死去人的心愿的限制和支配。① 然而限定继承权在今日欧洲的很多地方仍然受到尊重。限定继承法被认为是维持贵族血统,享受民事或军事荣誉的必要资格条件。这一阶层不但夺得了一种超乎其同胞之上的不正当的利益,而且还耻笑别人比自己贫穷,所以认为他们自己还应当再享有另一种不正当的利益。不过,英格兰的成文法是很厌恶这种永久不得转让的产业的,因此这种制度在那里比在欧洲其他各君主国要更受限制。尽管这种制度在英格兰也没有完全被废除。限定继承法仍然严格地支配着苏格兰现在的1/5以上(也许是1/3以上)的土地。

这样的话,个别的家族不但控制了大面积的荒地,而且极力集中保护这种权力防止其受到重新的分割。大地主们往往并非是大改良家。在产生这种野蛮制度的混乱时节,大地主集中精力忙于来保护已有的领土,扩大自身对邻国的管辖权和支配权。他们根本都没有空闲来开垦土地改良土地。在确立法制安定秩序之后,他们即使有了闲暇,也一般没有开垦和改良土地的愿望,重要的是没有这种必备的能力。倘若他全家和个人的开支超过了或恰巧相等于他的收入(这是常有的事情),他就没有富余的资本去投在这种用途上。如果他是有经济头脑的,那么他一般又觉得

<small>大地主是很少大改良家,</small>

---

① 这一段与《关于法律、警察、岁入及军备的演讲》第124页的论述很接近,不断产生荒谬。

ses, than in the improvement of his old estate. To improve land with profit, like all other commercial projects, requires an exact attention to small savings and small gains, of which a man born to a great fortune, even though naturally frugal, is very seldom capable. The situation of such a person naturally disposes him to attend rather to ornament which pleases his fancy, than to profit for which he has so little occasion. The elegance of his dress, of his equipage, of his house, and household furniture, are objects which from his infancy he has been accustomed to have some anxiety about. The turn of mind which this habit naturally forms, follows him when he comes to think of the improvement of land. He embellishes perhaps four or five hundred acres in the neighbourhood of his house, at ten times the expence which the land is worth after all his improvements; and finds that if he was to improve his whole estate in the same manner, and he has little taste for any other, he would be a bankrupt before he had finished the tenth part of it. There still remain in both parts of the united kingdom some great estates which have continued without interruption in the hands of the same family since the times of feudal anarchy. Compare the present condition of those estates with the possessions of the small proprietors in their neighbourhood, and you will require no other argument to convince you how unfavourable such extensive property is to improvement. ①

The occupiers were not likely to improve, as they were slaves attached to the land and incapable of acquiring property.

If little improvement was to be expected from such great proprietors, still less was to be hoped for from those who occupied the land under them. In the ancient state of Europe, the occupiers of land were all tenants at will. They were all or almost all slaves; but their slavery was of a milder kind than that known among the ancient Greeks and Romans, or even in our West Indian colonies. They were supposed to belong more directly to the land than to their master. They could, therefore, be sold with it, but not separately. They could marry, provided it was with the consent of their master; and he could not afterwards dissolve the marriage by selling the man and wife to

---

① [This remark follows *Lectures*, p. 228.]

宁可用一年的储蓄来购买新的地产比较合算,而不愿意去改良旧的地产。要通过改良土地来获利,也像其他各种商业计划一样,必须关注小的节省和小的赢利。一个出生在豪富人家的人,即使有着节俭的天性,也很不容易做到这一点。身处这种境遇的人,自然地让他去注意生活的装饰,而不会去注意自己并不需要的利润。他从小就习惯于追求衣着、陈设、住宅和家具的华丽,这些已成为他的目标和习惯。这种所形成的心态在想改良土地的时候照样也会支配着他的行动。他也许会花费比该地改良后所值大10倍的价钱来装饰住宅附近的四五百英亩的土地,如果按照这样的方法来改良他所有全部的地产,他会发现就算没有其他的一些嗜好,恐怕也会在没改良1/10以前他就会破产。现在联合王国的英格兰和苏格兰这两个地区自封建的无政府状态以来,仍然有些大地产继续在同一家族的控制下,至今没有改动。比较一下这些大地产与邻近的小地产的现状,你不需其他论证就会相信大地产是多么不利于改良①土地。

　　如果对土地的一些改良不能期望从这样的大地主那里获得,就更不用说从那些占有的土地比他们少的人那里获得了。在欧洲古代状态下,他们全都是可以随意任其退租的佃农。他们全是或几乎全是奴隶,只不过比起古希腊罗马、甚至西印度殖民地的奴隶而言,他们的劳役还要相对和缓一些。他们被认为比较直接地隶属于他们的土地,而不是隶属于他们的主人。因此,他们可以随同土地一起被出卖,但不能单独出卖。在得到了主人的同意之后他们还可以结婚。而且主人没有权利把他们夫妇拆散分

所有者能改因为他们附属于土地的,并且不能获得财产。可不会良,很不良。

---

① 参见《关于法律、警察、岁入及军备的演讲》,第228页。

different persons. If he maimed or murdered any of them, he was liable to some penalty, though generally but to a small one. They were not, however, capable of acquiring property. Whatever they acquired was acquired to their master, and he could take it from them at pleasure. Whatever cultivation and improvement could be carried on by means of such slaves, was properly carried on by their master. It was at his expence. The seed, the cattle, and the instruments of husbandry were all his. It was for his benefit. Such slaves could acquire nothing but their daily maintenance. It was properly the proprietor himself, therefore, that, in this case, occupied his own lands, and cultivated them by his own bondmen. This species of slavery still subsists in Russia, Poland, Hungary, Bohemia, Moravia, and other parts of Germany. It is only in the western and south-western provinces of Europe, that it has gradually been abolished altogether. ①

Slave labour is the dearest of all.

But if great improvements are seldom to be expected from great proprietors, they are least of all to be expected when they employ slaves for their workmen. The experience of all ages and nations, I believe, demonstrates that the work done by slaves, though it appears to cost only their maintenance, is in the end the dearest of any. A person who can acquire no property, can have no other interest but to eat as much, and to labour as little as possible. Whatever work he does beyond what is sufficient to purchase his own maintenance, can be squeezed out of him by violence only, and not by any interest of his own. In ancient Italy, how much the cultivation of corn degenerated,

---

① ['A small part of the West of Europe is the only portion of the globe that is free from slavery,' 'and is nothing in comparison with the vast continents where it still prevails.'—*Lectures*, p. 96.]

第三篇 第二章

别卖给不同的人,从而拆散他们的婚姻。如果主人残害或杀害了奴隶,他将要受到处分,不过惩罚一般都比较轻微。但是奴隶们不可能有蓄积的财产。他们所获得的一切都是主人拥有的,获取还是被取走都要听随主人的意愿。通过奴隶们从事的开垦和改良,实际上还是通过他们的主人来进行。费用的支出由主人来负担。种子、牲畜、劳动工具全都是主人的。改良的利益也由主人来获得。这些奴隶们除了日常维持生活的必需品之外,什么都不可能得到。因此,在这种情况下,正是这个土地所有者自己完全占有着土地,用奴隶来开垦这些土地。这种奴隶制度仍然存在于俄罗斯、波兰、匈牙利、波希米亚、摩拉维亚以及德意志其他部分。这种奴隶制度仅仅在欧洲西部和西南部各省已经逐步被完全消除。①

如果不指望从大地主那里得到什么大改良,那么,当他们雇用奴隶作为劳动者的时候,就根本不可能指望从他们那里得到大的改良了。我相信,所有时代和国家的经验展示了这样一个事实:所有由奴隶来完成的劳动,虽表面上看来似乎只花费了生活必须维持费用,但最终其代价是任何劳动中最高的。一个根本不能获得财产的人,除了尽可能多吃少干之外,他没有什么其他利益了。要想获得他所做的工作超过足以购买维持其生存的生活必需品之外的劳动量的话,仅仅能够通过暴力来压榨获得,不可能通过他们自身的利益来获得。普林尼和科拉麦拉曾评论过,在古代

奴隶劳动是最昂贵的。

―――――――

① 西欧的一小部分地方仅仅是全球废除奴隶制的一小部分地方,与仍存在奴隶制的大部分地区相比起来算不上什么。见《关于法律、警察、岁入及军备的演讲》,第96页。

— 843 —

how unprofitable it became to the master when it fell under the management of slaves, is remarked by both Pliny and Columella. ① In the time of Aristotle it had not been much better in ancient Greece. Speaking of the ideal republic described in the laws of Plato, to maintain five thousand idle men (the number of warriors supposed necessary for its defence) together with their women and servants, would require, he says, a territory of boundless extent and fertility, like the plains of Babylon. ②

<small>At present sugar and tobacco can afford slave cultivation, corn cannot.</small>

The pride of man makes him love to domineer, and nothing mortifies him so much as to be obliged to condescend to persuade his inferiors. Wherever the law allows it, and the nature of the work can afford it, therefore, he will generally prefer the service of slaves to that of freemen. The planting of sugar and tobacco can afford the expence of slave cultivation. The raising of corn, it seems, in the present times, cannot. In the English colonies, of which the principal produce is corn, the far greater part of the work is done by freemen. The late resolution of the Quakers in Pennsylvania to set at liberty all their negro slaves, may satisfy us that their number cannot be very great. Had they made any considerable part of their property, such a resolution could never have been agreed to. In our sugar colonies, on the contrary, the whole work is done by slaves, and in our tobacco colonies a very great part of it. The profits of a sugar-plantation in any of our West Indian colonies are generally much greater than those of any other cultivation that is known either in Europe or America: And the profits of a tobacco plantation, though inferior to those of sugar, are superior to those of corn, as has already been observed. ③ Both can afford the expence of slave cultivation, but sugar can afford it still

---

① [Pliny, H. N., lib. xviii., cap. iv.; Columella, *De re rustica*, lib. i., præfatio.]

② [*Politics*, 1265a.]

③ [Above, p. 158; *Lectures*, p. 225.]

意大利,当谷物种植由奴隶来管理的时候,谷物耕种退化到何种程度,主人就会变得何种不利。① 在亚里士多德时代的古希腊,耕种事业并没有变得好多少。所以,说起柏拉图法律中所描述理想共和国时,他说:为了维持5,000个(这认为是为了防御而所必要的战士人数)闲人以及他们的女人和奴仆,需要有一片像巴比伦平原那样极其广阔极其富饶的土地。②

人类的骄傲使得他热衷于成为统治者,并且没有什么比屈尊劝说下属更让他痛苦,感到羞辱的了。因此在法律允许的情况下,工作性质也允许的情况下,他一般倾向于奴隶提供的而不是自由人提供的服务。蔗糖与烟草的种植能够支付奴隶耕种的费用。但似乎目前的时代,种植谷物却不能做到这一点。英国的殖民地中,主要产物为谷物的绝大部分的工作是由自由人来完成的。宾夕法尼亚的贵格会议通过一个决定案,释放所有的黑人奴隶。这个决定案使我们相信他们所有的黑奴一定不多。倘若奴隶是他们财产的相当大的一部分的话,这样的决议是绝不可能被支持并通过的。截然不同的是,在我们以生产蔗糖为主的殖民地,所有的工作都是由奴隶来完成的;在生产烟草的殖民地,相当大部分的工作是由奴隶来做的。比起欧洲或美洲众所周知的其他耕种来说,西印度殖民地的任何地方,蔗糖种植的利润一般都要大得多。烟草种植的利润尽管比蔗糖种植的利润少,但是却比谷物种植的要多,前面已经提到过了。③ 这两种种植都可以支付

现在烟草和蔗糖能支付奴隶的耕种,谷物却不能。

---

① 普林尼:《自然史》第18卷第4章;科卢梅拉:《论乡间事》第1册,序言。

② 《政治学》,1265a。

③ 《关于法律、警察、岁入及军备的演讲》,第225页。

better than tobacco. The number of negroes accordingly is much greater, in proportion to that of whites, in our sugar than in our tobacco colonies.

<small>The slaves were succeeded by metayers.</small> To the slave cultivators of ancient times, gradually succeeded a species of farmers known at present in France by the name of Metayers. They are called in Latin, Coloni Partiarii. They have been so long in disuse in England that at present I know no English name for them. The proprietor furnished them with the seed, cattle, and instruments of husbandry, the whole stock, in short, necessary for cultivating the farm. The produce was divided equally between the proprietor and the farmer, after setting aside what was judged necessary for keeping up the stock, which was restored to the proprietor when the farmer either quitted, or was turned out of the farm. ①

<small>who are very different in that they can acquire property.</small> Land occupied by such tenants is properly cultivated at the expence of the proprietor, as much as that occupied by slaves. There is, however, one very essential difference between them. Such tenants, being freemen, are capable of acquiring property, and having a certain proportion of the produce of the land, they have a plain interest that the whole produce should be as great as possible, in order that their own proportion may be so. A slave, on the contrary, who can acquire nothing but his maintenance, consults his own ease by making the land produce as little as possible over and above that maintenance. It is probable that it was partly upon account of this advantage, and partly upon account of the encroachments which the sovereign, always jealous of the great lords, gradually encouraged their villains to make upon their authority, and which seem at last to have been such as rendered this species of servitude altogether inconvenient, that tenure in villanage gradually wore out through the greater part of Europe. The time and manner, however, in which so important a revolution was brought about, is one of the most obscure points in modern history. The church of Rome claims great merit in it; and it is certain that so early as the twelfth century, Alexander III. published a bull for the general emancipation of slaves. It seems, however,

---

① [lectures, pp. 100, 101.]

奴隶的耕种费用,但是蔗糖仍然能比栽种烟草更能提供这种费用。因此,蔗糖区域比烟草殖民地而言,黑人数量上比白种人相比要大得多。

继古代奴隶耕种时代之后,相继出现了在当今法兰西非常出名的一种农场主,他们被称为对分佃农。这种农场主,在拉丁文中叫做 Coloni Partarii(分益隶农)。他们在英格兰已经废除了非常久的时间,以至于现在我根本都不知道他们的英文名称。土地所有者给他们提供种子、牲畜、农具,综指旧时农耕必须的所有的原料。劳动产品在土地所有者和农场主之间进行平等的分配,被分配的产品不包括被认为维持原资本的必须部分。当农场主离开了农场或者被逐出农场的时候,这部分资本应该归还土地所有者。①

奴隶制度被对分佃农所继承。

佃农所占有的土地的耕种完全由地主来支付费用,和在奴隶耕种制下没有差别。然而两者之间存在一个最基本的区别。佃农属于自由人,他们可以占有财产,可以获得一定比例的土地产品,他们有一个非常明显的利益,尽可能地生产那些总量更多的产品,目的是为了自己所得的部分也越大。明显不同的是,除了可以获得维持生活的产品之外再不能获得其他产物的奴隶,出于考虑自己的舒适,生产出尽可能少的超出维持自身需求的产品。或许部分的是由于这种好处的考虑,部分的是由于统治者总是嫉妒大地主,逐渐鼓励他们的奴隶反抗他们地主的权力,这样最后使得这种对他们的奴役状态非常困难,以至于隶农身份及地位逐渐在欧洲大部分地区被废除。然而爆发的如此重大的一次变革,所产生的时间和方式是现代历史上最大的难以说清的事情之一。罗马教会声称是自己的丰功伟绩。当然,众所周知早在 12 世纪,

不同之处在于他们可以获得财产。

---

① 《关于法律、警察、岁入和军备的演讲》,第 100、101 页。

to have been rather a pious exhortation, than a law to which exact obedience was required from the faithful. Slavery continued to take place almost universally for several centuries afterwards, till it was gradually abolished by the joint operation of the two interests above mentioned, that of the proprietor on the one hand, and that of the sovereign on the other. A villain enfranchised, and at the same time allowed to continue in possession of the land, having no stock of his own, could cultivate it only by means of what the landlord advanced to him, and must, therefore, have been what the French call a Metayer.

<small>But they could have no interest to employ stock in improvement.</small> It could never, however, be the interest even of this last species of cultivators to lay out, in the further improvement of the land, any part of the little stock which they might save from their own share of the produce, because the lord, who laid out nothing, was to get one-half of whatever it produced. The tithe, which is but a tenth of the produce, is found to be a very great hindrance to improvement. A tax, therefore, which amounted to one-half, must have been an effectual bar to it. It might be the interest of a metayer to make the land produce as much as could be brought out of it by means of the stock furnished by the proprietor; but it could never be his interest to mix any part of his own with it. In France, where five parts out of six of the whole kingdom are said to be still occupied by this species of cultivators, ① the proprietors complain that their metayers take every opportunity of employing the masters cattle rather in carriage than in cultivation; because in the one case they get the whole profits to themselves, in the other they share them with their landlord. This species of tenants still subsists in some parts of Scotland. They are called steel-bow tenants. Those ancient English tenants, who are said by Chief Baron Gilbert and Doctor Blackstone to have been rather bailiffs

---

① [Probably Quesnay's estimate; cp. his article on 'Fermiers' in the *Encyclopedie*, reprinted in his *Euvres*, ed. Oncken, 1888, pp. 160, 171.]

亚历山大三世就颁布了一道普遍解放奴隶的赦令。然而这似乎只是一种虔诚的劝告,而不是一部必须来严格执行的法律。奴隶制度在随后的好几个世纪仍然普遍持续,直至上述两种利益的共同作用才把它废除。这两种利益一方面是地主的,另一方面是统治者的。一个被释放的奴隶,被允许急需拥有土地,没有自己的资本,耕种土地就只能通过地主的赊账,因此在法国很可能被称为对分佃农(亦称分益耕农)。

不过,这种耕种者不可能把从自己获得的产品中的一部分节约出资本,来投资于未来的土地改良中。因此,地主不做任何投资将会得到所产物品的一半。产品中的 1/10,即什一税,被认为是改良土地的最大障碍。那么,一种累计到一半的税率无疑将是土地改良的实质性障碍。产出和由地主提供的资本生产出来的产出一样,才符合对分佃农的利益的;但是将这种资本与自有的混合起来,却不可能符合他们的利益。在法兰西,据说全国有 5/6 的土地仍由对分佃农耕种。① 地主抱怨他们的对分佃农利用一切机会使用主人的牲畜来拖车,而不是耕田。因为运输的全部利润归他们自己,耕田的利润他们要和地主共同分享。在苏格兰的某些地方也残留着这种佃农。他们被称为由地主借给种子农具的佃户。那些古英格兰的佃农可能同属一类,大贵族吉尔伯特和布莱克斯顿博士曾说与其称其为土地管理者,还不如称其为地主

但是用资产去进行改良对他们没有可利益言。

---

① 或许是根据奎斯纳的估计。比较他在《百科全书》中所写的"佃农"词条,在《全书》翁肯编辑的重印版中,1888 年,第 160、171 页。

of the landlord than farmers properly so called, were probably of the same kind. ①

<small>Metayers were followed by farmers, who sometimes find it to their interest to improve when they have a lease, but leases were long insecure.</small>

To this species of tenancy succeeded, though by very slow degrees, farmers properly so called, who cultivated the land with their own stock, paying a rent certain to the landlord. When such farmers have a lease for a term of years, they may sometimes find it for their interest to lay out part of their capital in the further improvement of the farm; because they may sometimes expect to recover it, with a large profit, before the expiration of the lease. The possession even of such farmers, however, was long extremely precarious, and still is so in many parts of Europe. They could before the expiration of their term be legally outed of their lease, by a new purchaser; in England, even by the fictitious action of a common recovery. If they were turned out illegally by the violence of their master, the action by which they obtained redress was extremely imperfect. It did not always re-instate them in the possession of the land, but gave them damages which never amounted to the real loss. Even in England, the

<small>The forty-shilling freeholder vote in England contributes to the security of the farmer.</small>

country perhaps of Europe where the yeomanry has always been most respected, it was not till about the 14th of Henry the VIIth that the action of ejectment was invented, by which the tenant recovers, not damages only but possession, and in which his claim is not necessarily concluded by the uncertain decision of a single assize. This action has been found so effectual a remedy that, in the modern practice, when the landlord has occasion to sue for the possession of the land, he seldom makes use of the actions which properly belong to him as landlord, the writ of right or the writ of entry, ② but sues in the name of his tenant, by the writ of ejectment. In England, therefore, the security of the tenant is equal to that of the proprietor. In England besides a lease for life of forty shillings a year value is a freehold,

---

① [Gilbert, *treatise of Tenures*, 3rd ed., 1757, pp. 34 and 54; Blackstone, *Commentaries*, vol. ii., pp. 141, 142. The whole paragraph follows *Lectures*, p. 226, rather closely.]

② [Blackstone, *Commentaries*, iii., 197.]

的从仆更合适。①

　　继佃农之后的农场主才真正可以被称为农场主,尽管发展速度很慢,他们用自有资本耕种土地,支付一定的租金给地主。这种农场主租田都有一定年限的租约,他们有时发现抽出一部分资金来进行土地的改良可以给他们带来好处。因为他们有时希望能在租约到期之前收回投入的资金,并获得很大的利润。不过,这种农场主使用土地的权力在长期看来是极不稳定,如今欧洲的很多地方还是这样的。他们也可能在年限租约未到期之前被土地的新主人逐出来,这也不算违法。在英格兰,甚至可以通过一种虚构的普通诉讼解除公约。如果他们被地主用暴力非法的手段驱逐出来,农场主所能获得的赔偿也是极端不完善的。农场主并非总是可以重新获得原先使用的土地,但是带给他们的真正损失远远超过了赔偿金。即使在英格兰,这个自耕农总是受到最大尊重的欧洲国家,直到亨利七世十四年才实行了收回地产诉讼法,佃农不仅可以获得赔偿金而且可以重新占有土地。但他的这种请求权不一定通过一次审判就能得到结果。后来发现这种诉讼是一个如此有效的补救措施,以至于在近些年,当地主有机会对土地所有权提出诉讼的时候,他很少运用作为属于地主的合适的法令,这是属于地主的权力令和进入令,②但是常常用他的佃农名义,按退佃令去起诉。因此在英格兰,佃户的安全等同于地主的安全了。在英格兰,年租金 40 先令以上的终身租约,就是一

---

　　① 吉尔伯特:《论租佃》,第三版,1757 年,第 34、35 页;布莱克斯顿:《纪事》第 2 卷,第 141、142 页。整段与《关于法律、警察、岁入及军备的演讲》第 226 页极为相近。

　　② 布莱克斯顿:《纪事》,第 3 卷,第 197 页。

and entitles the lessee to vote for a member of parliament; and as a great part of the yeomanry have freeholds of this kind, the whole order becomes respectable to their landlords on account of the political consideration which this gives them. ① There is, I believe, no-where in Europe, except in England, any instance of the tenant building upon the land of which he had no lease, and trusting that the honour of his landlord would take no advantage of so important an improvement. Those laws and customs so favourable to the yeomanry, have perhaps contributed more to the present grandeur of England, than all their boasted regulations of commerce taken together.

<small>The law of Scotland is not quite so favourable.</small>

The law which secures the longest leases against successors of every kind is, so far as I know, peculiar to Great Britain. It was introduced into Scotland so early as 1449, by a law of James the IId. ② Its beneficial influence, however, has been much obstructed by entails; the heirs of entail being generally restrained from letting leases for any long term of years, frequently for more than one year. A late act of parliament③ has, in this respect, somewhat slackened their fetters, though they are still by much too strait. In Scotland, besides, as no leasehold gives a vote for a member of parliament, the yeomanry are upon this account less respectable to their landlords than in England.

<small>In the rest of Europe the farmer is less secure.</small>

In other parts of Europe, after it was found convenient to secure tenants both against heirs and purchasers, the term of their security was still limited to a very short period; in France, for example, to nine years from the commencement of the lease. It has in that country, indeed, been lately extended to twenty-seven, a period still too short to encourage the tenant to make the most important improvements. The proprietors of land were anciently the legislators of every part of Europe. The laws relating to land, therefore, were all calculated for what they supposed the interest of the proprietor. It was for

---

① [Lectures, pp. 227-228.]

② [Acts of 1449, c. 6, 'ordained for the safety and favour of the poor people that labours the ground.']

③ [10 Geo. III., c. 51.]

种终身保有的不动产,承租人就可以享有选举国会议员的权利,因为自耕农的大部分拥有这种不动产,由于这样给予他们在政治上的地位所以整个阶级变得备受尊重。① 我相信在欧洲除了英格兰,没有任何地方的佃农不签订土地租约而进行建筑的,并且可以相信地主,不去夺取这样一项重要的改良。这些法律和习俗对于自耕农如此有利,比起那些他们吹嘘的商业规定的总和来说,可能对目前英格兰的光荣伟大有更大的贡献。

确保最长租约不各受每种继承人侵害的法律,据我所知,为英格兰所特有。这种法律早在1449年就被詹姆士二世的一项法律②引进苏格兰。但是由于限制继承权,它所能带来的好处受到了很大的阻碍。限制继承权的继承者不能将超过一年期的土地出租出去。在这方面,国会的最新法案有点放松了对他们的这种束缚,尽管他们仍然受到过多的限制。③ 另外在苏格兰,如果不动产不能带给国会议员投票权,那自耕农在此基础上受到的尊重远远不如英格兰的地主对自耕农的尊重。

苏格兰的法律非常不利。

在欧洲的其他地方,在虽然发现保障佃农的权益不受继承人和购买者的损害是有利的,但是这种保障期限仍然非常有限。例如在法兰西的租约期为九年。实际上,直到最近才延长至27年,这个时间对于鼓励佃农进行最为重要的土地改良来说仍然太短。欧洲各地的地主自古以来都是立法家。因此与土地有关的法令

在欧洲的其余地方,农场主受保护很少。

---

① 见《关于法律、警察、岁人及军备的演讲》,第227~228页。
② 1449年的法律第3号,"为了在土地上劳动的穷人的安全和利益而颁"。
③ 乔治三世十年第51号法令。

his interest, they had imagined, that no lease granted by any of his predecessors should hinder him from enjoying, during a long term of years, the full value of his land. Avarice and injustice are always shortsighted, and they did not foresee how much this regulation must obstruct improvement, and thereby hurt in the long-run the real interest of the landlord. ①

<small>Customary services were vexatious to the farmer.</small> The farmers too, besides paying the rent, were anciently, it was supposed, bound to perform a great number of services to the landlord, which were seldom either specified in the lease, or regulated by any precise rule, but by the use and wont of the manor or barony. These services, therefore, being almost entirely arbitrary, subjected the tenant to many vexations. In Scotland the abolition of all services, not precisely stipulated in the lease,② has in the course of a few years very much altered for the better the condition of the yeomanry of that country.

<small>and so also were compulsory labour on the roads, purveyance</small> The public services to which the yeomanry were bound, were not less arbitrary than the private ones. To make and maintain the high roads, a servitude which still subsists, I believe, every-where, though with different degrees of oppression in different countries, was not the only one. When the king's troops, when his household or his officers of any kind passed through any part of the country, the yeomanry were bound to provide them with horses, carriages, and provisions, at a price regulated by the purveyor. Great Britain is, I believe, the only monarchy in Europe where the oppression of purveyance has been entirely abolished. It still subsists in France and Germany.

<small>and tallages.</small> The public taxes to which they were subject were as irregular and oppressive as the services. The ancient lords, though extremely unwilling to grant themselves any pecuniary aid to their sovereign, easily allowed him to tallage, as they called it, their tenants,③ and had not knowledge enough to foresee how much this must in the end affect their own revenue. The taille, as it still subsists in France, may serve

① [*Lectures*, pp. 226, 227.]
② [20 Geo. II., c. 50, § 21.]
③ [*Lectures*, p. 227.]

都是按他们所设想的地主的利益来计划的。正是为了他们所设想的利益,他们的前辈们不允许订立租约,阻止他们在较长时期享受土地的全部价值。贪婪和不公总是目光短浅,他们看不到这种规定必定阻碍土地的改良,因此在长期来说必然损害地主的真正利益。①

古代的农场主除了缴纳地租之外,还被认为一定要给地主提供很多的服务,这些服务在地租中既没有载明也不受到任何的明文的规定,但是受到庄园或领地的需要及习惯的约束。因此这些服务几乎完全是专横的,使佃农遭受了很多苦难。废除苏格兰的这些所有没有在租约中明确规定的服务,②在短短几年内就能够改善那个国家自耕农的境况。习惯性的奴役对农场主来说是一种痛苦

自耕农应服的公役与他们所受到的私役同样地专横。我相信,为了公路的修建和维护,尽管在不同国家的压迫程度不尽相同,但是这种奴役状态每个地方仍然存在,并且不是唯一的一个。当国王的军队,当他的任何军官和皇室路过它的领土的任何地方时,自耕农必定要给他们提供马匹、车辆、任何各种食物,价格由食物征发官来决定。我相信,在欧洲存在的王室食物征发权的压迫,只是在英国被完全废除了。在法国和德国,这些都仍然存在。强迫修路和征购粮食也是这样的

农场主所负担的公共赋税和劳役,都同样地既不规则,也很沉重。古代封建领主,虽然极不情愿给予他们的君主任何金钱上的帮助,但是却可以轻易地使他们在他们的佃农身上争取贡税。③他们没有足够的知识来预见这样的做法最终到底给他们和贡税

---

① 见《关于法律、警察、岁入及军备的演讲》,第226、227页。
② 乔治二世二十年第50号法令,第21节。
③ 见《关于法律、警察、岁入及军备的演讲》,第227页。

as an example of those ancient tallages. It is a tax upon the supposed profits of the farmer, which they estimate by the stock that he has upon the farm. It is his interest, therefore, to appear to have as little as possible, and consequently to employ as little as possible in its cultivation, and none in its improvement. Should any stock happen to accumulate in the hands of a French farmer, the taille is almost equal to a prohibition of its ever being employed upon the land. This tax besides is supposed to dishonour whoever is subject to it, and to degrade him below, not only. the rank of a gentleman, but that of a burgher, and whoever rents the lands of another becomes subject to it. No gentleman, nor even any burgher who has stock, will submit to this degradation. This tax, therefore, not only hinders the stock which accumulates upon the land from being employed in its improvement, but drives away all other stock from it. The ancient tenths and fifteenths,① so usual in England in former times, seem, so far as they affected the land, to have been taxes of the same nature with the taille.

Even under the best laws the farmer is at a disadvantage in improving, but large farmers are the principal improvers after small proprietors.

Under all these discouragements, little improvement could be expected from the occupiers of land. That order of people, with all the liberty and security which law can give, must always improve under great disadvantages. The farmer compared with the proprietor, is as a merchant who trades with borrowed money compared with one who trades with his own. The stock of both may improve, but that of the one, with only equal good conduct, must always improve more slowly than that of the other, on account of the large share of the profits which is consumed by the interest of the loan. The lands cultivated by the farmer must, in the same manner, with only equal good conduct,

---

① [Originally tenths and fifteenths of movable goods; subsequently fixed sums levied from the parishes, and raised by them like other local rates; see Cannan, *History of Local Rates*, 1896, pp. 13-14, 18-20, 22 note, 23 note.]

的利润带来多大的影响。法国现在仍然存在的租税可以说就是那些古代贡税的一个例子。这种对农场主利润所征收的税收,是根据农场主投在农场上的资本来估算的。因此,为了农场主他们自身的利益,他们尽可能假装所拥有的很少,结果,他耕种所用的资本也尽可能的少,土地的改良几乎就没有投入了。如果法国农场主的手中恰好积累了一定的资本,这种贡税就差不多相当于禁止他们在土地上进行投入。其他的税收被认为贬低了那些缴税者的身份,降低了他们的地位,不仅仅不如这些绅士的级别,还不如那些城市公民。凡是租借他们土地的人都要缴纳这种赋税。绅士和拥有自己资本的市民们,都不愿受这种耻辱。因此这种赋税不仅阻碍了在这片土地上所积累的资本来从事土地的改良,而且驱逐了其他的资本也不能改良这些土地。在英格兰以前的时代,古代的 1/10 税和 1/15 的赋税,①就他们对于土地的影响而言,似乎跟贡税有着同样的性质。

　　在这一切的挫抑政策之下,很难期望土地所有者进行一点点改良。即便法律给予了这个阶层的人民以自由和安全的保障,他们在改良土地时也处于极端不利的地位。农场主跟地主相比,就好像一个借钱经商的商人与一个自持资金的商人比较。借来的资金和自有的资金,两者都能因同样谨慎的运行而增长,但是其中的一种总是比另一种要增长得更慢一些,因为还要考虑贷款利息所吞噬的利润中的很大一部分。相同的,以同样谨慎的行为,

即便是最好的法律,农民在土地改良中也处于不利地位,但除了小农场主,大农场主是主要的土地改良者。

---

　　① 最初是对动产课征 1/10 和 1/15 的赋税,随后按固定数目向教区居民征税,他们像其他地方税一样缴纳;参阅坎南:《地方税捐史》,1896 年,第 14~15、18~20 及 22、23 页注解。

be improved more slowly than those cultivated by the proprietor; on account of the large share of the produce which is consumed in the rent, and which, had the farmer been proprietor, he might have employed in the further improvement of the land. ① The station of a farmer besides is, from the nature of things, inferior to that of a proprietor. Through the greater part of Europe the yeomanry are regarded as an inferior rank of people, even to the better sort of tradesmen and mechanics, and in all parts of Europe to the great merchants and master manufacturers. It can seldom happen, therefore, that a man of any considerable stock should quit the superior, in order to place himself in an inferior station. Even in the present state of Europe, therefore, little stock is likely to go from any other profession to the improvement of land in the way of farming. More does perhaps in Great Britain than in any other country, though even there the great stocks which are, in some places, employed in farming, have generally been acquired by farming, the trade, perhaps, in which of all others stock is commonly acquired most slowly. After small proprietors, however, rich and great farmers are, in every country, the principal improvers. There are more such perhaps in England than in any other European monarchy. In the republican governments of Holland and of Berne in Switzerland, the farmers are said to be not inferior to those of England.

<small>The common prohibition of the exportation of corn and the restraints on internal trade in agricultural produce were further discouragements to agriculture.</small>

The ancient policy of Europe was, over and above all this, unfavourable to the improvement and cultivation of land, whether carried on by the proprietor or by the farmer; first, by the general prohibition of the exportation of corn without a special licence, which seems to have been a very universal regulation; and secondly, by the restraints which were laid upon the inland commerce, not only of corn but of almost every other part of the produce of the farm, by the absurd laws against engrossers, regraters, and forestallers, and by the privileges of fairs and markets. It has already been observed in what manner the prohibition of the exportation of corn, together with some encouragement given to the importation of foreign corn, obstructed the cultivation of ancient Italy, naturally the most fertile country in Europe, and at that time the seat of the greatest empire in the world. To what degree such restraints upon the inland commerce of this com-

---

① [*Lectures*, p. 226.]

农场主开垦的土地必定要比土地所有者自有的那部分土地改良得更慢;因为产品的大部分都要作为地租来上缴,如果农场主就是土地所有者,他很可能用这部分来进行土地的改良。① 此外,从性质来看,农场主的地位当然比地主低。在欧洲的大部分地区,自耕农被认为是最下等的阶层,甚至连处境稍好的小商人和技师都不如。在欧洲的大部分地方,自耕农的地位不如大商人和大制造商,是相当普遍的情况了。因此很少出现一个拥有大量资金的人放弃自身的富贵地位去置身下层社会。所以,即使是在现在的欧洲,很难有资本从其他专业领域转到农业上来进行土地的改良。英国比其他国家拥有更多的转到农业方面来改良土地的资本。在许多地方,即使很多的资金用于农业,他们一般都是在农业上获得的,也许其中所有其他的资金通常积累的是最慢的。不过,除了小地主,在每一个国家里,富裕的大农场主是土地最主要的改良者。在欧洲君主国中,英格兰也许拥有最多的有这种情形。据说,在荷兰共和政府以及瑞士伯尔尼共和政府中,农场主的地位不低于英格兰的农场主。

　　除上述所有之外,欧洲古代的政策不利于土地的改良和开垦,不论进行改良和开垦是地主还是农场主来进行的。首先,禁止没有特许证的谷物的出口,这似乎是一个相当普遍的规定;其次,由于反对囤积居奇、垄断和零售的荒谬法律,对于内地贸易的限制,不仅是谷物甚至是几乎每一种农产品的限制。一直都这样评论,对于谷物出口的禁止,奖励外国谷物的进口,阻碍了古代意大利的土地的开垦,它天生就是欧洲土地最肥沃的国家,在那个

_{禁止谷物出口制品和农产品的国际贸易对农业的进一步抑制。}

---

① 见《关于法律、警察、岁入及军备的演讲》,第226页。

— 859 —

modity, joined to the general prohibition of exportation, must have discouraged the cultivation of countries less fertile, and less favourably circumstanced, it is not perhaps very easy to imagine.

时候,称为世界上最大帝国的中心。对于这种内陆商品贸易的限制的程度,以及对于一般出口的禁止,必定会挫伤土地不是很肥沃、环境不是很有利的国家土地的开垦,或许很难想象。

CHAPTER III

Of the Rise And Progress Of Cities and Towns, After The Fall Of The Roman Empire

The townsmen were not at first favoured more than the countrymen.
The inhabitants of cities and towns were, after the fall of the Roman empire, not more favoured than those of the country. They consisted, indeed, of a very different order of people from the first inhabitants of the ancient republics of Greece and Italy. These last were composed chiefly of the proprietors of lands, among whom the public territory was originally divided, and who found it convenient to build their houses in the neighbourhood of one another, and to surround them with a wall, for the sake of common defence. After the fall of the Roman empire, on the contrary, the proprietors of land seem generally to have lived in fortified castles on their own estates, and in the midst of their own tenants and dependants. The towns were chiefly inhabited by tradesmen and mechanics, who seem in those days to have been of servile, or very nearly of servile condition. The privileges which we find granted by ancient charters to the inhabitants of some of the principal towns in Europe, sufficiently shew what they were before those grants. The people to whom it is granted as a privilege, that they might give away their own daughters in marriage without the consent of their lord, that upon their death their own children, and not their lord, should succeed to their goods, and that they might dispose of their own effects by will, must, before those grants, have been either altogether, or very nearly in the same state of villanage with the occupiers of land in the country.

They were very nearly of servile condition.
They seem, indeed, to have been a very poor, mean set of people, who used to travel about with their goods from place to place, and from fair to fair, like the hawkers and pedlars of the present

第三章　论罗马帝国衰落后城镇的勃兴与发展

罗马帝国衰落后,城镇居民的境况并不比农村居民有利。实际上,城镇的居民由各种阶层组成,他们与来自古希腊共和国和古意大利的最初的居民很不相同。后者主要是由土地所有者组成,他们分割了公共土地,并且发现在彼此附近的领地建造房屋很方便,建以围墙,共同防御。大不相同的是,当罗马帝国衰落之后,地主似乎往往和他们的佃农和侍从们,居住在他们各自的坚固城堡中。城镇中主要居住的是小商人和技工,在那个时代,他们几乎处于一种被奴役的状态,或者几近奴役的状态。我们发现古代宪章赋予欧洲一些主要城镇的居民的权利,充分地显示了取得这些权利之前的一些情况。获得这些权利的人民,不经领主同意,他们可以自由嫁女;他们死后,他们自己的子女,而不是领主来继承他们的财物;无需批准,他们可以定立遗嘱来处置自己的遗产。可以见得在这种权利颁给之前,他们是和乡村土地占有者几乎一样,或竟全然一样,处于奴隶状态。

确实,他们似乎属于很穷很低劣的阶层。他们一般都带着自己的货物四处奔波,从一个集市到另一个集市,如同现在的沿街

> 最初城镇居民并不比乡村居民好。

> 他们近乎奴隶的状况。

times. ① In all the different countries of Europe then, in the same manner as in several of the Tartar governments of Asia at present, taxes used to be levied upon the persons and goods of travellers, when they passed through certain manors, when they went over certain bridges, when they carried about their goods from place to place in a fair, when they erected in it a booth or stall to sell them in. These different taxes were known in England by the names of passage, pontage, lastage, and stallage. Sometimes the king, sometimes a great lord, who had, it seems, upon some occasions, authority to do this, would grant to particular traders, to such particularly as lived in their own demesnes, a general exempt. on from such taxes. Such traders, though in other respects of servile, or very nearly of servile condition, were upon this account called Free-traders. They in return usually paid to their protector a sort of annual poll-tax. In those days protection was seldom granted without a valuable consideration, and this tax might, perhaps, be considered as compensation for what their patrons might lose by their exemption from other taxes. At first, both those polltaxes and those exemptions seem to have been altogether personal, and to have affected only particular individuals, during either their lives, or the pleasure of their protectors. In the very imperfect accounts which have been published from Domesday-book, of several of the towns of England, mention is frequently made sometimes of the tax which particular burghers paid, each of them, either to the king, or to some other great lord, for this sort of protection; and sometimes of the general amount only of all those taxes. ②

but arrived at liberty much earlier than the country people, acfauiring the farm of their town,

But how servile soever may have been originally the condition of the inhabitants of the towns, it appears evidently, that they arrived at liberty and independency much earlier than the occupiers of land in the country. That part of the king's revenue which arose from such poll-taxes in any particular town, used commonly to be let in farm, during a term of years for a rent certain, sometimes to the sheriff of

---

① [*Lectures*, p. 233.]

② See Brady's historical treatise of Cities and Burroughs, p. 3, &c. [Robert Brady, *Historical Treatise of Cities and Burghs or Boroughs*, 2nd ed., 1711. See, for the statements as to the position of townsmen and traders contained in these two paragraphs, esp. pp. 16, 18, and Appendix, p. 8. Cp. Hume, *History*, ed. of 1773, vol. i., p. 205, where Domesday and Brady are both mentioned. The note appears first in ed. 2.]

叫卖的小贩。① 那时欧洲不同的国家,跟现在亚洲的几个鞑靼政府一样,当这些旅行者经过某些城镇、某些桥梁,或是带着他们的货物从一个地方迁移到另一个地方,或者他们建立一个小亭子来出售这些货物的时候,过去常常就是在这些人或其货物上来征税。这些不同的税种在英格兰被称为过境税、过桥税、落地税和摊贩税。有的时候由国王,有的时候由某些似乎在某些场合有权力这样做的大领主来给予这些商人,尤其是居住在他们领土上的商人一些免税的普遍优惠。这些商人尽管在其他方面还是跟隶役没有什么差别,或是几乎完全一样,被称为自由商人。反过来他们经常交纳人头税给他们的保护者。在当时没有付出价值不菲的报酬是不可能的,可能这种赋税被认为是他们的保护者给其免税获得的一种补偿吧。起初,这种人头税和税收豁免似乎完全只限于个人,仅仅对个人的生活产生影响,或者在生之际或凭保护者的好恶。据英格兰土地清账书册的不完全统计,英格兰的几个城镇,有时常常提及某些市民,他们每个人为了这种保护给国王或大领主交纳人头税。有时,它只记录这些税收的总和。②

但是无论城镇居民起初的情况怎样卑贱,似乎很显然比农村的土地占有者更早获得自由和独立。国王收入中从人头税中获得的那部分,经常由国王规定一定的比额,在一定年限内包给该

但是比起乡村的人们,他们更早获得自由,他们所在的城镇承包税收权,

① 《关于法律、警察、岁入及军备的演讲》,第 233 页。
② 参见布雷迪的有关城市历史论文,第 3 页等。罗伯特·布雷迪:《关于城市和自治城市的历史论文集》,第 2 版,1711 年。关于这两段中提到的市民和商人的地位,特别参阅第 16、18 页和附录第 8 页。休谟的《英格兰史》,1773 年,第 1 卷,第 205 页,提到土地勘察记录和布雷迪。本书首见于第 2 版。

the county, and sometimes to other persons. The burghers themselves frequently got credit enough to be admitted to farm the revenues of this sort which arose out of their own town, they becoming jointly and severally answerable for the whole rent. ① To let a farm in this manner was quite agreeable to the usual economy of, I believe, the sovereigns of all the different countries of Europe; who used frequently to let whole manors to all the tenants of those manors, they becoming jointly and severally answerable for the whole rent; ② but in return being allowed to collect it in their own way, and to pay it into the king's exchequer by the hands of their own bailiff, and being thus altogether freed from the insolence of the king's officers; a circumstance in those days regarded as of the greatest importance.

first for a term of years and afterwards in perpetuity,

At first, the farm of the town was probably let to the burghers, in the same manner as it had been to other farmers, for a term of years only. In process of time, however, it seems to have become the general practice to grant it to them in fee, that is for ever, reserving a rent certain never afterwards to be augmented. The payment having thus become perpetual, the exemptions, in return for which it was made, naturally became perpetual too. Those exemptions, therefore, ceased to be personal, and could not afterwards be considered as belonging to individuals as individuals, but as burghers of a particular burgh, which, upon this account, was called a Free burgh, for the same reason that they had been called Free-burghers or Free-traders.

as well as other privileges equivalent to freedom,

Along with this grant, the important privileges above mentioned, that they might give away their own daughters in marriage, that their children should succeed to them, and that they might dispose of their own effects by will, were generally bestowed upon the burghers of the town to whom it was given. Whether such privileges had before been usually granted along with the freedom of trade, to particular' burghers, as individuals, I know not. I reckon it not improbable that they were, though I cannot produce any direct evidence of it. But however

---

① See Madox Firma Burgi, [1726,] p. 18. also [Madox,] History [and Antiquities] of the Exchequer, chap. 1o. sect. v. p. 223, first edition [1711.]

② [An instance is given in *Firma Burgi*, p. 21.]

市长官或其他人征收。这些市民自己经常获得足够的信用来被允许承包本市的这种税收,他们既联合起来又各自独立地对整个税收负责。① 这种包税方式,我相信对于欧洲所有不同国家的统治者的一般经济都是相当合适的;它们过去常常将整个领地全部承包给这个领地上的佃农,佃农们既联合起来又各自独立地来对整个税收负责。② 作为回报,它们又被允许以各自的方式去收税,并由经他们自己的官员之手,支付给国王的国库,因此可以免受国王官吏的蛮横无理;这种情况在当时被认为是非常重要的。

当初,市民获得承包税收权,跟其他农场主获得一样,限于特定的年限。随着时间的推移,这似乎演变成了一个普遍的做法,永久地承包给市民代征,确定一定税额,以后永远不能增加。税收因此就成为永久的,以此为条件的其他各种赋税的豁免也成了永久的。因此,那些豁免不限于个人,此后也不再能被看作属于个人,而是被看作是给予某个特定的市民群体中的市民,以此来看,被称为自由城市,同样的原因,他们被称为自由市民或自由商人。

当初限于特定的年限,后来变成了永久,

以上所述的赋予市民的权利,以及他们自由嫁女权,根据遗嘱自由处置自己遗产的权力,一般是一同赐给它应赋予的市民的。这样的特权在以前是否和自由贸易一同赋予给作为个人的特殊市民,这个我不知道。我想或许是这样的,尽管我提不出任何直接的证据。不过,无论怎样,贱奴制度及奴隶制度的主要属

连同其他权利就等同于自由了,

---

① 参见马多克斯:《自治城市》,1726 年,第 18 页。还有马多克斯:《国库的历史和古迹》,第 1 版,1711 年,第 10 章第 5 节,第 223 页。

② 在《自治城市》第 21 页提供了一个实例。

this may have been, the principal attributes of villanage and slavery being thus taken away from them, they now, at least, became really free in our present sense of the word Freedom.

<small>and a government of their own.</small>   Nor was this all. They were generally at the same time erected into a commonalty or corporation, with the privilege of having magistrates and a town-council of their own, of making bye-laws for their own government, of building walls for their own defence, and of reducing all their inhabitants under a sort of military discipline, by obliging them to watch and ward; that is, as anciently understood, to guard and defend those walls against all attacks and surprises by night as well as by day. In England they were generally exempted from suit to the hundred and county courts; and all such pleas as should arise among them, the pleas of the crown excepted, were left to the decision of their own magistrates. In other countries much greater and more extensive jurisdictions were frequently granted to them. ①

<small>It seems strange that sovereigns should have abandoned the prospect of increased revenue and have erected independent republics.</small>   It might, probably, be necessary to grant to such towns as were admitted to farm their own revenues, some sort of compulsory jurisdiction to oblige their own citizens to make payment. In those disorderly times it might have been extremely inconvenient to have left them to seek this sort of justice from any other tribunal. But it must seem extraordinary that the sovereigns of all the different countries of Europe, should have exchanged in this manner for a rent certain, never more to be augmented, that branch of their revenue, which was, perhaps, of all others the most likely to be improved by the natural course of things, without either expence or attention of their own:② and that they should, besides, have in this manner voluntarily erected a sort of independent republics in the heart of their own dominions.

In order to understand this, it must be remembered, that in those days the sovereign of perhaps no country in Europe was able to protect, through the whole extent of his dominions, the weaker part of

---

① See Madox Firma Burgi: See also Pfeffel in the remarkable events under Frederic Ⅱ. and his successors of the house of Suabia.

② [*Lectures*, p. 4o.]

性就这样从他们身上解除了,从我们现今"自由"这个词的含义来说,至少他们此时变得真正自由了。

还不仅如此。与此同时他们通常建成一个共同团体或自治机关,拥有选举市长和市议会的权利,有权为他们自己的政府制定内部规则,有权建筑城墙实行防御,有权使其所有的市民接受一种军事训练,迫使他们防御和防守。这也就是古代所理解的日夜都要保卫和防御这些城墙,防止一切进攻和袭击。在英格兰,他们一般可免于向州郡法庭提出诉讼;他们之间的所有诉讼除公诉外,均可由市长判决。在其他国家,常常赋予市长们更大得多和更广泛得多的司法权。①

还有一个自己的政府。

对于允许包征自己城镇税收的城市来说,有必要给予他们某种强制性的司法权,迫使他们的市民纳税。在那种混乱的年代,让他们从其他的法庭来寻求这种审判,或许是极端不方便的。此时,国家纷乱,如果要它们到别的法庭请求这种判决,势必极其困难。但很奇怪的是,欧洲各国的君主,为什么要通过这样的方式来交换一种固定的不能增加的租税,这种赋税在所有的税收中是最可能因为食物的自然发展过程而提高的,不用花费自己的钱财,不必投入自己的精力。此外,他们还按照这种方式在他们自己辖区的中心自动地建立了一种独立的共和政权。②

看起来很奇怪君主应该放弃税收可能的增加,建立独立的共和政权,

为了理解这一点,必须记住在那些时代一个没有君主能够在自己统治的整个辖区内保护受到大地主压迫的自己市民中的弱

---

① 参见马多斯克:《自治城市》。还可参见费福尔(Pfeffel)关于苏阿比亚(Suabia)弗雷德里克二世及其后继者的大事记。

② 见《关于法律、警察、岁人及军备的演讲》,第40页。

国民财富的性质与原理

but the towns were the natural allies of the sovereign against the lords. his subjects from the oppression of the great lords. Those whom the law could not protect, and who were not strong enough to defend themselves, were obliged either to have recourse to the protection of some great lord, and in order to obtain it to become either his slaves or vassals; or to enter into a league of mutual defence for the common protection of one another. The inhabitants of cities and burghs, considered as single individuals, had no power to defend themselves; but by entering into a league of mutual defence with their neighbours, they were capable of making no contemptible resistance. The lords despised the burghers, whom they considered not only as of a different order, but as a parcel of emancipated slaves, almost of a different species from themselves. The wealth of the burghers never failed to provoke their envy and indignation, and they plundered them upon every occasion without mercy or remorse. The burghers naturally hated and feared the lords. The king hated and feared them too; but though perhaps he might despise, he had no reason either to hate or fear the burghers. Mutual interest, therefore, disposed them to support the king, and the king to support them against the lords. They were the enemies of his enemies, and it was his interest to render them as secure and independent of those enemies as he could. By granting them magistrates of their own, the privilege of making byelaws for their own government, that of building walls for their own defence, and that of reducing all their inhabitants under a sort of military discipline, he gave them all the means of security and independency of the barons which it was in his power to bestow. Without the establishment of some regular government of this kind, without some authority to compel their inhabitants to act according to some certain plan or system, no voluntary league of mutual defence could either have afforded them any permanent security, or have enabled them to give the king any considerable support. By granting them the farm of their town in fee, he took away from those whom he wished to have for his friends, and, if one may say so, for his allies, all ground of jealousy and suspicion that he was ever afterwards to oppress them, either by raising the farm rent of their town, or by granting it to some other farmer.

  The princes who lived upon the worst terms with their barons, seem accordingly to have been the most liberal in grants of this kind to their burghs. King John of England, for example, appears to have

小部分。那些不受法律保护的市民,以及力量不足以保护自己的市民,他们只有两种选择:或者不得不求助于某些大地主的保护,为了达此目的,他们要么成为大地主的奴隶,要么成为他们的奴仆;或者为了共同防御,联合起来,成立一个共同的防御联盟。这些城镇和市区的市民,如果被看作单独的个人,是没有力量来保护自己的;但是一旦加入共同防御联盟,和邻居联合起来了,他们就可以是不可忽视的抵抗力量。大地主经常鄙视这些市民,认为他们不仅仅是另一个阶层的人,而且是被解放的奴隶,几乎是不同于自己的族类。市民的财富很可能会引起大地主的嫉妒和愤恨,他们每时每刻都毫不仁慈、毫不留情地从市民身上抢劫财物。市民憎恨又害怕大地主。国王也憎恶、害怕他们;但是尽管他也可能鄙视市民,但他没有嫉恨他们、畏惧他们的理由。所以,共同的利益使国王市民共建同盟,以对抗领主。市民是国王敌人的敌人,所以,国王为了他自己的利益,尽可能地给市民提供安全和独立。通过给予他们自己选举市长的权力,为自己的政府建立市政法律,建筑自己的防御围墙,减少市民的军事训练,尽其所有给予他们安全和独立的方法。如果没有建立这种正规的政府,如果没有某些权势来迫使他们的市民根据某些计划或体系行事,也就不会有共同的防御联盟给他们提供永久的安全,或者使他们给予国王相当的支持。通过将税收承包给市民来征收,国王就从自己想要使之成为自己的朋友,如果可以这样说的话,使之成为自己的同盟军的人心中驱除了一切的妒忌和猜测,不怕他以后会压迫他们,或是提高他们城市的租税,或是将其包给他的人去征收。

　　因此与领主关系最差的国王,似乎是在给予市民这种特权方面表现得最慷慨的。例如英格兰的国王约翰,对他的市民是最为

但是这些城镇是天生反对地主的国王的同盟军。

国民财富的性质与原理

The sovereigns who quarrelled most with the barons were the most liberal to the towns.

been a most munificent benefactor to his towns. ① Philip the First of France lost all authority over his barons. Towards the end of his reign, his son Lewis, known afterwards by the name of Lewis the Fat, consulted, according to Father Daniel, with the bishops of the royal demesnes, concerning the most proper means of restraining the violence of the great lords. ② Their advice consisted of two different proposals. One was to erect a new order of jurisdiction by establishing magistrates and a town council in every considerable town of his demesnes. The other was to form a new militia, by making the inhabitants of those towns, under the command of their own magistrates, march out upon proper occasions to the assistance of the king. It is from this period, according to the French antiquarians, ③ that we are to date the institution of the magistrates and councils of cities in France. It was during the unprosperous reigns of the princes of the house of Suabia that the greater part of the free towns of Germany received the first grants of their privileges, and that the famous Hanseatic league first became formidable. ④

The city militia was often able to overpower the neighbouring lords, as in Italy and Switzerland.

The militia of the cities seems, in those times, not to have been inferior to that of the country, and as they could be more readily assembled upon any sudden occasion, they frequently had the advantage in their disputes with the neighbouring lords. In countries, such as Italy and Switzerland, in which, on account either of their distance from the principal seat of government, of the natural strength of the country itself, or of some other reason, the sovereign came to lose the whole of his authority, the cities generally became independent republics, and conquered all the nobility in their neighbourhood; obliging them to pull down their castles in the country, and to live, like other peaceable inhabitants, in the city. This is the short history of the republic of Berne, as well as of several other cities in Switzerland. If you except Venice, for of that city the history is somewhat different, it

---

① See Madox [*Firma Burgi*, pp. 35, 150.].

② [1755, vol. iii. , pp. 512-513.]

③ [Possibly Du Cange (who is referred to in the margin of Daniel, p. 514, and by Hume, *History*, ed. 1773, vol. ii. , p. 118), *Glossarium*, s. v. Commune, communia, etc. , ' Primus vero ejus modi *Communias* in Francia Ludov. VII. [? VI.] rex multiplicavit et auxit. ']

④ See Pfeffel.

宽容的捐助者。① 法国的菲利普一世丧失了对于他的领地的统治。据神父丹尼尔说,在他统治末年他的儿子路易斯,后来被称为肥路易,与自己领地上所有的教主商榷,有关限制大地主暴力的最恰当的办法。② 主教们的意见可归纳为两种建议。一种是在其所有较大的领地上,通过选举市长和市政议会的方式来建立一个新的管辖体系。另一种是形成一支新的民兵,让这些城市的市民们在他们各自的市长的命令下,在合适的场合出来援助国王。据法国考古学家说,③法国开始市长制度和市政议会制度自此开始。正是在苏阿比亚王室的各国国王统治开始衰落的时候,德国的大部分自由城市被赋予了特权,著名的汉萨同盟首次变得难以对付。④

> 领主和领主争吵最激烈的君主,也是对城市最慷慨的君主。

在那个年代,城市的民兵似乎不比乡村的民兵地位低下,因为他们更容易在任何的紧急时刻集合起来,他们经常在与邻近地主的争议中处于优势地位。在意大利、瑞士等国家,考虑到距离首府很远,或者是城市自身的天然力量,也或者是其他什么原因,君主开始放弃他的统治,城市渐渐变成独立的共和国,并且征服当地贵族;迫使他们拆掉他们在城中的城堡,像其他和平居民一样居住在城镇内。这是伯尔尼民主国和瑞士其他城镇的简史。除了威尼斯之外,这个城市的历史稍有不同,所有意大

> 城市的民兵力量常比邻近的领主大,例如在意大利和瑞士。

---

① 参见马多斯克:《自治城市》,第35、150页。
② G. 丹尼尔(Daniel):《法兰西史》,1755年,第3卷,第512~513页。
③ 或许是杜坎的《辞典》中的"市自治体";丹尼尔:《法兰西史》第514页;休谟:《英格兰史》,1773年,第2卷,第118页,均曾提到杜坎。
④ 参见费福尔的书。

国民财富的性质与原理

is the history of all the considerable Italian republics, of which so great a number arose and perinhed, between the end of the twelfth and the beginning of the sixteenth century.

<small>In France and England the cities could not be taxed without their own consent.</small>   In countries such as France or England, where the authority of the sovereign, though frequently very low, never was destroyed altogether, the cities had no opportunity of becoming entirely independent. They became, however, so considerable, that the sovereign could impose no tax upon them, besides the stated farm-rent of the town, without their own consent. They were, therefore, called upon to send deputies to the general assembly of the states of the kingdom, where they might join with the clergy and the barons in granting, upon urgent occasions, some extraordinary aid to the king. Being generally too more favourable to his power, their deputies seem, sometimes, to have been employed by him as a counter-balance in those assemblies to the authority of the great lords, Hence the origin of the representation of burghs in the states general of all the great monarchies in Europe.

<small>In consequence of this greater security of the towns industry flourished and stock accumulated there earlier than in the country.</small>   Order and good government, and along with them the liberty and security of individuals, were, in this manner, established in cities, at a time when the occupiers of land in the country were exposed to every sort of violence. But men in this defenceless state naturally content themselves with their necessary subsistence; because to acquire more might only tempt the injustice of their oppressors. On the contrary, when they are secure of enjoying the fruits of their industry, they naturally exert it to better their condition and to acquire not only the necessaries, but the conveniencies and elegancies of life. That industry, therefore, which aims at something more than necessary subsistence, was established in cities long before it was commonly practised by the occupiers of land in the country. If in the hands of a poor cultivator, oppressed with the servitude of villanage, some little stock should accumulate, he would naturally conceal it with great care from his master, to whom it would otherwise have belonged, and take the first opportunity of running away to a town. The law was at that time so indulgent to the inhabitants of towns, and so desirous of diminishing the authority of the lords over those of the country, that if he could conceal himself there from the pursuit of his lord for a year, he was free for ever. ① Whatever stock, therefore, accumulated in the hands of

---

① [Lectures, p. 40.]

利共和国的历史也是这样的,在 12 世纪末到 16 世纪初期,他们的数目巨大,时起时落。

在英、法两国,虽然君主的权力有时很低微,但是从来没有全部失去过,城镇也没有机会获得完全的独立。然而他们的势力变得如此强大,以至于不经他们同意,除了城镇的前面所提到的承包税之外,君主不能够在他们身上征税。因此,他们被号召起来委派代表参加国家的议会,在会上他们可能和牧师和贵族联合起来,在紧急情况下给予国王特别的帮助。市民一般都是维护国王权威的,因此有时他们的代表似乎在会议中充当了反对大地主的力量。这就是市民代表出席欧洲各大君主国的国会的由来。

> 英、法两国的城市,没有市民同意不得对之征税。

在这种方式下,秩序、良好的政府以及带给个人的自由和安全,在各城镇确立了。这时乡村的土地占有者还是在忍受着各种暴力的压迫。但是处于无力抵抗状态之下的人们很自然地满足于获得必要的生活资料;获得更多的力量只会引发压迫者的更多不公平对待。相反,如果他们很放心地享受他们的劳动带给他们的成果的话,他们很自然会利用它来改善他们的条件,不仅仅获得必需品,而且是生活的便利品和娱乐品。因此,那个不仅以生活必需品为目标的劳动,在乡村土地所有者普遍那样去做以前,城市中就早已这样做了。一个受到奴役的贫穷的耕种者处于贱奴状态,如果稍有积蓄,他就会向他的主人隐藏,否则主人就会据为己有;当时的法律对城市的市民既如此宽纵,同时又如此希望削减乡村的权力,以至于农场主只要逃避了领主的追捕达到一年,他就永远自由了。① 所以,城市中的市民手中积累的所有辛

> 由于安全的原因,城市的繁荣,工商业和资本积累早于乡村。

---

① 见《关于法律、警察、岁入及军备的演讲》,第 40 页。

the industrious part of the inhabitants of the country, naturally took refuge in cities, as the only sanctuaries in which it could be secure to the person that acquired it.

<small>Cities on the seacoast or on navigable rivers are not dependent on the neighbouring country.</small>

The inhabitants of a city, it is true, must always ultimately derive their subsistence, and the whole materials and means of their industry, from the country. But those of a city, situated near either the seacoast or the banks of a navigable river, are not necessarily confined to derive them from the country in their neighbourhood. They have a much wider range, and may draw them from the most remote corners of the world, either in exchange for the manufactured produce of their own industry, or by performing the office of carriers between distant countries, and exchanging the produce of one for that of another. A city might in this manner grow up to great wealth and splendor, while not only the country in its neighbourhood, but all those to which it traded, were in poverty and wretchedness. Each of those countries, perhaps, taken singly, could afford it but a small part, either of its subsistence, or of its employment; but all of them taken together could afford it both a great subsistence and a great employment. There were, however, within the narrow circle of the commerce of those times, some countries that were opulent and industrious. Such was the Greek empire as long as it subsisted, and that of the Saracens during the reigns of the Abassides. Such too was Egypt till it was conquered by the Turks, some part of the coast of Barbary, and all those provinces of Spain which were under the government of the Moors.

<small>The cities of Italy were the first to grow opulent, being centrally situated and benefited by the crusades.</small>

The cities of Italy seem to have been the first in Europe which were raised by commerce to any considerable degree of opulence. Italy lay in the centre of what was at that time the improved and civilized part of the world. The crusades too, though, by the great waste of stock and destruction of inhabitants which they occasioned, they must necessarily have retarded the progress of the greater part of Europe, were extremely favourable to that of some Italian cities. The great armies which marched from all parts to the conquest of the Holy Land, gave extraordinary encouragement to the shipping of Venice, Genoa,

勤劳动的部分,都会向城市寻求庇护,因为这是唯一的可以保护所有者所得的避难所。

城市的市民最终还是必须从乡村中获得生活的必需品、所有的工业原料和工具,这一点确实是这样的。但是一个位于海边或沿河岸的城市,不一定要从邻近的乡村中获得这些物品。他们拥有更大的范围,可能从世界最遥远的地方来获得,或者用他们的劳动产品来交换,或者通过在相距很远的城市之间贩运,交换不同城市的产品。一个城市可能通过这种方式成长起来,日臻富强,尽管在邻近的乡村,在所有的与之进行贸易的城市仍处于贫穷和落后的状态。或许,其中的每一个城市可能只能提供生活必需品或就业机会的一小部分,但是所有的加起来可以提供大量的生活必需品和就业机会。然而,在那个时代里,狭小的商业圈子中,存在一些富裕勤劳的国家。例如希腊帝国只要在它存在的时候,以及亚巴西德统治下撒拉逊帝国时代。[1] 埃及直到它被土耳其征服之前,巴伯里海岸的一些地区,以及摩尔人统治下的西班牙各省,都是这样的。

在欧洲,意大利城市似乎最早的由商业来达到相当富裕程度。意大利位于当时世界先进和文明部分的中心地区。尽管十字军极大地破坏了他们所占有的资财,给人们也带来了伤害,毫无疑问地,他们阻碍了欧洲大部分地区的进步,但是对于意大利的这些城市却非常有利。为争夺圣地,来自世界各地的大军,给威尼斯、热那亚和比萨各地的航海业带来了极大的推动作用,有

---

〔1〕 撒拉逊人,原为叙利亚附近一游牧民族,后特指抵抗十字军的伊斯兰教阿拉伯人,现泛指伊斯兰教徒或阿拉伯人。

and Pisa, sometimes in transporting them thither, and always in supplying them with provisions. They were the commissaries, if one may say so, of those armies; and the most destructive frenzy that ever befel the European nations,① was a source of opulence to those republics.

<small>The cities imported manufactures and luxuries from richer countries, which were paid for by rude produce.</small>
The inhabitants of trading cities, by importing the improved manufactures and expensive luxuries of richer countries, afforded some food to the vanity of the great proprietors, who eagerly purchased them with great quantities of the rude produce of their own lands. The commerce of a great part of Europe in those times, accordingly, consisted chiefly in the exchange of their own rude, for the manufactured produce of more civilized nations. Thus the wool of England used to be exchanged for the wines of France, and the fine cloths of Flanders, in the same manner as the corn of Poland is at this day exchanged for the wines and brandies of France, and for the silks and velvets of France and Italy.

<small>Demand for such manufactured articles having become considerable, their manufacture was established in the cities.</small>
A taste for the finer and more improved manufactures, was in this manner introduced by foreign commerce into countries where no such works were carried on. But when this taste became so general as to occasion a considerable demand, the merchants, in order to save the expence of carriage, naturally endeavoured to establish some manufactures of the same kind in their own country. Hence the origin of the first manufactures for distant sale that seem to have been established in the western provinces of Europe, after the fall of the Roman empire.

<small>All countries have some manufactures.</small>
No large country, it must be observed, ever did or could subsist without some sort of manufactures being carried on in it; and when it is said of any such country that it has no manufactures, it must always be understood of the finer and more improved, or of such as are fit for distant sale. In every large country, both the clothing and houshold furniture of the far greater part of the people, are the produce of their own industry. This is even more universally the case in those poor

---

① ['The most signal and most durable monument of human folly that has yet appeared in any age or nation,' Hume, *History*, ed. of 1773, vol. i. , p. 292; 'this universal frenzy,' *ibid.* , p. 298, of ed. 1770, vol. i. , p. 327, but in his 1st ed. Hume wrote 'universal madness'.]

时在运输方面也是,并且经常给他们提供粮食供给。这些城市可以说是这些军队的补给库;曾经降临到欧洲许多国家的最具毁灭性的动乱,①成为了这些共和国的富裕的源泉。

商业城市的居民,通过进口富裕国家改良的制造品和昂贵的奢侈品,为满足大地主的虚荣心提供一些食物,大地主渴望用本国生产的大量产品、天然物品来进行交换。因此,在那个时代欧洲大部分地区的商业,主要是本国天然产品来交换更先进国家的制成品。英格兰的羊毛常常用于交换法国的葡萄酒和佛兰德的精制呢绒,同样的,波兰的玉米在当时用于交换法国的葡萄酒和白兰地,以及法国和意大利的丝绸和天鹅绒。

对于更精良更先进的制成品的嗜好,以这种方式由对外贸易引进没有这些工业的国家。但是当这些嗜好变成大众化成为大量需求的时候,商人们为了节省运费,很自然地努力在自己的国家来建立一些类似产品的制造场。因此,罗马帝国衰落之后的首批远距离国家之间的制成品销售起源于此。

必须注意的是,世界上不存在而且也绝对不会存在没有一点制造业的大国。当谈到那些没有制造业的国家时,必须应该理解为这些国家没有比较精良和比较先进的制成品,或者没有适于远距离销售的制造品。在所有的大国中,人们绝大部分的衣服和家具都是由他们自己国家的工业生产的。相对于制造业发达的较为富裕的国家,在贫穷的国家这些例子更为普遍,那里据说一般

---

① 休谟:《英格兰史》,1773年,第1卷,第292页:"在所有时代和所有国家曾经出现过的人类愚蠢的最显著、最持久的时刻。"《英格兰史》1770年,第1卷,第327页,休谟称之为"普遍的动乱"。

— 879 —

countries which are commonly said to have no manufactures, than in those rich ones that are said to abound in them. In the latter, you will generally find, both in the clothes and houshold furniture of the lowest rank of people, a much greater proportion of foreign productions than in the former.

Those manufactures which are fit for distant sale, seem to have been introduced into different countries in two different ways.

Sometimes manufactures for distant sale are introduced in imitation of foreign manufactures.

Sometimes they have been introduced, in the manner above mentioned, by the violent operation, if one may say so, of the stocks of particular merchants and undertakers, who established them in imitation of some foreign manufactures of the same kind. Such manufactures, therefore, are the offspring of foreign commerce, and such seem to have been the ancient manufactures of silks, velvets, and brocades, which flourished in Lucca, during the thirteenth century. They were banished from thence by the tyranny of one of Machiavel's heroes, Castruecio Castracani. In 1310, nine hundred families were driven out of Lucca, of whom thirty-one retired to Venice, and offered to introduce there the silk manufacture. ① Their offer was accepted; many privileges were conferred upon them, and they began the manufacture with three hundred workmen. Such too seem to have been the manufactures of fine cloths that anciently flourished in Flanders, and which were introduced into England in the beginning of the reign of Elizabeth; and such are the present silk manufacturesof Lyons and Spital-fields. Manufactures introduced in this manner are generally employed upon foreign materials, being imitations of foreign manufactures. When the Venetian manufacture was first established, the materials were all brought from Sicily and the Levant. The more ancient manufacture of Lucca was likewise carried on with foreign materials. The cultivation of mulberry trees, and the breeding of silkworms, seem not to have been common in the northern parts of Italy before the sixteenth century. Those arts were not introduced into France till

---

① See Sandi *Istoria Civile de Vinezia*, Part 2. vol. i. page 247, and 256.

第三篇 第三章

没有制造业。一般还能发现,在富裕国家中的最底层的人们,他们的衣服和家具比起穷国,有更大部分的是外国的产品。

那些适于远距离销售的制造品似乎通过两种途径被引入不同的国家。

有时他们被按照上述的方式引入,通过一次性地注入某些商人和资本家的大量资本(如果可以这样说的话),这些人模仿国外类似制造品来建立制造业。因此这些制造业是对外贸易的产物,例如 13 世纪在卢卡繁荣起来的古代的丝绸、天鹅绒和锻造业。从那时起在马基雅弗利的英雄之一斯特罗西奥·卡斯特拉卡尼的暴政之下,这些制造业被驱逐了。1310 年,900 多个家庭被逐出卢卡;其中的 31 家退往威尼斯,提议在那里引入丝织业。① 他们的建议被采纳,并且给予他们许多特权,他们开始雇用 300 多人来从事这种制造业。这与古代佛兰德精细呢绒制造业[1]的繁荣很类似,它们是在伊丽莎白统治初期被引入英格兰;现在里昂和斯皮塔菲尔德丝织业也如此。这样被引入的制造业一般使用国外的原料,模仿国外的制造业。当意大利的制造业最初被建立时,原料全部都从西西里和黎凡特运来。卢卡比较古老的制造业也同样使用国外的原料。桑树的种植,蚕的饲养在 16 世纪前的意大利北部似乎还不常见。直到查理九世这些工艺才

边注:适于远距离的销售被外国的制造业所模仿。

---

① 参见维特桑迪:《威尼斯共和国文明史纲要》,威尼斯,1755 年,第 2 编第 1 卷,第 247、256 页。

[1] 佛兰德:欧洲西北部一块历史上有名的地区,包括法国北部的部分地区、比利时西部地区和北海沿岸荷兰西南部的部分地带。几个世纪以来,作为一个服装业中心,它一直享有实际的独立权并且十分繁荣。低地国家的哈布斯堡战争导致了这一地区的最终分裂,并在两次世界大战中都遭受严重损失。

— 881 —

the reign of Charles IX. The manufactures of Flanders were carried on chiefly with Spanish and English wool. Spanish wool was the material, not of the first woollen manufacture of England, but of the first that was fit for distant sale. More than one half the materials of the Lyons manufacture is at this day foreign silk; when it was first established, the whole or very nearly the whole was so. No part of the materials of the Spital-fields manufacture is ever likely to be the produce of England. The seat of such manufactures, as they are generally introduced by the scheme and project of a few individuals, is sometimes established in a maritime city, and sometimes in an inland town, according as their interest, judgment or caprice happen to determine.

<small>Sometimes they have grown up out of the coarser home manufactures.</small> At other times manufactures for distant sale grow up naturally, and as it were of their own accord, by the gradual refinement of those houshold and coarser manufactures which must at all times be carried on even in the poorest and rudest countries. Such manufactures are generally employed upon the materials which the country produces, and they seem frequently to have been first refined and improved in such inland countries as were, not indeed at a very great, but at a considerable distance from the sea coast, and sometimes even from all water carriage. An inland country naturally fertile and easily cultivated, produces a great surplus of provisions beyond what is necessary for maintaining the cultivators, and on account of the expence of land carriage, and inconveniency of river navigation, it may frequently be difficult to send this surplus abroad. Abundance, therefore, renders provisions cheap, and encourages a great number of workmen to settle in the neighbourhood, who find that their industry can there procure them more of the necessaries and conveniencies of life than in other places. They work up the materials of manufacture which the land produces, and exchange their finished work, or what is the same thing the price of it, for more materials and provisions. They give a new value to the surplus part of the rude produce, by saving the expence of carrying it to the water side, or to some distant market; and they furnish the cultivators with something in exchange for it that is either useful or agreeable to them, upon easier terms than they could have obtained it before. The cultivators get a better price for their surplus produce, and can purchase cheaper other conveniencies which

被引入法国。佛兰德的制造业主要使用来自西班牙和英格兰的羊毛。西班牙羊毛不是英格兰毛织物最初采用的原料,却是最适于远地销售的毛织业最初所采用的材料。里昂一半以上的制造品原料是当时的国外丝绸;当它建立之初,全部的或几乎全部的都是这种情况。斯皮塔菲尔德制造业所用的材料似乎丝毫没有任何部分是英格兰的产物。这样的制造业因为一般是被少数个人的计划而引入的,因此有时候这种制造业的位置设立在海运城市,有时是在内陆城市,根据他们的利益、判断或幻想而决定的。

在其他的时候,适于远地销售的制造业,仿佛是自然而然地产生一样,甚至在最贫穷最原始的国家中,也是必须在所有的时候都在进行的比较粗糙的家庭制造业中逐渐改良而成的。这些制造业一般使用本国生产的原材料,并且它们往往首先在内陆离海岸线有相当距离甚至是离水运很远的国家里被加工和改良。内陆国家天然就土地肥沃、容易开垦,可以生产大量超过满足生产者自身生存需要的产品,把运费和河运的不便利因素计算在内,将这些富余产品运送出去也是很困难的事情。因此,物产丰富提供便宜的粮食,鼓励大量的工人定居邻近地区,工人们发现与其他地方比,他们在此处的生产可以获得更多的超过生活必需品和便利品的部分。这些工人从事本地生产的原材料的加工,以自己的最终产品或制成品价格(两者就是一回事)来交换更多的原材料和食物。他们通过节省运往水边或遥远市场的运输费,给天然物品剩余部分增加了一个新的价值。他们给耕种者提供一些物品,他们可以以比以前更容易获得的条件,用来交换对他们有用或是他们自己喜欢的物品。耕种者从他们提供的剩余产品中获得较高的价格,并且可以更加低廉地购买自己需要的其他便

<small>他们产生比较粗糙的家庭制造业。有时于</small>

they have occasion for. They are thus both encouraged and enabled to increase this surplus produce by a further improvement and better cultivation of the land; and as the fertility of the land had given birth to the manufacture, so the progress of the manufacture re-acts upon the land, and increases still further its fertility. The manufacturers first supply the neighbourhood, and afterwards, as their work improves and refines, more distant markets. For though neither the rude produce, nor even the coarse manufacture, could, without the greatest difficulty, support the expence of a considerable land carriage, the refined and improved manufacture easily may. In a small bulk it frequently contains the price of a great quantity of rude produce. A piece of fine cloth, for example, which weighs only eighty pounds, contains in it, the price, not only of eighty pounds weight of wool, but sometimes of several thousand weight of corn, the maintenance of the different working people, and of their immediate employers. The corn, which could with difficulty have been carried abroad in its own shape, is in this manner virtually exported in that of the complete manufacture, and may easily be sent to the remotest corners of the world. In this manner have grown up naturally, and as it were of their own accord, the manufactures of Leeds, Halifax, Sheffield, Birmingham, and Wolverhampton. Such manufactures are the offspring of agriculture. In the modem history of Europe, their extension and improvement have generally been posterior to those which were the offspring of foreign commerce. England was noted for the manufacture of fine cloths made of Spanish wool, more than a century before any of those which now flourish in the places above mentioned were fit for foreign sale. The extension and improvement of these last could not take place but in consequence of the extension and improvement of agriculture, the last and greatest effect of foreign commerce, and of the manufactures immediately introduced by it, and which I shall now proceed to explain.

利品。耕种者既被鼓励能够通过进一步改良和更好的开垦来增加这些剩余产品的生产。由于土地肥沃,制造业因此而产生,所以制造业的改良又对土地起作用,进一步又提高土地的肥沃程度。制造业最初仅仅供应邻近的地区,后来随着工艺的改进和提高,可以给更远的市场提供产品。因为天然物品,甚至粗糙的制成品,必然要克服极大的困难才能弥补长途陆运的费用,而改良的工艺品或制造品却很容易做到。它往往在较小的体积中包含了大量天然物品的价格。例如,一匹精制呢绒,虽然仅重 80 磅,但所包含的价值,却不只是 80 磅羊毛的价格,有时甚至会是几千镑谷物的价值,这是各种工人及其直接雇主的维持费用。很难按照其原来形态运往国外的谷物,按照这种方式的话实际上是以完全制成品的形式出口,而且很容易就可以运往世界上最远的角落了。利兹(Leeds)、哈利法克斯、雪菲尔德、伯明翰、乌维汉普顿等地的制造业,[1]就是按照这个方式,自然而然地发展起来的。这些制造业是农业的产物。在欧洲的现代史上,他们的延伸和改进,一般晚于那些由对外贸易促成的制造业。英格兰制造业以西班牙羊毛为原料而制造的精致呢绒非常出名,一个多世纪之前这些呢绒现在盛行于上述地区,适于对外贸易。后述的各种扩大和改良,只能发生在农业的延伸和改良之后,以及直接引入的制造业的影响,我将进一步加以说明。

---

[1] 利兹(Leeds),英国英格兰中北部城市,在曼彻斯特的东北部。1626 年被合并,它是一个主要商业、运输、通讯及工业中心。哈利法克斯(Halifax),英格兰东北部、曼彻斯特东北部的享有自治特权的城市,是一个工业中心。乌维汉普顿(Wolverhampton),英格兰中西部的自治市镇,位于伯明翰西北。它是一座高度工业化的城市。

CHAPTER IV

How The Commerce Of The Towns Contributed To The Improvement Of The Country

The rise of towns benefited the country, The increase and riches of commercial and manufacturing towns, contributed to the improvement and cultivation of the countries to which they belonged, in three different ways.

First, by affording a great and ready market for the rude produce of the country, they gave encouragement to its cultivation and further because they afforded (1) already market for its produce, improvement. This benefit was not even confined to the countries in which they were situated, but extended more or less to all those with which they had any dealings. To all of them they afforded a market for some part either of their rude or manufactured produce, and consequently gave some encouragement to the industry and improvement of all. Their own country, however, on account of its neighbourhood, necessarily derived the greatest benefit from this market. Its rude produce being charged with less carriage, the traders could pay the growers a better price for it, and yet afford it as cheap to the consumers as that of more distant countries.

(2) because merchants bought land in the country and improved it, Secondly, the wealth acquired by the inhabitants of cities was frequently employed in purchasing such lands as were to be sold, of which a great part would frequently be uncultivated. Merchants are commonly ambitious of becoming country gentlemen, and when they do, they are generally the best of all improvers. A merchant is accustomed to employ his money chiefly in profitable projects; whereas a mere country gentleman is accustomed to employ it chiefly in expence. The one often sees his money go from him and return to him again with a profit: the other, when once he parts with it, very seldom expects to see any more of it. Those different habits naturally affect their temper and disposition in every sort of business. A merchant is commonly a bold; a country gentleman, a timid undertaker. The one

第四章　城镇商业怎样对农村的改良做出贡献

工商业城镇的增加与富裕,通过三种途径来对所属农村的改良与耕种做出贡献。

> 城市的出现对乡村有益,

第一,通过为乡村的天然产品提供一个巨大的方便的市场,他们鼓励了农村的开垦与进一步的改进。这些利益不仅限于他们所在的城市,而且在于或多或少延伸到与其通商的那些城市。对于所有这些乡村来说,他们提供了天然产品或是制成品的部分市场,并且随之鼓励了产业和产业的改进。然而他们自己的乡村,由于邻近城市,可能从这个市场上获得最大的利益。它的天然产品因为运费较低,商人可以为耕种者支付更好的价格,也能以较低的价格支付给更远的乡村的消费者。

> (1)因为他们为乡村产品提供了市场,

第二,城市的市民所占有的财富,常常被用来购买诸如土地这样的资本来出售,其中的大部分往往未被开垦。商人一般都有成为乡绅的野心,当他们的愿望实现的时候,他们一般都成为最好的改良者。商人习惯于投入自己的钱财主要是在有利可图的计划上,然而一个普通的乡绅,习惯于投资于开支上。一个常常看着自己的钱离开自己,然后带回来一些利润;另外一个,当他把钱投出去的时候,很少再希望看到它。这些不同的习惯很自然会影响他们在每件事情中的脾气和性情。商人一般很胆大;绅士一

> (2)因为商人在乡村购买土地并进行改良,

— 887 —

is not afraid to lay out at once a large capital upon the improvement of his land, when he has a probable prospect of raising the value of it in proportion to the expence. The other, if he has any capital, which is not always the case, seldom ventures to employ it in this manner. If he improves at all, it is commonly not with a capital, but with what he can save out of his annual revenue. Whoever has had the fortune to live in a mercantile town situated in an unimproved country, must have frequently observed how much more spirited the operations of merchants were in this way, than those of mere country gentlemen. The habits, besides, of order, economy and attention, to which mercantile business naturally forms a merchant, render him much fitter to execute, with profit and success, any project of improvement.

and (3) because order and good government were introduced.

Thirdly, and lastly, commerce and manufactures gradually introduced order and good government, and with them, the liberty and security of individuals, among the inhabitants of the country, who had before lived almost in a continual state of war with their neighbours, and of servile dependency upon their superiors. This, though it has been the least observed, is by far the most important of all their effects. Mr. Hume is the only writer who, so far as I know, has hitherto taken notice of it.

Before foreign commerce and fine manufactures are introduced great proprietors are surrounded by bands of retainers,

In a country which has neither foreign commerce, nor any of the finer manufactures, a great proprietor, having nothing for which he can exchange the greater part ot the produce of his lands which is over and above the maintenance of the cultivators, consumes the whole in rustic hospitality at home. If this surplus produce is sufficient to maintain a hundred or a thousand men, he can make use of it in no other way than by maintaining a hundred or a thousand men. He is at all times, therefore, surrounded with a multitude of retainers and dependants, who having no equivalent to give in return for their maintenance, but being fed entirely by his bounty, must obey him, for the same reason that soldiers must obey the prince who pays them. Before the extension of commerce and manufactures in Europe, the hospitality of the rich and the great, from the sovereign down to the smallest baron, exceeded every thing which in the present times we can easily

般很胆怯。一个不担心立马投入大量资本到他的土地改良上,如果他觉得很有希望按照费用的比例来提高土地价值。另一个如果拥有资本,往往没有资本,很少冒险用这种方式运用资金。如果他最终改良了,一般也不是用资本进行的,而是用他年收入中节省的部分来进行的。无论谁有幸主宰位于一个荒村的商业中心城镇,一定经常看到商人按照这种方式来运作,比起乡绅来说要活跃得多了。另外,商业经营自然形成商人的秩序、节省和谨慎等习惯,使得他们更适于执行任何的改良计划,获得成功和利润。

第三,也是最后一点,商业和制造业逐步引入了良好的秩序和管理,随之在居民中引入了个人的自由和安全。在乡村中的居民里,有些人以前一向处在与其邻人战争的状态中,处于对他们上级的奴役依附状态下。尽管很少受到注意,但是这也是所有影响中最为重要的。就我所知,休谟先生是唯一注意到了这一点的作家。

(3) 还因为秩序和好的管理被引入。

在既没有对外贸易又没有精细制造业的乡村,一个大地主土地上的产出超过维持耕种者基本维持费的绝大部分,没有东西可以用来交换,他就用乡村式的家庭款待来花费这部分剩余。如果这部分剩余足够养活上百或上千人,他除了用来维持 100 人或 1000 人之外,没有其他的使用办法。因此,他总是被大群的仆人依附和围绕着,这些人没法给予所得的维持费以回报,只能靠他的施舍为生,所以必须服从于他,这个道理跟士兵必须服从于给他们军饷的君主一样。欧洲的工商业发展扩张之前,从国王到小的贵族,富人和贵族的家庭款盛都超过了现代所有我们所能想到的规模。威斯敏斯特大厅是威廉·鲁弗斯的餐厅,对于他的同伴来说

在国外商业和精细制造业被引入之前,大地主被大群的侍从围绕着。

form a notion of. Westminster hall was the dining-room of William Rufus, and might frequently, perhaps, not be too large for his company. It was reckoned a piece of magnificence in Thomas Becket, that he strowed the floor of his hall with clean hay or rushes in the season, in order that the knights and squires, who could not get seats, might not spoil their fine clothes when they sat down on the floor to eat their dinner. ① The great earl of Warwick is said to have entertained every day at his different manors, thirty thousand people; and though the number here may have been exaggerated, it must, however, have been very great to admit of such exaggeration. ② A hospitality nearly of the same kind was exercised not many years ago in many different parts of the highlands of Scotland. It seems to be common in all nations to whom commerce and manufactures are little known. I have seen, says Doctor Pocock, an Arabian chief dine in the streets of a town where he had come to sell his cattle, and invite all passengers, even common beggars, to sit down with him and partake of his banquet. ③

and tenants at will were just as dependent as' retainera.

The occupiers of land were in every respect as dependent upon the great proprietor as his retainers. Even such of them as were not in a state of villanage, were tenants at will, who paid a rent in no respect equivalent to the subsistence which the land afforded them. A crown, half a crown, a sheep, a lamb, was some years ago in the

① [Evidently from Hume, *History*, ed. of 1773, vol. i., p. 384.]

② ['No less than 30,000 persons are said to have daily lived at his board in the different manors and castles which he possessed in England.' —Hume, *History*, ed. of 1773, vol. iii., p. 182. In *Lectures*, p. 42, it had been '40,000 people, besides tenants'.]

③ ['An Arab prince will often dine in the street, before his door, and call to all that pass, even beggars, in the usual expression, Bismillah, that is, In the name of God; who come and sit down, and when they have done, give their Hamdellilah, that is, God be praised. For the Arabs are great levellers, put everybody on a footing with them; and it is by such generosity and hospitality that they maintain their interest.' -Richard Pococke, *Description of the East*, 1743, vol. i., p. 183.]

常常或许不是很大。据说托马斯·贝克特[1]有过这样的壮举:他将他的大厅地板用干净的草或灯芯草铺满,以便于骑士们和先生们找不到座位,当他们席地而坐用餐时不至于弄脏他们的华丽衣服。① 据说沃里克公爵每天在不同的庄园里款待3万宾客;尽管这个数字也许夸张了点,但是数目一定很大才会有这样的夸张。② 几乎同样的款筵在苏格兰高地许多不同的地方,前几年也都出现过。似乎在所有没有制造业和商业的国家,这也是非常常见的事情。波科克博士说过,他曾见一阿拉伯酋长在他售卖牲畜的市场上就餐,并且邀请所有的行人过客,甚至普通的乞丐,也跟他坐在一起共享筵席。③

土地占有者每个方面都依附于大地主,就像他的奴仆一样。即使那些不是处于奴隶状态的人,也是可以随意令其退租的佃农,他们缴纳的地租无论在哪方面都不等价于土地提供给他们的

并且可以随意令其退租的佃农跟奴仆一样具有依赖性。

---

① 显然引自休谟:《英格兰史》,1773年,第1卷,第384页。
② "据说每天都有不少于3万人都在他所拥有的位于英格兰的不同庄园和城堡里聚餐。"见休谟:《英格兰史》,1773年,第3卷,第182页。《关于法律、警察、岁入及军备的演讲》的第42页中说除了佃户还有4万人。
③ 一个阿拉伯君主经常坐在自家门前,当街进餐,邀请所有的过客甚至乞丐,往往说这是以真主的名义采取的行为;过来坐下进餐的人,经常感谢真主。因为阿拉伯人是伟大的平等主义者,他们将所有人放在平等的位置上,通过这种慷慨和款待来维持他们的利益。见理查德·波科克:《东方素描》,1743年,第1卷,第183页。

[1] 托马斯·贝克特(Thomas Becket)(1118? ~1170):英国的罗马天主教殉教者。1154年后任亨利二世的主教管区秘书室教士,他被指派为坎特伯雷大主教(1162年)并失宠于国王。由于侵占国王基金被起诉(1164年),贝克特逃离这个国家。他刚一回来(1170年)就被卷入亨利指定他的儿子为约克大主教的争论中,并在坎特伯雷大教堂里被四个爵士谋杀。

highlands of Scotland a common rent for lands which maintained a family. In some places it is so at this day; nor will money at present purchase a greater quantity of commodities there than in other places. In a country where the surplus produce of a large estate must be consumed upon the estate itself, it will frequently be more convenient for the proprietor, that part of it be consumed at a distance from his own house, provided they who consume it are as dependent upon him as either his retainers or his menial servants. He is thereby saved from the embarrassment of either too large a company or too large a family. A tenant at will, who possesses land sufficient to maintain his family for little more than a quit-rent, is as dependent upon the proprietor as any servant or retainer whatever, and must obey him with as little reserve. Such a proprietor, as he feeds his servants and retainers at his own house, so he feeds his tenants at their houses. The subsistence of both is derived from his bounty, and its continuance depends upon his good pleasure.

The power of the ancient barons was founded on this. Upon the authority which the great proprietors necessarily had in such a state of things over their tenants and retainers, was founded the power of the ancient barons. They necessarily became the judges in peace, and the leaders in war, of all who dwelt upon their estates. They could maintain order and execute the law within their respective demesnes, because each of them could there turn the whole force of all the inhabitants against the injustice of any one. No other person had sufficient authority to do this. The king in particular had not. In those ancient times he was little more than the greatest proprietor in his dominions, to whom, for the sake of common defence against their common enemies, the other great proprietors paid certain respects. To have enforced payment of a small debt within the lands of a great proprietor, where all the inhabitants were armed and accustomed to stand by one another, would have cost the king, had he attempted it by his own authority, almost the same effort as to extinguish a civil war. He was, therefore, obliged to abandon the administration of justice through the greater part of the country, to those who were capable of administering it; and for the same reason to leave the command of the country militia to those whom that militia would obey.

生活资料。几年前在苏格兰高地一带,一克朗、半克朗、一只羊、一只羊羔足以维持一家人的土地。现在有很多地方也是这样的;那里的钱也不会比其他地方购买数量更多的商品。在乡村大地产生产的剩余产品必须由这个大地产自身消费,对于所有者来说,这样往往比较便利。其中有一部分要在远离他家的地方消费,只要消费者是依附于他的人或者是他的仆人。因此,他可以避免伴侣太多家庭太大这样的尴尬。一个可以随意令其退租的佃农,拥有足够多的土地来维持他的家庭,仅仅支付一点免役税即可,像其他仆人或奴仆必须毫无保留地服从于地主一样,佃农依附于土地所有者。这样一个土地所有者,就像他在自己的家中供养着它的奴隶和仆人一样,他在佃农的屋里也养活着他们。两处的生活必需品都来自他的施舍,这种施舍是否继续维持下去完全依靠他的高兴与否来决定。

大地主们在这种状态下对于其佃农和奴仆所拥有的必然的权威是建立在古代贵族的权力上的。在所有居住在他们的领地上的人们中,他们在和平时期是裁判,战争时期是统领。在他们各自的领地之内,他们能继续维持秩序,执行法令,因为他们中的任何一个人都可能使全部居民的全部力量来跟任何不公平的行为抗衡。没有任何其他人有足够的权力这样做。国王尤其做不到这一点。在古代时期,国王只不过是领土上最大的地主。为了共同抵抗他们的敌人,其他的地主给予他一定的尊重。为了在一个大地主的领地内迫使偿还小额债务,那里所有的居民都全副武装,习惯于并肩相助,如果他试图靠自己的权威,那么几乎要花费他试图消灭一场战争的力量。因此,他必须放弃国家大部分地区的司法行政权;同样的道理,放弃对于乡村民兵的指挥

古代贵族的权利就是建立在这个基础之上。

| 国民财富的性质与原理

It was anterior to and independent of the feudal law.
It is a mistake to imagine that those territorial jurisdictions took their origin from the feudal law. Not only the highest jurisdictions both civil and criminal, but the power of levying troops, of coining money, and even that of making bye-laws for the government of their own people, were all rights possessed allodially by the great proprietors of land several centuries before even the name of the feudal law was known in Europe. The authority and jurisdiction of the Saxon lords in England, appear to have been as great before the conquest, as that of any of the Norman lords after it. But the feudal law is not supposed to have become the common law of England till after the conquest. ① That the most extensive authority and jurisdictions were possessed by the great lords in France allodially, long before the feudal law was introduced into that country, is a matter of fact that admits of no doubt. That authority and those jurisdictions all necessarily flowed from the state of property and manners just now described. Without remounting to the remote antiquities of either the French or English monarchies, we may find in much later times many proofs that such effects must always flow from such causes. It is not thirty years ago since Mr. Cameron of Loehiel, a gentleman of Lochabar in Scotland, without any legal warrant whatever, not being what was then called a lord of regality, nor even a tenant in chief, but a vassal of the duke of Argyle, and without being so much as a justice of peace, used, notwithstanding, to exercise the highest criminal jurisdiction over his own people. He is said to have done so with great equity, though without any of the formalities of justice; and it is not improbable that the state of that part of the country at that time made it necessary for him to assume this authority in order to maintain the public peace. That gentleman, whose rent never exceeded five hundred pounds a year, carried, in 1745, eight hundred of his own people into the rebellion with him. ②

---

① [Hume, *History*, ed. of 1773, i., 224.]

② ['The Highlands of Scotland have long been entitled by law to every privilege of British subjects; but it was not till very lately that the common people could in fact enjoy those privileges.'—Hume, *History*, vol. i., p. 214, ed. of 1773. Cp. *Lectures*, p. 116.]

权,交给能驯服民兵的人去统辖。

假定这种地方的司法行政权起源于封建法律的说法,其实是错误的。欧洲的大地主们在封建法律建立之前的好几个世纪,就已经完全拥有了最高民事和刑事司法行政权,招募军队、铸造硬币权利,甚者还包括为了治理自己的臣民制定法律的权利。英格兰撒克逊地主的权力和司法权,在其被征服以前似乎与被征服以后的诺曼地主差不多大。但是在被征服之前,封建法律并不被认为已经成为了英格兰的惯律。① 最广泛的权利和这些司法权天生就掌握在法国的大地主手中,在封建法律被引入法国之前就是这样的,这是一个毋庸置疑的事实。那些权力和司法权都必定形成于前面所描述的财产状况和风俗习惯。我们不需要上述寻访法兰西和英国君主国古老的遗迹来寻求证据,在后来较晚的时代,就有了许多证据表明这样的影响必定总是源于这样的原因。不到30年前,洛基尔的卡梅伦先生,他是苏格兰洛巴赫的一位绅士,既非一个贵族地主也非一个大佃农,只是亚盖尔公爵的一个家臣,尽管他既不是治安官员也没有获得正式的委任状,却对其民众执行最高的刑事裁判权。据说他非常公平地判决,尽管没有司法仪式;在那个时候那个地区的这种状态,他承担这种权威来维护公共安全是合适的。这位每年地租从来不超过500镑的绅士,1745年带领他自己的800人和他一起参加了起义。②

封建法律的引入,可以被看作是减缓大地主权力的一种尝

<small>这是在封建法律建立之前,并且与之无关。</small>

---

① 休谟:《历史》,1773年,第1卷,第224页。
② 休谟:《英格兰史》,1773年,第1卷,第214页:"在苏格兰高地,早已通过法律授予不列颠的臣民们所有的特权,但普通人民直到最近才在事实上享受这些特权。"

国民财富的性质与原理

It was moderated by the feudal caw,

The introduction of the feudal law, so far from extending, may be regarded as an attempt to moderate the authority of the great allodial lords. ① It established a regular subordination, accompanied with a long train of services and duties, from the king down to the smallest proprietor. During the minority of the proprietor, the rent, together with the management of his lands, fell into the hands of his immediate superior, and, consequently, those of all great proprietors into the hands of the king, who was charged with the maintenance and education of the pupil, and who, from his authority as guardian, was supposed to have a right of disposing of him in marriage, provided it was in a manner not unsuitable to his rank. But though this institution necessarily tended to strengthen the authority of the king, and to weaken that of the great proprietors, it could not do either sufficiently for establishing order and good government among the inhabitants of the country; because it could not alter suffieiently that state of property and manners from which the disorders arose. The authority of government still continued to be, as before, too weak in the head and too strong in the inferior members, and the excessive strength of the inferior members was the cause of the weakness of the head. After the institution of feudal subordination, the king was as incapable of restraining the violence of the great lords as before. They still continued to make war according to their own discretion, almost continually upon one another, and very frequently upon the king; and the open country still continued to be a scene of violence, rapine, and disorder.

and undermined by foreign com. merce.

But what all the violence of the feudal institutions could never have effected, the silent and insensible operation of foreign commerce and manufactures gradually brought about. These gradually furnished the great proprietors with something for which they could exchange the whole surplus produce of their lands, and which they could consume themselves without sharing it either with tenants or retainers. All for ourselves, and nothing for other people, seems, in every age of the world, to have been the vile maxim of the masters of mankind. As soon, therefore, as they could find a method of consuming the whole value of their rents themselves, they had no disposition to share them with any other persons. For a pair of diamond buckles perhaps, or for something as frivolous and useless, they exchanged the maintenance, or what is the same thing, the price of the maintenance of a thousand men for a year, and with it the whole weight and authority which it could give them. The buckles, however, were to be all their own,

———

① [*Lectures*, pp. 38, 39.]

— 896 —

试,其目的绝不是想扩大其权力。① 它建立了一套正规的隶属等级制度,伴随着一长串的职责和义务,从国王到小地主。在地主还未成年的时候,地租和土地管理的权利一起落入他最直接的上级手中,接着,这些地租和土地管理的权利落入了国王手中。国王负责这些未成年地主的维持和教育,从作为监护人的权力出发,他被认为有权力为之办理婚事,但要采取适合其身份的方式。虽然这种机制肯定会加强国王的权威,并且削弱大地主的权力,但是这种制度对于在乡村的居民中建立秩序和政府管理可能是不够的;因为他不可能充分改变财富的状态和风俗习惯,这是产生混乱的根源。政府的权力仍如同以前一样,头部过小,下级人员权力过大,这是头部过小的原因。封建等级制度建立之后,国王不能像以前一样限制大地主的暴力行为。他们仍然根据自己的判断来发动战争,几乎彼此不断地作战,甚至常常对国王作战;广大的乡村仍然是一片暴力、抢劫和混乱的局面。

贵族的权利被封建法律所减弱,

  但是所有封建制度的强制力所不能做到的,对外贸易和制造业的无声无息和不知不觉的运作却逐渐实现了。这些可以逐步给大地主提供用以交换他们土地上生产剩余的物品,并且他们可以独自享用这些物品,而不与他们的佃农或奴仆分享。所有一切唯我独尊,不顾他人,似乎是这个世界上所有年代人类主子们可耻的格言。因此,只要他们发现了消耗他们所有租金的方法,他们就没有性情与其他任何人来分享。为了一对钻石纽扣,或许是为了一些同样没有价值的无用的东西,他们用可以维持上千人生活一年的维持品来交换,或用类似的东西,随之就是这种维持品

也被对外贸易所削弱。

---

① 《关于法律、警察、岁入及军备的演讲》,第 38、39 页。

and no other human creature was to have any share of them; whereas in the more ancient method of expence they must have shared with at least a thousand people. With the judges that were to determine the preference, this difference was perfectly decisive; and thus, for the gratification of the most childish, the meanest and the most sordid of all vanities, they gradually bartered their whole power and authority. ①

At present a rich man maintains in all as many persons as an ancient baron, but he contributes only a small portion of the maintenance of eachperson.

In a country where there is no foreign commerce, nor any of the finer manufactures, a man of ten thousand a year cannot well employ his revenue in any other way than in maintaining, perhaps, a thousand families, who are all of them necessarily at his command. In the present state of Europe, a man of ten thousand a year can spend his whole revenue, and he generally does so, without directly maintaining twenty people, or being able to command more than ten footmen not worth the commanding. Indirectly, perhaps, he maintains as great or even a greater number of people than he could have done by the ancient method of expence. For though the quantity of precious pro. ductions for which he exchanges his whole revenue be very small, the number of workmen employed in collecting and preparing it, must necessarily have been very great. Its great price generally arises from the wages of their labour, and the profits of all their immediate employers. By paying that price he indirectly pays all those wages and profits, and thus indirectly contributes to the maintenance of all the workmen and their employers. He generally contributes, however, but a very small proportion to that of each, to very few perhaps a tenth, to many not a hundredth, and to some not a thousandth, nor even a ten thousandth part of their whole annual maintenance. Though he contributes, therefore, to the maintenance of them all, they are all more or less independent of him, because generally they can all be maintained without him.

When the great proprietors of land spend their rents in maintaining their tenants and retainers, each of them maintains entirely all

① [Hume, *History*, ed. of 1773, vol. iii. , p. 400; vol. v. , p. 488.]

所能带来的全部力量和权威。然而,钻石纽扣完全属于他们自己,没有其他任何人可以与他来分享;然而按照古老的花费方法,他们必须至少要和1000人共享。对于决定取舍而言,这种区别是完全明确的;因此,为了满足最幼稚的最卑鄙的最低劣的虚荣心,他们逐渐地用他们的权利和权威来进行交换。①

在既无对外贸易又无精细制造业的国家,一个年收入有10000的人,除了维持1000个家庭之外,没有其他途径很好地来消费其收入,这1000个家庭必然听命于他。在现在欧洲的状态下,一个年收入有10000的人可以花费他所有的收入,并且他一般也会这样做,不直接地养活20人,或对10个以上的仆人发号施令。可能采用间接的方式,他所能养活的人数或许同采取古老的花销方式养活的人数同样多,甚至会更多。尽管以前他的全部收入所能交换的产品数量很少,但被雇用来收集和制造产品的工人数量必然会很大。产品的昂贵的价格一般是由于这些工人的劳动工资以及所有直接雇员的利润导致的。通过支付这个价格,他间接地支付了所有工资和利润,因此间接地维持了所有工人和雇员。然而,一般来说他只对每个人每年的基本生活费贡献非常少的一部分,对极少人是1/10,对许多人不到1/100,对部分人不到1/1000,甚至对有些人不到1/10000。因此,尽管他对维持他们所有的生活有所贡献,他们却全都或多或少地不依赖于他,因为一般而言,没有他,他们照样可以生存。

当大地主花费他们的地租来养活他们的佃农和奴仆时,他们

现代富人跟古族多但仅持一个人维持的很部分。

的维贵样人他了代的贡了一献每个人维的品持很的小部分。

---

① 休谟:《历史》,1773年,第3卷,第400页;第5卷,第488页。

his own tenants and all his own retainers. But when they spend them in maintaining tradesmen and artificers, they may, all of them taken together, perhaps, maintain as great, or, on account of the waste which attends rustic hospitality, a greater number of people than before. Each of them, however, taken singly, contributes often but a very small share to the maintenance of any individual of this greater number. Each tradesman or artificer derives his subsistence from the employment, not of one, but of a hundred or a thousand different customers. Though in some measure obliged to them all, therefore, he is not absolutely dependent upon any one of them.

<small>To meet their new expenses the great proprietors dismissed their retainers and their unnecessary tenants, and gave the remaining tenants long leases,</small>

The personal expence of the great proprietors having in this manner gradually increased, it was impossible that the number of their retainers should not as gradually diminish, till they were at last dismissed altogether. The same cause gradually led them to dismiss the unnecessary part of their tenants. Farms were enlarged, and the occupiers of land, notwithstanding the complaints of depopulation, reduced to the number necessary for cultivating it, according to the imperfect state of cultivation and improvement in those times. By the removal of the unnecessary mouths, and by exacting from the farmer the full value of the farm, a greater surplus, or what is the same thing, the price of a greater surplus, was obtained for the proprietor, which the merchants and manufacturers soon furnished him with a method of spending upon his own person in the same manner as he had done the rest. The same cause continuing to operate, he was desirous to raise his rents above what his lands, in the actual state of their improvement, could afford. His tenants could agree to this upon one condition only, that they should be secured in their possession, for such a term of years as might give them time to recover with profit whatever they should lay out in the further improvement of the land. The expensive vanity of the landlord made him willing to accept of this condition; and hence the origin of long leases.

<small>thus making them independent.</small>

Even a tenant at will, who pays the full value of the land, is not altogether dependent upon the landlord. The pecuniary advantages which they receive from one another, are mutual and equal, and such a tenant will expose neither his life nor his fortune in the service of the proprietor. But if he has a lease for a long term of years, he is altogether independent; and his landlord must not expect from him even

每个人都完全拥有了他自己的佃农和奴仆。但是当他们花钱来维持商人和工匠的时候,相比以前来说,他们可能总体上会维持相同或者更多的人,因为乡村的款筵必然会造成浪费。然而他们每一个人,单独来看,往往为更多人数的维持品贡献了很小的部分。每个商人和工匠从顾客那里获得他的维持品,不是从一个人那里,而是从上百上千的顾客那里获得的。因而,虽然在某种程度上依仗它们全体,但是也不是绝对地依靠他们中的每一个人。

以这种方式,大地主的个人消费就逐渐增大起来。他们的奴仆的数量不可能不慢慢减少,直到最后完全消失。同样的原因使他们解雇他们奴仆中不必要的部分。农场扩大了,尽管对于雇员数量减少存在抱怨,土地所有者仍然按照那个时代开垦和改良的不完全状态,将雇用人数减少到耕种田地的必要数量。由于取消了不必要的人数,并且从农场主身上索取农田的最大价值,土地所有者获得了巨大的剩余,或者同样可以说是更多的剩余的价值,商人和制造业者很快将会给他提供一种方法,像他对其余的产品一样,以同样的方式自己花费剩余产品。同样的原因仍在起作用,他非常盼望将他的地租提高到他的土地实际改良状态能够提供的水平之上。他的佃农仅仅在一种情况下可能同意这样,那就是他们必须确保他们的占用,租佃的期限要足以使他们回收在进一步改良土地上投入的资本。地主在开支方面的虚荣心使他愿意接受这个条件,这也就是产生其租赁的来源。

为了满足他们的支出,他们主雇的奴仆不必要的部分,新出,地解雇他们奴仆中不必要的部分,给予其佃农的长期租赁,

一个可以随意令其退租的佃农,他支付了土地的全部价值,并非完全依靠地主。他们从彼此身上获得的金钱利润是相互的、共同的,一个佃农将不会在为地主服务中使自己的生命和财产受到影响。但是如果他获得了一个长期的租赁时期,他就完全独

因此使得他们独立起来。

the most trifling service beyond what is either expressly stipulated in the lease, or imposed upon him by the common and known law of the country.

<small>The great proprietors thus became insignificant.</small>

The tenants having in this manner become independent, and the retainers being dismissed, the great proprietors were no longer capable of interrupting the regular execution of justice, or of disturbing the peace of the country. Having sold their birth-right, not like Esau for a mess of pottage in time of hunger and necessity, but in the wantonness of plenty, for trinkets and baubles, fitter to be the play-things of children than the serious pursuits of men, they became as insignificant as any substantial burgher or tradesman in a city. A regular government was established in the country as well as in the city, nobody having sufficient power to disturb its operations in the one, any more than in the other.

<small>Old families are rare in commercial countries.</small>

It does not, perhaps, re]ate to the present subject, but I cannot help remarking it, that very old families, such as have possessed some considerable estate from father to son for many successive generations, are very rare in commercial countries. In countries which have little commerce, on the contrary, such as Wales or the highlands of Scotland, they are very common. The Arabian histories seem to be all full of genealogies, and there is a history written by a Tartar Khan, which has been translated into several European languages, and which contains scarce any thing else; a proof that ancient families are very common among those nations. In countries where a rich man can spend his revenue in no other way than by maintaining as many people as it can maintain, he is not apt to run out, and his benevolence it seems is seldom so violent as to attempt to maintain more than he can afford. But where he can spend the greatest revenue upon his own person, he frequently has no bounds to his expence, because he frequently has no bounds to his vanity, or to his affection for his own person. In commercial countries, therefore, riches, in spite of the most violent regulations of law to prevent their dissipation, very seldom remain long in the same family. Among simple nations, on the contrary, they frequently do without any regulations of law: for among

立;并且除了租约中明确规定的或国家在习惯法和成文法中规定的之外,他的地主不能期望从他们身上获得额外的最些微的服务。

<small>大地主因此变得不足道。他们也得不到。</small>

这样佃农就已经独立,奴仆也已经解雇,大地主不能再扰乱司法的正常执行,也不能扰乱国家的安宁。出售了他们与生俱来的权力之后,不是像伊骚那样在饥饿和必要的时候,付出了巨大的代价来得到眼前小利,而是在资财丰富的放荡中,为了更适合小孩玩的而不适合人们认真追求的无关紧要的小玩意儿,他们变成了跟城市中大量的商人或市民一样的无足轻重了。乡村和城市都建立了正规的政府,没有人有足够的能量来扰乱它在乡村发挥作用,也没有人能扰乱它在城市中的作用。

这个可能与我现在所说的主题无关,但是我还是忍不住要提及一下,有一个非常古老的家庭,以父传子的方式传承了很多代人,他们拥有相当数量的土地,在商业国家很罕见了。相反,在商业较少的国家,例如在威尔士和苏格兰高地,它们就非常普遍。阿拉伯历史似乎充满着贵族世系;一位鞑靼可汗写了一部历史,并且被翻译成多种欧洲文字,除此之外就没有包含其他东西。有证据表明古代家庭在这些国家中非常普遍。在一些国家,富人除了维持他尽可能能维持的人数之外就没有别的途径花费他的开支,他不容易破产,他的善行似乎很少去试图维持超过他的能力所能维持的人数。但是如果他能将收入的最大部分花费在自己身上的时候,他经常就无限制地支出,因为他的虚荣心或者对他自己的爱心经常都是无止境的。因此,在商业国家中,尽管存在最严格的法律规定防止他们的挥霍浪费,富裕还是很少在同一个家庭中长久维持下去。相反的是,在俭朴的国家中,却很少存在

<small>古老的家族在商业国家已经罕见了。</small>

国民财富的性质与原理

nations of shepherds, such as the Tartars and Arabs, the consumable nature of their property necessarily renders all such regulations impossible.

<small>A revolution was thus insensibly brought about,</small> A revolution of the greatest importance to the public happiness, was in this manner brought about by two different orders of people, who had not the least intention to serve the public. To gratify the most childish vanity was the sole motive of the great proprietors. The merchants and artificers, much less ridiculous, acted merely from a view <small>and commerce and manufactures became the cause of the improvement of the country.</small> to their own interest, and in pursuit of their own pedlar principle of turning a penny wherever a penny was to be got. Neither of them had either knowledge or foresight of that great revolution which the folly of the one, and the industry of the other, was gradually bringing about.

It is thus that through the greater part of Europe the commerce and manufactures of cities, instead of being the effect, have been the cause and occasion of the improvement and cultivation of the country.

<small>This order of things is both slow and uncertain compared with the natural order, as may be shown by the rapid progress of the North American colonies.</small> This order, however, being contrary to the natural course of things, is necessarily both slow and uncertain. Compare the slow progress of those European countries of which the wealth depends very much upon their commerce and manufactures, with the rapid advances of our North American colonies, of which the wealth is founded altogether in agriculture. Through the greater part of Europe, the number of inhabitants is not supposed to double in less than five hundred years. In several of our North American colonies, it is found to double in twenty or five-and-twenty years. In Europe the law of primogeniture, and perpetuities of different kinds, prevent the division of great estates, and thereby hinder the multiplication of small proprietors. A small proprietor, however, who knows every part of his little territory, who views it all with the affection which property, especially small property, natur. ally inspires, and who upon that account takes pleasure not only in cultivating but in adorning it, is generally of all improvers the most industrious, the most intelligent, and the most successful. The same regulations, besides, keep so much land out of the market, that there are always more capitals to buy than there is land to sell, so that what is sold always sells at a monopoly price. The rent never pays the interest of the purchase-money, and is besides burdened with repairs and other occasional charges, to which the interest of money is not liable. To purchase land is every-where in

第三篇　第四章

法律法规：例如鞑靼和阿拉伯那样的游牧民族，他们财富的消费本质必定不可能提供所有的法规。

　　对于公众的幸福最重要的革命被两个不同的阶级以这种方式完成，他们丝毫不考虑公众的幸福。为了使这种小孩式的虚荣心得到满足，是大地主唯一的动机。商人和工匠没有他们那样可笑，仅仅从他们自身的利益来行动，追求他们自己的小贩原则，在能赚到一个便士的地方就去赚一便士。这两种人对大革命都不了解也没有远见，一个愚蠢，一个勤劳，但最终就把这次革命逐渐完成了。

（旁注：革命因此不知不觉地产生，并且商业和制造业成为乡村改良的原因。物种事这种自相顺序说明了这一点。对来说顺序既很慢又很不确定，北美殖民地的发展就证明了这一点。）

　　因此在欧洲大部分地方，城市商业和制造业是乡村改良与开发的诱因，而非它的结果。

　　但是，由于与事物自然发展过程相反，这种顺序必定很慢而且很不确定。那些欧洲国家它们的财富非常依赖于它们的商业和制造业，北美殖民地的财富完全建立在农业的基础上，将前者缓慢的发展进程与后者快速的进步相比较。欧洲大部分地区居民的数量在近五百年中没有增加一倍。在北美殖民地中的几个地方，却在20年或25年中增加了一倍。在欧洲长子继承权的法律和各种永久所有权阻碍了财产的分割，也因此阻碍了小地主的增加。然而，小地主非常了解他的每一部分小片领地，他带着热情看待他的土地，尤其是小土地，感情自然流露，他不仅是喜欢开垦它，而且还喜欢装点它。他是所有改良者中最勤勉的，最聪明的，最成功的。另外，同样的规定使许多财产不能进入市场进行交易，以至于购买土地的资金多于可以出售的土地，因此，土地总是以垄断价格来出售。地租从来没有用于支付购买土地费用的利息，并且另外还要负担维修和其他意外费用，是在购款利息以

Europe a most unprofitable employment of a small capital. For the sake of the superior security, indeed, a man of moderate circumstances, when he retires from business, will sometimes chuse to lay out his little capital in land. A man of profession too, whose revenue is derived from another source, often loves to secure his savings in the same way. But a young man, who, instead of applying to trade or to some profession, should employ a capital of two or three thousand pounds in the purchase and cultivation of a small piece of land, might indeed expect to live very happily, and very independently, but must bid adieu, for ever, to all hope of either great fortune or great illustration, which by a different employment of his stock he might have had the same chance of acquiring with other people. Such a person too, though he cannot aspire at being a proprietor, will often disdain to be a farmer. The small quantity of land, therefore, which is brought to market, and the high price of what is brought thither, prevents a great number of capitals from being employed in its cultivation and improvement which would otherwise have taken that direction. In North America, on the contrary, fifty or sixty pounds is often found a sufficient stock to begin a plantation with. The purchase and improvement of uncultivated land, is there the most profitable employment of the smallest as well as of the greatest capitals, and the most direct road to all the fortune and illustration which can be acquired in that country. Such land, indeed, is in North America to be had almost for nothing, or at a price much below the Value of the natural produce; a thing impossible in Europe, or, indeed, in any country where all lands have long been private property. If landed estates, however, were divided equally among all the children, upon the death of any proprietor who left a numerous family, the estate would generally be sold. So much land would come to market, that it could no longer sell at a monopoly price. The free rent of the land would go nearer to pay the interest of the purchase-money, and a small capital might be employed in purchasing land as profitably as in any other way.

and the slow progress of England in agriculture in spite of favours accorded to it

England, on account of the natural fertility of the soil, of the great extent of the sea-coast in proportion to that of the whole country, and of the many navigable rivers which run through it, and afford the conveniency of water carriage to some of the most inland parts of it, is perhaps as well fitted by nature as any large country in Europe, to be the seat of foreign commerce, of manufactures for distant sale,

外的。在欧洲购买土地是小资本最没有利润的用途。确实,为了特别的安全,一个中等状况的人,不再经商以后有时选择将其少量的资金投入到土地上。一个专业人士,从其他的途径获得自己的利润,他也喜欢以同样的方式确保自己钱财的安全。但是一个小青年,如果不做生意或其他职业,而愿意用两三千镑资金来购买和开垦一小片土地,当然也可以希望非常独立地幸福生活,但恐怕对于成为大富翁和大名人的愿望却要永别了。如果他把资本用于别的用途,他就可望和别人一样有这样的机会。这样的人尽管他不能立志成为地主,但也不会愿意成为农场主。因此少量被带入市场进行交易的土地以高价成交,阻碍了大量资金用于土地的开垦和改良,否则资金应该用到这个用途上来的。相反在北美,50镑或60镑的资本就足够用来开办一个农场。未开垦土地的购买与改良既是最大资本也是最小资本最有利的用途,也是在那个国家所能得到的最直接的成为大富翁和大名人的道路。实际上这样的土地在北美几乎可以无代价地来获得,或者以低于自然产物价值很多的价格来购买到;实际上这种事情在欧洲是不可能的;在其他任何土地已经私有化的国家也是不可能的。但是,土地财产平均地分给所有子女的家庭,当一家之主一死,土地一般都被出售。这样的土地可以进入市场交易,也不会以垄断价格来出售。土地的自由租金会越来越接近购买资金所支付的利息,购买土地的小资金也和其他用途上的资金一样有利可图。

  英格兰由于土壤天然肥沃,海岸线相比于整个国家很大,许多的可通航河流穿过这个国家,可以为该国大部分的内地提供水运的便利,跟欧洲的很多大国一样,是天然的对外贸易位置,适于经营远地销售的制造业,适于上述情况所能引起的种种改良。自

尽管赋予了很多鼓励,但是英格兰农业进步缓慢,

and of all the improvements which these can occasion. From the beginning of the reign of Elizabeth too, the English legislature has been peculiarly attentive to the interests of commerce and manufactures, and in reality there is no country in Europe, Holland itself not excepted, of which the law is, upon the whole, more favourable to this sort of industry. Commerce and manufactures have accordingly been continually advancing during all this period. The cultivation and improvement of the country has, no doubt, been gradually advancing too: But it seems to have followed slowly, and at a distance, the more rapid progress of commerce and manufactures. The greater part of the country must probably have been cultivated before the reign of Elizabeth; and a very great part of it still remains uncultivated, and the cultivation of the far greater part, much inferior to what it might be. The law of England, however, favours agriculture not only indirectly by the protection of commerce, but by several direct encouragements. Except in times of scarcity, the exportation of corn is not only free, but encouraged by a bounty. In times of moderate plenty, the importation of foreign corn is loaded with duties that amount to a prohibition. The importation of live cattle, except from Ireland, is prohibited at all times,① and it is but of late that it was permitted from thence. ② Those who cultivate the land, therefore, have a monopoly against their countrymen for the two greatest and most important articles of land produce, bread and butcher's meat. These encouragements, though at bottom, perhaps, as I shall endeavour to show hereafter, altogether illusory, sufficiently demonstrate at least the good intention of the legislature to favour agriculture. But what is of much more importance than all of them, the yeomanry of England are rendered as secure, as independent, and as respectable as law can make them. No country, therefore, in which the right of primogeniture takes place, which pays tithes, and where perpetuities, though contrary to the spirit of the law, are admitted in some cases, can give more encouragement to agriculture than England. Such, however, notwithstanding, is the state of its cultivation. What would it have been, had the law given no direct encouragement to agriculture besides what arises indirectly from the progress of commerce, and had left the yeomanry in the same condition as in most other countries of Europe? It is now more than two

---

① [18 Car. II., c. 2.]
② [32 Geo. II., c. 11, § 1; 5 Geo. III., c. 10; 12 Geo. III., c. 2.]

伊丽莎白即位以来,英国立法尤为注意工商业的利益;实际上,欧洲没有一个国家,荷兰也不例外,其法律总的来说对这种产业更为有利。因此,商业和制造业在这整个时期内继续进步。乡村的开发和改良也毫无疑问地在进步,但是似乎进步很慢,商业和制造业就要更加迅速了。乡村的大部分土地肯定在伊丽莎白统治时期以前就开垦了;但是很大一部分还没有被开垦,并且绝大部分的开垦还没有达到应有的程度。不过,英格兰的法律不仅通过保护商业而间接支持农业,而且有很多的对农业的直接补贴。除了收成不好的年份之外,谷物出口不仅自由,而且可以得到奖金。在收获一般的年份,外国谷物的进口会受到关税的限制,几近禁止。除了来自爱尔兰的之外,活牲口的进口一向都是被禁止的,①而且准许从爱尔兰进口也是不久以前的事。② 因此,开垦土地的人在两种最大最重要的土地生产物即面包与家畜上,享有一种垄断的权力。这些津贴,尽管如我在随后所要予以说明的那样,实际上完全是幻想,但是还是充分地表明了立法机关支持农业的良好愿望。但是比所有这一切更为重要的是,英格兰的自耕农享有的安全、独立和尊重,是法律可能做到的。因此没有一个实行长子继承权的国家,还在征收什一税的国家,尽管与法律精神想违背,永久权在那里仍然有效的国家,能比英格兰更鼓励农业,然而尽管如此,英格兰的耕种情况仍是如此。除了间接地从商业中得到的鼓励之外,假使法律没有给予农业直接的鼓励,假使自耕农

---

① 查理二世十八年第 2 号法令。
② 乔治二世三十二年第 2 号法令第 1 节;乔治三世五年第 10 号法令;乔治三世十二年第 2 号法令。

hundred years since the beginning of the reign of Elizabeth, a period as long as the course of human prosperity usually endures.

<small>and the still slower progress of France,</small> France seems to have had a considerable share of foreign commerce near a century before England was distinguished as a commercial country. The marine of France was considerable, according to the notions of the times, before the expedition of Charles the VIIIth to Naples. The cultivation and improvement of France, however, is, upon the whole, inferior to that of England. The law of the country has never given the same direct encouragement to agriculture.

<small>Spain and Portugal.</small> The foreign commerce of Spain and Portugal to the other parts of Europe, though chiefly carried on in foreign ships, is very considerable. That to their colonies is carried on in their own, and is much greater, on account of the great riches and extent of those colonies. But it has never introduced any considerable manufactures for distant sale into either of those countries, and the greater part of both still remains uncultivated. The foreign commerce of Portugal is of older standing than that of any great country in Europe, except Italy.

<small>Italy alone was improved throughout by foreign commerce and exported manufactures.</small> Italy is the only great country of Europe which seems to have been cultivated and improved in every part, by means of foreign commerce and manufactures for distant sale. Before the invasion of Charles the VIIIth, Italy, according to Guicciardin, was cultivated not less in the most mountainous and barren parts of the country, than in the plainest and most fertile. The advantageous situation of the country, and the great number of independent states which at that time subsisted in it, probably contributed not a little to this general cultivation. It is not impossible too, notwithstanding this general expression of one of the most judicious and reserved of modern historians, that Italy was not at that time better cultivated than England is at present.

The capital, however, that is acquired to any country by commerce and manufactures, is all a very precarious and uncertain possession, till some part of it has been secured and realized in the cultivation and improvement of its lands. A merchant, it has been said very properly, is not necessarily the citizen of any particular country. It is in a great measure indifferent to him from what place he carries on his trade; and a very trifling disgust will make him remove his capital,

跟欧洲大部分国家的状况一样,情况将会怎样呢?伊丽莎白即位迄今已两百余年了,这期间已经是人类繁荣阶段通常所能持续的最长时期了。

在英格兰以商业城市而出名之前,法国在近一个世纪之前就似乎在对外贸易中占有相当的分量。根据当时的概念,法国的海运在查理第八次远征那不勒斯以前似乎很大。然而法国的开垦和改良从总体上说要落后于英格兰。这个国家的法律从来没有直接鼓励过农业的发展。法国也同样进步很慢。

西班牙与葡萄牙对欧洲其他各国的对外贸易,尽管主要是由外国船舶装运,但数量很可观。对于他们殖民地的对外贸易,一般自己运输并且数量非常巨大,因为殖民地富饶广大。但是它从来没有引入任何巨大的适于远距离销售的制造业,并且这两国的土地亦尚有大部分未曾开垦。除了意大利,欧洲各国中意大利的对外贸易最为悠久。西班牙和葡萄牙亦是如此。

通过远距离的对外贸易和制造业,意大利成为了欧洲唯一的每一个部分都被开垦的大国。据古西亚迪尼说,在查理第八侵入以前,意大利最多山、最贫瘠的乡村跟最平坦最肥沃的地方一样已经被开垦。这个国家所处的相当有利的地位和大量的独立城邦,可能对于一般的开垦也是有贡献的。但是有一位贤明的近代历史学家这样说,那时意大利的土地开垦不比今日的英格兰,这也不是不可能的。只有意大利通过对外贸易和制造业出口被彻底改良。

然而任何国家的工商业需要的资本,都是非常不稳定、不确定的财产,其某一部分已在土地耕种与改良事业上得到保障和实现。一个商人不一定是某一个国家特定的公民,这种说法非常恰当。他在哪里进行他的贸易活动,这一点在很大程度上不是他所

<small>The national capital acquired by commerce and manufactures is an uncertain possession till realised in the improvement of land.</small> and together with it all the industry which it supports, from one country to another. No part of it can be said to belong to any particular country, till it has been spread as it were over the face of that country, either in buildings, or in the lasting improvement of lands. No vestige now remains of the great wealth, said to have been possessed by the greater part of the Hans towns, except in the obscure histories of the thirteenth and fourteenth centuries. It is even uncertain where some of them were situated, or to what towns in Europe the Latin names given to some of them belong. But though the misfortunes of Italy in the end of the fifteenth and beginning of the sixteenth centuries greatly diminished the commerce and manufactures of the cities of Lombardy and Tuscany, those countries still continue to be among the most populous and best cultivated in Europe. The civil wars of Flanders, and the Spanish government which succeeded them, chased away the great commerce of Antwerp, Ghent, and Bruges. But Flanders still continues to be one of the richest, best cultivated, and most populous provinces of Europe. The ordinary revolutions of war and government easily dry up the sources of that wealth which arises from commerce only. That which arises from the more solid improvements of agriculture, is much more durable, and cannot be destroyed but by those more violent convulsions occasioned by the depredations of hostile and barbarous nations continued for a century or two together; such as those that happened for some time before and after the fall of the Roman empire in the western provinces of Europe.

关心的；一件很细小的令他反感的事情都可能使他抽回资金，并且从一国抽走它所支持的整个行业的资金转而投入到另一国去。没有哪部分资金可以说是属于任何特定的国家，它扩散到一国地面上，或是在建筑上，或是在最近改良的土地上。据说汉萨同盟大部分城镇都拥有大量财富，除了13、14世纪模糊的历史外，没留下一点痕迹。甚至它们中某些城市位于哪里，其中有些拉丁文名称属于欧洲的哪些城镇，也是不确定的。但是15世纪末16世纪初意大利所遭受的灾难，极大地打击了伦巴迪亚和托斯卡纳各城市的工商业，但这些地方仍然是欧洲人口最多、开垦得最好的地方。佛兰德的内战之后，以及西班牙的统治，赶走了安特卫普、根特、布鲁日的大商业。[1] 但是佛兰德现在仍是欧洲最富裕、开垦最好、人口最多的地方之一。战争与政治所造成的变革往往会耗尽仅仅来源于商业的资财。而来源于农业改良的坚实财富，就是牢不可破的，除非遭受持续一两个世纪的敌对和野蛮民族引发的武力动荡；例如欧洲西部省份罗马帝国衰败前后发生的动荡。

旁注：通过商业制造获得的民族资本现在改良土地以前是不确定的财产。

---

〔1〕 安特卫普市（Antwerp），比利时北部一城市，位于布鲁塞尔以北的斯特尔特河边。它是欧洲最繁忙的港口之一，从15世纪开始就是一个钻石工业中心。根特（Ghent），比利时西部布鲁塞尔西北偏西的一座城市，建于7世纪。该城市是中世纪的一个羊毛生产中心并一直保持独立。直到1584年被哈布斯堡人占领。布鲁日（Bruges），比利时西北部一城市，通过运河与北海相连。建于9世纪，13世纪时成为汉萨同盟的主要成员之一。现今以"桥之城"闻名，成为受欢迎的游览胜地。

BOOK IV
Of Systems Of Political Economy

INTRODUCTION

<small>The first object of political economy is to provide subsistence for the people.</small> Political economy, considered as a branch of the science of a statesman or legislator, proposes two distinct objects: first, to provide a plentiful revenue or subsistence for the people, or more properly to enable them to provide such a revenue or subsistence for themselves; and secondly, to supply the state or commonwealth with a revenue sufficient for the public services. It proposes to enrich both the people and the sovereign. ①

<small>Two different systems proposed for this end will be explained.</small> The different progress of opulence in different ages and nations, has given occasion to two different systems of political economy, with regard to enriching the people. The one may be called the system of commerce, the other that of agriculture. I shall endeavour to explain both as fully and distinctly as I can, and shall begin with the system of commerce. It is the modern system, and is best understood in our own country and in our own times.

---

① [For other definitions of the purpose or nature of political economy see the index, s. v.]

第四篇　论政治经济学体系

引　言

　　政治经济学,通常被视为政治家或立法者的科学的一门分支。它提出两种不同的目标:第一,为人民提供充足的国家收入和生活物资,或者更恰当地说使人民能够为自己提供收入和生活物资;第二,为国家或联邦提供足够维持公共服务的收入。其目的在于既要富裕人民,也要富裕国家。①

> 政治经济学的第一个目标是为人民提供生活资料。

　　在不同时代,不同国家,就增加人民财富而言,其增长进程的不同也导致了两种不同的政治经济学体系。其中一种被称为重商主义体系,另外一种是重农主义体系。我将尽力充分地对这两种体系进行清晰明了地阐述,我将从重商主义体系开始谈起。它是一个现代化的体系,而且它在我们国家和现代是最为人们所了解的。

> 为此目的而提出的两种不同的体系将在以下做出说明。

---

① 政治经济学的目的或性质的其他定义请参阅索引。

CHAPTER I

Of The Principle Of The Commercial Or Mercantile System

<small>Wealth and money in common language are considered synonymous.</small> That wealth consists in money, or in gold and silver, is a popular notion which naturally arises from the double function of money, as the instrument of commerce, and as the measure of value. In consequence of its being the instrument of commerce, when we have money we can more readily obtain whatever else we have occasion for, than by means of any other commodity. The great affair, we always find, is to get money. When that is obtained, there is no difficulty in making any subsequent purchase. In consequence of its being the measure of value, we estimate that of all other commodities by the quantity of money which they will exchange for. We say of a rich man that he is worth a great deal, and of a poor man that he is worth very little money. A frugal man, or a man eager to be rich, is said to love money; and a careless, a generous, or a profuse man, is said to be indifferent about it. To grow rich is to get money; and wealth and money, in short, are, in common language, considered as in every respect synonymous.

<small>Similarly the Tartars thought wealth consisted of cattle.</small> A rich country, in the same manner as a rich man, is supposed to be a country abounding in money; and to heap up gold and silver in any country is supposed to be the readiest way to enrich it. For some time after the discovery of America, the first enquiry of the Spaniards, when they arrived upon any unknown coast, used to be, if there was any gold or silver to be found in the neighbourhood ? By the information which they received, they judged whether it was worth while

第一章　论商业体系或贸易体系的原理

　　财富是由货币和金银构成的,这一流行观念自然而然地源自于货币的双重职能,即,既作为商业活动的媒介,又作为价值尺度。货币作为商业媒介,其结果是当我们有了货币时,相比于用其他任何商品作为交换媒介,我们更容易得到我们所需要的任何东西。我们总是发现,得到货币是最重要的事情。只要有了货币,以后要买什么东西都毫不费力。而货币作为价值尺度,据此我们可以根据商品所能交换的货币数量,来衡量其他所有商品的价值。我们谈到一个富人的时候,是指他有很多钱;谈到一个穷人的时候是说他没什么钱。一个节俭的人或者一个迫切想变富裕的人,人们说他爱钱;一个粗心大意,慷慨大方,或者奢侈浪费的人,人们说他不关心钱。发财致富就是要拥有货币,简而言之,在普通语言中财富和货币在各个方面都被视为同义词。

　　就像一名富人一样,一个富裕的国家被认为是拥有很多钱的国家。在任何一个国家,聚集金银都被视作致富的最便捷的方法。在美洲大陆发现后的一段时间里,西班牙人每到达一个不知名的海岸,通常首先要询问的就是在附近能否发现黄金或白银。

to make a settlement there, or if the country was worth the conquering. Plano Carpino, a monk sent ambassador from the king of France to one of the sons of the famous Gengis Khan, says that the Tartars used frequently to ask him, if there was plenty of sheep and oxen in the kingdom of France?① Their enquiry had the same object with that of the Spaniards. They wanted to know if the country was rich enough to be worth the conquering. Among the Tartars, as among all other nations of shepherds, who are generally ignorant of the use of money, cattle are the instruments of commerce and the measures of value. Wealth, therefore, according to them, consisted in cattle, as according to the Spaniards it consisted in gold and silver. Of the two, the Tartar notion, perhaps, was the nearest to the truth.

<small>Locke thought gold and silver the most substantial part of the wealth of a nation.</small> Mr. Locke remarks a distinction between money and other moveable goods. All other moveable goods, he says, are of so consumable a nature that the wealth which consists in them cannot be much depended on, and a nation which abounds in them one year may, without any exportation, but merely by their own waste and extravagance, be in great want of them the next. Money, on the contrary, is a steady friend, which, though it may travel about from hand to hand, yet if it can be kept from going out of the country, is not very liable to be wasted and consumed. Gold and silver, therefore, are, according to him, the most solid and substantial part of the moveable wealth of a nation, and to multiply those metals ought, he thinks, upon that ac-

---

① [There seems to be a confusion between Plano-Carpini, a Franciscan sent as legate by Pope Innocent IV. in 1246, and Guillaume de Rubruquis, another Franciscan sent as ambassador by Louis IX. in 1253.]

第四篇 第一章

根据所获得的消息,他们再做出判断,是否值得在此地驻扎建立殖民地或者这个国家是否值得征服占领。普拉诺·卡皮诺是被法国国王作为大使派往著名的成吉思汗一个儿子那里的一名僧侣,他曾说:鞑靼人经常会问他法兰西王国是否有很多的牛羊。① 他们的询问和西班牙人的询问目的是相同的,他们想知道这个国家是否很富有,值得去征服。在鞑靼人中,就像在所有其他游牧民族中一样,他们一般对使用货币一无所知,牲畜是商业媒介和价值尺度。因此对他们而言,财富就是由牲畜构成的,正如对西班牙人而言财富是由金银构成的一样,在这两者当中,鞑靼人的观念可能是最接近于事实的。

洛克先生对货币和其他可移动商品做出了区分。他说,所有其他可移动商品都具有易消耗掉的本质,因而不能过分依赖由该类商品构成的财富。如果一个国家一年内拥有充足的此类动产商品,也没有进口,而仅仅是由他们自己去消费和挥霍,那么来年都有可能极度缺乏这些动产商品。相反的,货币是一个稳定的商品。虽然它可能会从一个人手中被转移到另外一个人手中,但如果能保持货币不外流出国家,那么它就不大可能被浪费和消耗掉。因而,根据洛克先生的观点,金银是一个国家可移动财富中最固定最坚实的一部分。所以他认为,增加那些金属财富应当是

洛克先生认为金银是财家可移动富中最固的部分。

---

① 似乎把教皇英诺森四世于1246年派遣作为大使的修道士普拉诺—卡皮尼和路易九世于1253年派遣作为大使的修道士纪尧姆·得·卢布诺奎混淆了。

count, to be the great object of its political economy. ①

<small>Others say that it is necessary to have much money in order to maintain fleets and armies abroad.</small> Others admit that if a nation could be separated from all the world, it would be of no consequence how much, or how little money circulated in it. The consumable goods which were circulated by means of this money, would only be exchanged for a greater or a smaller number of pieces; but the real wealth or poverty of the country, they allow, would depend altogether upon the abundance or scarcity of those consumable goods. But it is otherwise, they think, with countries which have connections with foreign nations, and which are obliged to carry on foreign wars, and to maintain fleets and armies in distant countries. This, they say, cannot be done, but by sending abroad money to pay them with; and a nation cannot send much money abroad, unless it has a good deal at home. Every such nation, therefore, must endeavour in time of peace to accumulate gold and silver, that, when occasion requires, it may have wherewithal to carry on foreign wars.

<small>So all European nations have tried to accumulate gold and silver.</small> In consequence of these popular notions, all the different nations of Europe have studied, though to little purpose, every possible means of accumulating gold and silver in their respective countries. Spain and Portugal, the proprietors of the principal mines which supply Europe with those metals, have either prohibited their exportation under the severest penalties, or subjected it to a considerable duty. The like prohibition seems anciently to have made a part of the policy of most other European nations. It is even to be found, where we <small>At first by a prohibition of exportation,</small> should least of all expect to find it, in some old Scotch acts of parliament, which forbid under heavy penalties the carrying gold or silver *forth of the kingdom.* ② The like policy anciently took place both in France and England.

---

① [There is very little foundation for any part of this paragraph. It perhaps originated in an inaccurate recollection of pp. 17, 18 and 77 – 79 of *Some Considerations* (1696 ed.), and § § 46 – 50 of *Civil Government*. It was probably transferred bodily from the *Lectures* without verification. See *Lectures*, p. 198.]

② [The words 'forth of the realm' occur in (January) 1487, c. 11. Other acts are 1436, c. 13; 1451, c. 15; 1482, c. 8.]

第四篇 第一章

一国政治经济学的伟大目标。①

其他一些人则承认,如果一个国家能同整个世界隔离开,那么国内流通的货币是多是少就无关紧要了。通过这种货币来流通的可消耗商品,只不过是换来数量或多或少的货币而已。他们认为国家的真实财富或贫穷完全取决于这些可消耗商品的丰富或稀缺。但是,他们认为,对于那些同外国有联系的国家,和因必须进行对外战争而不得不在遥远的国度维持供应船队和军队的国家,情况就完全不同了。而要在遥远的外国维持供应军队就只能把货币送往外国以支付费用,否则别无他法。而一个国家除非在国内就拥有大量货币,否则将无法往国外输送许多货币。因此,每一个这样的国家就必须在和平时期努力储蓄金银,以便在必要之时有足够的钱财进行对外战争。

由于这些流行的观念,尽管收效甚微,欧洲所有国家都在研究如何在本国内使用一切可能的手段积累金银。西班牙和葡萄牙作为向欧洲国家提供金银金属的主要矿山的所有者,曾以最严酷的惩罚或者对出口金银课以重税,来禁止金银的出口。相似的禁令似乎在古代就是大多数其他欧洲国家的政策的一部分。我们甚至在一些古代苏格兰议会的法案里,也完全出乎意料地发现了类似的禁令:对携带金银前往王国以外②者处以重罚。法兰西

---

① 这一段的所有论述都论据不足。它或许来源于对一些著作的不精确记忆:《对降低利率和提高币值后果的思考》(1696年版),第17、18页和77~79页;《文官政府》,第46~50节。它也可能是未加证实地从《关于法律、警察、岁入及军备的演讲》处得来,见《关于法律、警察、岁入及军备的演讲》,第198页。

② "forth of the realm"这种说法出现于1487年第11号法律。其他还有1436年第13号、1451年第15号和1482年第8号法律。

921

国民财富的性质与原理

<small>but merchants found this inconvenient.</small> When those countries became commercial, the merchants found this prohibition, upon many occasions, extremely inconvenient. They could frequently buy more advantageously with gold and silver than with any other commodity, the foreign goods which they wanted, either to import into their own, or to carry to some other foreign country. They remonstrated, therefore, against this prohibition as hurtful to trade.

<small>and therefore argued that exportation did not always diminish the stock in the country,</small> They represented, first, that the exportation of gold and silver in order to purchase foreign goods, did not always diminish the quantity of those metals in the kingdom. That, on the contrary, it might frequently increase that quantity; because, if the consumption of foreign goods was not thereby increased in the country, those goods might be re-exported to foreign countries, and, being there sold for a large profit, might bring back much more treasure than was originally sent out to purchase them. Mr. Mun compares this operation of foreign trade to the seed-time and harvest of agriculture. "If we only behold," says he, "the actions of the husbandman in the seed-time, when he casteth" away much good corn into the ground, we shall account him rather "a madman than a husbandman. But when we consider his labours" in the harvest, which is the end of his endeavours, we shall find the "worth and plentiful increase of his actions."①

<small>and that the metals could be retained only by attention to the balance of trade.</small> They represented, secondly, that this prohibition could not hinder the exportation of gold and silver, which, on account of the smallness of their bulk in proportion to their value, could easily be smuggled abroad,② That this exportation could only be prevented by a

---

① [*England's Treasure by Forraign Trade, or the Ballance of our Forraign Trade is the Rule of our Treasure*, 1664, chap. iv., ad fin.]

② [*Mun England's Treasure*, chap. vi.]

第四篇 第一章

和英格兰在古代也采取了类似的政策。

当这些国家成为商业国时,商人们发现在许多场合这种禁令都极其不方便。他们用金银通常比用其他任何商品都能更加便利地购买到他们所需要的外国商品,以进口输入他们本国或运往其他国家。因此,他们抗议这种禁令,认为其损害贸易。

<small>但是发现禁止出口金银会带来不便,商人们</small>

他们提出,第一,出口金银以购买外国商品并不总是会减少国内这种金属的数量。相反的,它通常可能会增加国内金银的数量。因为如果外国商品在国内的消费没有因此而增加,那些商品可以再次出口到国外并以巨额利润出售,这样就可以带回比原来送往国外以购买商品的财富更加多得多的财富。孟先生把这种对外贸易的运作比作农业的播种和收获。他说:"如果我们仅仅看到农夫在播种时期的行为,他把许多优良的谷粒撒到地里,那么我们会认为他是一个疯子而不是一个农夫。但是当我们把这看作他在收获中的劳动,而这种劳动也正是他努力的结果时,我们将会发现他的劳动的价值和巨大的增值。"①

<small>因此,他们争辩说,出口并不总会减少金银储备。</small>

他们提出,第二,这种禁令制止不了金银的出口,因为相对于金银的价值而言,金银的体积很小,是很容易走私到国外的。②这种出口只能通过对被他们称作贸易差额的东西给予适当关注

<small>只有通过关注贸易差额才能保持国内的金银。</small>

---

① 《英国通过对外贸易得到的财富,或我们对外贸易的差额是我们财富的尺度》,1664 年,第四章直到最后。

② 孟,上面所引用的书《英国通过对外贸易得到的财富,或我们对外贸易的差额是我们财富的尺度》,第六章。

proper attention to, what they called, the balance of trade. ① That when the country exported to a greater value than it imported, a balance became due to it from foreign nations, which was necessarily paid to it in gold and silver, and thereby increased the quantity of those metals in the kingdom. But that when it imported to a greater value than it exported, a contrary balance became due to foreign nations, which was necessarily paid to them in the same manner, and thereby diminished that quantity. That in this case to prohibit the exportation of those metals could not prevent it, but only by making it more dangerous, render it more expensive. That the exchange was thereby turned more against the country which owed the balance, than it otherwise might have been; the merchant who purchased a bill upon the foreign country being obliged to pay the banker who sold it, not only for the natural risk, trouble and expence of sending the money thither, but for the extraordinary risk arising from the prohibition. But that the more the exchange was against any country, the more the balance of trade became necessarily against it; the money of that country becoming necessarily of so much less value, in comparison with that of the country to which the balance was due. That if the exchange between England and Holland, for example, was five per cent. against England, it would require a hundred and five ounces of silver in England to purchase a bill for a hundred ounces of silver in Holland: that a hundred and five ounces of silver in England, therefore, would be worth only a hundred ounces of silver in Holland, and would purchase only a proportionable quantity of Dutch goods: but that a hundred ounces of silver in Holland, on the contrary, would be worth a hundred and five ounces in England, and would purchase a proportionable quantity of English goods: that the English goods which were sold to Holland would be sold so much cheaper; and the Dutch goods which were sold to England, so much dearer, by the difference of the exchange; that the one would draw so much less Dutch money to England, and the other so much more English money to Holland, as this difference amounted to: and that the balance of trade, therefore, would

---

① ['Among other things relating to trade there hath been much discourse of the balance of trade; the right understanding whereof may be of singular use.'—Josiah Child, *New Discourse of Trade*, 1694, p. 152, chap. ix., introducing an explanation. The term was used before Mun's work was written. See Palgrave's *Dictionary of Political Economy*, s. v. Balance of Trade, History of the theory.]

才能予以制止。① 当一个国家出口的价值大于其进口的价值时，就产生了对外贸易顺差，这一差额必须由外国用金银来支付，这样就增加了本国金银的数量。但是当一个国家进口的价值大于其出口的价值时，相反地就会产生对外贸易逆差，同样的，这一差额也必须以金银支付给外国，这样，就减少了本国国内金银的数量。在这种情况下，禁止金银的出口不起作用，只能使这种出口更加危险，更加昂贵。这样，汇兑将比原来更加不利于有贸易逆差的国家，购买外国汇票的商人对于出售外国汇票的银行要承担的责任既包括把货币送往国外的自然风险、麻烦和费用，还包括由于禁令出口而产生的特殊风险。但是，对于任何一个国家而言，汇兑对其越不利，贸易收支平衡必然对其也就越不利，相对于贸易顺差的国家而言，贸易逆差的国家的货币必然变得更不值钱。例如，如果英格兰与荷兰之间的汇兑有5%不利于英格兰，那么英格兰就需要105盎司白银才能购得荷兰100盎司白银的汇票。因此，英格兰105盎司白银只值荷兰100盎司白银，也就只能购买到相应数量的荷兰商品；但是相反，荷兰100盎司白银却值英格兰105盎司白银，将能够购买到相应数量的英格兰商品；出售给荷兰的英国商品价格较便宜，而出售给英国的荷兰商品价格较贵，这个价格之差是由汇兑的差价决定的；按照这个差价英格兰从荷兰得到的荷兰货币就少一些，而荷兰从英格兰得到的英格

---

① "在与贸易相关的其他方面，已有许多关于贸易差额的论述；关于它的正确理解可能会单独使用。"——乔赛亚·蔡尔德《贸易新论》，1694年，见第九章第152页，引入这一解释。贸易差额这个词语，在孟的著作出版以前已经使用，参见帕尔格雷夫《政治经济学词典》，"贸易差额，这一理论的历史"。

| 国民财富的性质与原理

Their arguments were partly sophistical,

necessarily be so much more against England, and would require a greater balance of gold and silver to be exported to Holland.

Those arguments were partly solid and partly sophistical. They were solid so far as they asserted that the exportation of gold and silver in trade might frequently be advantageous to the country. They were solid too, in asserting that no prohibition could prevent their exportation, when private people found any advantage in exporting them. But they were sophistical in supposing, that either to preserve or to augment the quantity of those metals required more the attention of government, than to preserve or to augment the quantity of any other useful commodities, which the freedom of trade, without any such attention, never fails to supply in the proper quantity. They were sophistical too, perhaps, in asserting that the high price of exchange necessarily increased, what they called, the unfavourable balance of trade, or occasioned the exportation of a greater quantity of gold and silver. That high price, indeed, was extremely disadvantageous to the merchants who had any money to pay in foreign countries. They paid so much dearer for the bills which their bankers granted them upon those countries. But though the risk arising from the prohibition might occasion some extraordinary expence to the bankers, it would not necessarily carry any more money out of the country. This expence would generally be all laid out in the country, in smuggling the money out of it, and could seldom occasion the exportation of a single six-pence beyond the precise sum drawn for. The high price of exchange too would naturally dispose the merchants to endeavour to make their exports nearly balance their imports, in order that they might have this high exchange to pay upon as small a sum as possible. The high price of exchange, besides, must necessarily have operated as a tax, in raising the price of foreign goods, and thereby diminishing their consumption. It would tend, therefore, not to increase, but to diminish, what they called, the unfavourable balance of trade, and consequently the exportation of gold and silver.

but they convinced parliaments and councils.

Such as they were, however, those arguments convinced the people to whom they were addressed. They were addressed by merchants to parliaments, and to the councils of princes, to nobles, and to country gentlemen; by those who were supposed to understand trade, to those who were conscious to themselves that they knew nothing

兰货币就多一些。所以，贸易差额必然更加不利于英格兰，从而要求向荷兰出口更多金银。

这些论证一部分是合理的，而一部分则是诡辩。他们宣称贸易中的金银出口常常是有利于国家的，这一点是合理的；他们宣称当私人发现出口金银有利可图时，禁令就不能够阻止其出口，这一点也是合理的。但是，他们认为保持或增加本国内的金银数量要比保持或增加其他任何有用商品更需要政府的更多关注，这一点就是诡辩了。因为对于其他任何有用商品，无需任何这种关注，自由贸易的原则总会确保这些商品的适量供应。他们宣称高汇价必然增加他们所谓的贸易逆差，或者造成金银更大数量的出口，这一点可能也是诡辩。高汇价对于那些必须向外国支付货币的商人来说，确实是不利的。对银行为他们开具的外国汇票他们所支付的价格要贵得多。虽然由于禁令所产生的风险可能会给银行造成意外的费用，但是却不一定要把更多的货币带出国外。这种费用一般都是在走私货币出国时在国内支付的，不会超出汇兑数目一分钱。高汇价也自然而然促使商人竭力保持出口和进口之间基本平衡，以便他们为这个高汇价支付的数量尽可能少点。除此之外，高汇价必然会起到税收的作用，提高外国商品的价格，从而减少了外国商品的消费。因此，高汇价将不仅不会增加，反而只会减少他们所说的所谓贸易逆差，因而也减少了金银的出口。

然而，尽管如此，这些论证还是说服了它的听众们，这些论证是由商人们向国会、向王公会议、向贵族和乡绅们讲述的；是由那些被认为懂得贸易的人向那些自知对贸易一无所知的人讲述的。经验向贵族和乡绅表明，同时也向商人表明对外贸易能使国家致

国民财富的性质与原理

<small>The exportation of foreign coin and bullion was permitted by France and England, and the exportation of Dutch coin by Holland.</small> about the matter. That foreign trade enriched the country, experience demonstrated to the nobles and country gentlemen, as well as to the merchants; but how, or in what manner, none of them well knew. The merchants knew perfectly in what manner it enriched themselves. It was their business to know it. But to know in what manner it enriched the country, was no part of their business. This subject never came into their consideration, but when they had occasion to apply to their country for some change in the laws relating to foreign trade. It then became necessary to say something about the beneficial effects of foreign trade, and the manner in which those effects were obstructed by the laws as they then stood. To the judges who were to decide the business, it appeared a most satisfactory account of the matter, when they were told that foreign trade brought money into the country, but that the laws in question hindered it from bringing so much as it otherwise <small>That treasure was obtained by foreign trade became a received maxim.</small> would do. Those arguments therefore produced the wished-for effect. The prohibition of exporting gold and silver was in France and England confined to the coin of those respective countries. The exportation of foreign coin and of bullion was made free. In Holland, and in some other places, this liberty was extended even to the coin of the country. The attention of government was turned away from guarding against the exportation of gold and silver, to watch over the balance of trade, as the only cause which could occasion any augmentation or diminution of those metals. From one fruitless care it was turned away to another care much more intricate, much more embarrassing, and just equally fruitless. The title of Mun's book, England's Treasure in Foreign Trade, became a fundamental maxim in the political economy, not of England only, but of all other commercial countries. The inland or home trade, the most important of all, the trade in which an equal capital affords the greatest revenue, and creates the greatest employment to the people of the country, was considered as subsidiary only to foreign trade. It neither brought money into the country, it was said, nor carried any <small>Gold and silver will be imported without any attention of government</small> out of it. The country therefore could never become either richer or poorer by means of it, except so far as its prosperity or decay might indirectly influence the state of foreign trade.

A country that has no mines of its own must undoubtedly draw its gold and silver from foreign countries, in the same manner as one that has no vineyards of its own must draw its wines. It does not seem

第四篇　第一章

富。但是该怎样或用何种方式，他们谁都不知道。对外贸易是以何种方式使他们自己致富的，商人们十分清楚。了解这一点也是他们的事情，但是弄清楚对外贸易是以何种方式使国家致富则不是他们的事了。除了当他们向国家申请对对外贸易法律作某些变更时，他们是绝不会考虑这个问题的。于是对对外贸易的有利作用以及现行法律如何妨碍了这种有利作用，就有必要说些什么了。对于应就此事做出决策的裁决者，当他们被告知对外贸易给国家带来货币，但是现行有关法律却阻碍了它给国家带来本该带来的货币量时，他们觉得这是个非常令人满意的说明。因而那些辩论就产生了预期的效果。在法国和英国，禁止金银出口的禁令仅局限于各自的铸币上。外国铸币和金银条仍可自由出口。在荷兰和其他一些地方，这种出口的自由甚至可以延伸到本国的铸币。政府的注意力也从监视金银的出口转向监视贸易差额，把其作为唯一会使得金银增加或减少的原因，从而从一种毫无结果的关注转向另外一种更加复杂、更加困窘且同样毫无结果的关注。孟的著作《英国在对外贸易中的财富》不仅成为了英国而且也成为了其他所有商业国家政治经济学的一个基本信条。内陆贸易或国内贸易是最重要的一种贸易，在这种贸易中等量的资本能获取最大量的收入，能为国内人民创造最大的就业机会，而这种贸易却只是被视作对外贸易的附属物。据说，这种贸易既不能为国家带来货币，也不会使国内货币外流，所以国家不会因国内贸易而致富或变穷，除了国内贸易的繁荣或衰落可能间接影响对外贸易的状况这一点以外。

一个没有自己矿山的国家毫无疑问必须从外国进口金银，就如一个自己没有葡萄园的国家必须从外国进口葡萄酒一样。然

法国和英国允许外国铸币和金银条出口，荷兰允许本国铸币出口。

由对外贸易获得财富变成了公认的教条。

无需政府任何关注，金银也可进口。

necessary, however, that the attention of government should be more turned towards the one than towards the other object. A country that has wherewithal to buy wine, will always get the wine which it has occasion for; and a country that has wherewithal to buy gold and silver, will never be in want of those metals. They are to be bought for a certain price like all other commodities, and as they are the price of all other commodities, so all other commodities are the price of those metals. We trust with perfect security that the freedom of trade, without any attention of government, will always supply us with the wine which we have occasion for; and we may trust with equal security that it will always supply us with all the gold and silver which we can afford to purchase or to employ, either in circulating our commodities, or in other uses.

_{They can be imported more easily than other commodities when there is an effectual demand.} The quantity of every commodity which human industry can either purchase or produce, naturally regulates itself in every country according to the effectual demand, or according to the demand of those who are willing to pay the whole rent, labour and profits which must be paid in order to prepare and bring it to market. But no commodities regulate themselves more easily or more exactly according to this effectual demand than gold and silver; because, on account of the small bulk and great value of those metals, no commodities can be more easily transported from one place to another, from the places where they are cheap, to those where they are dear, from the places where they exceed, to those where they fall short of this effectual demand. If there were in England, for example, an effectual demand for an additional quantity of gold, a packet-boat could bring from Lisbon, or from wherever else it was to be had, fifty tuns of gold, which could be coined into more than five millions of guineas. But if there were an effectual demand for grain to the same value, to import it would require, at five guineas a tun, a million of tuns of shipping, or a thousand ships of a thousand tuns each. The navy of England would not be sufficient.

_{When their quantity exceeds the demand it is impossible to prevent their exportation.} When the quantity of gold and silver imported into any country exceeds the effectual demand, no vigilance of government can prevent their exportation. All the sanguinary laws of Spain and Portugal are

而，政府似乎没有必要更多地关注这个目标、更少地关注另外一个目标。有足够资金购买葡萄酒的国家，总是能在它需要之时购买到葡萄酒；有足够资金购买金银的国家，绝不会短缺金银。像所有其他商品一样，金银也是以一定的价格购买的，正如金银是所有其他商品的价格一样，所有其他商品也是金银的价格。我们完全有十足的把握相信，没有政府的任何关注自由贸易将总是能够供应给我们所需要的葡萄酒，我们也可以同样完全有十足把握地相信自由贸易将总能够供应我们在商品流通或其他用途中所能够购买或使用的金银。

  人类的勤劳能够购买或生产的每一种商品的数量，在每一个国家自然是根据有效需求来调节的，或是根据愿意生产商品并支付将其送入市场所必须预支的全部地租、劳动和利润的人的需求来调节的。但是没有任何其他商品比金银更加容易、更加准确地根据这种有效需求来调节自己。因为金银的体积小而价值大，没有其他的商品能更加容易地从一个地方运输到另一个地方、从便宜的地方运输到昂贵的地方、从超过有效需求的地方运输到有效需求不足的地方。例如，如果英格兰有黄金的额外有效需求，那么一艘邮轮就会从里斯本或其他任何有黄金的地方运来50吨黄金，可以铸成五百多万几尼。但是如果是对同等价值的谷物的有效需求，那么，进口这批谷物，按每吨五几尼的价格，将需要100万吨的航运，或载重1000吨的船只1000艘，英格兰的海军船只也不够用。

<small>当有有效需求时，金银比其他商品更容易进口。</small>

  当任何一个国家进口的金银数量超过有效需求时，政府的警惕并不能阻止出口。西班牙和葡萄牙所有残酷的法律都不能使金银留在国内。从秘鲁和巴西不断进口的金银超过了这两个国

<small>当金银数量超过需求时，不可能阻止其出口；</small>

not able to keep their gold and silver at home. The continual importations from Peru and Brazil exceed the effectual demand of those countries, and sink the price of those metals there below that in the neighbouring countries. If, on the contrary, in any particular country their quantity fell short of the effectual demand, so as to raise their price above that of the neighbouring countries, the government would have no occasion to take any pains to import them. If it were even to take pains to prevent their importation, it would not be able to effectuate it. Those metals, when the Spartans had got wherewithal to purchase them, broke through all the barriers which the laws of Lycurgus opposed to their entrance into Lacedemon. All the sanguinary laws of the customs are not able to prevent the importation of the teas of the Dutch and Gottenburgh East India companies; because somewhat cheaper than those of the British company. A pound of tea, however, is about a hundred times the bulk of one of the highest prices, sixteen shillings, that is commonly paid for it in silver, and more than two thousand times the bulk of the same price in gold, and consequently just so many times more difficult to smuggle.

It is partly owing to the easy transportation of gold and silver from the places where they abound to those where they are wanted, that the price of those metals does not fluctuate continually like that of the greater part of other commodities, which are hindered by their bulk from shifting their situation, when the market happens to be either over or under-stocked with them. The price of those metals, indeed, is not altogether exempted from variation, but the changes to which it is liable are generally slow, gradual, and uniform. In Europe, for example, it is supposed, without much foundation, perhaps, that, during the course of the present and preceding century, they have been constantly, but gradually, sinking in their value, on account of the continual importations from the Spanish West Indies. ① But to make any sudden change in the price of gold and silver, so as to raise or lower at once, sensibly and remarkably, the money price of all other commodities, requires such a revolution in commerce as that occasioned by the discovery of America.

---

① [The absence of any reference to the long Digression in bk. i., chap. xi., suggests that this passage was written before the Digression was incorporated in the work. Contrast the reference below, vol. ii., p. 9.]

家的有效需求,使得这两国金银价格低于邻国金银价格。反之,如果任何一个国家金银数量不能满足其有效需求时,就会导致金银价格提高得高于邻国价格,那么也无需政府费力去进口金银了。如果政府费力去阻止金银进口,那也是办不到的。当斯巴达人有足够的资金购买金银时,金银就冲破了莱克尔加斯法律为阻止金银进入老斯巴达而设置的一切障碍。所有残酷的海关法律,都不能阻止荷兰和戈登堡东印度公司茶叶的进口,因为它比不列颠东印度公司的茶叶稍微便宜。然而,一磅茶叶的最高价格以白银计通常是16先令,而一磅茶叶的体积大约是16先令白银体积的100倍,是相同价格黄金体积的两千多倍,因此走私茶叶比走私金银也要困难这么多倍。

当金银供应少于有效需求时,同样也不能阻止金银的进口。

部分的是因为金银易于从丰富的地方运输到匮乏的地方,所以金银的价格不像其他大部分商品的价格那样不断地波动。当其他商品在市场出现过剩或短缺时,由于其体积的原因而不能自由流动。的确,金银的价格也不是完全没有变化的,只是这种变化通常是缓慢的、逐渐的和统一的。例如,在欧洲,有人认为(或许是没有根据的)在本世纪和上世纪,由于从西班牙所属西印度群岛不断进口金银,金银的价值不断地下降。① 但是为了使所有其他商品的货币价格当即明显地、显著地提高或降低,而对金银的价格做出任何突然的改变,这就需要在商业中进行一场像发现美洲大陆那样的革命。

正是这种运输使得金银的价格统一。

尽管如此,如果一个有足够资金购买金银的国家在任何时候

---

① 这里没有提到第一编第十一章中的很长的题外话论述,表明在题外话论述编入本书以前这一段已经完成了。比较下面第二卷的援引。

> If, notwithstanding all this, gold and silver should at any time fall short in a country which has wherewithal to purchase them, there are more expedients for supplying their place, than that of almost any other commodity. If the materials of manufacture are wanted, industry must stop. If provisions are wanted, the people must starve But if money is wanted, barter will supply its place, though with a good deal of inconveniency. Buying and selling upon credit, and the different dealers compensating their credits with one another once a month or once a year, will supply it with less inconveniency. A well-regulated paper money will supply it, not only without any inconveniency, but, in some cases, with some advantages. Upon every account, therefore, the attention of government never was so unnecessarily employed, as when directed to watch over the preservation or increase of the quantity of money in any country.

If they did fall short, their place could be supplied by paper.

> No complaint, however, is more common than that of a scarcity of money. Money, like wine, must always be scarce with chose who have neither wherewithal to buy it, nor credit to borrow it. Those who have either, will seldom be in want either of the money, or of the wine which they have occasion for. This complaint, however, of the scarcity of money, is not always confined to improvident spendthrifts. It is sometimes general through a whole mercantile town, and the country in its neighbourhood. Over-trading is the common cause of it. Sober men, whose projects have been disproportioned to their capitals, are as likely to have neither wherewithal to buy money, nor credit to borrow it, as prodigals whose expence has been disproportioned to their revenue. Before their projects can be brought to bear, their stock is gone, and their credit with it. They run about everywhere to borrow money, and every body tells them that they have none to lend. Even such general complaints of the scarcity of money do not always prove that the usual number of gold and silver pieces are not circulating in the country, but that many people want those pieces who have nothing to give for them. When the profits of trade happen to be greater than ordinary, over-trading becomes a general error both among great and small dealers. They do not always send more money abroad than usual, but they buy upon credit both at home and abroad, an unusual quantity of goods, which they send to some distant market, in hopes that the returns will come in before the de-

The common complaint of scarcity of money only means difficulty in borrowing.

出现金银短缺,那么相比其他商品的短缺,有更多的应急手段保障金银的供应。如果生产资料短缺,产业必须停工。如果食物短缺,人民一定挨饿。但如果货币短缺,尽管会有诸多不便,但物物交换可以填补其空缺。通过赊账进行买卖,商人们可以每月一次或每年一次清偿彼此的债务,来填补货币短缺,而且也较方便。如果用一种调节得当的纸币去填补货币短缺,不但不会有任何不便之处,而且在某些情况下还有一些好处。因此,从各方面来讲,政府对于保持或增加一个国家的货币数量的关注是完全不必要的。

<small>如果金银短缺,可以用纸币来填补其位置。</small>

然而,没有什么抱怨比对货币短缺的抱怨更普遍了。货币也像葡萄酒一样,对于那些既没有足够资金购买它又没有信用借到它的人来说必然总是短缺的。对于那些拥有两者中任何一样的人来说,在他们需要货币或葡萄酒时总不会短缺。不过,对货币短缺的这种抱怨并不总是限于没有远见的浪费者。有时候在整个商业城市及其周围的农村,都有这种抱怨。其共同原因是过度的贸易。理智冷静的人,如果他们的计划与资本不相称,他们就既无足够的资金去购买货币,也没有信用去借到货币,就像支出与收入不成比例的浪费者一样。在他们的计划完成以前,他们的资金就耗尽了,信用亦失去了。他们到处奔走去借钱,每个人都告诉他们无钱可借。即使是这种情况的对货币缺乏的普遍抱怨,也并不总能证明国内流通的金银币数量不正常,而只是能够证明许多人想要这些金银币而却没有可以用来交换的东西。当商业利润大于普通利润时,贸易过度便成了大小商人都会犯的共同错误。他们并不总是将比平常更多的货币送往国外,而是在国内和国外赊购了超过寻常数量的货物,并把它们送到某个远方的

<small>抱怨货币短缺只意味着借款困难。普遍货币短缺是</small>

mand for payment. The demand comes before the returns, and they have nothing at hand, with which they can either purchase money, or give solid security for borrowing. It is not any scarcity of gold and silver, but the difficulty which such people find in borrowing, and which their creditors find in getting payment, that occasions the general complaint of the scarcity of money.

<small>Money makes but a small part of the national capital.</small> It would be too ridiculous to go about seriously to prove, that wealth does not consist in money, or in gold and silver; but in what money purchases, and is valuable only for purchasing. Money, no doubt, makes always a part of the national capital; but it has already been shown that it generally makes but a small part, and always the most unprofitable part of it.

<small>It is easier to buy than to sell simply because money is the instrument of commerce.</small> It is not because wealth consists more essentially in money than in goods, that the merchant finds it generally more easy to buy goods with money, than to buy money with goods; but because money is the known and established instrument of commerce, for which every thing is readily given in exchange, but which is not always with equal readiness to be got in exchange for every thing. The greater part of goods besides are more perishable than money, and he may frequently sustain a much greater loss by keeping them. When his goods are upon hand too, he is more liable to such demands for money as he may not be able to answer, than when he has got their price in his coffers. Over and above all this, his profit arises more directly from selling than from buying, and he is upon all these accounts generally much more anxious to exchange his goods for money, than his money for goods. But though a particular merchant, with abundance of goods in his warehouse, may sometimes be ruined by not being able to sell them in time, a nation or country is not liable to the same accident. The whole capital of a merchant frequently consists in perishable goods destined for purchasing money. But it is but a very small part of the annual produce of the land and labour of a country which can ever be destined for purchasing gold and silver from their neighbours. The far greater part is circulated and consumed among themselves; and even

市场,期望在要求支付货款以前回收本利。在回收本利以前,就要求支付货款了,而他们手头什么也没有,没有东西可以用来购买货币,或为借款提供坚实担保。这并不是什么金银的短缺,而只是这些人感到借款的困难,以及他们的债权人感到收回借款的困难,造成了对货币缺乏的普遍抱怨。

如果要去认真严肃地证明财富不是由货币或金银构成的,而是由货币所购买的东西构成的,并且货币只有用于购买时才有价值,那就太荒谬可笑了。无疑货币总是构成国家资本的一部分,但是,我们已经指出,它一般只构成国家资本的一小部分,而且总是最无利可图的一部分。

并非是因为财富更主要的是由货币构成,而不是由货物构成,商人才感到用货币购买货物通常比用货物购买货币更容易;而是因为货币是公认的确立起来的交易媒介,一切东西与之相交换都很容易,但是一切东西却并不能同样如此容易地和它相交换。此外,绝大部分货物都比货币易于腐烂,保存货物常常会遭受更大的损失。当货物在手中时,他更可能遇到一些支付货币的要求,而他无法满足要求,但当他把货物出手获得它们的价钱放在钱柜里时,就不会有这种可能性了。除此之外,他的利润更直接地产生于出售货物而不是购买货物,基于这一切原因,他通常更急切想把货物换成货币,而不是把货币换成货物。但是,虽然某一个商人在仓库里保存大量货物,有时可能因未能及时出售货物而遭遇破产,但是一个国家不可能遭遇相同的事故。一个商人的全部资本通常包括预定用来换取货币的易于腐烂的货物,但是一个国家的土地和劳动年产物中只有极少的一部分是预定用来同邻国金银相交换的,其中绝大部分是在国内流通和消费的。即

of the surplus which is sent abroad, the greater part is generally destined for the purchase of other foreign goods. Though gold and silver, therefore, could not be had in exchange for the goods destined to purchase them, the nation would not be ruined. It might, indeed, suffer some loss and inconveniency, and be forced upon some of those expedients which are necessary for supplying the place of money. The annual produce of its land and labour, however, would be the same, or very nearly the same, as usual, because the same, or very nearly the same consumable capital would be employed in maintaining it. And though goods do not always draw money so readily as money draws goods, in the long-run they draw it more necessarily than even it draws them. Goods can serve many other purposes besides purchasing money, but money can serve no other purpose besides purchasing goods. Money, therefore, necessarily runs after goods, but goods do not always or necessarily run after money. The man who buys, does not always mean to sell again, but frequently to use or to consume; whereas he who sells, always means to buy again. The one may frequently have done the whole, but the other can never have done more than the one-half of his business. It is not for its own sake that men desire money, but for the sake of what they can purchase with it.

The durability of a commodity is no reason for accumulating more of it than is wanted. Consumable commodities, it is said, are soon destroyed; whereas gold and silver are of a more durable nature, and, were it not for this continual exportation, might be accumulated for ages together, to the incredible augmentation of the real wealth of the country. Nothing, therefore, it is pretended, can be more disadvantageous to any country, than the trade which consists in the exchange of such lasting for such perishable commodities. We do not, however, reckon that trade disadvantageous which consists in the exchange of the hard-ware of England for the wines of France; and yet hard-ware is a very durable commodity, and were it not for this continual exportation, might too be accumulated for ages together, to the incredible augmentation of the pots and pans of the country. But it readily occurs that the number of such utensils is in every country necessarily limited by the use which there is for them; that it would be absurd to have more pots

第四篇 第一章

使是送往国外的剩余部分,其中大部分一般也是预定用来购买其他外国的货物。因此,即使预定用来交换金银的货物没有交换到金银,国家也不会破产。的确,它可能遭受某些损失和不便,不得不采取为填补货币短缺所必须采取的应急措施。但是,它的土地和劳动年产物还是和通常情况一样,或者几乎一样,因为相同的或者几乎相同的可消费资本将用于维持国家。虽然以货物交换货币并不总像以货币交换货物那么容易,但从长远来看,以货物交换货币比以货币交换货物更有必要。货物除了购买货币外,还有许多其他的用途,但货币除了购买货物之外没有其他的用途。因此,货币必然追逐货物,但货物并不总是或并不必然追逐货币。购买货物的人并不总是要再出售,而常常是使用或消费,而出售货物的人总是要再购入。前者买进货物常常可能就做完了他的全部工作,而后者售出货物至多只完成了工作的一半。人们并不是为了货币本身而想要得到货币,而是为了货币所能购买到的东西才想要得到货币。

人们都说,可消费商品很快就损坏,而金银则更具耐久性,如果不是由于不断的出口,可以将金银长年积累起来,使国家的真实财富增加到让人难以置信的程度。因此,有人认为,对于任何一个国家而言,不利的事情莫过于用这种耐久性商品去交换那些易于腐烂的商品的贸易了。但是,我们并不认为用英格兰的铁器去交换法兰西的葡萄酒是不利的贸易;虽然铁器是非常耐用持久的商品,如果不是由于不断的出口,也可以将它长年积累起来,使国家锅盘的数量增加到让人难以置信的程度。但是通常的情况是每个国家这类用具的数量必然被该国对它们的用途所限制;锅盘的数量超过用来烹调当地通常消费的食物所需锅盘的数目,将

商品的耐久性并不是我们积累这种商品超过需求的理由。

— 939 —

and pans than were necessary for cooking the victuals usually consumed there; and that if the quantity of victuals were to increase, the number of pots and pans would readily increase along with it, a part of the increased quantity of victuals being employed in purchasing them, or in maintaining an additional number of workmen whose business it was to make them. It should as readily occur that the quantity of gold and silver is in every country limited by the use which there is for those metals; that their use consists in circulating commodities as coin, and in affording a species of houshold furniture as plate; that the quantity of coin in every country is regulated by the value of the commodities which are to be circulated by it: increase that value, and immediately a part of it will be sent abroad to purchase, wherever it is to be had, the additional quantity of coin requisite for circulating them: that the quantity of plate is regulated by the number and wealth of those private families who chuse to indulge themselves in that sort of magnificence: increase the number and wealth of such families, and a part of this increased wealth will most probably be employed in purchasing, wherever it is to be found, an additional quantity of plate: that to attempt to increase the wealth of any country, either by introducing or by detaining in it an unnecessary quantity of gold and silver, is as absurd as it would be to attempt to increase the good cheer of private families, by obliging them to keep an unnecessary number of kitchen utensils. As the expence of purchasing those unnecessary utensils would diminish instead of increasing either the quantity or goodness of the family provisions; so the expence of purchasing an unnecessary quantity of gold and silver must, in every country, as necessarily diminish the wealth which feeds, clothes, and lodges, which maintains and employs the people. Gold and silver, whether in the shape of coin or of plate, are utensils, it must be remembered, as much as the furniture of the kitchen. Increase the use for them, increase the consumable commodities which are to be circulated, managed, and prepared by means of them, and you will infallibly increase the quantity; but if you attempt, by extraordinary means, to increase the quantity, you will as infallibly diminish the use and even the quantity too, which in those metals can never be greater than what the use requires. Were they ever to be accumulated beyond this quantity, their transportation is so easy, and the loss which attends their lying idle and unemployed so great, that no law could prevent their being immediately sent out of the country.

是可笑的事情；如果食物的数量增加了，锅盘的数量会自然随之增加，即用增加的食物的一部分用来购买锅盘，或者用于维持增添的制造锅盘的工人的生活费用。同样普遍的情况，是每个国家的金银数量是受到这些金银用途的制约的；它们的用途在于作为铸币去流通商品，以及作为金银餐具，一种家具。每个国家铸币的数量是由通过它进行流通的商品的价值来调控的；增加了流通的商品的价值，其中一部分立刻会被送往国外到可以购买到铸币的地方去购买商品流通所必需的额外数量的铸币。金银餐具的数量是由沉溺于这种豪华东西的私人家庭的数量和财富所调节的；增加这种家庭的数量和财富，那么所增加财富的一部分将很可能在能购买的地方用于购买额外的金银餐具。企图通过引入国内或保持国内不必要的金银数量来增加国家财富，就像企图通过强迫一些私人家庭保留不必要数量的厨房用具来增添他们的快乐一样荒谬可笑。正如购买那些不必要的用具的开支将会减少而不是增加家庭食物的数量和质量一样，购买不必要的数量的金银的开支要每一个国家也必然会减少用于吃、穿、住方面及用于维持人民生活并为他们提供就业机会的财富。必须记住，黄金和白银无论是以铸币形式还是以金银餐具形式存在，都是与厨房用具一样的用具。增加金银的用途，增加通过它们来流通、经营和生产的可消费商品的数量，那么你一定会增加金银的数量；但是如果你试图通过特别的方法来增加金银数量，那么你一定会减少它们的用途，甚至减少其数量，这些金属的数量绝不会多于其用途所需。如果它们积累到超过这个数量，由于它们的运输如此容易，而且任其闲置不用的损失如此巨大，因而任何法律都阻止不了它们被立即运送出国。

国民财富的性质与原理

<small>Accumulation of gold and silver is not necessary for carrying on distant wars,</small> It is not always necessary to accumulate gold and silver, in order to enable a country to carry on foreign wars, and to maintain fleets and armies in distant countries. Fleets and armies are maintained, not with gold and silver, but with consumable goods. The nation which, from the annual produce of its domestic industry, from the annual revenue arising out of its lands, labour, and consumable stock, has wherewithal to purchase those consumable goods in distant countries, can maintain foreign wars there.

<small>which may be paid for by exporting: (1) gold and silver, (2) manufactures, or (3) rude produce.</small> A nation may purchase the pay and provisions of an army in a distant country three different ways; by sending abroad either, first, some part of its accumulated gold and silver; or secondly, some part of the annual produce of its manufactures; or last of all, some part of its annual rude produce.

<small>The gold and silver consists of money in circulation, plate, and money in the treasury.</small> The gold and silver which can properly be considered as accumulated or stored up in any country, may be distinguished into three parts; first, the circulating money; secondly, the plate of private families; and last of all, the money which may have been collected by many years parsimony, and laid up in the treasury of the prince.

<small>Little can be spared from the money in circulation;</small> It can seldom happen that much can be spared from the circulating money of the country; because in that there can seldom be much redundancy. The value of goods annually bought and sold in any country requires a certain quantity of money to circulate and distribute them to their proper consumers, and can give employment to no more. The channel of circulation necessarily draws to itself a sum sufficient to fill it, and never admits any more. Something, however, is generally withdrawn from this channel in the case of foreign war. By the great number of people who are maintained abroad, fewer are maintained at home. Fewer goods are circulated there, and less money becomes necessary to circulate them. An extraordinary quantity of paper money, of some sort or other too, such as exchequer notes, navy bills, and bank bills in England, is generally issued upon such occasions, and by supplying the place of circulating gold and silver, gives an opportunity of sending a greater quantity of it abroad. All this, however, could afford but a poor resource for maintaining a foreign war, of great expence and several years duration.

为了使一个国家能够进行对外战争,并且能在遥远的国家维持其海陆军,并不总是必须积累金银。海陆军不是依靠金银而是依靠消费品维持生活的。一个国家从它的国内产业的年产物中,从它土地、劳动和消费资本的年收入中拿出一部分,就有足够的财力在遥远的国家购买这些消费品,就能够维持那里的对外战争了。

一个国家可以通过以下三种不同的方式在遥远的国家为军队购买饷给和食物:首先,将所积累的金银的一部分出口到国外;其二,将其制造业年产物的一部分出口到国外;其三,将每年的原产物的一部分送往国外。

在任何一个国家可正当地被看作积累或贮存的金银可以被分为三部分:第一,流通中的货币;第二,私人家庭的金银器具;第三,经过多年节俭积累起来存贮在国库中的货币。

从一国流通中的货币很少能节省下许多东西,因为在流通中的货币里很少有剩余。在任何一个国家,每年买卖的货物的价值要求一定数量的货币进行流通并把货物分配到适当的消费者手中,此外就不能使用更多的货币了。流通的渠道必然会吸引足够数量的货币去填充,而不能容纳更多。然而,在进行对外战争的情况下,一般要从这个渠道撤走一些东西。由于在国外维持大量人员的生活,在国内所维持的人数就少一些。在国内流通的货物较少一些,流通所需货币也就少一些。大量额外数量的纸币,这种或那种如财政部债券、海军债券、英格兰银行债券等,一般在这种场合发行,填补了流通中金银的空缺,并为更大量的金银送往国外提供了机会。但是所有这些对于维持耗资巨大历时经年的对外战争也只能提供一点微薄的资源。

| 国民财富的性质与原理

<small>plate has never yielded much:</small> The melting down the plate of private families, has upon every occasion been found a still more insignificant one. The French, in the beginning of the last war, did not derive so much advantage from this expedient as to compensate the loss of the fashion.

<small>accumulation in the treasury has been abandoned.</small> The accumulated treasures of the prince have, in former times, afforded a much greater and more lasting resource. In the present times, if you except the king of Prussia, to accumulate treasure seems to be no part of the policy of European princes.

The funds which maintained the foreign wars of the present century the most expensive perhaps which history records, seem to have had little dependency upon the exportation either of the circulating money, or of the plate of private families, or of the treasure of the <small>The foreign wars of the century have evidently not been paid for from the money in circulation</small> prince. The last French war cost Great Britain upwards of ninety millions, including not only the seventy-five millions of new debt that was contracted,① but the additional two shillings in the pound land tax, and what was annually borrowed of the sinking fund. More than two-thirds of this expence were laid out in distant countries; in Germany, Portugal, America, in the ports of the Mediterranean, in the East and West Indies. The kings of England had no accumulated treasure. We never heard of any extraordinary quantity of plate being melted down. The circulating gold and silver of the country had not been supposed to exceed eighteen millions. Since the late recoinage of the gold, however, it is believed to have been a good deal under-rated. Let us suppose, therefore, according to the most exaggerated computation which I remember to have either seen or heard of, that, gold and silver together, it amounted to thirty millions.② Had the war been carried on, by means of our money, the whole of it must, even according to this computation, have been sent out and returned again at least twice, in a period of between six and seven years. Should this be supposed, it would afford the most decisive argument to demonstrate how unnecessary it is for government to watch over the preservation of money, since upon this supposition the whole money of the country must have gone from it and returned to it again, two different times in so short a period, without any body's knowing any thing of the matter. The channel of circulation, however, never appeared more empty than usual during any part of this period. Few

---

① [Present State of the Nation (see next page and note), p. 28.]
② [Lectures, p. 199.]

每次这种情况下熔化私人家庭的金银餐具就更显得微不足道。在上次战争开始时,法国从这种应紧举措中得到的好处,还不足以弥补铸造带来的损失。

<small>金银器具也从来没有提供过多少;</small>

在过去的时代,国家积累的金银财宝曾提供过更多、更持久的资源。在当今,如果把普鲁士国王除外,积累金银财宝似乎已不再是欧洲君主们政策的一部分了。

<small>已经放弃再使用国库积累的办法。</small>

用来维持本世纪对外战争——或许是历史记载的花费最大的战争——的资金,似乎并不怎么依靠出口流通中的货币,或出口私人家庭的金银器具或国库中存贮的金银财宝。上次对法战争耗费大不列颠 9000 万镑以上,不仅包括新发行的 7500 万镑公债,①而且还有附加的每镑两先令的土地税,以及每年向还债基金的借款。这部分开支的 2/3 以上用在了遥远的国家,用在德国、葡萄牙、美洲,以及地中海各港口、东西印度群岛。英格兰国王没有积累财宝,我们也从未听说过有特别大数量的金银器具被熔化。国内流通的金银并未超过 1800 万镑。可是,人们相信自从上次金币重铸以来这个数字是被大大低估了。因此,根据我所见到或听到的最夸张的估算,我们可以假定流通中的金银币总共达到了 3000 万镑。② 如果战争是通过我们的货币进行的,那么根据这个计算,在六七年间的时间里,全部的货币一定是被运出又送回了至少两次。如果假设是这样的话,那它就提供了最有决定性的论证,来证明政府不需要去监视货币的保存。因为根据这个假设,国家所有的货币送出去又收回来,在这么短的一段时期

<small>本世纪的对外战争很明显是由不流通中的货币支付的。</small>

---

① 《国家的现状》(参阅下页及注释),第 28 页。
② 《关于法律、警察、岁入及军备的演讲》,第 199 页。

people wanted money who had wherewithal to pay for it. The profits of foreign trade, indeed, were greater than usual during the whole war; but especially towards the end of it. This occasioned, what it always occasions, a general over-trading in all the ports of Great Britain; and this again occasioned the usual complaint of the scarcity of money, which always follows over-trading. Many people wanted it, who had neither wherewithal to buy it, nor credit to borrow it; and because the debtors found it difficult to borrow, the creditors found it difficult to get payment. Gold and silver, however, were generally to be had for their value, by those who had that value to give for them.

<small>but by commodities.</small> The enormous expence of the late war, therefore, must have been chiefly defrayed, not by the exportation of gold and silver, but by that of British commodities of some kind or other. When the government, or those who acted under them, contracted with a merchant for a remittance to some foreign country, he would naturally endeavour to pay his foreign correspondent, upon whom he had granted a bill, by sending abroad rather commodities than gold and silver. If the commodities of Great Britain were not in demand in that country, he would endeavour to send them to some other country, in which he could purchase a bill upon that country. The transportation of commodities, when properly suited to the market, is always attended with a considerable profit; whereas that of gold and silver is scarce ever attended with any. When those metals are sent abroad in order to purchase foreign commodities, the merchant's profit arises, not from the purchase, but from the sale of the returns. But when they are sent abroad merely to pay a debt, he gets no returns, and consequently no profit. He naturally, therefore, exerts his invention to find out a way of paying his foreign debts, rather by the exportation of commodities than by that of gold and silver. The great quantity of British goods exported during the course of the late war, without bringing back any returns, is accordingly remarked by the author of The Present State of the Nation. ①

---

① [*The Present State of the Nation, particularly with respect to its Trade, Finances, etc. . etc.*, *addressed to the King and both Houses of Parliament*, 1768 (written under the direction of George Grenville by William Knox), pp. 7, 8.]

里已经两次了,而且任何人对此都一无所知。而流通渠道在这段时期中从未显得比平常更加空虚,有足够资金购买货币的人很少有人感到货币短缺。的确,在整个战争期间,特别是战争临近结束时,对外贸易的利润比平时大些。这就造成了,并且会经常造成大不列颠所有港口普遍的贸易过度,这又造成了对货币短缺的普通抱怨,这种抱怨总是紧随贸易过度而出现。许多人想要得到货币,但他们既没有足够的财力去购买,又没有信用可以借到它。因为债务人感到难以借贷,债权人感到难以收回借款。可是拥有可以换取金银的价值的人,一般都用他们的价值去换取金银。

因此,上次战争的巨大费用,必定主要不是由出口金银来支付的,而是由出口大不列颠这种或那种的商品来支付的。当政府或在政府领导下工作的人同商人签约汇款到某一国家时,那么这位商人自然会努力向接受期票的外国代理人出口商品而不是金银。如果那个国家不需要大不列颠的商品,他将努力将其运往别的其他国家,这样他就能交换到所需款项。当输送的商品适合市场需求时,便能获得可观的利润,而输送金银则很少获取什么利润。当这些金属送往国外的目的是为了购买外国商品时,那么商人的利润不是由购买产生,而是从出售买进的货物产生的。但当金银送往国外仅仅是为了偿还债务时,则不会有任何回收,因而也就没有利润。因此,他自然会努力想方设法寻求一种偿还外国债务的办法,即通过出口商品而不是出口金银。因此,《国家的现状》一书的作者①指出,上次战争期间,出口的大批量大不列颠

而是由商品支付的。

———————
① 《国家的现状,特别是它的贸易、金融等,向国王和议会两院提出》,1768 年在乔治·格伦维尔指导下由威廉·诺克斯执笔,第 7、8 页。

| 国民财富的性质与原理

Part of the bullion which circulates from country to country may have been employed, but it must have been purchased with commodities.   Besides the three sorts of gold and silver above mentioned, there is in all great commercial countries a good deal of bullion alternately imported and exported for the purposes of foreign trade. This bullion, as it circulates among different commercial countries in the same manner as the national coin circulates in every particular country, may be considered as the money of the great mercantile republic. The national coin receives its movement and direction from the commodities circulated within the precincts of each particular country: the money of the mercantile republic, from those circulated between different countries. Both are employed in facilitating exchanges, the one between different individuals of the same, the other between those of different nations. Part of this money of the great mercantile republic may have been, and probably was, employed in carrying on the late war. In time of a general war, it is natural to suppose that a movement and direction should be impressed upon it, different from what it usually follows in profound peace; that it should circulate more about the seat of the war, and be more employed in purchasing there, and in the neighbouring countries, the pay and provisions of the different armies. But whatever part of this money of the mercantile republic, Great Britain may have annually employed in this manner, it must have been annually purchased, either with British commodities, or with something else that had been purchased with them; which still brings us back to commodities, to the annual produce of the land and labour of the country, as the ultimate resources which enabled us to carry on the war. It is natural indeed to suppose, that so great an annual expence must have been defrayed from a great annual produce. The expence of 1761, for example, amounted to more than nineteen millions. No accumulation could have supported so great an annual profusion. There is no annual produce even of gold and silver which could have supported it. The whole gold and silver annually imported into both Spain and Portugal, according to the best accounts, does not commonly much exceed six millions sterling, which, in some years, would scarce have paid four months expence of the late war.

货物未带回任何收入。

　　除了上面所提到的这三种金银外,在所有大商业国还有大量的金条和银条,为了进行对外贸易而不断交替地进口和出口。这些金银条在各商业国之间流通,就像各国的国家铸币在每个国家内流通一样,它们可以被看作是大商业共和国的货币。国家铸币的流动和方向,受每个国家境内所流通的商品的支配;而这个大商业共和国的货币则受在不同国家之间流通的商品的支配。两者都是用来方便交易的,国家铸币是为了便于同一国家内不同个人之间的交易,大商业共和国货币则是为了便于不同国家之间的不同个人之间的交易。大商业共和国此种货币的一部分可以用于或许已经用于进行上次战争。在一次全面战争中,人们很自然会认为货币的流动和方向因迫于战争影响,而不同于和平时期通常的流动和方向;它应该更多地在战场周边流通,应当更多地用于在那里以及在邻国购买不同军队的饷给和食物。但是每年不论大不列颠使用大商业共和国多大部分的此种货币,它一定是利用不列颠的商品,或者利用不列颠商品交换的其他东西来购买的;这仍然把我们带回到商品上,带回到国家土地和劳动的年产物上,这是能够使我们进行战争的最后资源。的确,我们自然可以认为,如此巨额的一个年度开支必定由巨大的年产物支付。例如,1761年的支出达到了1900万镑以上。没有任何财富积累能够支撑得了如此巨额的年度开支,甚至也没有任何金银的年产量能够支撑得了这样巨额的年度开支。根据最可靠的记录,每年输入西班牙和葡萄牙两国的全部金银也通常不超过600万英镑,在某些年份里,这还不够维持上次战争中四个月的费用。

　　最适于运往远方国家,以便在那里购买军队的饷给和食物,

国民财富的性质与原理

The finer manufactures are the most convenient commodities for the purpose.

The commodities most proper for being transported to distant countries, in order to purchase there, either the pay and provisions of an army, or some part of the money of the mercantile republic to be employed in purchasing them, seem to be the finer and more improved manufactures; such as contain a great value in a small bulk, and can, therefore, be exported to a great distance at little expence. A country whose industry produces a great annual surplus of such manufactures, which are usually exported to foreign countries, may carry on for many years a very expensive foreign war, without either exporting any considerable quantity of gold and silver, or even having any such quantity to export. A considerable part of the annual surplus of its manufactures must, indeed, in this case be exported, without bringing back any returns to the country, though it does to the merchant; the government purchasing of the merchant his bills upon foreign countries, in order to purchase there the pay and provisions of an army. Some part of this surplus, however, may still continue to bring back a return. The manufacturers, during the war, will have a double demand upon them, and be called upon, first, to work up goods to be sent abroad, for paying the bills drawn upon foreign countries for the pay and provisions of the army; and, secondly, to work up such as are necessary for purchasing the common returns that had usually been consumed in the country. In the midst of the most destructive foreign war, therefore, the greater part of manufactures may frequently flourish greatly; and, on the contrary, they may decline on the return of the peace. They may flourish amidst the ruin of their country, and begin to decay upon the return of its prosperity. The different state of many different branches of the British manufactures during the late war, and for some time after the peace, may serve as an illustration of what has been just now said.

No foreign war of great expence or duration could conveniently be carried on by the exportation of the rude produce of the soil. The expence of sending such a quantity of it to a foreign country as might purchase the pay and provisions of an army, would be too great. Few countries too produce much more rude produce than what is sufficient for the subsistence of their own inhabitants. To send abroad any great quantity of it, therefore, would be to send abroad a part of the necessary subsistence of the people. It is otherwise with the exportation of manufactures. The maintenance of the people employed in them is kept at home, and only the surplus part of their work is exported. Mr. Hume frequently takes notice of the inability of the ancient kings of

或购买用来购买军队的饷给和食物的一部分大商业共和国的货币，似乎是比较精细、比较先进的制造品。它们体积虽小，但包含的价值巨大，因而无需多大花费就可出口到遥远的地方。一个国家的工业每年能生产大量的这种剩余产品，通常出口到外国，那么这个国家就可以进行一场持续多年且耗资巨大的对外战争，不必出口数量可观的金银，甚至也不必拥有如此可观数量的可供出口的金银。的确，在这种场合，其每年生产的剩余产品中的相当可观一部分必须出口，不能给国家带来任何回报，尽管给商人带来一些回报。政府向商人购买外国期票，以便在那里购买军队的饷给和食物。然而，这种剩余的一部分仍然会继续带来回报。在战争期间，制造业将有双重要求：第一，要生产出送往国外的货物，以偿付为购买军队的饷给和食物而对外国开出的期票；第二，要生产为购买本国国内已经消费了的外国商品。因此，在最具破坏性的对外战争中，大部分的制造业通常特别繁荣。相反，回到和平时期它们可能会衰落下去。它们可能在国家衰败时期繁荣，却在国家恢复兴旺后开始衰退。在上次战争期间及恢复和平后的一段时间里，不列颠制造业的许多部门的不同情况，可以作为以上所说的一个例证。

更加精细的制造品是达到此种目的的最方便的商品。

耗资巨大、旷日持久的对外战争，不能靠出口土地的原产物而便利地进行下去。将如此大量的原产物送往国外的费用都足以购买军队的饷给和食物了，因而这个费用太大。很少国家生产的原产物能大大超出足以维持本国居民生活的需要。因此，把大量原产物送往国外，就是把维持人民生活必须的一部分生活资料送往国外。而出口制造品则不同，制造业中雇佣工人的基本生活维持费用留在了国内，而只是将其产品的剩余

|国民财富的性质与原理|

Rude produce is inconvenient

England to carry on, without interruption, any foreign war of long duration. ① The English, in those days, had nothing wherewithal to purchase the pay and provisions of their armies in foreign countries, but either the rude produce of the soil, of which no considerable part could be spared from the home consumption, or a few manufactures of the coarsest kind, of which, as well as of the rude produce, the transportation was too expensive. This inability did not arise from the want of money, but of the finer and more improved manufactures. Buying and selling was transacted by means of money in England then, as well as now. The quantity of circulating money must have borne the same proportion to the number and value of purchases and sales usually transacted at that time, which it does to those transacted at present; or rather it must have borne a greater proportion, because there was then no paper, which now occupies a great part of the employment of gold and silver. Among nations to whom commerce and manufactures are little known, the sovereign, upon extraordinary occasions, can seldom draw any considerable aid from his subjects, for reasons which shall be explained hereafter. ② It is in such countries, therefore, that he generally endeavours to accumulate a treasure, as the only resource against such emergencies. Independent of this necessity, he is in such a situation naturally disposed to the parsimony requisite for accumulation. In that simple state, the expence even of a sovereign is not directed by the vanity which delights in the gaudy finery of a court, but is employed in bounty to his tenants, and hospitality to his retainers. But bounty and hospitality very seldom lead to extravagance; though vanity almost always does. ③ Every Tartar chief, accordingly, has a treasure. The treasures of Mazepa, chief of the Cossacks in the Ukraine, the famous ally of Charles the XIIth, are said to have been very great. The French kings of the Merovingian race had all treasures. When they divided their kingdom among their different children, they divided their treasure too. The Saxon princes, and the first kings after the conquest, seem likewise to have accumu-

---

① [History, chaps. xix. and xx., vol. iii., pp. 103, 104, 165 in ed. of 1773.]

② [Below, p. 396.]

③ [This sentence and the nine words before it are repeated below, vol. ii. p. 393.]

部分出口到国外。休谟先生常常注意到,英格兰古代国王无力连续地进行一场长期的对外战争。① 在那时,英格兰没有足够的财力为驻在外国的军队购买饷给和食物,而只有土地的原产物,除去国内消费也没有多少剩余,也有少量粗糙的制造品,其运输费用和土地原产物一样过于昂贵。这种无能为力不是由于缺乏货币,而是缺乏更加精细的、更加先进的制造品。和现在一样,在当时的英格兰,买卖是通过货币的方式进行的。流通中货币的数量和当时通常进行的买卖次数和买卖价值的比例关系,也一定和现在的买卖交易的比例关系是一样的,或者其比例还要更大一些,因为当时没有纸币,而在现今纸币代替了金银的大部分用途。在对商业和制造业几乎一无所知的国家里,君主在特殊场合很少能获得其臣民的重大援助,其原因将在后面做出解释。② 因此,正是在这样的国家里,君主通常竭力积累金银财宝,作为应付这种紧急情况的唯一资源。除了这种需要之外,他在这种状况下自然倾向于为积累所要求的节俭。在那种简朴的情况下,即使是君主的支出,也不是用来满足宫廷豪华的虚荣喜好,而是用来赏赐佃户、款待侍从。但是赏赐和款待很少导致铺张浪费,③而虚荣则总是会导致铺张浪费。因此,每一位鞑靼酋长都有财宝。马捷帕,乌克兰哥萨克的酋长,是查理十二世著名的盟友,据说他的财宝很多。法国梅罗文加王朝的各位国王都有财宝。当他们把王国分给他们的子女时,也把财宝分给了子女们。撒克逊的君们,

旁注:原产物不方便

---

① 《英格兰史》,1773 年,第 3 卷,第 19、20 章,第 103、104、165 页。
② 下面第 396 页。
③ 之前的这一句话和 9 个单词在下面第 2 章第 393 页重复提到。

lated treasures. The first exploit of every new reign was commonly to seize the treasure of the preceding king, as the most essential measure for securing the succession. The sovereigns of improved and commercial countries are not under the same necessity of accumulating treasures, because they can generally draw from their subjects extraordinary aids upon extraordinary occasions. They are likewise less disposed to do so. They naturally, perhaps necessarily, follow the mode of the times, and their expence comes to be regulated by the same extravagant vanity which directs that of all the other great proprietors in their dominions. The insignificant pageantry of their court becomes every day more brilliant, and the expence of it not only prevents accumulation, but frequently encroaches upon the funds destined for more necessary expences. What Dercyllidas said of the court of Persia, may be applied to that of several European princes, that he saw there much splendor but little strength, and many servants but few soldiers. ①

The principal benefit of foreign trade is not the importation of gold and silver, but the carrying out of surplus produce for which there is no demand and bringing back something for which there is.

The importation of gold and silver is not the principal, much less the sole benefit which a nation derives from its foreign trade. Between whatever places foreign trade is carried on, they all of them derive two distinct benefits from it. It carries out that surplus part of the produce of their land and labour for which there is no demand among them, and brings back in return for it something else for which there is a demand. It gives a value to their superfluities, by exchanging them for something else, which may satisfy a part of their wants, and increase their enjoyments. By means of it, the narrowness of the home market

---

① ['Dercyllidas' appears to be a mistake for Antiochus. See Xenophon, *Hellenica*, vii., L, § 38]

第四篇 第一章

以及征服后的最初几位国王,似乎同样都积累了财宝。每一位新君主即位后所做的第一件大事,就是掠夺上一位国王的财宝,作为确保王位继承最必要的措施。先进的商业国的君主们没有必要积累财宝,因为在特殊场合他们一般能够从他们的臣民那里得到重大援助。他们同样不太倾向于这样做,他们自然而然地,或许必然地追随时代的潮流,他们的花销受到铺张浪费的虚荣心的支配,这种虚荣心同样支配着他们领地内所有其他大领主的奢侈花销。他们宫廷上无足轻重的装饰变得日渐华丽,其支出不仅妨碍了积累,而且常常占用了预定用于其他更必要的开支的资金。德西利达期所说的关于波斯宫廷的话,也可适用于其他几个欧洲国王的宫廷;他在那里看到的是豪华多而实力少,仆人多而军人少。①

进口金银不是一个国家从对外贸易中获取的最主要的好处,更不是唯一的好处。不论在任何地方进行对外贸易,所有各方都能从中得到两种不同的好处。它把当地没有需求的土地和劳动年产物的剩余部分送往外地,同时带回了本地所需要的别的东西。它通过交换剩余产品获取其他东西,从而使剩余产品具有了价值,而交换来的其他东西可以满足他们的

---

① 可能错把"安提克"当作了"德西利达斯"。参阅色诺芬(Xenophon)《长征记》,vii., 1,第38节。

[1]色诺芬:约公元前434~前355年,希腊将军,历史学家。苏格拉底的门徒,在进攻波斯的战役中加入居鲁士二世的军队。居鲁士死后,色诺芬率领着希腊军队到了黑海,这次严峻的经历成了他远征记的素材。

does not hinder the division of labour in any particular branch of art or manufacture from being carried to the highest perfection. By opening a more extensive market for whatever part of the produce of their labour may exceed the home consumption, it encourages them to improve its productive powers, and to augment its annual produce to the utmost, and thereby to increase the real revenue and wealth of the society. These great and important services foreign trade is continually occupied in performing, to all the different countries between which it is carried on. They all derive great benefit from it, though that in which the merchant resides generally derives the greatest, as he is generally more employed in supplying the wants, and carrying out the superfluities of his own, than of any other particular country. To import the gold and silver which may be wanted, into the countries which have no mines, is, no doubt, a part of the business of foreign commerce. It is, however, a most insignificant part of it. A country which carried on foreign trade merely upon this account, could scarce have occasion to freight a ship in a century.

It is not by the importation of gold and silver, that the discovery of America has enriched Europe. By the abundance of the American mines, those metals have become cheaper. A service of plate can now be purchased for about a third part of the com, or a third part of the labour, which it would have cost in the fifteenth century. With the same annual expence of labour and commodities, Europe can annually purchase about three times the quantity of plate which it could have purchased at that time. But when a commodity comes to be sold for a third part of what had been its usual price, not only those who purchased it before can purchase three times their former quantity, but it is brought down to the level of a much greater number of purchasers, perhaps to more than ten, perhaps to more than twenty times the former number. So that there may be in Europe at present not only more than three times, but more than twenty or thirty times the quantity of plate which would have been in it, even in its present state of improvement, had the discovery of the American mines never been made. So far Europe has, no doubt, gained a real conveniency, though surely a very trifling one. The cheapness of gold and silver renders those metals rather less fit for the purposes of money than they were before. In order to make the same purchases, we must load ourselves with a greater quantity of them, and carry about a shilling in our pocket where a groat would have done before. It is difficult to say

<small>The discovery of America has benefited Europe not by the cheapening of gold and silver, out by opening up of a new market which improved the productive powers of labour.</small>

部分需求，增加了他们的享受。通过对外贸易，国内狭小的市场就不至于阻碍工艺的任何部门或制造业的任何部门的劳动分工达到最完善的程度。通过为超出国内消费那部分的劳动产品开辟一个更为广阔的市场，鼓励了各国提高生产力，并最大限度地增加其年产量，从而增加了社会的实际收入和财富。对外贸易一直不断地为进行贸易的所有国家提供这种重大而重要的服务。各方都能从中得到巨大好处，虽然其中商人所在国通常得到的好处最大，因为他一般更多的是从事于供应本国的需求，把本国而不是别的国家的剩余产品出口出去。向没有金银矿山的国家输送他们所需要的金银，无疑是对外贸易业务的一部分。不过它是极其无关紧要的一部分，一个仅为此原因而进行对外贸易的国家，一个世纪里也几乎装不了一船金银。

美洲的发现使欧洲富裕起来，不是通过金银的进口。由于美洲矿山的丰富，金银变得更便宜。现在购买一套金银餐具，只需要15世纪所值谷物的1/3，或所费劳动的1/3。花费同样的劳动和商品，现在欧洲每年所能购买到的金银器具大约是15世纪时的3倍之多。但是当一种商品仅以平常价格的1/3出售时，不仅以前购买它的人现在可以买到以前数量的3倍之多，而且会使购买者的人数大增，或许增至过去的10倍还多，或许20倍还不止。所以如果美洲的矿山迄今为止还没有被发现，那么在现今的进步状态下，欧洲所拥有的金银器具也不仅可以达到以前的3倍还多，甚至可以达到20倍或30倍以上。因此，毫无疑问欧洲获得了一种实在的便利，虽然肯定是一种微不足道的便利。金银的廉价使得它们不如以前那样适合于作货币的用途。为了进行相同的

| 国民财富的性质与原理

which is most trifling, this inconveniency, or the opposite conveniency. Neither the one nor the other could have made any very essential change in the state of Europe. The discovery of America, however, certainly made a most essential one. By opening a new and inexhaustible market to all the commodities of Europe, it gave occasion to new divisions of labour and improvements of art, which, in the narrow circle of the ancient commerce, could never have taken place for want of a market to take off the greater part of their produce. The productive powers of labour were improved, and its produce increased in all the different countries of Europe, and together with it the real revenue and wealth of the inhabitants. The commodities of Europe were almost all new to America, and many of those of America were new to Europe. A new set of exchanges, therefore, began to take place which had never been thought of before, and which should naturally have proved as advantageous to the new, as it certainly did to the old continent. The savage injustice of the Europeans rendered an event, which ought to have been beneficial to all, ruinous and destructive to several of those unfortunate countries.

<small>The discovery of the sea passage to the East Indies would have been still more advantageous if the trade to the East Indies had been free.</small>   The discovery of a passage to the East Indies, by the Cape of Good Hope, which happened much about the same time, opened, perhaps, a still more extensive range to foreign commerce than even that of America, notwithstanding the greater distance. There were but two nations in America, in any respect superior to savages, and these were destroyed almost as soon as discovered. The rest were mere savages. But the empires of China, Indostan, Japan, as well as several others in the East Indies, without having richer mines of gold or silver, were in every other respect much richer, better cultivated, and more advanced in all arts and manufactures than either Mexico or Peru, even though we should credit, what plainly deserves no credit, the exaggerated accounts of the Spanish writers, concerning the ancient state of those empires. But rich and civilized nations can always exchange to a much greater value with one another, than with savages and barbarians. Europe, however, has hitherto derived much

第四篇 第一章

购物，我们现在必须携带数量更多的金银，以前只需要携带一枚四便士的银币，而如今要带一先令在口袋里。很难说哪一种最微不足道，是这种不方便，还是与之相反的那种方便。两者都不可能对欧洲的状况做出任何根本的变革。然而，美洲的发现无疑带来了一个最根本的变革。通过为欧洲所有商品开辟一个崭新的无限广阔的市场，它引起了新的劳动分工和工艺的改进，而在古代狭小的商业圈里这是根本不可能发生的，原因在于缺乏一个可以吸纳他们大部分产品的市场。在欧洲各国，劳动生产力提高了，产品产量增加了，居民的实际收入和财富也增加了。欧洲的商品对于美洲而言，几乎是崭新的，而美洲的许多商品对于欧洲来说也是崭新的。因此，一系列新的交易产生了，这是以前从未想到过的，而且自然而然地可以证明，就像肯定对旧大陆有利一样，它们对新大陆也肯定有利。欧洲人野蛮不公正的行为，使得这样一件本来对所有各方都有利的事件，给几个不幸的国家造成了毁灭性和破坏性的后果。

经由好望角通往东印度的航道也几乎在同时被发现了，相比于美洲的发现，这一航道的发现也许为对外贸易开辟了更为广阔的领域，尽管距离远一些。在美洲只有两个民族在各方面都优于野蛮人，而这两个民族几乎一经发现就被消灭了。其余的民族不过是野蛮人。但是中国、印度斯坦和日本，以及东印度的其他几个帝国，除了没有更加丰富的金银矿之外，在其他各个方面都比墨西哥或秘鲁更加富有，土地耕种得更好，所有的工艺和制造业更加先进，即使我们相信西班牙作家有关这些帝国古代状况夸张的描写（显然是不值得信赖的）。但是，富裕、文明的民族彼此之间的交易要比它们和野蛮民族之间的交易的价值大得多。不过，

如果对东印度的贸易是自由的，那么发现通往东印度的海道会更加有利；

less advantage from its commerce with the East Indies, than from that with America. The Portuguese monopolized the East India trade to themselves for about a century, and it was only indirectly and through them, that the other nations of Europe could either send out or receive any goods from that country. When the Dutch, in the beginning of the last century, began to encroach upon them, they vested their whole East India commerce in an exclusive company. The English, French, Swedes, and Danes, have all followed their example, so that no great nation in Europe has ever yet had the benefit of a free commerce to the East Indies. No other reason need be assigned why it has never been so advantageous as the trade to America, which, between almost every nation of Europe and its own colonies, is free to all its subjects. The exclusive privileges of those East India companies, their great riches, the great favour and protection which these have procured them from their respective governments, have excited much envy against them. This envy has frequently represented their trade as altogether pernicious, on account of the great quantities of silver, which it every year exports from the countries from which it is carried on. The parties concerned have replied, that their trade, by this continual exportation of silver, might, indeed, tend to impoverish Europe in general, but not the particular country from which it was carried on; because, by the exportation of a part of the returns to other European countries, it annually brought home a much greater quantity of that metal than it carried out. Both the objection and the reply are founded in the popular notion which I have been just now examining. It is, therefore, unnecessary to say any thing further about either. By the annual exportation of silver to the East Indies, plate is probably somewhat dearer in Europe than it otherwise might have been; and coined silver probably purchases a larger quantity both of labour and commodities. The former of these two effects is a very small loss, the latter a very small advantage; both too insignificant to deserve any part of the public attention. The trade to the East Indies, by opening a market to the commodities of Europe, or, what comes nearly to the same thing, to the gold and silver which is purchased with those commodities, must necessarily tend to increase the annual production of European commodities, and consequently the real wealth and revenue of Europe. That it has hitherto increased them so little, is probably

迄今为止,欧洲从与东印度的贸易中得到的好处远远少于从与美洲贸易中得到的好处。葡萄牙垄断东印度贸易大约一个世纪,欧洲其他国家只有间接地通过葡萄牙人才能将货物输送到东印度或从东印度得到货物。当荷兰人在上世纪初开始侵占东印度时,他们将他们全部的东印度商业赋予一个公司独家经营。英国人、法国人、瑞典人和丹麦人全部都仿效荷兰人的做法,所以欧洲没有一个大国获得了与东印度进行自由贸易的好处。为什么对东印度的贸易从来没有像对美洲的贸易那么有利,并不需要指出任何其他理由:几乎每个欧洲国家和它自己殖民地间的贸易,对它自己的臣民都是自由的。那些东印度公司的专有特权,它们的巨大财富,它们从各自政府所获得的巨大恩惠和保护,激起了对它们的众多嫉妒。这种嫉妒常常表现为认为这种贸易完全是有害的,因为与东印度公司的贸易每年要从开展贸易的国家出口大量白银。有关方面回答说,由于不断的出口白银,他们的贸易确实可能会使欧洲普通地变穷,但是不会使进行贸易的某一国家变穷,因为通过把带回来的货物的一部分出口到其他欧洲国家,它每年带回本国的白银数量比带出去的多得多。反对的意见及其答复其根据都是建立在我刚才分析的那些流行观点上。因此,无需再对两者多说什么了。由于每年向东印度出口白银,在欧洲银餐具可能比原来贵一些;银币可能相比以前购买到更多的劳动和商品。这两种影响中的前一种是很小的损失,后一种是很小的好处。两者都是无关紧要的,不足以引起公众的注意。对东印度的贸易,通过为欧洲商品开辟了市场,或者说几乎是一回事,为用这些商品所购买的金银开辟了市场,也必定会增加欧洲商品的年产量,从而增加欧洲的实际财富和收入。迄今为止,增加之所以如

向东印度出口白银没有害处。

owing to the restraints which it every-where labours under.

<small>Writers who begin by including lands, houses and consumable goods in wealth often forget them later.</small> I thought it necessary, though at the hazard of being tedious, to examine at full length this popular notion that wealth consists in money, or in gold and silver. Money in common language, as I have already observed, frequently signifies wealth; and this ambiguity of expression has rendered this popular notion so familiar to us, that even they, who are convinced of its absurdity, are very apt to forget their own principles, and in the course of their reasonings to take it for granted as a certain and undeniable truth. Some of the best English writers upon commerce set out with observing, that the wealth of a country consists, not in its gold and silver only, but in its lands, houses, and consumable goods of all different kinds. In the course of their reasonings, however, the lands, houses, and consumable goods seem to slip out of their memory, and the strain of their argument frequently supposes that all wealth consists in gold and silver, and that to multiply those metals is the great object of national industry and commerce.

<small>Wealth being supposed to consist in gold and silver, political economy endeavoured to diminish imports and encourage exports,</small> The two principles being established, however, that wealth consisted in gold and silver, and that those metals could be brought into a country which had no mines only by the balance of trade, or by exporting to a greater value than it imported; it necessarily became the great object of political economy to diminish as much as possible the importation of foreign goods for home consumption, and to increase as much as possible the exportation of the produce of domestic industry. Its two great engines for enriching the country, therefore, were restraints upon importation, and encouragements to exportation.

The restraints upon importation were of two kinds.

<small>by restraints upon importation</small> First, Restraints upon the importation of such foreign goods for home consumption as could be produced at home, from whatever country they were imported.

Secondly, Restraints upon the importation of goods of almost all kinds from those particular countries with which the balance of trade was supposed to be disadvantageous.

Those different restraints consisted sometimes in high duties, and <small>and encouragements to exportation,</small> sometimes in absolute prohibitions.

Exportation was encouraged sometimes by drawbacks, sometimes by bounties, sometimes by advantageous treaties of commerce with

此之少,或许是由于贸易在各地所受的限制。

虽然有些冗长乏味,我仍以为有必要对财富是由货币或金银构成的这一流行观念进行详细的分析。我已经指出过,在普通语言里货币常常意味着财富。这一说法的模糊不清使得这个流行观念对我们来说如此熟悉,甚至那些深信其荒谬的人也很轻易地忘记了他们自己的原则,而且在他们的推理过程中也假定它是一个确定的不可否认的真理。一些优秀的关于商业方面的英格兰作家一开头就指出一个国家的财富不仅包括它的金银,而且也包括它的土地、房屋和各种不同的消费品。然而在他们推理过程中,土地、房屋和消费品似乎又从他们的记忆中消失了,他们的论证常常假定全部财富即由金银构成,增加金银就是国家工商业的伟大目标。

> 在开头将地、房屋和消费品包括在财富之作们,后来常忘了这些。

确立了两个原则:财富由金银构成;金银要进口到一个没有金银矿山的国家,只有通过贸易差额即出口价值大于进口价值。原则一经确定,政治经济学的伟大目标必然是:尽可能减少供国内消费的外国货物的进口,尽可能增加国内产业产品的出口。因此,使国家富裕的两大引擎就是限制进口,鼓励出口。

> 被认为由金银构成的财富,政治经济学竭力鼓励出口,减少进口。

对进口的限制有两种。

第一,对于国内能够生产的供本国消费的外国货物,不论来自哪个国家,限制其进口。 > 限制进口

第二,限制进口所有贸易差额不利于本国的国家的货物。

这些不同的限制,有时是高关税,有时则是绝对禁止。

对于出口的鼓励有时是通过退税,有时是通过奖金,有时通过和外国签订有利的通商条约,有时是在遥远国家建立殖民地。 > 鼓励出口

是在两种不同的场合采取退税的方式。当已被课征关税或

foreign states, and sometimes by the establishment of colonies in distant countries.

Drawbacks were given upon two different occasions. When the home-manufactures were subject to any duty or excise, either the whole or a part of it was frequently drawn back upon their exportation; and when foreign goods liable to a duty were imported in order to be exported again, either the whole or a part of this duty was sometimes given back upon such exportation.

Bounties were given for the encouragement either of some beginning manufactures, or of such sorts of industry of other kinds as were supposed to deserve particular favour.

By advantageous treaties of commerce, particular privileges were procured in some foreign state for the goods and merchants of the country, beyond what were granted to those of other countries.

By the establishment of colonies in distant countries, not only particular privileges, but a monopoly was frequently procured for the goods and merchants of the country which established them.

<small>which restraints and encouragements will be considered in the next six chapters.</small> The two sorts of restraints upon importation above-mentioned, together with these four encouragements to exportation, constitute the six principal means by which the commercial system proposes to increase the quantity of gold and silver in any country by turning the balance of trade in its favour. I shall consider each of them in a particular chapter, and without taking much further notice of their supposed tendency to bring money into the country, I shall examine chiefly what are likely to be the effects of each of them upon the annual produce of its industry. According as they tend either to increase or diminish the value of this annual produce, they must evidently tend either to increase or diminish the real wealth and revenue of the country.

货物税的国内制造品出口时,往往退还所纳税额的全部或一部分;已被课征关税的外国货物重新出口时,有时会退还所纳税额的全部或一部分。

津贴是为了鼓励某些刚起步的制造业或某种值得特别关注的工业而颁发的。

通过有利的通商条约,为本国的货物和商人获得在外国的某些特权,这是其他国家的货物和商人所不享有的。

在遥远的国家建立殖民地,不仅可以使殖民的国家的货物和商人获得特权,而且常常是垄断权。

上述对进口的两种限制,加上对出口的四种鼓励,共同构成了重商主义体系提出的六种主要方法,通过这六种方法使贸易差额有利于本国从而增加本国金银数量。我将在以后的每一章中对每一种方法加以探讨,不再过多注意它们假定的能把货币带回本国的趋势,我将主要研究它们每一种方法对本国产业年产量可能产生的影响。根据它们增加或减少年产物价值的趋势,它们显然必定会趋向于增加或减少国家的实际财富和收入。